WRITERS &POLITICS

WRITERS & POLITICS

A PARTISAN REVIEW READER

EDITED BY EDITH KURZWEIL & WILLIAM PHILLIPS

Routledge & Kegan Paul
Boston, London, Melbourne and Henley

This selection first published in 1983
by Routledge & Kegan Paul Ltd
9 Park Street, Boston, Mass. 02108, USA,
39 Store Street, London WC1E 7DD,
296 Beaconsfield Parade, Middle Park,
Melbourne, 3206, Australia, and
Broadway House, Newtown Road,
Henley-on-Thames, Oxon RG9 1EN.

Printed in the United States of America
This selection and introductions copyright
© Edith Kurzweil and William Phillips 1983
Selections copyright © Partisan Review 1938, 1941, 1952, 1954,
1960, 1966, 1967, 1972, 1973, 1974, 1976, 1978, 1980

Library of Congress Cataloging in Publication Data

Main entry under title:

Writers and politics.

1. Politics and literature – Addresses, essays, lectures.
I. Kurzweil, Edith.
II. Phillips, William, 1907 Nov. 14–.
III. Partisan review (New York, N.Y.: 1937)
PN51.W73 1983   814'.54'080358   82-16533

ISBN 0-7100-9316-0

Contents

Preface vii
Acknowledgments viii
Notes on Contributors ix
Introduction: Writers and Politics 1

Part I Literary and Political Theories 13

Introduction 15
1 Tradition and the Modern Age 19
Hannah Arendt *Vol. 21, no. 1, 1954*
2 Art and Revolt 42
Albert Camus *Vol. 19, no. 3, 1952*
3 Art and Politics 56
Leon Trotsky *Vol. 5, no. 3, 1938*
4 The Idea of the Avant-Garde 64
Richard Gilman *Vol. 39, no. 3, 1972*
5 The Intelligentsia 79
Arthur Koestler *Vol. 11, no. 3, 1944*
6 Toward a Portrait of the French Intellectual 93
Victor Brombert *Vol. 27, no. 3, 1960*
7 Modernism and Capitalism 116
Daniel Bell *Vol. 45, no. 2, 1978*

Part II Political Emphases 133

Introduction 135
8 Reading from Left to Right 138
Dwight Macdonald *Vol. 8, no. 1, 1941*
9 Murti-Bing 148
Czeslaw Milosz *Vol. 18, no. 5, 1951*

10 Radical Questions and the American
   Intellectual 165
   Irving Howe *Vol. 33, no. 2, 1966*
11 Old and New Classes 192
   Edith Kurzweil *Vol. 47, no. 4, 1966*

Part III Emphasis on Literature and Art 197

   Introduction 199
12 The Intellectuals' Tradition 202
   William Phillips *Vol. 8, no. 6, 1941*
13 Writers and Politics 212
   Stephen Spender *Vol. 34, no. 3, 1967*
14 Protest in Art 235
   Barbara Rose *Vol. 40, no. 2, 1973*

Part IV Writers' Political Documents 247

   Introduction 249
15 Sartre versus Camus: A Political Quarrel 254
   Nicola Chiaromonte *Vol. 19, no. 6, 1952*
16 Yugoslav Report 261
   Susan Sontag *Vol. 33, no. 1, 1966*
17 Cold War Blues: Notes on the Culture of the
   Fifties 269
   Morris Dickstein *Vol. 41, no. 1, 1974*
18 While America Burns 293
   William Barrett and William Phillips *Vol. 43, no. 3, 1976*
19 Neoconservatism: Pro and Con 302
   Nathan Glazer, Peter Steinfels, James Q. Wilson,
   and Norman Birnbaum *Vol. 47, no. 4, 1980*

Preface

Politics and literature – they almost have become one word; and the common acceptance of their connection has been one of the cultural contributions of *Partisan Review*.

The essays in this volume reflect the politics and literary tendencies of *Partisan Review* since its beginnings. But they also represent, we feel, an important sector of opinion in America and Europe – opinion that might be characterized as among the best nondoctrinaire, nonconformist and open-minded writing of the time. The selection is a joint effort: William Phillips, one of the founding editors, originally solicited many of the pieces for the magazine; Edith Kurzweil read some of them for the first time, and was impressed by the fact that so much of the material is still alive. We had a wealth of material to choose from, but decided to take no more than one article by any one person, to stay as close to our subject as possible, and to be representative of what the magazine stands for – independence of thought, openness to new ideas, and quality. This is not to say that everything we publish is of equal value, but only that it is lively and serious. In retrospect, we must have succeeded, given that so many of the most respected figures of our time were first printed in *Partisan Review*.

We hope that our readers will be stimulated, and that some of them might look to the magazine for other pieces of similar interest and importance.

E.K. W.P.

June 1982

Acknowledgments

Although all the selections in this volume first appeared in *Partisan Review*, the editors and publishers gratefully acknowledge as follows permission to reprint in this collection those whose copyrights have in the meantime reverted to their authors:

To Harcourt Brace Jovanovich for "Tradition and the Modern Age" by Hannah Arendt; to Madame Albert Camus and the translator, Joseph Frank, for "Art and Revolt" by Albert Camus; to Miriam Chiaromonte for "Sartre versus Camus" by Nicola Chiaromonte; and to the Houghton Library, Harvard University, for permission to reprint Leon Trotsky's letter entitled "Art and Politics." "The Intelligentsia" by Arthur Koestler is reprinted by permission of the Sterling Lord Agency, Inc., New York, copyright © 1944, and A. D. Peters & Co. Ltd., London. "The Pill of Murti-Bing" from *The Captive Mind* by Czeslaw Milosz, translated by Jane Zielonko, copyright © 1953 by Czeslaw Milosz, is reprinted by permission of Alfred A. Knopf, Inc., New York, and Secker & Warburg Ltd., London.

The articles and pieces by Richard Gilman, Victor Brombert, Daniel Bell, Dwight Macdonald, Irving Howe, Stephen Spender, Barbara Rose, Susan Sontag, Morris Dickstein, William Barrett, Nathan Glazer, Peter Steinfels, James Q. Wilson, and Norman Birnbaum are reprinted here with the knowledge and authorization of their authors.

Notes on Contributors

William Barrett was an editor of *Partisan Review* from 1945 to 1952. His most recent book is *The Truants* (Doubleday, 1982).

Daniel Bell is Henry Ford II Professor of Social Sciences at Harvard University. His most recent work is *The Winding Passage: Essays and Sociological Journeys*.

Norman Birnbaum is a University Professor at Georgetown University and an advisor to the United Auto Workers, to several members of the House and Senate, and to the member parties of the Socialist International.

Victor Brombert is the Henry Putnam University Professor of Romance and Comparative Literatures at Princeton University. His most recent book, *The Romantic Prison* (1978), was awarded the Harry Levin Prize in Comparative Literature.

Morris Dickstein teaches English and American literature at Queens College, and is the author of *Gates of Eden: American Culture in the Sixties* (1977).

Richard Gilman, professor at the Yale School of Drama, was recently elected president of the American branch of PEN International.

Nathan Glazer is Professor of Education and Sociology at Harvard University, co-editor of *The Public Interest*, and author of *Remembering the Answers*, among other books.

Irving Howe is editor of *Dissent*, Distinguished Professor of English at the City University of New York, and author of books in literary criticism and social history.

Arthur Koestler lives in England; his works are now being republished in a collection of twenty volumes.

Dwight Macdonald is a journalist who lives in New York and is best known for his literary and film criticism.

Czeslaw Milosz, 1981 Nobel Prize winner, is Professor of Comparative Literature at the University of California at Berkeley.

Barbara Rose is an art critic. Her latest book is *Lee Krasner/Jackson Pollock: A Working Relationship*.

Susan Sontag writes fiction and essays. She now lives mostly in New York City, and is working on her third novel.

Stephen Spender, the well-known poet and critic, lives in London.

Peter Steinfels is Executive Editor of *Commonweal* magazine and author of *The Neoconservatives* (Simon & Schuster, 1978).

James Q. Wilson is Professor of Government at Harvard. His most recent book is *The Politics of Regulation* (Basic Books, 1980).

Introduction:
Writers and Politics

The relation of writers to politics is a modern question. It arose out of a sense of history and historical change, and a concern over whether writers, as part of the intelligentsia, are on the side of the old order or a new one. Toward the end of the eighteenth century, particularly in the climate of the French revolution, writers, philosophers and social thinkers, all of whom might be included under the heading of intellectuals, tended to become spokesmen for radical or conservative movements and ideologies – ideologies that affected the fate of nations and societies. Indeed, as Arthur Koestler pointed out, the modern concept of the intelligentsia as a body of writers and thinkers whose ideas were partly independent and partly a reflection of social interests stems from the French *philosophes* and encyclopedists who had a more or less common view of society and a common interest in transforming it. Before then, the politics of writers were usually personal, or idiosyncratic, or factional in their support of one or another ruling figure or institution. They were generally not part of a movement nor subversive. It was not until Marx separated intellectuals into those who were contained within the ideological superstructure of existing society and those who broke away to ally themselves with the forces making for a new society – it was not until then that the politics of intellectuals were seen to be related to different class interests. The contemporary division of intellectuals into radicals and conservatives owes much to Marx.

As Victor Brombert points out, the term "intellectuals" first came into use in France at the end of the nineteenth century. Since then it has been fraught with all kinds of negative as well as honorific associations. Intellectuals – and writers as a subspecies – have been put down as dreamers, elitists, radicals, bleeding hearts, do-gooders, traitors. Hence such unflattering names as egghead, highbrow, longhair, and the dual attitude toward professors. At the same time, writers and intellectuals have acquired an aura that combines wisdom and morality. They have been looked up to as thinkers who transcended the limits of any discipline and any national interest and were therefore able to generalize about global issues. Their habitat was the "truth" and their terrain was nothing less than all of humanity.

In many circles, particularly on the left, intellectuals and writers have been assigned the role of acting as the conscience of the world. Big claims, often leading to self-inflation and to the kind of overconfidence that permits intellectuals to cling to false theories. Such have been the contradictions of the modern world that writers with a political bent have been able to play the parts of both prophet and false guide.

Writers have also been associated with rebellion, especially by the left – rebellion against old forms, conventional values, bourgeois society, injustice, blind governmental authority. As Trotsky, Camus, Gilman, among others, have argued in the essays in this volume, the really important writers were rebels in their medium and in their social vision. And this has come to be the definition of the "alienated" and *avant-garde* writer. The politics of avant-gardism and alienation are not always clear, particularly in an age of political ambiguity and chaos, except in the broadest sense of being nonconformist. And they are further confused, as critics of the current scene have argued, by the influence of the media, with their stress on originality and *far-outness*, and their receptiveness to almost any form of subversion.

Moreover, with the recent refinements in literary and social criticism, we can no longer speak of the relation of writers to politics as though it were a single subject. We have to distinguish between the political views and activities of writers and the political meaning of their work, and to recognize the changing relations between the two. Furthermore, in either case, a seeming lack of politics could be politically significant. But to decipher the visible or hidden politics of a novel or poem requires a much more complex and subtle understanding than to interpret the political alignments of writers in their role as citizens, even though their views are often ambiguous and evasive. Beyond the influence of the New Critics and the various formalist schools, the main emphasis of modern criticism has been on the intricacies of the text.

The question not only of the politics of writers but of the politics of their writing is further complicated today by the radical demands that writers be engaged and responsible. In addition, these complications are multiplied by the chaos of modern politics, in which much of what goes by the name of "left" politics has been badly compromised, and by the belief – which has its source and its justification in the radical movement – that writers, either in their public life or in their work, should be both political and have the "correct" politics. It was, it will be recalled, in reaction to this politicalization of intellectuals that Julien Benda wrote his famous polemic, *The Treason of the Clerks*.

In any event, it was not until the twentieth century that writers attached themselves in significant numbers to large-scale political movements. It was in our own era that writers as a class, so to speak, supported Communist, Socialist, and Fascist parties, and also acquired group identities as anti-Fascists, anti-Communists, and conservatives. Political ideologies had taken shape as forces that were thought to be able to preserve existing society or transform it completely. And writers who were not reticent in announcing their views came to be known as spokesmen for the competing alignments. Furthermore, the process of exposure was accelerated by the media, which enlarged the public face of writers and intellectuals. And because politics, with the growth of mass parties and unions, had become crucial for large sections of the population, the opinions of the newly created writer-celebrities became part of the political bombardment to sway people's minds. The enormous growth of instant communication had not only created a more informed population, but also a more confused one, susceptible to all kinds of conflicting and demagogic influences as well as to serious and legitimate ones. The perfection of communication meant that everyone was open to everyone else's opinion; and though some people qualified as intellectual gurus, there was no accepted method of distinguishing between genuine gurus and fake ones.

There is, indeed, a certain amount of irony in the contradiction between the lofty role assigned to intellectuals in the development of Western thought and the patently false position taken by many intellectuals today – an irony dramatically indicated in the very title of a piece by Harold Rosenberg, "A Herd of Independent Minds," which was a put down of what he claimed were the conservative reflexes of contemporary writers. It is not easy to explain this disparity, for we are talking about the blunders – and often the mindlessness – of our intellectual elites. As we have been reminded over again, it is our writers, scientists, and social critics who have not only created those ideas and works which represent the peaks of our civilization, but have also, we are told, acted as the conscience of our society. How is it that these, by definition our great minds, have so frequently in recent times subscribed to untenable ideologies, ideologies that fly in the face of common sense? It is true that elite errors have usually been errors on a high level, and often not so much false as intellectually perverse. As Orwell once remarked, there is a certain kind of nonsense that can be learned only in college. A formal explanation, but one that cannot be dismissed easily, is that mistakes made on the higher reaches of professional thinking are not the same as mistakes made out of ignorance, though they are sometimes superficially – or in their consequences – indistinguishable. But a more substantive and historical explanation would be that what Marx termed false consciousness has usually come from ideological pressures, which intellectuals both transmit and are the victims of. And it is mostly in the modern era that ideology has not only stimulated but also distorted political activity as well as political thought.

The Russian revolution may be said to mark the dividing line between the accepted political categories of the past and the modern era of misshapen politics – mostly on the left. For the Soviet regime created a confusion of realms by attaching many of the old aims and the old rhetoric of socialism to the nationalistic interests of the Soviet Union. There had been some twisting of ideology by Hitler and Mussolini in their manipulation of the appeals of socialism, but they had almost no influence on the thinking of the left, or on the politics of either nationalist or liberation movements in Africa or Asia. The Communist doctrines fostered by the Russians, however, encompassed all kinds of causes and beliefs that had nothing to do with Socialist ideals. So great has been the confusion spread by Russian tactics that many conservatives now insist the old terms "left" and "right," "radical" and "conservative," are no longer valid or useful. To some extent, this is true of current politics on the left, but it does not follow that these terms have lost their original meaning, and one is inclined to believe that to obliterate all distinctions can serve only those conservatives who deny they are conservatives, and claim that their views are arrived at empirically and through common sense, not ideologically.

In any event, it is the myth that the Soviet Union represents a progressive force, despite its manipulations of Marxist doctrine to suit its own national interests – it is this stubborn myth that affects the politics of many left intellectuals. It is also the failure to comprehend the real intentions of the Soviet Union that leads some European intellectuals to underestimate the threat from the East and to exaggerate the aggressive aims of the West. On the other hand, conservative intellectuals in reaction to the somersaults on the left have swung to a defense of all capitalist institutions and almost any policies that appear to be anti-Communist, many of which add up to little more than right-wing rhetoric. The result has been a tendency toward the extremes of political thought, leaving a vacuum at the center, where one would normally expect to find intellectual independence and political sanity. This makes for discontinuity and tends to reduce the politics of writers and intellectuals to apologia for special interests.

But not all the confusion can be blamed on the Soviet equation of socialism with totalitarianism. A certain amount of eccentricity, amateurism, academicism, improvisation, free-wheeling liberationism, and theoretical cultism has moved into the intellectual spotlight. These are not all the same thing. But they have this in common: that they tend to destabilize thinking and force us to question the authority of the professionals in various fields. Examples come easily to mind. One of the early "liberators" was Wilhelm Reich, with his celebration of the orgasm and his promotion of the orgone box. More recently, Laing and Szasz have tried to make psychosis normal. In the realm of cultural and literary critcism, the black aesthetic was fashionable for a time, and currently some feminist critics have pushed valid complaints to ideological extremes by making all aesthetic – and intellectual – history a function of gender. In philosophy, linguistics, and literary criticism, the later structuralists and deconstructionists built some very esoteric and self-contained theories about the nature of reading and writing, about psychoanalysis, and about the role of language in the formation of thought. The most far-out figure is Jacques Lacan, who made of psychoanalysis a personal instrument for his own blend of Freud, Marx, and semiotics. One interesting aspect of this new intellectual wave is that it has found its way into American universities where it is treated as a new academic discipline.

These theoretical lunges, that create the impression our minds have lost their moorings, are not political. But they are part of the political climate, in the sense that they represent the accommodation of our thinking to organized movements and popular pressures. It is one of the modern ironies that ideas which are fashionable should be presented in a form that appears to be original. Perhaps in a culture dominated by the media it is essential that trendy movements acquire a far-out or esoteric look. Thus Lacan, even after his death, is not only the latest cult-figure in certain academic and therapeutic circles, but has the appearance of a perverse sage and the voice of a lonely prophet. And the various popular forms of therapy present themselves as advances in knowledge and treatment. The result is intellectual chaos – a cacophony of contradictory opinions spreading all over the political and ideological map. However, the significant aspect of this situation is not the vast number and variety of views – this was perhaps inevitable in a society both highly specialized and dedicated to mass education and communication – but the failure to distinguish between these widely differing views.

What has been lost, then, is the power to discriminate. In the United States, which takes the lead in the West in both cultural progression and regression, the lack of distinction has been ideologized under the headings of pluralism, relativism, and regionalism – all of which barely conceal the aim of giving equal weight to all ideas. The rationalization, utilized by almost every liberation movement, has been that art, thought, and politics have up to now been perpetuated by a thin line of cultural elites.

But, in addition to the intellectual effects of a false notion of cultural democracy, the political and literary world has actually become enormously more complex. Hence to talk about the relation of writers to politics today means to scan a wide spectrum of opinions and commitments. It becomes a survey of endless variations of belief on the right, the left, and the center. The range of modern intellectual politics might be indicated by citing the view of some of our major figures: for example, Eliot's traditionalism, Yeats's eccentric conservatism, Solzhenitsyn's panslavic clericalism, Brecht's manipulated Marxism, Marquez's third world socialism, Naipaul's third world scepticism, Camus's radical liberalism, Mailer's radical conservatism, Orwell's democratic socialism. But, of course, the major figures, despite their diversity, are fairly clear in their differences, and do not sacrifice tradition to originality. It is the less gifted writers and the trendy movements that give the appearance of an unbounded freedom of self-expression – and no common denominator except an enormous capacity for self-indulgence.

When it comes to the relation of literature, itself, to politics, we are in a much more complex and problematic sphere. Our findings here are bound to be more tentative, and dependent on critical assumptions, textual interpretations, and semantic questions. In a sense, all literature, indeed all of life, is political – if our definition of politics is broad enough. Even the lack of politics – or political neutrality – can be seen as a political stance. But narrowing the definition of "politics" does not make matters less difficult, for the politics of writing may not coincide with the known politics of the writer. In fact, the two may be opposed, since, as we know, the political attitudes that we can reconstruct in a literary work are dredged up from layers of consciousness far below those exhibited in daily life. Brecht, for example, was not always as orthodox in his plays as in his political statements. Similarly, the psychological twists of Dostoevsky's fiction are not prescribed by his Christian beliefs. There are other problems, too. When we talk about politics in literature, we are ostensibly talking about so-called content. Yet there is no critical agreement on the importance – or the place – of content in literature. On the contrary, the tendency of modern criticism has been to regard the content as inseparable from form. This means that it is difficult if not impossible to isolate content in order to interpret it or to evaluate it. Furthermore, some critics have gone so far as to deny content its own existence, or even, like Valéry, to speak of form as content. But, regardless of how we conceive of the meaning of content and form and of the relation of the two, there still remains the question of how to interpret and evaluate the politics of a work.

Take the poetry of Pound, perhaps the most politically controversial figure among modern writers. Assuming we can isolate his politics from the rest of his views, which is not so simple a matter as some brash critics seem to think, how much weight are they to be given in estimating Pound as a poet? Both sides have been argued: that the poetry is to be judged as poetry, apart from the politics; and, on the other hand, that the anti-Semitism, the Fascist sympathies, and the crude economics reduce the scale of the poetry. In essence, the former position removes poetry from history, while the latter assumes that poetry cannot be judged by purely formal considerations. Probably a more balanced view is that Pound's retrograde politics are interwoven with his other attitudes, and that these are all connected with the formal properties of his poems, with, for example, the choppiness and the lack of coherence of the verse. This is not to deny Pound's contribution to the language and sensibility of modern poetry. But the fact is that Pound's primitive and perverse idea of history is reflected in the formal lack of unity of the *Cantos*.

In literature as in life, the political extremes are easier to identify and to talk about. It is the middle registers that defy our interpretive powers and challenge our suppositions. We have less trouble in identifying the politics of out-and-out conservative or radical works. It is often the liberals, with their mixed premises and feelings, who, following the modern mode of combining right and left sentiments, present us with critical difficulties. Norman Mailer, for example, who calls himself a "conservative radical," has gone with the left on such popular issues as Vietnam, civil rights, and human rights, but has taken more traditional stands on sex, feminism, and power. He has the style of a revolutionary, but, as in D. H. Lawrence, it is a mystique of change that he exudes. Essentially, what Lawrence and Mailer explore is the perverse and underground order of things. There are many other instances of political ambiguity, which is not surprising when one considers that writing draws on different states of consciousness, some in opposition to the others. Conrad, for example, was a conservative, but his sense of adventure, of evil, of the waywardness and gloom of existence, brought other notes into his fiction. Camus, on the other hand, was a radical, at least in his human sympathies and in his apparent belief in a metaphysic of permanent revolution. But his feeling for gratuitous acts and for the small tragedies of life gave a certain timeless, and in that sense, a conservative aura to his writing. Henry James is another example of a novelist whose politics were not pure. In *The Princess Casimassima*, his explicitly political novel, James merged the theme of revolution with one of his basic motifs, the style of the aristocratic mind. His leading characters are the alienated plebian, Hyacinth, and the alienated princess, Casimassima, thus adding the idea of class as a way of life to its political definition.

In his attitude toward revolutionaries, Henry James would have to be classified as a conservative, though he did have doubts about the ability of the upper classes to defend their civilization. Dostoevsky and Conrad were similarly conservative in raising the spectre of anarchy in their fiction. But other ideas complicated their original conceptions. Conrad was the less complex political thinker. But in *The Secret Agent*, which would seem to be a straightforward story of human destruction and self-destruction by a group of simpleminded anarchists and a paid agent of the French government, acting as a provocateur, Conrad gives his novel a nonpolitical aspect by blending the abstract force of destiny with the mindlessness of his characters. Dostoevsky is much more complex – and historically clairvoyant. Nietzsche called Dostoevsky a great psychologist; but he was also probably the greatest political novelist. His achievement was to integrate his uncanny sense of the depths of morbid and perverse psychology with his equally perverse but remarkable insight into the extremes of revolutionary thinking. Hence what at first sight might appear to be an embittered and reactionary exposé of radical ideology is actually an apocalyptic vision of twentieth-century Communism. It is surely one of the ironies of intellectual history that only a wildly tortured mind could have foreseen the transformation of progressive thought into a system of organized repression.

In our own time, there have been a number of so-called progressive novelists: Henri Barbusse, Romain Rolland, Upton Sinclair, Jack London, John Steinbeck. Their achievement was largely to convert into fiction the advanced beliefs of their time; but they did not create a distinguished body of writing. Nor did the proletarian novelists in the thirties, who were inspired by the Communist slogans that defined literature as a revolutionary weapon, and produced books that were propagandistic and ideologically narrow. However, the outstanding political writers of fiction have not been the orthodox radicals but those who came out of the wave of disillusionment and disgust with the course of the Russian revolution. Such novelists as Malraux (in his later work), Koestler, Orwell, and Solzhenitsyn were quite direct and explicit in their politics, which consisted essentially of a probe of the Communist mentality – the mentality that managed to integrate the ideals of socialism with their total betrayal. In *Man's Fate*, Malraux accepted the revolutionary principle, though he saw it as an extension of personal will, and prophetically connected it with tragedy. (*Man's Hope* unfortunately did not question the Stalinist terror against the independent left in Spain.) Koestler's *Darkness at Noon* probed further into the revolutionary logic that kept presumably independent minds loyal to the regime. And Orwell in *1984* completed the cycle that traced the transformation of belief by projecting the complete regimentation and thought control that the ideal society of the future would achieve. Ignazio Silone's novels, on the other hand, were concerned with the demoralizing effects of Communist manipulation on the simpler Italian people. They were essentially pastoral political tragedies.

Solzhenitsyn, possibly the greatest of the modern political writers, might be said to have documented some of the things that

Orwell fantasized. Solzhenitsyn's politics, which amount to a call for a return to prerevolutionary Russia, are easy to disagree with. But they have inspired a powerful body of work, part fictional, part documentary, that is the blackest – and most depressing – indictment of the Soviet regime. Yet the incredible force of the writing and of Solzhenitsyn, himself, does help to keep alive a spirit of human possibilities, even though they may not be our own choice.

An interesting aspect of the political novel is the break of sophisticated political fiction – from Dostoevsky to Solzhenitsyn – with the traditional relation of events to character. In the typical eighteenth- and nineteenth-century novel, the *deus ex machina* was destiny, abstract, uncontrollable destiny, which was either a matter of accident in a writer like Fielding or Jane Austen, or an inscrutable cosmic law in a writer like Zola or Hardy. In the fiction of anti-Communist disillusionment, however – as in Communist fiction too – social forces determine human fate, though the individual is a co-conspirator with society. In this sense, the modern political novel might be said to represent an inversion of Marx's famous remark that man makes his own history, but not out of the whole cloth. For Koestler, Orwell, and Solzhenitsyn – and for Dostoevsky – history is made by the totalitarian components of the revolutionary will to save the world.

Such are the main lines in the relation of writers to politics. But politics today has taken on a broader meaning, and covers more facets of public life. Hence there is one other aspect of intellectual politics – the world of liberation movements – in which writers have had a conspicuous relation to politics. For these liberation movements, in addition to making their political presence felt, have invaded the territories of the arts. The feminist and black power movements are the most prominent of these modern political forces; and both of those have not only produced their own literature but have rewritten literary history. A number of good writers have come out of the consciousness surrounding these trends, such as Ralph Ellison, James Baldwin, Toni Morrison, Doris Lessing; but the aesthetic claims of these tendencies do confront us with some large critical questions. In the last analysis, it is true, new movements establish their power and credibility not by persuasion but by success, that is, by supplanting accepted tradition and principles. But, in the meantime, they present us with works and ideas whose value is primarily in support of the cause, not literary – at least not by prevailing standards; standards, by the way, which both movements tend to reject, for they regard them largely as part of the dominant white, male culture. Obviously, if one is guided only by current standards, one may not be receptive to new or radical productions. On the other hand, the total rejection of traditional criteria allows for no standards of judgment, and opens the way to accepting the claims on its own terms of any new work by any person or political group. The result amounts to aesthetic as well as political anarchy – a situation which some exponents of liberation do not find uncongenial. Clearly, the answer to the dilemmas posed by the new aesthetics lies somewhere in between rigid adherence to tradition and a complete rejection of it. This is not the place to indicate how such a resolution could be made. But it could be noted that a compromise with existing standards might not be entirely compatible with the position of both the radical feminists and the proponents of the black aesthetic.

However, aside from the problems raised by extreme aesthetic views, in dealing generally with the question of the political components of liberation, one's approach depends on the school of criticism one invokes. But it is quite evident in some of the recent excursions into critical method that theory is no substitute for taste and judgment – even if one concedes that both of these "amateurish" faculties are not totally independent of the culture. Still, some general observations are in order. Clearly, the Marxist approach has been most aware of the political side of literature, though only a few Marxists – like Walter Benjamin and Arnold Hauser – have avoided the vulgarizing and reductive applications of the doctrine which the more orthodox Marxists have fallen into. The main error of the Marxists – and of many political critics of literature – has been to ignore the importance of the medium, which has a history of its own and stands between writers' beliefs and their sensibility. On the other hand, the later structuralists and the deconstructionists – such as Barthes, Hartman, de Man, Greimas, Culler – have tried to give politics its due by extending the text into the wider domains of public and private existence. But this is a very special and eccentric view of the texts of literature, of the social context, and of the meaning of political life. In fact, it might be said to be tautologous, in that the stretching of the text into all the possibilities of our real and imaginary worlds is bound to include the dimension of politics. In our own time, it is the social critics, critics like Lionel Trilling, Irving Howe, Alfred Kazin, Philip Rahv, and Stephen Spender, who have been most successful in bringing a historical and political perspective to bear on narrower textual questions. Indeed, Stephen Spender's essay in this volume on the politics of English writers is a model of how to combine literary subtlety with political sophistication.

Part I

Literary and Political Theories

Introduction

Both writing and politics, though in very different fashion and addressed – at least in their immediacy – to different constituencies, expect to "reinvent the world." But no one, so far, has pinpointed exactly how this is done, or has agreed even whether writers – another catch-all category ranging from novelists, poets, and playwrights to essayists, cultural or political commentators, and reviewers – can substantially change the course of politics rather than be carried along by the events which, however indirectly, inspire them. We do not have an agreed upon "theory" on the subject. In fact, the propensity to look for such a theory, that is, for systematic categorization of the interaction between writers and their subject, is itself an Anglo-Saxon phenomenon that parallels to some extent the German tradition, and differs from the French intellectual habit to construct "systems of thought." Some of the overall traditions, of course, become evident in the essays which follow, as do the universal problems the authors address – problems that reach beyond national cultures to all of Western thought. For the most part, the present is assessed in terms of this past, even though each writer's political vantage point, or prejudice, is bound to dictate the logic of his/her argument. In addition, the training of a writer determines the specific tradition and range, and his/her focus and subject. So in spite of the fact that all these writers span a variety of disciplines, we are immediately aware that Hannah Arendt is a philosopher, that Albert Camus and Arthur Koestler are primarily novelists, that Victor Brombert and Richard Gilman are literary critics, that Leon Trotsky's perspective on art is determined by political reality, and that Daniel Bell is a sociologist.

Hannah Arendt locates the beginning of political thinking in Plato and Aristotle, and argues that this tradition ended with Marx, with his "conscious rebellion," which, however, still remained "strictly within a traditional framework." He broke with the past, "leaping from theory into action, from contemplation into labor, and from philosophy into politics." Kierkegaard and Nietzsche, though coming from different perspectives (the former reacted against Descartes's philosophy of doubt and the latter inverted Platonism), continues Arendt, completed this break, and were as concerned with reasserting the dignity of the individual in modern society as Marx. All three of them addressed the incompatibility of traditional beliefs with modern science (the most formidable enemy of religion), a fact that had been observed by all nineteenth-century writers and now was pushed to the point of questioning the specifically human qualities of social life – qualities that were being eroded with the introduction of the division of labor.

Whereas Arendt's focus is on Marx's and Nietzsche's political philosophy, and on the "devaluation of values," Camus takes off from their ideas on art, arguing that art ought to give us an understanding of revolt, but can never induce it. For artistic creation cannot be too self-conscious, cannot occur with a revolutionary aim. Summarizing periods of artistic ferment in relation to political events, he finds that great art never was created during revolutionary periods, or by revolutionaries, because the creation of a novel or a painting "supposes some sort of rejection of the real, though not a simple flight." Camus, of course, struggled with this issue his whole life, not only in his fiction but also in his political stance, as when he felt compelled to break with friends such as Sartre and Merleau-Ponty to free himself from the restrictions of Communist ideology while remaining on the left. Artistic works, in their attempts to overcome mortality, by allying themselves with "the beauty of the world and being against the forces of death and oblivion," he concluded, are themselves creative revolts.

This emphasis on the autonomy of art parallels Trotsky's formulation that every new art, though rooted in rebellion, and revolutionary in character, must be free of political messages. It cannot be in the service of a political elite – be it bourgeois or Communist. Socialist realism, and other messages disguised as art, he argues, have nothing to do with artistic creation: they are propaganda full of lies and hypocrisy. Art must remain faithful to itself and cannot "be commanded." Trotsky's "letter" was written in 1938, two years before he was killed by an agent of the Stalinists he attacked.

Richard Gilman's essay, written thirty-four years later, again addresses the death of art which had been predicted since Hegel. He argues against this assertion, claiming that there is always an avant-garde if only we are willing to recognize its existence. He chides the intelligentsia for attaching itself to the ideological content of art works, and thus for "taming" or co-opting these works, although he also attacks much of what is new as "bad, shapeless, chaotic, nihilistic, above all lacking in that large coherent vision of experience and society that was one of modernism's hallmarks." Because big literary works such as *Ulysses* or *The Waste Land* are no longer written, and "post-modernist" writing is on a smaller scale, "marked by ugliness, a pleasure in outrage, and the spirit of the haphazard," states Gilman, critics forget that there is "*serious* funk or pop, earnest grotesquerie, and the emergence of a vocabulary based on verbal 'dreck.'" All of these are efforts of the current avant-garde and represent the "risk of the impractical" and of "art being new."

Gilman already takes for granted Koestler's definition of the intelligentsia – the part of the nation that aspires to independent thinking, that debunks the existing hierarchy of values and tries to replace them with new ones. These new values, maintains Koestler, always contain a prophetic element, which then is picked up and adapted by a group or class that has won a political struggle. Thus "the intelligentsia is a kind of sensitive porous membrane stretched between media of different properties." Koestler goes on to demonstrate how this happened, beginning with the Encylopedists; how as the Third Estate began to lose its progressive character, there was a decline in the quality of the intelligentsia's thinking – allegedly introduced by neurosis due to the hostile pressures from the rest of society. His theory, though heavily bolstered by Freud, of course, was tied to his own politics, and thus was directed against the Bloomsbury group and all the other fellow-travelling intellectuals who refused to acknowledge the collapse of the Marxist revolution, who, in 1944, saw the Soviet Union through pink glasses, and who, also, had forgotten that the first "allegiance" of the intelligentsia is to independence of thought.

Brombert, focusing on French intellectuals, questions Koestler's affirmation that the Encylopedists were the first modern intellectuals, by quoting Julien Benda for whom they were the first traitors to the philosophical spirit, and Raymond Aron who pointed out that they were also the first ones to use the pen for a living. The word intellectual itself, continues Brombert, bears the ideological traces of its origin. And Benda, according to Brombert, regularly denounces those on the right, while allowing the left to "follow the dictates of their conscience . . . in the name of justice and out of a pure sense of moral duty." Novelists, too, he points out, have written about intellectuals ever since the nineteenth century, and about the ferment amongst them – elaborating on all the conflicts, illusions, failures, and ambitions which lend themselves to caricature and to depicting the intellectual-novelist as hero.

Brombert, a literary critic, indicates that we can best understand the intellectuals' role by exploring the many subtleties of a literary work. Bell, though fully conversant with literary traditions and criticism, subordinates them and, instead, looks to sociological meanings. Assailing the tendency of Americans to view politics from a one-dimensional perspective that pigeonholes intellectuals in relation to their attitudes towards Marxism – a Marxism suffering from the weight of its own history – he focuses on the role of capitalism as it actually emerged, and on Max Weber's and Werner Sombart's respective themes of *asceticism* and *acquisitiveness*. Since Marx's predictions of revolution were wrong, Bell looks at the ensuing cultural fragmentations and contradictions and finds himself to be a socialist in economics (he advocates minimum social security, adequate medical care, and self-respect for all), a liberal in politics (individual needs take precedence over group needs), and a conservative in culture (he respects artistic tradition and judgments based on quality). Modernism, responsible for the surge of creativity between about 1850 and 1930, and begun as an "attack on orthodoxy . . . [to] become the regnant orthodoxy of the day," he notes, has been trivialized. Gilman, among others, would agree, although he perceives continuing experimentation in the modernist spirit. Bell, on the other hand, perceives the exhaustion of modernism, "the aridity of communist life, to the tedium of the unrestrained self, and the prevalent meaninglessness of political chants," as indicative of an entire era.

Whether we look to the empty or the full half of the proverbial cup, Bell's notions that the need for economic limits might also push for limits in cultural spheres, at least in life-styles, are provocative. But this argument gets us back into politics, into discussions of conservatism versus radicalism, and away from the centrality of art, of the avant-garde, and of free-floating intellectuals.

Chapter 1
Tradition and the Modern Age*
Hannah Arendt

Our tradition of political thought has its definite beginning in the teachings of Plato and Aristotle. I believe it came to a
no less definite end in the theories of Karl Marx. The beginning was
made when in *The Republic,* in the allegory of the cave, Plato described the sphere of human affairs—all that belongs to the living
together of men in a common world—in terms of darkness, confusion,
and deception which those aspiring to true being must turn away
from and abandon if they want to discover the clear sky of eternal
ideas. The end came with Marx's declaration that philosophy and
its truth are not located outside the affairs of men and their common
world but precisely in them, and can be "realized" only in the
sphere of living-together, which he called Society, through the emergence of "socialized men" (*vergesellschaftete Menschen*). Political
philosophy necessarily implies the attitude of the philosopher toward
politics; its tradition began with the philosopher turning away from
politics and then returning in order to impose his standards on human affairs. The end came when a philosopher turned away from
philosophy so as to "realize" it in politics. This was Marx's attempt,
expressed, first, in his decision (in itself philosophical) to abjure
philosophy, and, secondly, in his intention to "change the world" and
thereby the philosophizing minds, the "consciousness" of men.

The beginning and the end of the tradition have this in common: that the elementary problems of politics never come as clearly
to light in their immediate and simple urgency as when they are
first formulated and when they receive their final challenge. The
beginning, in Jacob Burckhardt's words, is like a "fundamental

* This essay is drawn from a series of lectures delivered under the auspices of
the Christian Gauss Seminars in Criticism at Princeton University.

chord" which sounds in its endless modulations through the whole history of Western thought. Only beginning and end are, so to speak, pure or unmodulated; and the fundamental chord therefore never strikes its listeners more forcefully and more beautifully than when it first sends its harmonizing sound into the world and never more irritatingly and jarringly than when it still continues to be heard in a world whose sounds—and thought—it can no longer bring into harmony. A random remark which Plato made in his last work: "The beginning is like a god which as long as it dwells among men saves all things" (*arché gar kai theos en anthrôpois hidrymené sôdzei panta*, Laws VI, 775), is true of our tradition; as long as its beginning was alive, it could save and bring all things into harmony. By the same token, it became destructive as it came to its end—to say nothing of the aftermath of confusion and helplessness which came after the tradition ended and in which we live today.

In Marx's philosophy, which did not so much turn Hegel upside down as invert the traditional hierarchy of thought and action, of contemplation and labor, and of philosophy and politics, the beginning made by Plato and Aristotle proves its vitality by leading Marx into flagrantly contradictory statements, mostly in that part of his teachings usually called utopian. The most important are his prediction that under conditions of a "socialized humanity" the "state will wither away," and that the productivity of labor will become so great that labor somehow will abolish itself, thus guaranteeing an almost unlimited amount of leisure time to each member of the society. These statements, in addition to being predictions, contain of course Marx's ideal of the best form of society. As such they are not utopian, but rather reproduce the political and social conditions of the same Athenian city-state which was the model of experience for Plato and Aristotle, and therefore the foundation on which our tradition rests. The Athenian *polis* functioned without a division between rulers and ruled, and thus was not a state if we use this term, as Marx did, in accordance with the traditional definitions of forms of government, that is, one-man rule or monarchy, rule by the few or oligarchy, and rule by the majority or democracy. Athenian citizens, moreover, were citizens only insofar as they possessed leisure time, had that freedom from labor which Marx predicts for the future. Not only in Athens, but throughout antiquity and up to the modern age, those who labored were not citizens and those who were citizens were first of all those who did not labor or who possessed more than their labor power. This similarity becomes even more striking when we look into the actual content of Marx's ideal society. Leisure time is seen to exist under the condition of statelessness, or under conditions where, in Lenin's famous phrase which renders Marx's thought very precisely, the administration of society has become so simplified that every cook is qualified to take over its machinery. Obviously, under such circumstances the whole business of politics, which is now the simplified "administration of things" (Engels), could be of interest only to a cook. This, to be sure, is very different from actual conditions in antiquity, where, on the contrary, political duties were considered so difficult and time-consuming that those engaged in them could not be permitted to undertake any tiring activity. (Thus, for instance, the shepherd could qualify for citizenship but the peasant could not, or the painter, but not the sculptor, was still recognized as something more than a *banausos,* the distinction being drawn in either case simply by applying the criterion of effort and fatigue.) It is against the time-consuming political life of an average full-fledged citizen of the Greek *polis* that the philosophers, especially Aristotle, established their ideal of *scholé,* of leisure time, which in antiquity never meant freedom from ordinary labor, a matter of course anyhow, but time free from political activity and the business of the state.

In Marx's ideal society these two different concepts are inextricably combined: the classless and state-less society somehow realizes the general ancient conditions of leisure from labor and, at the same time, leisure from politics. This is supposed to come about when the "administration of things" has taken the place of government and political action. This twofold leisure from labor as well as politics had been for the philosophers the condition of a *bios theôrétikos,* a life devoted to philosophy and knowledge in the widest sense of the word. Lenin's cook, in other words, lives in a society providing her with as much leisure from labor as the free ancient citizens enjoyed in order to devote their time to *politeuesthai,* as well as as much leisure from politics as the Greek philosophers had demanded for the few who wanted to devote all their time to *philosophein.* The combination of a state-less (apolitical) and almost labor-less society loomed so large in Marx's imagination as the very expression of an ideal humanity because of the traditional connotation of leisure as *scholé* and *otium*, that is, a life devoted to aims higher than work or politics.

Marx himself regarded his so-called utopia as simple prediction, and it is true that this part of his theories contains a great many developments which have come fully to light only in our time. Government in the old sense has given way in many respects to administration and the constant increase in leisure for the masses is a fact in all industrialized countries. Marx clearly perceived certain trends inherent in the era ushered in by the Industrial Revolution, although he was wrong in assuming that these trends would assert themselves only under conditions of socialization of the means of production. The hold which the tradition had over him lies in his viewing this development in an idealized light, and in understanding it in terms and concepts having their origin in an altogether different historical period. This blinded him to the authentic and very perplexing problems inherent in the modern world and gives his accurate predictions their utopian quality. But the utopian ideal of a classless, state-less and labor-less society is born out of the marriage of two altogether non-utopian elements: the perception of certain trends in the present which can no longer be understood in the framework of the tradition, and the traditional concepts and ideals by which Marx himself understood and integrated them.

Marx's own attitude to the tradition of political thought was one of conscious rebellion. In a challenging and paradoxical mood he therefore framed certain key statements which, containing his political philosophy, underlie and transcend the strictly scientific part of his work (and as such curiously remain the same throughout his life, from the early writings to the last volume of *Das Kapital*). Crucial among them are the following: "Labor is the creator of man" (in a formulation by Engels, who, contrary to an opinion current among some Marx scholars, usually renders Marx's thought adequately and succinctly). "Violence is the midwife of history" (which occurs in both the writings of Marx and of Engels in many variations). Finally, there is the famous last thesis on Feuerbach: "The philosophers have only interpreted the world differently; the point is, however, to change it," which, in the light of Marx's thought, one could render more adequately as: The philosophers have interpreted the world long enough; the time has come to change it. For this last statement is in fact only a variation of another, also occurring in an early manuscript: "You cannot *aufheben* (i.e., elevate, conserve, and abolish in the Hegelian sense) philosophy without realizing it." In the later work the same attitude to philosophy appears in the many predictions that the working class will be the heir of classical philosophy.

None of these statements can be understood in and by itself. Each acquires its meaning by contradicting some traditionally accepted truth whose plausibility up to the beginning of the modern age had been beyond doubt. "Labor created man" means first that labor and not God created man; secondly, it means that man, insofar as he is human, creates himself, that his humanity is the result of his own activity; it means, thirdly, that what distinguishes man from animal, his *differentia specifica*, is not reason, but labor, that he is not an *animal rationale*, but an *animal laborans;* it means, fourthly, that it is not reason, until then the highest attribute of man, but labor, the traditionally most despised human activity, which contains the humanity of man. Thus Marx challenges the traditional God, the traditional estimate of labor, and the traditional glorification of reason.

"Violence is the midwife of history" means that the hidden forces of development of human productivity, insofar as they depend upon free and conscious human action, come to light only through the violence of wars and revolutions. Only in those violent periods does history show its true face and dispel the fog of mere ideological, hypocritical talk. Again the challenge to tradition is clear. Violence is traditionally the *ultima ratio* in relationships between nations and the most disgraceful of domestic actions, being always considered the outstanding characteristic of tyranny. (The few attempts to save violence from disgrace, chiefly by Machiavelli and Hobbes, are of great relevance for the problem of power and quite illuminative of the early confusion of power with violence, but they exerted remarkably little influence on the tradition of political thought prior to our own time.) To Marx, on the contrary, violence or rather the possession of the means of violence is the constituent element of all forms of government; the state is the instrument of the ruling class by means of which it oppresses and exploits, and the whole sphere of political action is characterized by the use of violence.

The Marxian identification of action with violence implies another fundamental challenge to tradition which may be more difficult to perceive, but of which Marx, who knew Aristotle very well, must have been aware. The twofold Aristotelian definition of man as a *dzôon politikon* and a *dzôon logon echon,* a being attaining his highest possibility in the faculty of speech and the life in a *polis,* was designed to distinguish the Greek from the barbarian and the free man from the slave. The distinction was that Greeks living together in a *polis* conducted their affairs by means of speech, through persuasion, and not by means of violence through mute coercion. Barbarians were ruled by violence and slaves by labor, and since violent action and toil are alike in that they do not need speech to be effective, barbarians and slaves are *aneu logou,* that is, they do not live with each other primarily by means of speech. Labor was to the Greeks essentially a non-political, private affair, but violence is related to and establishes a contact, albeit negative, with other men. Marx's glorification of violence therefore contains the more specific denial of *logos,* of speech, the diametrically opposite and traditionally most human form of intercourse. Marx's theory of ideological superstructures ultimately rests on this anti-traditional hostility to speech and the concomitant glorification of violence.

For traditional philosophy it would have been a contradiction in terms to "realize philosophy" or to change the world in accordance with philosophy—for Marx's remark about interpreting and changing the world implies that one can change the world only now, after philosophers have interpreted it and because of that. Philosophy may prescribe certain rules of action, though no great philosopher ever took this to be his most important concern. Essentially, philosophy from Plato to Hegel was "not of this world," whether it is Plato describing the philosopher as the man whose body only inhabits the city of his fellow men, or Hegel admitting that from the point of view of common sense, philosophy is a world stood on its head, a *"verkehrte Welt."* The challenge to tradition, this time not merely implied but directly expressed in Marx's statement, lies in the prediction that the world of common human affairs, where we orient ourselves and think in common-sense terms, will one day become identical with the realm of ideas where the philosopher moves, or that philosophy, which has always been only "for the few," will one day be the common-sense reality for everybody.

These three statements are framed in traditional terms which they, however, explode; they are formulated as paradoxes and meant to shock us. They are in fact even more paradoxical and led Marx into greater perplexities than he himself had anticipated. Each contains one fundamental contradiction which remained insoluble in his own terms. If labor is the most human and most productive of man's activities, what will happen when after the revolution "labor is abolished" in "the realm of freedom," when man has succeeded in emancipating himself from it? What productive and what essentially human activity will be left? If violence is the midwife of history and violent action therefore the most dignified of all forms of human action, what will happen when, after the conclusion of class struggle and the disappearance of the state, no violence will even be possible? How will man be able to act at all in a meaningful authentic way? Finally, when philosophy has been both realized and abolished in the future society, what kind of thought will be left?

Marx's inconsistencies are well known and noted by almost all Marx scholars. They usually are summarized as discrepancies "between the scientific point of view of the historian and the moral point of view of the prophet" (Edmund Wilson), between the historian seeing in the accumulation of capital "a material means for the increase of productive forces" (Marx) and the moralist who denounced those who performed "the historical task" (Marx) as exploiters and dehumanizers of man. This and similar inconsistencies are minor when compared with the fundamental contradiction between the glorification of labor and action as against contemplation and thought *and* of a state-less, that is, action-less and (almost) labor-less society. For this can neither be blamed on the natural difference between a revolutionary young Marx and the more scientific insights of the older historian and economist, nor resolved through the assumption of a dialectical movement which needs the negative or evil to produce the positive or the good.

Such fundamental and flagrant contradictions rarely occur in second-rate writers, in whom they can be discounted. In the work of great authors they lead into the very center of their work and are the most important clue to a true understanding of their problems and new insights. In Marx, as in the case of other great authors of the last century, a seemingly playful, challenging, and paradoxical mood conceals the perplexity of having to deal with new phenomena in terms of an old tradition of thought outside of whose conceptual framework no thinking seemed possible at all. It is as though Marx, not unlike Kierkegaard and Nietzsche, tried desperately to think against the tradition using its own conceptual tools. Our tradition of political thought began when Plato discovered that it is somehow inherent in the philosophical experience to turn away from the common world of human affairs; it ended when nothing was left of this experience but the opposition of thinking and acting, which, depriving thought of reality and action of sense, makes both meaningless.

II

The strength of this tradition, its hold on Western man's thought, has never depended on his consciousness of it. Indeed, only twice in our history do we encounter periods in which men are conscious and over-conscious of the fact of tradition, identifying age as such with authority. This happened, first, when the Romans adopted classical Greek thought and culture as their own spiritual tradition and thereby decided historically that tradition was to have a permanent formative influence on European civilization. Before the Romans such a thing as tradition was unknown; with them it became and after them it remained the guiding thread through the past and the chain to which each new generation knowingly or unknowingly was bound in its understanding of the world and its own experience. Not until the Romantic period do we again encounter an exalted consciousness and glorification of tradition. (The discovery of antiquity in the Renaissance was a first attempt to break the fetters of tradition, and by going to the sources themselves to establish a past over which tradition would have no hold.) Today tradition is sometimes considered an essentially romantic concept, but romanticism did no more than place the discussion of tradition on the agenda of the nineteenth century; its glorification of the past only served to mark the moment when the modern age was about to change our world and general circumstances to such an extent that a matter-of-course reliance on tradition was no longer possible.

The end of a tradition does not necessarily mean that traditional concepts have lost their power over the minds of men. On the contrary, it sometimes seems that this power of well-worn notions and categories becomes more tyrannical as the tradition loses its living force and as the memory of its beginning recedes; it may even reveal its full coercive force only after its end has come and men no longer even rebel against it. This at least seems to be the lesson of the twentieth-century aftermath of formalistic and compulsory thinking, which came after Kierkegaard, Marx, and Nietzsche, by consciously inverting the traditional hierarchy of concepts, had challenged the basic assumptions of traditional religion, traditional political thought, and traditional metaphysics. However, neither the twentieth-century aftermath nor the nineteenth-century rebellion against tradition actually caused the break in our history. This sprang from a chaos of mass-perplexities on the political scene and of mass-opinions in the spiritual sphere which the totalitarian movements, through terror and ideology, crystallized into a new form of government and domination. Totalitarian domination as an established fact, which in its unprecedentedness cannot be comprehended through the usual categories of political thought, and whose "crimes" cannot be judged by traditional moral standards or punished within the legal framework of our civilization, has broken the continuity of occidental history. The break in our tradition is now an accomplished fact. It is neither the result of anyone's deliberate choice nor subject to further decision.

The attempts of great thinkers after Hegel to break away from patterns of thought which had ruled the West for more than two thousand years may have foreshadowed this event and certainly can help to illuminate it, but they did not cause it. The event itself marks the division between the modern age—rising with the natural sciences in the seventeenth century, reaching its political climax in the revolutions of the eighteenth, and unfolding its general implications after the Industrial Revolution of the nineteenth—and the world of the twentieth century, which came into existence through the chain of catastrophes touched off by the First World War. To hold the thinkers of the modern age, especially the nineteenth-century rebels against tradition, responsible for the structure and conditions of the twentieth century is even more dangerous than it is unjust. The implications apparent in the actual event of totalitarian domination go far beyond the most radical or most adventurous ideas of any of these thinkers.

Their greatness lay in the fact that they perceived their world as one invaded by new problems and perplexities which our tradition of thought was unable to cope with. In this sense their own departure from tradition, no matter how emphatically they proclaimed it (like children whistling louder and louder because they are lost in the dark), was no deliberate act of their own choosing either. What frightened them about the dark was its silence, not the break in tradition. This break, when it actually occurred, dispelled the darkness, so that we can hardly listen any longer to the overloud, "pathetic" style of their writing. But the thunder of the eventual explosion has also drowned the preceding ominous silence that still answers us whenever we dare to ask, not, "what are we fighting *against*" but "what are we fighting *for*?"

Neither the silence of the tradition nor the reaction of thinkers against it in the nineteenth century can ever explain what actually happened. The non-deliberate character of the break gives it an irrevocability which only events, never thoughts, can have. The rebellion against tradition in the nineteenth century remained strictly within a traditional framework; and on the level of mere thought, which could hardly be concerned then with more than the essentially negative experiences of foreboding, apprehension, and ominous silence, only radicalization, not a new beginning and reconsideration of the past, was possible.

Kierkegaard, Marx, and Nietzsche stand at the end of the tradition just before the break came. Their immediate predecessor was Hegel. He it was who for the first time saw the whole of world history as one continuous development, and this tremendous achievement implied that he himself stood outside all authority-claiming systems and beliefs of the past, that he was held only by the thread of continuity in history itself. The thread of historical continuity was the first substitute for tradition; by means of it, the overwhelming mass of the most divergent values, the most contradictory thoughts and conflicting authorities, all of which had somehow been able to function together, were reduced to a unilinear dialectically consistent development actually designed to repudiate not tradition as such, but the authority of all traditions. Kierkegaard, Marx, and Nietzsche remained Hegelians insofar as they saw the history of past philosophy as one dialectically developed whole; their great merit was that they radicalized this new essence in the only way it could still be further developed, namely in leaps and reversals.

Kierkegaard, Marx, and Nietzsche are for us like guideposts to a past which has lost its authority. They were the first who dared to think without the guidance of any authority whatsoever; yet, for better and worse, they were still held by the categorical framework of the great tradition. In some respects we are better off. We need no longer be concerned with their scorn for the "educated philistines," who all through the nineteenth century tried to make up for the loss of authentic authority with a spurious glorification of culture. To most people today, this culture looks like a field of ruins which, far from being able to claim any authority, can hardly command their interest. This fact may be deplorable, but implicit in it is the great chance to look upon the past with eyes undistracted by any tradition, with a directness which has disappeared from occidental reading and hearing ever since the Romans submitted to Greek civilization.

III

The leaps and inversions of the rebels against tradition were all caused by some new experience which they tried almost instantaneously to overcome and resolve into something old. Kierkegaard's leap from doubt into belief was a reversal and a distortion of the traditional relationship between reason and faith. It was the answer to the modern loss of faith, not only in God but in reason as well, which was inherent in Descartes' *De omnibus dubitandum est,* with its underlying suspicion that things may not *be* as they appear and that an evil spirit may willfully and forever hide truth from the minds of man. Marx's leap from theory into action, and from contemplation into labor, came after Hegel had transformed metaphysics into a philosophy of history and changed the philosopher into the historian to whose backward glance eventually, at the end of time, the meaning of becoming and motion, not of being and truth, would reveal itself. Nietzsche's leap from the non-sensuous transcendent realm of ideas and measurements into the sensuousness of life, his "inverted Platonism" or "trans-valuation of values," as he himself would call it, was the last attempt to turn away from the tradition, an attempt which succeeded only in turning tradition upside down.

Different as these rebellions against tradition are in content and intention, their results have an ominous similarity: Kierkegaard, jumping from doubt into belief, carried doubt into religion, transformed the attack of modern science on religion into an inner-religious struggle, so that since then sincere religious experience has seemed possible only in the tension between doubt and belief, in torturing one's beliefs with one's doubts and relaxing from this torment in the violent affirmation of the absurdity of both the human condition and man's belief. No clearer symptom of this modern religious situation can be found than the fact that Dostoevsky, perhaps the most experienced psychologist of modern religious beliefs, portrayed pure faith in the character of Myshkin, *The Idiot.*

Marx, when he leaped from philosophy into politics, carried the theories of dialectics into action, making political action more theoretical, more dependent upon what we today would call an ideology, than it ever had been before. Since, moreover, his springboard was not philosophy in the old metaphysical sense, but as specifically Hegel's philosophy of history as Kierkegaard's springboard had been Descartes' philosophy of doubt, he superimposed the "law of history" upon politics and ended by losing the significance of both, of action no less than of thought, of politics no less than of philosophy, when he insisted that both were mere functions of society and history.

Nietzsche's inverted Platonism, his insistence on life and the sensuously and materially given as against the suprasensuous and transcendent ideas which, since Plato, had been supposed to measure, judge, and give meaning to the given, ended in what is commonly called nihilism. Yet Nietzsche was no nihilist, but on the contrary was the first to try to overcome the nihilism inherent not in the notions of the thinkers but in the reality of modern life. What he discovered in his attempt at "trans-valuation" was that within this categorical framework the sensuous loses its very *raison d'être* when it is deprived of its background of the suprasensuous and transcendent. This insight in its elementary simplicity is relevant for all the turning-about operations in which the tradition found its end. "The deposition of the suprasensuous removes also the mere sensuous and its differentiation. . . . The deposition ends in senselessness" (Martin Heidegger, "Nietzsches Wort 'Gott is tot' " in *Holzwege*).

What Kierkegaard wanted was to assert the dignity of faith against modern reason and reasoning, as Marx desired to assert again the dignity of human action against modern historical contemplation and relativization, and as Nietzsche wanted to assert the dignity of human life against the impotence of modern man. The traditional oppositions of *fides* and *intellectus* and of *theôria* and *praxis* took their respective revenges upon Kierkegaard and Marx, just as the opposition between the transcendent and the sensuously given took its revenge upon Nietzsche, not because these oppositions still had roots in valid human experience, but, on the contrary, because they had become mere concepts outside of which, however, no comprehensive thought seemed possible at all.

That these three outstanding and conscious rebellions against a tradition which had lost its *arché*, its beginning and principle, should have ended in self-defeat, is no reason to question the greatness of the enterprises nor their relevance to the understanding of the modern world. Each attempt, in its particular way, took account of those traits of modernity which were incompatible with our tradition, and this even before modernity in all its aspects had fully revealed itself. Kierkegaard knew that the incompatibility of modern science with traditional beliefs does not lie in any specific scientific findings, all of which can be integrated into religious systems and absorbed by religious beliefs for the reason that they will never be able to answer the questions which religion raises. He knew that this incompatibility lay, rather, in the conflict between a spirit of doubt and distrust which ultimately can trust only what it has made itself and the traditional unquestioning confidence in what has been given and appears in its true being to man's reason and senses. Modern science, in Marx's words, would "be superfluous if the appearance and essence of things coincided." Because our traditional religion is essentially a revealed religion and holds, in harmony with ancient philosophy, that truth is what reveals itself, that truth *is* revelation (even though the meanings of this revelation may be as different as the philosophers' *alétheia* and *délôsis* are from the early Christians' eschatological expectations for an *apokalypsé* in the Second Coming), modern science has become much more formidable an enemy of religion than traditional philosophy, even in its most rationalistic versions, ever could be. Yet Kierkegaard's attempt to save faith from the onslaught of modernity made even religion modern, that is, subject to doubt and distrust. Traditional beliefs disintegrated into absurdity when Kierkegaard tried to reassert them on the assumption that man cannot trust the truth-receiving capacity of his reason or his senses.

Marx knew that the incompatibility between classical political thought and modern political conditions lay in the accomplished fact of the French and Industrial Revolutions, which together had raised labor, traditionally the most despised of all human activities, to the highest rank of productivity and pretended to be able to assert the time-honored ideal of freedom under unheard-of conditions of universal equality. He knew that the question was only superficially posed in the idealistic assertions of the equality of man, the inborn dignity of every human being, and only superficially answered by giving laborers the right to vote. This was not a problem of justice that could be solved by giving the new class of workers its due, after which the old order of *suum cuique* would be restored and function as in the past. There is the fact of the basic incompatibility between the traditional concepts making labor itself the very symbol of man's subjection to necessity and the modern age which saw labor elevated to express man's positive freedom, the freedom of productivity. It is from the impact of labor, that is to say, of necessity in the traditional sense, that Marx endeavored to save philosophical thought, deemed by the tradition to be the freest of all human activities. Yet when he proclaimed that "you cannot abolish philosophy without realizing it," he thus began subjecting thought also to the inexorable tyranny of necessity, to the "iron law" of productive forces in society.

Nietzsche's devaluation of values, like Marx's labor theory of value, arises from the incompatibility between the traditional "ideas," which, as transcendent units, had been used to recognize and measure human thoughts and actions, and modern society, which had dissolved all such standards into relationships between its members, establishing them as functional "values." Values are social commodities that have no significance of their own but, like other commodities, exist only in the ever-changing relativity of social linkages and commerce. Through this relativization both the things which man produces for his use and the standards according to which he lives undergo a decisive change: they become entities of exchange and the bearer of their "value" is society and not man, who produces and uses and judges. The "good" loses its character as an idea, the standard by which the good and the bad can be measured and recognized; it has become a value which can be exchanged with other values, such as those of expediency or of power. The holder of values can refuse this exchange and become an "idealist," who prices the value of "good" higher than the value of expediency; but this does not make the "value" of good any less relative.

The term "value" owes its origin to the sociological trend which even before Marx was quite manifest in the relatively new science of classical economy. Marx was still aware of the fact, which the social sciences have since forgotten, that nobody "seen in his isolation produces values," but that products "become values only in their social relationship." His distinction between "use value" and "exchange value" reflects the distinction between things as men use and produce them and their value in society, and his insistence on the greater authenticity of use values, his frequent description of the rise of exchange value as a kind of original sin at the beginning of market production, reflect his own helpless and, as it were, blind recognition of the inevitability of an impending "devaluation of all values." The birth of the social sciences can be located at the moment when all things, "ideas" as well as material objects, were equated with values so that everything derived its existence from and was related to society, the *bonum* and *malum* no less than tangible objects. In the dispute as to whether capital or labor is the source of values, it is generally overlooked that at no time prior to the incipient Industrial Revolution was it held that values, and not things, are the result of man's productive capacity, or everything that exists related to society and not to man "seen in his isolation." The notion of "socialized men," whose emergence Marx projected into the future classless society, is in fact the underlying assumption of classical as well as Marxian economy.

It is therefore only natural that the perplexing question which has plagued all later "value-philosophies," where to find the one supreme value by which to measure all others, should first appear in the economic sciences which, in Marx's words, try to "square the circle—to find a commodity of unchanging value which would serve as a constant standard for others." Marx believed he had found this standard in labor-time, and insisted that use values "which can be acquired without labor have no exchange value" (though they retain their "natural usefulness"), so that the earth itself is of "no value"; it does not represent "objectified labor." With this conclusion we come to the threshold of a radical nihilism, to that denial of everything given of which the nineteenth-century rebellions against tradition as yet knew little and which rises only in twentieth-century society.

Nietzsche seems to have been unaware of the origin as well as of the modernity of the term "value" when he accepted it as a key notion in his assault on tradition. But when he began to devaluate the current values of society, the implications of the whole enterprise quickly became manifest. Ideas in the sense of absolute units had become identified with social values to such an extent that they simply ceased to exist once their value-character, their social status, was challenged. Nobody knew his way better than Nietzsche through the meandering paths of the modern spiritual labyrinth, where recollections and ideas of the past are hoarded up as though they had always been values which society depreciated whenever it needed better and newer commodities. Also, he was well aware of the profound nonsense of the new "value-free" science which was soon to degenerate into scientism and general scientific superstition and which never, despite all protests to the contrary, had anything in common with the Roman historians' attitude of *sine ira et studio*. For while the latter demanded judgment without scorn and truth-finding without zeal, the *"wertfreie Wissenschaft,"* which could no longer judge because it had lost its standards of judgment and could no longer find truth because it doubted the existence of truth, imagined that it could produce meaningful results if only it abandoned the last remnants of those absolute standards. And when Nietzsche proclaimed that he had discovered "new and higher values," he was the first to fall prey to delusions which he himself had helped to destroy, accepting the old traditional notion of measuring with transcendent units in its newest and most hideous form, thereby again carrying the relativity and exchange-ability of values into the very matters whose absolute dignity he had wanted to assert—power and life and man's love of his earthly existence.

IV

Self-defeat, the result of all three challenges to tradition in the nineteenth century, is only one and perhaps the most superficial thing Kierkegaard, Marx, and Nietzsche have in common. More important is the fact that each of their rebellions seems to be concentrated on the same, ever-repeated subject: Against the alleged abstractions of philosophy and its concept of man as an *animal rationale*, Kierkegaard wants to assert concrete and suffering men; Marx confirms that man's humanity consists of his productive and active force which in its most elementary aspect he calls labor-power; and Nietzsche insists on creation and power. In complete independence of one another—none of them ever knew of the others' existence—they arrive at the conclusion that this enterprise in terms of the tradition can be achieved only through a mental operation best described in the images and similes of leaps, inversions and turning concepts upside down. (Kierkegaard speaks of his leap from doubt into belief; Marx turns Hegel, or rather "Plato and the whole Platonic tradition" (Sidney Hook), "right side up again," leaping "from the realm of necessity into the realm of freedom"; and Nietzsche understands his philosophy as "inverted Platonism" and "transformation of all values.")

The turning operations with which the tradition ends bring the beginning to light in a twofold sense: the very assertion of one side of the opposites—*fides* against *intellectus, praxis* against *theôria,* sensuous perishable life against permanent unchanging suprasensuous truth—necessarily brings to light the repudiated opposite and shows that both have meaning and significance only in this opposition. Furthermore, to think in terms of such opposites is not a matter of course, but is grounded in a first great turning operation on which all others ultimately are based because it established the opposites in whose tension the tradition moves. This first turning-about is Plato's *periagôgé holés tés psychés,* the turning-about of the whole human being, which he tells—as though it were a story with beginning and end and not merely a mental operation—in the parable of the cave in the *Republic.*

The story of the cave unfolds in three stages: the first turning-about takes place in the cave itself when one of the inhabitants frees himself from the fetters which chain the cave dwellers' "legs and necks" so that "they can only see before them," their eyes glued to the screen on which shadows and images of things appear; he now turns around to the rear of the cave where an artificial fire illuminates the things in the cave as they really are. There is, second, the turning from the cave to the clear sky where the ideas appear as the true and eternal essences of the things in the cave, illuminated by the sun, the idea of ideas, enabling man to see and the ideas to shine forth. Finally there is the necessity of returning to the cave, of leaving the realm of eternal essences and moving again in the realm of perishable things and mortal men. Each of these turnings is accompanied by a loss of sense and orientation: the eyes accustomed to the shadowy appearances on the screen are blinded by the fire in the cave; the eyes then adjusted to the dim light of the artificial fire are blinded by the light that illuminates the ideas; finally, the eyes adjusted to the light of the sun must readjust to the dimness of the cave.

Behind these turnings-about, which Plato demands only of the philosopher, the lover of truth and light, lies another inversion indicated generally in Plato's violent polemics against Homer and the Homeric religion, and in particular in the construction of his story as a kind of reply to and reversal of Homer's description of Hades in the eleventh book of the *Odyssey*. The parallel between the images of the cave and Hades (the shadowy, unsubstantial, senseless movements of the soul in Homer's Hades correspond to the ignorance and senselessness of the bodies in the cave) is unmistakable because it is stressed by Plato's use of the words *eidôlon,* image, and *skia,* shadow, which are Homer's own key words for the description of life after death in the underworld. The reversal of the Homeric "position" is obvious; it is as though Plato were saying to him: not the life of bodyless souls, but the life of the bodies takes place in an underworld; compared to the sky and the sun, the earth is like Hades; images and shadows are the objects of bodily senses, not the surroundings of bodyless souls; the true and real is not the world in which we move and live and which we have to part from in death, but the ideas seen and grasped by the eyes of the mind. In a sense, Plato's *periagôgé* was a turning-about by which everything that was commonly believed in Greece in accordance with the Homeric religion came to stand on its head. It is as though the underworld of Hades had risen to the surface of the earth. But this reversal of Homer did not actually turn Homer upside down or downside up, since the dichotomy within which such an operation alone can take place is of Platonic origin and quite alien to the Homeric world. No turning about of the tradition can therefore ever land us in the original Homeric "position." It is true that Plato set forth his doctrine of ideas solely for political purposes in the form of a reversal of Homer; but thereby he established the framework within which such turning operations are not far-fetched possibilities but predetermined by the conceptual structure itself. The development of philosophy in late antiquity in the various schools, which fought each other with a fanaticism unequaled in the pre-Christian world, consists of turnings-about and shifting emphases on one of two opposite terms, made possible by Plato's separation of a world of mere shadowy appearance and the world of eternally true ideas. He himself had given the first example in the *periagôgé* from the cave to the sky. When Hegel finally, in a last gigantic effort, had gathered together into one consistent self-developing whole the various strands of traditional philosophy as they had developed from Plato's original concept, the same splitting up into two conflicting schools of thought, though on a much lower level, took place, and right-wing and left-wing, idealistic and materialistic, Hegelians could for a short while dominate philosophical thought.

The significance of Kierkegaard's, Marx's, and Nietzsche's challenges to the tradition—though none of them would have been possible without the synthesizing achievement of Hegel and his concept of history—is that they constitute a much more radical turning-about than the mere upside-down operations with their weird oppositions between sensualism and idealism, materialism and spiritualism, and even immanentism and transcendentalism imply. If Marx had been merely a "materialist" who brought Hegel's "idealism" down to earth, his influence would have been as short-lived and limited to scholarly quarrels as that of his contemporaries. Hegel's basic assumption was that the dialectical movement of thought is identical with the dialectical movement of matter itself. Thus he hoped to bridge the abyss which Descartes had opened between man, defined as *res cogitans,* and the world, defined as *res extensa,* between cognition and reality, thinking and being. The spiritual homelessness of modern man finds its first expressions in this Cartesian perplexity and the Pascalian answer. Hegel claimed that the discovery of the dialectical movement as a universal law ruling both human reason and affairs *and* the inner "reason" of natural events, accomplished even more than a mere correspondence between *intellectus* and *res,* whose coincidence pre-Cartesian philosophy had defined as truth. By introducing the Spirit and its self-realization in movement, Hegel believed he had demonstrated an ontological identity of matter and idea. To Hegel, therefore, it would have been of no great importance whether one started this movement from the viewpoint of consciousness, which at one moment begins to "materialize," or whether one chose as starting point matter, which, moving in the direction of "spiritualization," becomes conscious of itself. (How little Marx doubted these fundamentals of his teacher appears from the role he ascribed to self-consciousness in the form of class-consciousness in history.) In other words, Marx was no more a "dialectical materialist" than Hegel was a "dialectical idealist"; the very concept of dialectical *movement,* as Hegel conceived it as a universal law, and as Marx accepted it, makes the terms "idealism" and "materialism" as philosophical systems meaningless. Marx, especially in his earlier writings, is quite conscious of this and knows that his repudiation of the tradition and of Hegel does not lie in his "materialism," but in his refusal to assume that the difference between man and animal life is *ratio* or thought, that, in Hegel's words, "man is essentially spirit." His turning-about, like Kierkegaard's and Nietzsche's, goes to the core of the matter; they all question the traditional hierarchy of human capabilities or, to put it another way, they ask again what the specifically human quality of man is; they do not intend to build systems or *Weltanschauungen* on this or that premise.

The allegory of the cave is told by Plato in the context of a strictly political dialogue searching for the best form of government in the sense of the best way to organize the living-together of men. As such, the story contains not so much Plato's doctrine of ideas as the relationship and applicability of this doctrine to the political realm of a common world, and, at the same time, tells the story of the philosopher in this world as though it were his concentrated biography, the life of *the* philosopher. Important in our context is the fact that the transcendence of the ideas, their existence outside the cave of human affairs, does not imply an absolute transcendence in the sense of other-worldliness; the ideas transcend only the common world of living-together. (It is true that Plato in the concluding myth of the *Republic,* as in the concluding myths of *Gorgias* and *Phaidon,* established a tangible, physical hereafter; but these myths were meant as myths, and not as parables or truth; they were given, not as part of his own political philosophy, which he taught his pupils, but as the corresponding fairytale for the multitude unable to perceive truth. These myths, far from being able to explain the cave allegory, are invented precisely because the cave parable is for the few and not supposed to convince the many.) Plato's doctrine of ideas is not political in origin; but once he had discovered them, he hoped to use them for political purposes as absolute standards, units of measurement by which one could judge a realm where everything seems to dissolve into relationships and to be relative by definition. It is perfectly true that, in the words of Werner Jaeger, "the idea that there is a supreme art of measurement and that the philosopher's knowledge of values is the ability to measure, runs through all of Plato's work right down to the end"—true to the extent that his work is concerned with politics. And it is here that the transcendence of the ideas has its origin; they are transcendent in terms of the world of the *polis* and no more so than the yardstick is transcendent in terms of the matter which it is supposed to measure; the standard necessarily transcends everything to which it is applied. Not the ideas themselves, but the non-religious concept of transcendence in philosophy, is political in origin. In other words, the dichotomy between the relativity of human affairs (*ta tôn anthrôpôn pragmata*), their futility, mortality, and ever-changing motion, and absolute truth whose permanent light illuminates this futility.

What distinguishes the life in the cave from the life under the sky of ideas is that the former is characterized by activities in which men are related and communicate with each other, that is *lexis,* speech, and *praxis,* action, while the latter is characterized by *blepein eis to aléthestaton,* contemplating the truest in solitude and ultimately in speechlessness (*rhéton gar oudamôs estin hôs alla mathémata,* "it can never be articulated in words like other things we learn"). In the parable of the cave, Plato does not even mention speech and action, but depicts the lives of the inhabitants as though they too were interested only in seeing: first the images on the screen, then the things themselves in the dim light of the fire in the cave, until finally those who want to see the truth must leave the common world of the cave altogether and embark upon their new adventure all by themselves. In other words, the whole realm of human affairs is seen from the viewpoint of a philosophy which assumes that even those who inhabit the cave of ordinary human affairs are human only insofar as they too want to see, though deceived by shadows and images.

This dichotomy, between seeing the truth in solitude and speechlessness and being caught in the web of relationships and interdependencies of human affairs through speaking and acting, became authoritative for the tradition of political thought. It is at the basis of our common understanding of the relationship between thought and action and as such was not dependent upon an acceptance of Plato's doctrine of ideas; it depended much rather on a general attitude which Plato expressed in another random remark and which Aristotle later quoted almost verbatim, namely that the beginning of all philosophy is *thaumadzein,* the surprised wonder at everything that is as it is. This surprise and wonder separate the few from the many and alienate them from the affairs of man. Aristotle, therefore, without accepting Plato's doctrine of ideas, and even repudiating Plato's ideal state, still followed him in the main by separating the *bios theôrétikos* from the *bios politikos* and by basing the rules for the latter on the experiences of the former. The priority of seeing over doing and speaking, of the *vita contemplativa* over the *vita activa,* could be challenged only in the modern age, when an altogether new "scientific spirit" had begun to doubt that things are as they appear, replacing experience, the reasoning but non-interfering observation of appearances, with the modern experiment, where we prescribe conditions in order to know, until the search for truth eventually ended in the conviction of the modern world that man can know only what he makes himself.

Since the rise of modern science, whose spirit is expressed in the Cartesian philosophy of doubt and mistrust, the conceptual framework of the tradition has not been secure. The dichotomy between contemplation and action, and the hierarchy which ruled that truth is ultimately perceived only in speechless and actionless seeing, could not be upheld under the conditions of science becoming active and *doing* in order to know. When the trust that things appear as they really are was gone, the concept of truth as revelation had become doubtful and with it the unquestioning faith in a revealed God. The notion of theory changed its meaning. It no longer meant a system of reasonably connected truths which as such had not been made but given to reason and the senses. Rather it became the modern scientific theory which is a working hypothesis, changing in accordance with the results it produces and depending for its validity not on what it "reveals" but on whether it "works." By the same process, Plato's ideas lost their autonomous power to illuminate the world and the universe. First they became what they had been for Plato only in their relationship to the political realm, standards and measurements—the regulating, limiting forces of man's own reasoning mind, as they appear in Kant. Then, after the priority of reason over doing, of the mind prescribing its rules to the actions of men, had been lost in the transformation of the whole world by the Industrial Revolution—a transformation the success of which seemed to prove that man's doings and fabrications prescribe their rules to reason—these ideas finally became mere values whose validity is determined not by one or many men but by society as a whole in its everchanging functional needs.

These values in their ex- and inter-changeability are the only "ideas" left to (and understood by) "socialized men." These are men who have decided never to leave what to Plato was "the cave" of everyday human affairs, and never to venture on their own into a world and a life which, perhaps, the ubiquitous functionalization of modern society has deprived of one of its most elementary characteristics—the instilling of wonder at that which is as it is. This very real development is reflected and foreshadowed in Marx's political thought. Turning the tradition upside down within its own framework, he did not actually get rid of Plato's ideas, though he did record the darkening of the clear sky where those ideas, as well as many other presences, had once become visible to the eyes of men.

Chapter 2
Art and Revolt
Albert Camus

Art, like revolt, is a movement which exalts and denies at the same time. "No artist can tolerate the real," said Nietzsche. This is true; but no artist can do without the real. Creation is a demand for unity and a refusal of the world. But it refuses the world because of what it lacks, and in the name of that which, sometimes, it is. Revolt can be observed in art in its pure state, in its primitive composition, outside history. Art, then, should give us a perspective on the content of revolt.

We must note, however, the hostility to art shown by all revolutionary reformers. Plato is still moderate. He only impugns the deceitful function of language and exiles poets from his republic. For the rest, he placed beauty about the world. But the revolutionary movement of modern times coincides with a process of placing art on trial which is not yet finished. The Reformation chooses morality and exiles beauty. Rousseau denounces art as a corruption added by society to nature. Saint-Just thunders against the theater and, in the excellent program that he drew up for the "Feast of Reason," desires that reason be personified by a figure "virtuous rather than beautiful." The French Revolution did not give birth to any artist; only to a great journalist, Desmoulins, and a clandestine writer, the Marquis de Sade. The one poet of his time [André Chenier] is guillotined by the Revolution. The only great prose writer [Chateaubriand] is exiled to London and pleads for Christianity and the throne. A bit later, the Saint-Simonians will demand an art "socially useful." "Art for progress" is a commonplace which runs through the century and that Hugo took up, though he did not succeed in making it convincing. Only Vallés, in pronouncing a malediction on art, brings to it an imprecatory tone which has an authentic ring.

This is also the tone of the Russian Nihilists. Pisarev proclaims the decadence of aesthetic values in the interest of pragmatic ones. "I would much prefer to be a Russian shoemaker than a Russian Raphael." A pair of shoes is more useful than Shakespeare for Pisarev. The Nihilist Nekrassov, himself a great and unhappy poet, nonetheless affirms that he prefers a bit of cheese to Pushkin. Tolstoy's excommunication of art is famous. Revolutionary Russia finally turned its back on those marble statues of Venus and Apollo, still gilded by the Italian sun, that Peter the Great had bought for his summer garden in St.Petersburg. Misery, sometimes, turns away from painful images of happiness.

The ideology of the Germans is no less severe in its accusations. According to the revolutionary interpreters of Hegel's *Phenomenology,* there will be no art in a just society. Beauty will be lived, no longer imagined. The real, completely rational, will be enough by itself to satisfy all desires. Art is not for all time; on the contrary it is determined by its epoch, and it expresses, Marx will say, the privileged values of the dominant class. There is only one revolutionary art, which is, precisely, art placed in the service of the revolution. By creating beauty outside of history, art obstructs the only effort which is rational: the transformation of history itself into an absolute beauty. The Russian shoemaker, from the moment that he becomes conscious of his revolutionary role, is the creator of final beauty. Raphael has only created a fleeting beauty which will be incomprehensible to the new humanity.

Marx asks himself, it is true, how it is that Greek beauty can still be beautiful for us. He answers that this beauty expresses the naive infancy of a world, and that we have, in the midst of our adult struggles, a nostalgia for that infancy. But the masterpieces of the Renaissance, Rembrandt, Chinese art—how can they all still be beautiful for us? No matter! The condemnation of art has definitely begun, and is followed up today with the embarrassed complicity of artists and intellectuals themselves, dedicated to the calumny of their art and their intelligence. In the battle between Shakespeare and the shoemaker, it is not the shoemaker who execrates Shakespeare and beauty; on the contrary, it is those who continue to read Shakespeare rather than make shoes—who could never make them in any case. The artists of our time resemble the

repentent noblemen of nineteenth-century Russia; their bad conscience is their alibi. But the last thing that an artist ought to
experience before his art is repentence. This goes beyond a simple
and necessary humility—this pretense at relegating beauty to the
end of time, and, while waiting, depriving the world and the shoemaker of that extra nourishment from which one has benefited
himself.

This ascetic madness, however, has its reasons which interest
us for their own sake. They translate, on the plane of aesthetics,
the battle between revolution and revolt. In every revolt there is
revealed a metaphysical demand for unity, the impossibility of possessing this unity, and the fabrication of a replacement. This also
defines art. The exigence of revolt, to tell the truth, is in part an
aesthetic one. All the thinking inspired by revolt is illuminated by
a rhetoric or a closed universe. The rhetoric of ramparts in Lucre-
tius, the convents and bolted castles of Sade, the isle of the romantic cliff, the solitary heights of Nietzsche, the elemental ocean of
Lautréamont; the terrifying castles that are reborn among the
Surrealists, battered by a storm of flowers; the prison, the nation
entrenched within itself, the concentration camp, the domination
of slave overseers—all these light up in their fashion the same need
of coherence and unity. Within these closed worlds, man can finally
know and rule.

This movement is also that of all the arts. The artist remakes
the world to his advantage. Nature's symphonies do not know any
pauses. The world is never silent; its muteness itself eternally repeats the same notes, according to vibrations that escape us. As
for those that we hear, they bring us sounds, rarely an accord, never
a melody. Yet music exists, in which symphonies finish and melody
gives its form to sounds which, by themselves, have none; where
a privileged arrangement of notes, lastly, brings out of natural disorder a unity satisfying the heart and the spirit.

"I believe more and more," writes Van Gogh, "that one
should not judge God on the basis of this world. It's a sketch of
his that didn't come off." Every artist tries to remake this sketch
and to give it the style it lacks. The greatest and most ambitious
of all the arts, sculpture, desperately tries to fix the fleeting figure
of man in his three dimensions, to organize the disorder of gesture

into the unity of a grand style. Sculpture does not reject imitation, which on the contrary it needs. But it does not primarily seek
imitation. What it seeks, in its great periods, is the typical gesture,
the expression or look which will recapitulate all the gestures and
all the looks in the world. Its purpose is not to imitate but to stylize,
and to imprison in a significant expression the passing fury of the
body or the infinite pliability of attitudes. Only then does it erect,
on the pediment of tumultuous cities, the model, the type, whose
immobile perfection will quiet, for a moment, the incessant fever
of men. The lover deprived of love will then be able to wander
among the Greek Korés and grasp that which, in the body and
face of women, survives all degradation.

The principle of painting is also in a choice. "Genius itself,"
writes Delacroix, "reflecting on its art, is nothing but the gift of
generalizing and choosing." The painter isolates his subject, which
is the first way of unifying it. Landscapes flit by, disappear from
memory or destroy one another. This is why the landscape painter
or the painter of still lifes isolates in space and time that which,
normally, changes with changing light, loses itself in an infinite perspective or vanishes under the impact of other values. The first step
of the landscape painter is to make the various parts of his picture
agree with each other. He eliminates as much as he selects. Similarly,
the painting of subjects isolates, in time as well as space, an action
which normally loses itself in another action. The painter then proceeds to immobilize his subject. The great creators are those who,
like Piero della Francesca, give the impression that this fixation has
just been accomplished, that the projector has just stopped turning.
All their figures then give the impression that, by the miracle of art,
they continue to be alive while ceasing to be perishable. Long after
his death, Rembrandt's philosopher continues to meditate, between
light and shadow, on the same question.

"How empty a thing is painting, which pleases us by its re-
semblances with objects that cannot please us!" Delacroix, who
cites this famous phrase of Pascal, writes "strange" instead of
"empty," and with good reason. These objects cannot please us
because we do not see them; they are buried and negated in a
perpetual becoming. Who looked at the hands of the whipper during the flagellation, or at the olive trees on the way of Calvary?

But there they are: depicted, stolen from the incessant movement of the Passion; and the sorrow of Christ, imprisoned in images of violence and beauty, cries freshly to us every day in the indifferent halls of museums. The style of a painter is a conjunction of nature and history; a presence imposed on that which perpetually passes. Art realizes, with no apparent effort, that reconciliation of the particular and the universal of which Hegel dreamed. Perhaps this is the reason why epochs like our own, enraptured by unity, turn toward the primitive arts where stylization is most intense and unity most exciting. The strongest stylization is always found at the beginning and the end of artistic epochs; this explains the power of negation and transposition that has stirred up all of modern painting in a disorganized impulse toward being and unity. The admirable lamentation of Van Gogh is the proud and despairing outcry of all artists. "I can very well, in life and in painting also, do without God. But I cannot, suffering creature that I am, do without something greater than myself, something that is my life, the power to create."

But the revolt of the artist against the real—and this makes it suspect to a totalitarian revolution—contains the same affirmation as the spontaneous revolt of the oppressed. The revolutionary spirit, born of total negation, felt instinctively that there was in art a consent as well as a refusal; that contemplation threatened to outweigh action, beauty to outweigh injustice, and that, in certain cases, beauty was in itself an injustice without remedy. Besides, no art can exist on a total refusal. Just as all thought means something, even the thought of no-meaning, so there is no art of no-sense. Man can take on himself the denunciation of the world's total injustice and demand a total justice that he will be alone in creating. But he cannot affirm the total ugliness of the world. To create beauty, he must at the same time refuse the real and exalt certain of its aspects. Art questions the real, but does not shun it. Nietzsche was able to refuse all transcendence, moral or divine, by saying that such transcendence led to a calumniation of this world and this life. But there is perhaps a living transcendence, promised us by beauty, which may make us love and prefer to any other our own limited and mortal world. Art thus brings us back to the origins of revolt, in the degree to which it tries to give form to a value escaping in a perpetual becoming; but which the artist senses and wishes to snatch from history. We can show this even more clearly by reflecting on the art which, precisely, proposes to enter into the flux and give it a style: the novel.

It is possible to separate the literature of consent, which roughly coincides with the centuries of antiquity and classicism, from the literature of dissidence that begins with modern times. In the former, the novel is a rarity. When it exists, with rare exceptions, it is not concerned with history but with fantasy (*Theagena and Charides* or *L'Astrée*). They are tales, not novels. With the second kind of literature, on the contrary, the novel as a genre develops, and it has not ceased enriching and extending itself up to our own day simultaneously with the movement of criticism and revolution. The novel is born at the same time as the spirit of revolt, and it translates the same ambition on the aesthetic plane.

"A make-believe story, written in prose," says Littré of the novel. Is it nothing but that? A Catholic critic, Stanislas Fumet, has nonetheless written: "Art, whatever its aim, enters into a guilty rivalry with God." It is more precise, indeed, to speak of a rivalry with God—so far as the novel is concerned—than to speak of a rivalry with the civil register. Thibaudet expressed a similar idea when he said, apropos of Balzac: "The 'Human Comedy' is an 'Imitation' of God the Father." The effort of great literature seems to be to create closed universes or self-sufficient types. The Occident, in its great creations, does not limit itself to retracing everyday life. Without ceasing, it conjures up great images and throws itself feverishly in their pursuit.

After all, to write and read a novel are unusual actions. It is not inevitable, or necessary, for one to construct a story by a new arrangement of true facts. Even if the vulgar explanation were true, that this gives pleasure to the writer and reader, we should still ask by what necessity the majority of men find pleasure and interest in make-believe stories. Revolutionary criticism condemns the pure novel as the escape of an idle imagination. Ordinary language, in its turn, labels the untruthful recital of a bungling journalist as being "like a novel." Not so long ago, it was customary, against all the laws of probability, to say that young girls were like "those in novels." By this, one understood that these ideal creatures paid no attention to the realities of existence. Speaking generally, it has always been thought that the world of the novel was separate from that of life, and that the former, in embroidering the latter, also betrayed it. The simplest and most common way of regarding the novel, as a form of expression, thus consists in viewing it as an exercise in escape. Common sense is at one with revolutionary criticism.

But what is one escaping by means of the novel? A reality judged to be too crushing? Happy people also read novels, and it is well known that extreme suffering takes away the taste for reading. On the other hand, the novelistic universe certainly has less weight and presence than that other universe in which beings of flesh assail us unceasingly. By what mystery, however, does Adolphe seem a personage more familiar than Benjamin Constant, and the Count Mosca more familiar than our professional moralists? Balzac, one day, cut short a long conversation on politics and the fate of the world by saying: "And now let's get back to talking about serious things," meaning that he wanted to talk about his novels. The unquestionable gravity of the novelistic world, our obstinacy, indeed, in taking seriously the innumerable myths that the novelistic genius has proposed to us for two centuries, cannot be adequately explained by a taste for escape. Certainly, the activity of writing novels supposes some sort of rejection of the real. But this rejection is not a simple flight. Should one see in it the movement of retreat proper to the tender-minded soul who, according to Hegel, creates for himself, in his disillusion, a factitious world where morality reigns supreme? The edifying novel, however, falls considerably short of being great literature; and the best of the rose-colored novels, *Paul et Virginie,* is a saddening work that offers no consolation.

The contradiction is this: man refuses the world as it is, without consenting to escape it completely. In fact, men stick to the world and, in the immense majority, do not wish to leave it. Far from always wishing to forget it, they suffer, on the contrary, from not possessing it enough: strange citizens of the world exiled in their own country! Except for blazing moments of plenitude, all reality is unfinished for them. Their acts escape them to merge into other acts, return to judge them under unfamiliar guises, flow like the waters of Tantalus toward a river-mouth yet unknown. To know where the river culminates, to dominate the current, finally to grasp life as destiny—this is the true nostalgia of men, in the very heart of their homeland. But that vision which, in knowledge at least, would finally reconcile them with themselves can only appear—if it appears at all—in the fugitive moment before death: everything finishes there. To be completely in the world for once, it is necessary never to be there again.

Here is the source of that misguided envy that so many men have for the lives of others. Looking at these existences from the outside, one lends them a coherence and a unity which, in truth, they cannot have, but which appears evident to the observer. He sees only the outline of these lives, without taking account of the complicating details. We make art out of these existences. In an elementary way, we novelize them. Everyone, in this sense, seeks to make of his life a work of art. We desire that love shall last and we know that it does not last; and even if, by a miracle, it should last a lifetime, it would still be unfinished. Perhaps, in this insatiable need to continue, we should better understand earthly suffering if we knew it were eternal. It seems, sometimes, that great spirits are less frightened by pain than by the thought that it will not persist. For lack of an indefatigable happiness, a prolonged suffering would at least constitute a destiny. But no: our worst tortures will some day cease. One morning, after so much despair, an irrepressible desire to live will announce to us that all is finished, and that suffering has no more meaning than happiness.

A bent toward possession is merely another form of the desire to endure; this is what causes the impotent delirium. No being, not even the one we love most and who most returns our love, is ever in our possession. In this inhuman world, where lovers sometimes die in solitude and are always divided, the total possession of another being, an absolute communion for the duration of a lifetime, is an impossible demand. And a bent toward possession can be so insatiable that it may survive love itself. To love, then, means to sterilize the beloved. The shameful suffering of the lover is not so much that he is no longer loved as that he knows the other can and will love again. At the extremity, each man devoured by the distraught desire to endure and to possess wishes, for the beings that he loves, sterility or death. This is the true revolt. Those who have not demanded, at least for one day, the absolute purity of the world and other beings, who have not trembled with nostalgia and impotence before this impossibility, who have not destroyed themselves in a love that continually throws them back on their nostalgia for the absolute—these will never be able to understand the reality of revolt and its fury of destruction. But other beings are always escaping us, and we are escaping them; they are without fixed contours. Life, from this point of view, is without style. It is nothing but a movement unsuccessfully pursuing its form. Man, thus torn apart, seeks in vain for a form to give him limits within which he can be king. Let just one living thing have its form in this world, and he will be reconciled!

There is no being, finally, who, starting from an elementary level of consciousness, does not exhaust himself seeking formulas or attitudes that will give his existence the unity it lacks. Whether in pretending or in acting, the dandy or the revolutionary both require a unity of being, and of being in this world. Like those pathetic and miserable love affairs, which sometimes drag on interminably because one of the partners is waiting to find the word, the gesture, the situation that will make the adventure a thing of the past—ended in just the right way—each one of us creates or gives himself an epigraph. It is not enough to live; one must have a destiny—and without waiting for death. It is thus true to say that man has the idea of a world better than the present one. But better does not mean different; better means unified. That fever which impels the heart beyond our scattered world—a world, however, which it cannot do without—is the fever of unity. It does not finish up as a mediocre escape but as the most obstinate reclamation. Religion or crime, all human effort finally obeys this irrational desire and pretends to give human life a form it does not possess. The same movement that can lead to the adoration of Heaven or the destruction of man can also lead to the creation of novels; and this gives the latter activity its seriousness.

What is a novel, indeed, if not that universe where action finds its form, where the final words are spoken, where beings are given over totally to other beings, where all life takes on the aspect of destiny?[1] The world of the novel is nothing but the correction of our own world, following man's profound desire. For we are still in the same world; the suffering is the same, the deception and the love. The heroes speak our language; have our weaknesses, our strengths. Their universe is neither more beautiful nor more edifying than ours. But they at least pursue their destiny to its end, and no hero is so overwhelming as the one who follows his passion to its farthest limits: Kirilov and Stavrogin, Mme. Graslin, Julien Sorel or the Prince de Clèves. It is here that we lose their measure, for they finish what we shall never accomplish.

Mme. de Lafayette drew the *Princesse de Clèves* from bitterest experience. She is herself, without doubt, Mme. de Clèves and yet she is not. Where is the difference? The difference is that Mme. de Lafayette did not enter a convent and that nobody in her entourage expired for love. No doubt she knew the agonizing moments of that unequaled love. But it did not have any final point, she outlived and prolonged it by ceasing to live in it; and nobody, not even herself, would have known its shape if she had not given it the naked embodiment of her faultless language. There is no story more "like a novel" and more beautiful than that of Sophie Tonska and Casimir in *Les Pleiades* of Gobineau. Sophie, a beautiful and sensitive woman (who enables one to understand Stendhal's confession that "only women of marked temperament can make me happy"), forces Casimir to reveal his love. Accustomed to being loved, she becomes impatient with Casimir who sees her every day and yet never drops his irritating calm. Casimir avows his love, indeed, but as if he were exposing some legal argument. He has studied Sophie, knows her as well as he knows himself, and is convinced that this love—without which he cannot live—has no future. He has thus decided to inform her, at one and the same time, of his love and its futility, and to make her a present of his fortune— she is wealthy herself, and this gesture is of no importance—on condition that she provide him with a modest pension to enable him to live in the suburbs of a city chosen at random (the city is Vilna),

---

1. Even if the novel speaks only of nostalgia, despair, the unachieved, it still creates the form and the salvation. To name despair is already to go beyond it. The literature of desperation is a contradiction in terms.

there to await death in poverty. Casimir recognizes, for the rest, that the idea of taking a pension from Sophie is a concession to human weakness, the only concession he will allow himself, with, from time to time, the dispatch of a blank page in an envelope on which will be written the name of Sophie. After being indignant, then disturbed, then melancholy, Sophie finally accepts; everything takes place as Casimir had foreseen. He dies, at Vilna, of his unhappy love. The world of the novel has its own logic. A good story cannot do without the imperturbable continuity which is never in the situations of real life, but that one finds in the elaboration of a reverie that takes reality as its point of departure. If Gobineau had gone to Vilna, he would probably have been bored and left, or he would have managed to make himself comfortable. But Casimir is a stranger to the need for change and to moments of recovery. He goes to the extreme, like Heathcliff in *Wuthering Heights,* who wished to go beyond even death and attain Hell itself.

Here is, then, an imaginary world, but a world created by the correction of the one we know; a world where sorrow can, if it wishes, last until death, where passions are never sidetracked, where beings are in the grip of an unchanging idea and are always in each other's thoughts. Man finally gives himself the form and the pacifying limit that he pursues in vain in his natural condition. The novel manufactures destiny to order. This is how it competes with creation and, temporarily, triumphs over death. A detailed analysis of the most famous novels would show that, in differing perspectives, the essence of the novel is in this perpetual correction—always going in the same direction—that the artist gives to his experience. Far from being moral or purely formal, this correction aims first of all at unity and in this way translates a metaphysical need. The novel, at this level, is primarily an exercise of the intelligence in the service of a nostalgic sensibility in revolt. We can study this search for unity in the French novel of analysis, and in Melville, Balzac, Dostoevsky or Tolstoy. But a brief confrontation between the two efforts that are situated at the opposite extremes of the world of the novel—the creation of Proust and the American novel of recent years—will be enough for our purposes.

The American novel[2] seeks to find its unity in reducing man either to the elementary, or to his external reactions and behavior. It does not choose a feeling or passion of which it will give a privileged image, as in the French classic novels. It rejects analysis and the search for a fundamental psychological lever that will explain and sum up the conduct of a character. This is why the unity of the American novel is nothing but a unity of lighting. Its technique consists in describing men externally in their most unimportant gestures, in reproducing their speech without commentary even to its repetitions,[3] in acting as if men were entirely defined by their everyday automatisms. At this mechanical level, in truth, men resemble each other; and we can thus explain this curious universe where all the people seem interchangeable, even to the particularities of their physique. This technique is called realist only through a misunderstanding. Aside from the fact that realism in art is an incomprehensible notion, it is clear that the world of the American novel does not aim at the pure and simple reproduction of reality; it aims at the most arbitrary kind of stylization. The unity thus obtained is a degraded unity, a leveling of beings and of the world. It seems that, for these novelists, it is the interior life which deprives human actions of their unity and which alienates beings from each other. In part, this suspicion is well-founded. But the revolt at the source of this art can only find its satisfaction, not by denying the interior life completely, but by constructing a unity that uses the interior life as a starting point. To deny it completely is to have recourse to an imaginary man. The pitch-black novel is also a rose-colored one, and it has the formal pretensions of the latter. It too edifies, after its fashion.[4] The life of the body, reduced to itself, paradoxically produces an abstract and gratuitous universe, in its turn constantly denied by reality. This novel, purged of inner life, and in which man seems to be observed as if under glass, finishes

2. Naturally, I am dealing with the "tough-guy" novel of the thirties and forties, not with the admirable blossoming of American literature in the nineteenth century.

3. Even in Faulkner, the great writer of this generation, the interior monologue reproduces only the outer covering of thought.

4. Bernardin de Saint-Pierre and the Marquis de Sade, in different registers, are the creators of the propaganda novel.

logically by portraying the pathological because it began by taking the so-called average man as its special subject. One can thus explain the considerable number of "innocents" utilized in this universe. The innocent is the ideal subject for such an undertaking since he is completely defined by his behavior. He is the symbol of this despairing universe, where unhappy automatons live in the most mechanical kind of coherence, a universe which the American novelists have raised up as a pathetic—though sterile—protest in the face of the modern world.

With regard to Proust, his effort was to start from reality, stubbornly contemplated, and to create a closed, irreplaceable world that belonged to him alone and would commemorate his victory over the flight of time and death. But his methods are opposite. They consist, above all, in a calculated choice, a meticulous collection of privileged instants that the novelist chooses from his most personal past. Immense dead spaces are thus rejected because they have left no trace in recollection. If the world of the American novel is that of men without memory, the world of Proust is nothing but memory. Only, it is the most difficult and demanding of memories, which refuses the dispersion of the world and draws out of a rediscovered scent the secret of an old—and yet new—universe. Proust chose the interior life, and in the interior life what was most interior, against the forgetfulness of the real; that is, the mechanical, the blindness of the world. But out of this refusal of the real he did not draw its negation. He did not commit the error, parallel to that of the American novel, of suppressing the mechanical. On the contrary, he reunites, in a superior unity, the souvenir of the past and the sensation of the present, the foot which slips and the blissful days of earlier years.

It is difficult to return to the haunts of happiness and of youth. The budding young girls laugh and chatter eternally before the ocean, but he who contemplates them loses, little by little, the right to love them, as those whom he had once loved lose the status of being. This melancholy is that of Proust. It was powerful enough in him to burst forth into a refusal of all being. But a relish for the sun-lit aspects of the world bound him to it at the same time. He did not consent to give up forever the joys of his carefree holidays. He took as his task to re-create them anew, and to show, in the teeth of death, that the past could be found again at the end of time; in an imperishable present, truer and richer than it had ever been. The psychological analysis of the *Temps Perdu* is thus only a powerful means to an end. Proust's real greatness is to have written the *Temps Retrouvé,* which reorganizes a scattered world and gives it meaning at the very level of anguish itself. His difficult victory, on the eve of death, is to have been able to draw from the incessant flight of time, uniquely by means of memory and intelligence, the rapturous symbols of man's unity. The surest challenge that a work of this kind can fling at creation is to present itself as a whole, a closed and unified world. This defines those works created without flinching.

It has been said that the world of Proust is without God. If this is true, it is not because he never speaks of God but because this world has ambitions to be closed and perfect by itself, and to give to eternity the visage of man. The *Temps Retrouvé,* at least by intention, is an eternity without God. The work of Proust, from this point of view, appears as one of the boldest and most significant attempts of man to overcome his mortal condition. It showed that the art of the novel re-made creation itself, the creation which is both imposed by man and refused by him. In one of its aspects at least, this art consists in choosing the created against the creator. But, more profoundly still, it allies itself to the beauty of the world and its being against the forces of death and oblivion. It is thus that revolt is creative.

(Translated from the French by Joseph Frank)

Chapter 3
Art and Politics
Leon Trotsky

A Letter to the Editors of **PARTISAN REVIEW**

Y OU HAVE BEEN kind enough to invite me to express my views on the state of present-day arts and letters. I do this not without some hesitation. Since my book *Literature and Revolution* (1923), I have not once returned to the problem of artistic creation and only occasionally have I been able to follow the latest developments in this sphere. I am far from pretending to offer an exhaustive reply. The task of this letter is to correctly pose the question.

Generally speaking, art is an expression of man's need for an harmonious and complete life, that is to say, his need for those major benefits of which a society of classes has deprived him. That is why a protest against reality, either conscious or unconscious, active or passive, optimistic or pessimistic, always forms part of a really creative piece of work. Every new tendency in art has begun with rebellion. Bourgeois society showed its strength throughout long periods of history in the fact that, combining repression and encouragement, boycott and flattery, it was able to control and assimilate every "rebel" movement in art and raise it to the level of official "recognition." But each time this "recognition" betokened, when all is said and done, the approach of trouble. It was then that from the left wing of the academic school or below it—i.e. from the ranks of a new generation of bohemian artists—a fresher revolt would surge up to attain in its turn, after a decent interval, the steps of the academy. Through these stages passed classicism, romanticism, realism, naturalism, symbolism, impressionism, cubism, futurism . . . Nevertheless, the union of art and the bourgeoisie remained stable, even if not happy, only so long as the bourgeoisie itself took the initiative and was capable of maintaining a regime both politically and morally "democratic." This was a question of not only giving free rein to artists and playing up to them in every possible way, but also of granting special privileges to the top layer of the working class, and of mastering and subduing the bureaucracy of the unions and workers' parties. All these phenomena exist in the same historical plane.

The decline of bourgeois society means an intolerable exacerbation of social contradictions, which are transformed inevitably into personal contradictions, calling forth an ever more burning need for a liberating art. Furthermore, a declining capitalism already finds itself completely incapable of offering the minimum conditions for the development of tendencies in art which correspond, however little, to our epoch. It fears superstitiously every new word, for it is no longer a matter of corrections and reforms for capitalism but of life and death. The oppressed masses live their own life. Bohemianism offers too limited a social base. Hence new tendencies take on a more and more violent character, alternating between hope and despair. The artistic schools of the last few decades—cubism, futurism, dadaism, surrealism—follow each other without reaching a complete development. Art, which is the most complex part of culture, the most sensitive and at the same time the least protected, suffers most from the decline and decay of bourgeois society.

To find a solution to this impasse through art itself is impossible. It is a crisis which concerns all culture, beginning at its economic base and ending in the highest spheres of ideology. Art can neither escape the crisis nor partition itself off. Art cannot save itself. It will rot away inevitably— as Grecian art rotted beneath the ruins of a culture founded on slavery— unless present-day society is able to rebuild itself. This task is essentially revolutionary in character. For these reasons the function of art in our epoch is determined by its relation to the revolution.

But precisely in this path history has set a formidable snare for the artist. A whole generation of "leftist" intelligentsia has turned its eyes for the last ten or fifteen years to the East and has bound its lot, in varying degrees, to a victorious revolution, if not to a revolutionary proletariat. Now, this is by no means one and the same thing. In the victorious revolution there is not only the revolution, but there is also the new privileged class which raises itself on the shoulders of the revolution. In reality, the "leftist" intelligentsia has tried to change masters. What has it gained?

The October revolution gave a magnificent impetus to all types of Soviet art. The bureaucratic reaction, on the contrary, has stifled artistic creation with a totalitarian hand. Nothing surprising here! Art is basically a function of the nerves and demands complete sincerity. Even the art of the court of absolute monarchies was based on idealization but not on falsification. The official art of the Soviet Union—and there is no other over there— resembles totalitarian justice, that is to say, it is based on lies and deceit. The goal of justice, as of art, is to exalt the "leader," to fabricate an heroic myth. Human history has never seen anything to equal this in scope and impudence. A few examples will not be superfluous.

The well known Soviet writer, Vsevolod Ivanov, recently broke his silence to proclaim eagerly his solidarity with the justice of Vyshinsky. The general extermination of the old Bolsheviks, "those putrid emanations of capitalism," stimulates in the artists a "creative hatred" in Ivanov's words. Romantic, cautious by nature, lyrical, none too outspoken, Ivanov recalls Gorki, in many ways, but in miniature. Not a prostitute by nature, he preferred to remain quiet as long as possible but the time came when silence meant civil and perhaps even physical annihilation. It is not a "creative hatred" that guides the pen of these writers but paralyzing fear.

Alexis Tolstoy, who has finally permitted the courtesan to master the artist, has written a novel expressly to glorify the military exploits of Stalin and Voroshilov at Tsaritsin. In reality, as impartial documents bear witness, the army of Tsaritsin—one of the two dozen armies of the revolution— played a rather sorry role. The two "heroes" were relieved of their posts.* If the honest and simple Chapayev, one of the real heroes of the civil war is glorified in a Soviet film, it is only because he did not live until the "epoch of Stalin" which would have shot him as a Fascist agent. The same Alexis Tolstoy is now writing a drama on the theme of the year 1919: "The Campaign of the Fourteen Powers." The principal heroes of this piece, according to the words of the author, are Lenin, Stalin and Voroshilov. Their images [of Stalin and Voroshilov!] haloed in glory and heroism, will pervade the whole drama." Thus, a talented writer who bears the name of the greatest and most truthful Russian realist, has become a manufacturer of "myths" to order!

Very recently, the 27th of April of this year, the official government paper *Izvestia,* printed a reproduction of a new painting representing Stalin as the organizer of the Tiflis strike in March 1902. However, it appears from documents long known to the public, that Stalin was in prison at that time and besides not in Tiflis but in Batum. This time the lie was too glaring! *Izvestia* was forced to excuse itself the next day for its deplorable blunder. No one knows what happened to the unfortunate picture, which was paid for from State funds.

Dozens, hundreds, thousands of books, films, canvases, sculptures immortalize and glorify such historic "episodes." Thus the numerous pictures devoted to the October revolution do not fail to represent a revolutionary "Center," with Stalin at its head, which never existed. It is necessary to say a few words concerning the gradual preparation of this falsification. Leonid Serebriakov, shot after the Piatakov-Radek trial, drew my attention in 1924 to the publication in *Pravda,* without explanation, of extracts from the minutes of the Central Committee of the latter part of 1917. An old secretary of the Central Committee, Serebriakov had numerous contacts behind the scenes with the party apparatus, and he knew well enough the object of this unexpected publication: it was the first step, still a cautious one,

---

* See, for example, the article of N. Narkine, "Voroshilov and the Red Army" in Leon Trotsky's *The Stalin School of Falsification.*

towards the principal Stalinist myth, which now occupies so great a place in Soviet art.

From an historical distance the October insurrection seems much more planned and monolithic than what it proved to be in reality. In fact, there were lacking neither vacillations, search for solutions, nor impulsive beginnings which led nowhere. Thus, at the meeting of the Central Committee on the 16th of October, improvised in one night, in the absence of the most active leaders of the Petrograd Soviets, it was decided to round out the general-staff of the insurrection with an auxiliary "Center" created by the party and composed of Sverdlov, Stalin, Bubnov, Uritzky and Djerjinsky. At the very same time at the meeting of the Petrograd Soviet, a Revolutionary Military Committee was formed which from the moment of its appearance did so much work towards the preparation of the insurrection that the "Center," appointed the night before, was forgotten by everybody, even by its own members. There were more than a few of such improvisations in the whirlwind of this period.* Stalin never belonged to the Military Revolutionary Committee, did not appear at Smolny, staff headquarters of the revolution, had nothing to do with the practical preparation of the insurrection, but was to be found editing *Pravda* and writing drab articles, which were very little read. During the following years nobody once mentioned the "Practical Center." In memoirs of participants in the insurrection—and there is no shortage of these—the name of Stalin is not once mentioned. Stalin himself, in an article on the anniversary of the October insurrection, in the *Pravda* of November 7, 1918, describing all the groups and individuals who took part in the insurrection, does not say a word about the "Practical Center." Nevertheless, the old minutes, discovered by chance in 1924 and falsely interpreted, have served as a base for the bureaucratic legend. In every compilation, bibliographical guide, even in recently edited school books, the revolutionary "Center" has a prominent place with Stalin at its head. Furthermore, no one has tried, not even out of a sense of decency, to explain where and how this "Center" established its headquarters, to whom it gave orders and what they were, and whether minutes were taken where they are. We have here all the features of the Moscow trials.

With the docility which distinguishes it, Soviet art so-called, has made this bureaucratic myth into one of its favorite subjects for artistic creation. Sverdlov, Djerjinsky, Uritsky and Bubnov are represented in oils or in tempera, seated or standing around Stalin and following his words with rapt attention. The building where the "Center" has headquarters, is intentionally depicted in a vague fashion, in order to avoid the embarrassing question of the address. What can one hope for or demand of artists who

---

* This question is fully developed in my *History of the Russian Revolution* in the chapter entitled "Legends of the Bureaucracy."

are forced to follow with their brushes the crude lines of what they themselves realize is an historical falsification?

The style of present-day official Soviet painting is called "socialist realism." The name itself has evidently been invented by some high functionary
in the department of the arts. This "realism" consists in the imitation of
provincial daguerreotypes of the third quarter of the last century; the "socialist" character apparently consists in representing, in the manner of pre-
tentious photography, events which never took place. It is impossible to read
Soviet verse and prose without physical disgust, mixed with horror, or to
look at reproductions of paintings and sculpture in which functionaries
armed with pens, brushes, and scissors, under the supervision of functionaries armed with Mausers, glorify the "great" and "brilliant" leaders, actually devoid of the least spark of genius or greatness. The art of the Stalinist
period will remain as the frankest expression of the profound decline of the
proletarian revolution.

This state of things is not confined, however, within the frontiers of
the U.S.S.R. Under the guise of a belated recognition of the October revolution, the "left" wing of the western intelligentsia has fallen on its knees
before the Soviet bureaucracy. As a rule, those artists with some character
and talent have kept aloof. But the appearance in the first ranks, of the
failures, careerists and nobodys is all the more unfortunate. A rash of
Centers and Committees of all sorts has broken out, of secretaries of both
sexes, inevitable letters from Romain Rolland, subsidized editions, ban-
quets and congresses, in which it is difficult to trace the line of demarcation
between art and the G.P.U. Despite this vast spread of activity, this mili-
tarized movement has not produced one single work that was able to outlive
its author or its inspirers of the Kremlin.

In the field of painting, the October revolution has found her greatest
interpreter not in the U.S.S.R. but in faraway Mexico, not among the official
"friends," but in the person of a so-called "enemy of the people" whom
the Fourth International is proud to number in its ranks. Nurtured in the
artistic cultures of all peoples, all epochs, Diego Rivera has remained Mexican in the most profound fibres of his genius. But that which inspired him
in these magnificent frescoes, which lifted him up above the artistic tradition, above contemporary art in a certain sense, above himself, is the mighty
blast of the proletarian revolution. Without October, his power of creative
penetration into the epic of work, oppression and insurrection, would never
have attained such breadth and profundity. Do you wish to see with your
own eyes the hidden springs of the social revolution? Look at the frescoes
of Rivera. Do you wish to know what revolutionary art is like? Look at the
frescoes of Rivera.

Come a little closer and you will see clearly enough, gashes and spots
made by vandals: catholics and other reactionaries, including, of course,

Stalinists. These cuts and gashes give even greater life to the frescoes. You have before you, not simply a "painting," an object of passive esthetic contemplation, but a living part of the class struggle. And it is at the same time a masterpiece!

Only the historical youth of a country which has not yet emerged from the stage of struggle for national independence, has allowed Rivera's revolutionary brush to be used on the walls of the public buildings of Mexico. In the United States it was more difficult. Just as the monks in the Middle Ages, through ignorance, it is true, erased antique literary productions from parchments to cover them with their scholastic ravings, just so Rockefeller's lackeys, but this time maliciously, covered the frescoes of the talented Mexican with their decorative banalities. This recent palimpsest will conclusively show future generations the fate of art degraded in a decaying bourgeois society.

The situation is no better, however, in the country of the October revolution. Incredible as it seemed at first sight, there was no place for the art of Diego Rivera, either in Moscow, or in Leningrad, or in any other section of the U.S.S.R. where the bureaucracy born of the revolution was erecting grandiose palaces and monuments to itself. And how could the Kremlin clique tolerate in its kingdom an artist who paints neither icons representing the "leader" nor life-size portraits of Voroshilov's horse? The closing of the Soviet doors to Rivera will brand forever with an ineffaceable shame the totalitarian dictatorship.

Will it go on much longer—this stifling, this trampling under foot and muddying of everything on which the future of humanity depends? Reliable indications say no. The shameful and pitiable collapse of the cowardly and reactionary politics of the Popular Fronts in Spain and France, on the one hand, and the judicial frame-ups of Moscow, on the other, portend the approach of a major turning point not only in the political sphere, but also in the broader sphere of revolutionary ideology. Even the unfortunate "friends"—but evidently not the intellectual and moral shallows of *The New Republic* and *Nation*—are beginning to tire of the yoke and whip. Art, culture, politics need a new perspective. Without it humanity will not develop. But never before has the prospect been as menacing and catastrophic as now. That is the reason why panic is the dominant state of mind of the bewildered intelligentsia. Those who oppose an irresponsible skepticism to the yoke of Moscow do not weigh heavy in the balance of history. Skepticism is only another form, and not the best, of demoralization. Behind the act, so popular now, of impartially keeping aloof from the Stalinist bureaucracy as well as its revolutionary adversaries, is hidden nine times out of ten a wretched prostration before the difficulties and dangers of history. Nevertheless, verbal subterfuges and petty maneuvers will be of no use. No one will be granted either pardon or respite. In the face of the era of wars and revolutions which is drawing near, everyone will have to give an answer: philosophers, poets, painters as well as simple mortals.

In the June issue of your magazine I found a curious letter from an editor of a Chicago magazine, unknown to me. Expressing (by mistake, I hope) his sympathy for your publication, he writes: "I can see no hope however [?] from the Trotskyites or other anemic splinters which have no mass base." These arrogant words tell more about the author than he perhaps wanted to say. They show above all that the laws of development of society have remained a seven times sealed book for him. Not a single progressive idea has begun with a "mass base," otherwise it would not have been a progressive idea. It is only in its last stage that the idea finds its masses—if, of course, it answers the needs of progress. All great movements have begun as "splinters" of older movements. In the beginning, Christianity was only a "splinter" of Judaism; protestantism a "splinter" of Catholicism, that is to say decayed Christianity. The group of Marx and Engels came into existence as a "splinter" of the Hegelian Left. The Communist International germinated during the war from the "splinters" of the Social Democratic International. If these pioneers found themselves able to create a mass base, it was precisely because they did not fear isolation. They knew beforehand that the quality of their ideas would be transformed into quantity. These "splinters" did not suffer from anemia; on the contrary, they carried within themselves the germs of the great historical movements of tomorrow.

In very much the same way, to repeat, a progressive movement occurs in art. When an artistic tendency has exhausted its creative resources, creative "splinters" separate from it, which are able to look at the world with new eyes. The more daring the pioneers show in their ideas and actions, the more bitterly they oppose themselves to established authority which rests on a conservative "mass base," the more conventional souls, skeptics, and snobs are inclined to see in the pioneers, impotent eccentrics or "anemic splinters." But in the last analysis it is the conventional souls, skeptics and snobs who are wrong—and life passes them by.

The Thermidorian bureaucracy, to whom one cannot deny either a certain animal sense of danger or a strong instinct of self-preservation, is not at all inclined to estimate its revolutionary adversaries with such wholehearted disdain, a disdain which is often coupled with lightness and inconsistency. In the Moscow trials, Stalin, who is not a venturesome player by nature, staked on the struggle against "Trotskyism," the fate of the Kremlin oligarchy as well as his own personal destiny. How can one explain this fact? The furious international campaign against "Trotskyism," for which a parallel in history will be difficult to find, would be absolutely inexplicable if the "splinters" were not endowed with an enormous vitality. He who does not see this today will see it better tomorrow.

As if to complete his self-portrait with one brilliant stroke, your Chicago correspondent vows—what bravery!—to meet you in a future concentration camp—either fascist or "communist." A fine program! To tremble at the thought of a concentration camp is certainly not admirable. But is it much better to foredoom oneself and one's ideas to this grim hospitality? With the Bolishevik "amoralism" which is characteristic of us, we are ready to suggest that gentlemen—by no means anemic—who capitulate before the fight and without a fight really deserve nothing better than the concentration camp.

It would be a different matter if your correspondent simply said: in the sphere of literature and art we wish no supervision on the part of "Trotskyists" any more than from the Stalinists. This protest would be, in essence, absolutely just. One can only retort that to aim it at those who are termed "Trotskyists" would be to batter in an open door. The ideological base of the conflict between the Fourth and Third Internationals is the profound disagreement not only on the tasks of the party but in general on the entire material and spiritual life of mankind.

The real crisis of civilization is above all the crisis of revolutionary leadership. Stalinism is the greatest element of reaction in this crisis. Without a new flag and a new program it is impossible to create a *revolutionary* mass base; consequently it is impossible to rescue society from its dilemma. But a truly revolutionary party is neither able nor willing to take upon itself the task of "leading" and even less of commanding art, either before or after the conquest of power. Such a pretension could only enter the head of a bureaucracy—ignorant and impudent, intoxicated with its totalitarian power —which has become the antithesis of the proletarian revolution. Art, like science, not only does not seek orders, but by its very essence, cannot tolerate them. Artistic creation has its laws—even when it consciously serves a social movement. Truly intellectual creation is incompatible with lies, hypocrisy and the spirit of conformity. Art can become a strong ally of revolution only in so far as it remains faithful to itself. Poets, painters, sculptors and musicians will themselves find their own approach and methods, if the struggle for freedom of oppressed classes and peoples scatters the clouds of skepticism and of pessimism which cover the horizon of mankind. The first condition of this regeneration is the overthrow of the domination of the Kremlin bureaucracy.

May your magazine take its place in the victorious army of socialism and not in a concentration camp!

Coyoacan, D. F., June 18, 1938   LEON TROTSKY.

(Translated by Nancy and Dwight Macdonald)

Chapter 4
The Idea of the Avant-Garde
Richard Gilman

> Art, seen in relation to its supreme
> destination, remains a thing of the
> past. It has hence lost for us what
> once made it true and vital, its for-
> mer reality and necessity. — HEGEL

> The history of art is drawing to a
> close. — HAROLD ROSENBERG

If art is always dying, there is never any scarcity of theories
to explain why this should be so, but there is a shortage of insights into
the states of mind in which the obituaries arise. Art hasn't yet died, and
Harold Rosenberg is as likely to be proven wrong as was Hegel, that
philosopher so intent on systems and abstract perfections that he was
oblivious to what was happening almost in his very presence. In the
1830s in Germany Georg Buchner was writing plays that would inau-
gurate a new era of sensibility and that go on informing literary imagination to this moment.

There is something especially ironic about the charge leveled against
certain critics of being "trendy" for championing new forms, when the
really fashionable intellectual pose is that of a steely-eyed, not-to-be-
taken-in defender of civilization against the new barbarians. The irony
is of course compounded by the fact that these pundits at the parapets
are mostly erstwhile evangelists for art and for new art in particular,
and that in defending the past against the present and future they
betray their own pasts and the nature of the human activity we call
art or imagination or creativity, which whatever its transformations is
not likely to die and whose essence is to change — which can look like
dying.

What has been described as the new conservatism in the arts is a complex matter, at least as much a question of political and social stances as of aesthetic ones. In fact, there is almost nothing useful or relevant being said in the aesthetic realm by the new conservatives, who are masters of everything that had *once been* pertinent, which is to say they look at new artistic phenomena with the principles and from the vantage points of the past. More than that, they are engaged in jealously protecting the past, as though it were all there was, or rather as though if the present were acknowledged it would wipe out intellectual history and obliterate our imaginative heritage.

In a piece in this issue by John Bayley (which the editors permitted me to see while I was preparing this piece) the astonishing thesis is offered that the critic ought never to deal with contemporary writers, unless they have already found their "niches," in other words unless, their status and qualities having been fixed and assured, they are already in effect dead. Bayley's idea of art as a refuge or strong room in which to recuperate from life and gain perspective is one with which I have a good deal of sympathy, but to argue from this that only the art of the past provides such refuge is to make impossible any sane consideration of how art comes into being and affects us. For if Bayley is right, then art would always be produced for the future, artists would never be addressing their own contemporaries, and critics would be like scholars working away in museums. As of course so many savants who think like Bayley are.

But Bayley is not really thinking. He is reacting to what he and other cultural tories, new or old, detest in the present atmosphere, its "nihilism," its "mindlessness," its contempt for tradition and for established (sanctified) forms and its hurly-burly insistence on striking out afresh. He is objecting to the "new sensibility," not least to its non-literary orientation, and like Saul Bellow, Philip Rahv, George P. Elliot and so many other defenders of the faith, he cannot accept that others may be at work, neither to endorse nor to anathematize, but to try to understand it. Nor can he see the deadly stasis which the new conservative position implies.

I would like in this essay to examine this curious state of arrest, to try to account for or anyway offer some possible light on the latest "art is dead" epiphany and, more cogently, since the chief current of the moment is not so much that art is dead but that only dead art is art, to investigate the belief that there is something called the "avant—garde" which is finished, that experiment is no longer holy and is even wicked, and that the chief malefactors are artists and critics who want to be "with it."

With what? Nothing has more widely corrupted recent intellectual and aesthetic discussion than the so-called assimilation of the far-out by the mass media. To grant that there are any number of poseurs and operators who are only too willing to be assimilated, that nothing is too extreme for *Life* and *Newsweek* to exhibit if not endorse, that *The New Yorker* publishes Borges and Donald Barthelme and television offers Grotowski and the Open Theater, that the powers of communications seem to make a plaintive bit of naiveté out of a plea like Gide's that he not be "understood too quickly" — to grant all this is not to have settled the question. For the critic it is really to have posed the issues: how do you distinguish the living from the stillborn, the personal from the appropriated, art from sensation? Where there is so much inauthenticity does anything authentic remain? And what is authenticity?

The thing I think we have to try to keep in mind is that the mass media haven't so much assimilated the avant-garde as surrounded it; and in that encirclement there is as little true understanding, as little recognition of what is being done by artists as there ever was in bourgeois society. The uses that are made of things don't always define them, although I would be foolish not to grant that creative acts are affected by the atmosphere surrounding them. But in any case the avant-garde hasn't been destroyed by the mass media; what has been injured, perhaps mortally, is an *idea* of the avant-garde, sometimes promulgated by its practitioners but more often by its camp followers, the idea that it is to be defined not by what it does but by how it acts, that it always moves directly against the social tide and by means of ever more intensive shocks and more extreme propositions, that it cannot (through some higher spirituality) be bought and that it exists to render the world speechless. Art will continue to be satisfyingly unsociable and new art even more, but there isn't any reason to think it a bad thing that the high-flying, quasi-religious righteousness of avant—gardism has been brought down to earth.

Fifteen years ago Richard Chase began an essay in this magazine by remarking that "it is the custom nowadays to pronounce the avant—garde dead." In the piece, which has often been reprinted, Chase went on to argue that at the very least the obituary was premature, as it had been so many times before, but probably would be in error for as far into the future as anybody could see. To broadcast it or give credence to it betrayed a lack of understanding of what the avant—garde is and does for, as he wrote, "the fact seems to be that under modern conditions the avant-garde is a permanent movement" upon whose presence the health and indeed the fate of the general culture heavily depends.

Under modern conditions. If they have held reasonably constant, if what we understand by the term has remained coherent, then we ought to be in a position to make a judgment about Chase's judgment, to decide, a cultural generation after he wrote, how much acceptance we can still give (if we ever gave any) to his theories and whether, if what we call the avant-garde has really gone on showing a life, there is anything inspiriting or efficacious in its doing so.

Is it possible to agree that the "modern conditions" Chase saw prevailing in 1957 have not disappeared but have intensified and spread? This is the assumption I begin with, anyway. Technology has deepened its bite and widened its grip. Television has pushed formally communicated experience further away from the verbal and literary and from the private to the public, and so has the recent flourishing of the kind of film that purports to be "where it's at." Education, bad then, is worse now, or at least a dismal awareness of its badness has become widespread. Politics, after a moment of seeming generosity and hopefulness, has become more estranging than ever. There have of course been new appearances: the black insurgency, the "counterculture," participatory democracy as a rough impulse, new cults of bodily awareness, the rehabilitation and dissemination of the erotic as a style of life and a kind of knowledge.

Yet these new phenomena, whatever their healing action may prove to be, have so far only exacerbated our condition. And what out of long habit we think of when we speak about the modern as a spirit and the time of our experience remains largely intact. A set of clichés, a wearisome catalog, perhaps, but not yet dislodged: alienation, fragmentation, the continual erosion of traditions, change as a first principle, the sense of the world as a place of unprecedented dilemmas and unheard-of enticements. Whatever is being drawn up to come next, we still feel ourselves largely defined by our distance from a simpler and, to the wholly nostalgic among us, a more "human" past, and yet like men and women at any time we are able to imagine the future only as the present extended, as the permanently modern.

But if the modern in Chase's sense remains, "modernism," its erstwhile towering system or principle of formal artistic expression, quite clearly doesn't. Looking around, it isn't hard to detect a widespread conviction that this time, after all the false alarms, the obituary Chase spoke of is accurate. Where art in the most general sense isn't held to be exhausted, no longer of any use, certainly the kind of art accepted in this century as high seriousness, the art Harold Rosenberg has described as "the tradition of the new," is widely considered to have become extinct, or to have become merely a manner by which the recent past is aped or else, in a concession that really concedes nothing, to exist in writers like Beckett or Borges or musicians like Stockhausen, but in sterility and futurelessness, like a prince without an heir.

The "experimental," that which was once nearly synonymous with avant-gardism and was bathed in an air of intrepidity, takes its lumps in the journals — the *serious* ones — and is now thought cranky, eccentric, unattached to any living body of imagination. The imagination is itself distrusted and where it isn't decried is made to stay at home, kept under watch and handed domestic chores. The young new conservative editor of *The New York Times Book Review* extols Updike and sees Borges, John Hawkes, Donald Barthelme, William Gass, John Barth, Claude Simon, Michel Butor and Alain Robbe-Grillet as all having something "febrile" about their work, "a parodistic element . . . and irony so hyper-developed it becomes a form of suicide." Saul Bellow spends a day reading the literary quarterlies and is made "uncomfortable, then queasy, then indignant, contemptuous and finally quite bleak. . . ." Moreover, "reality" commends itself to the creative sensibility, not only to that of the young but also to that of many older persons who show signs of being exhausted by their years of struggle on behalf of an art and a literature that gained its soul from the refusal of reality, of the reality any naked eye could apprehend.

Oh, art has undoubtedly lost some of its former prestige, and avant-garde art, which gained its own prestige from being the only art that mattered, seems to have fallen on bad days. Yet was the prestige of the avant-garde very much higher at the time of Chase's essay? He was writing at a moment and in a climate which one might think looked nearly as inimical as our own to the flourishing of a vanguard. The Eisenhower years, the ostensibly silent generation, the apparent renewal of vigor and the consolidation of many bourgeois and "middle" values, the malaise caused by the Bomb: culture, as Chase said, seemed suspended, hovering disconsolately between the expiring impulses of the great contemporary movement and whatever new artistic and intellectual forces were gathering to replace them.

But the indications were bleak, particularly in literature, which was Chase's main concern. Thomas Mann, the last of the European colossi of the novel, had died two years before. In America, Hemingway, Faulkner and Cummings were all within a few years of their deaths and were creatively pretty much played out; Wallace Stevens had died the same year as Mann. There were only two literary phenomena of any consequence in Europe: the existentialist, which was rather more a matter of philosophic redirection and search for morale and of literary purposefulness than of imaginative achievement; and "the absurd," which was almost wholly confined to the theater and which, moreover, represented the stage's catching up with developments that had long been visible in the other arts. The only presence in America was that of the Beats, which except for the poetry of Allen Ginsberg was a notably sad and ineffectual enterprise by any previous standard of literary élan.

Yet despite such grounds for pessimism Chase, a not easily stampeded critic and obviously no trend-follower, offered his conviction that the avant-garde would sooner or later reassert its "recurring impulse to experimentation, its search for radical values, its historical awareness, its flexibility and receptivity to experience, its polemical intransigence." Such a litany of qualities and sources for action was, for that time or for any time, as complete an expression of faith in the avant-garde and as thorough a description of its adherents' conception of its nature and purposes as anybody could ask for. Disillusionment was setting in, but Chase was evidently not of its party.

There was a great deal at stake. Avant-garde art had come to be what kept civilization going in the face of its desire for sleep, its complacency and deadly entropic drift. It isn't too much to say that a step beyond Chase, in the most zealously evangelical circles, avant-garde art had come to represent what Victor Hugo, even before the modern era, had described literature as being: "civilization itself." Historically art had moved from a celebratory or archival function to guardianship of the very powers of human self-definition; and in the modern age, reversing the classic disposition of things, avant-garde art was what determined those definitions for society and people of consciousness.

The accelerating decline from this high station on the part of art and especially of literature, from which most had been asked and expected, a decline which as I hope to show may prove a very good thing, is one chief source of the present talk about the death of the avant-garde. It isn't that things have radically changed but that they haven't changed enough; the modern world has witnessed its own perpetuation, largely unaffected by the modernist sensibility, unaltered by the great novels and poems. A time comes when unmet expectations produce a reaction or even a revulsion — and this revulsion is a powerful element of the new conservatism.

This is the only way, it seems to me, that we can account for the peculiar note of rancor in so many recent pronouncements on the state of the avant-garde by its one-time exponents and supporters. For, in addition to this rancor, which used to be the property only of declared and predictable enemies — passed-over artists and critics, upholders of the eternal verities, subsidized spotters of the barbarian at the gates, moralists and academic preservationists — we can observe something else even more surprising, and that is a tone of pleasure. The avant-garde is finished, done for, kaput; and people who spent years singing its praises and insisting on its necessity are rushing to help pile the dirt on the coffin. Well, rancor and pleasure in another's bad turn of fortune are marks of both the unrequited lover and the disappointed investor.

If avant-garde art is civilization itself or the principle on which civilization can go forward or be renewed (as successive waves of futurists of all descriptions have most ardently insisted) then something a great deal broader than aesthetic issues is clearly in question. In this idea of the redemptive or socially propulsive power of art, of which Chase's catalog is actually a rather restrained expression, one can discern that fusion or at least affinity of political and social energies, values and aspirations with literary and aesthetic ones which has characterized thinking and writing about the avant-garde ever since it became a self-conscious and publicly celebrated (or decried) activity, which is to say ever since it took on or, more accurately, was given a name.

We tend to forget, as the very term becomes an emblem or an epithet, that the notion of a vanguard implies an aggressive, military-like movement toward an objective, that it implies conquest. In the life of the avant-garde this movement may be seen as having been roughly divided into three parts or, to keep the military metaphor, columns. The most violently apocalyptic one was advancing toward nothing less than the full transformation of social, political and personal life, through imaginative exploration and discovery, the creation of opposing values, the reconstruction of consciousness and the erection of models for true, liberated behavior. A much more modest progress was toward the creation of alternate realms of existence, to be inhabited by all imagination-summoned refugees from modern social horror and psychic oppression. Young persons who during the twenties, thirties or forties, say, were struck by art like Saul by the Paraclete, fell mostly under one or the other of these two sways, as did the majority of humanist critics.

The third column, impelled by an even more total repudiation of the art of the past than the other two, yet notably chaste and "uncommitted," was moving into the elaboration of wholly self-contained new artifacts, into an "aestheticism" whose orthodoxy is summed up in Malevich's Suprematist Manifesto:

> The difference between the new, non-objective ("useless") art and the art of the past lies in the fact that the full artistic value of the latter comes to light (becomes recognized) only after life, in search of some new expedient, has forsaken it, whereas the unapplied artistic element of the new art outstrips life and shuts the door on "practical utility." And so there the new non-objective art stands — the expression of pure feeling, seeking no practical values, no ideas, no "promised land."

Such "useless" art would of course undermine the notion of the avant-garde as continuous since, having arrived at pure, noncontingent, unappliable works, it would have to rid itself of all nonaesthetic categories, including those of progress, discovery and cultural renewal. This appears in fact to have happened from time to time, the outcome of a theory or not: with Mallarmé, *Finnegans Wake,* Mondrian, etc. And it is an element in the decline of the avant-garde, if not in substance then in public and critical estimation of its existence and vitality. For absolute art, or what would seem from the perspective of a confinement in time to be absolute — pure, nonmatrixed theater such as certain Happenings attempted to be, John Cage's music, Ad Reinhart's Black paintings, Beckett's *How It Is* — appears to many people to block artistic energy instead of renewing it, to obscure the human element in art and to make newness seem a kind of sterility or death.

Throughout the modern period there have been points at which many supposedly avant-garde cultural critics have refused to endorse the most extreme ideas and products of this impulse toward an almost wholly self-contained art or have drawn the line within the ongoing tradition of the new: *Ulysses* but not *Finnegans Wake,* Pollock but not Newman. For the entirely or chiefly aesthetic, art as autonomous and nonutilitarian, leaves society and general culture to their own devices and deprives cultural critics of any validated principle of commentary and interpretation.

This is why there has always been greater intellectual enthusiasm for a more usable art, one that *does* seek the promised land which Malevich's pronunciamento so strenuously repudiated. But as has been observed often enough, the responsibility for bringing about palpable new existence through a revolution in consciousness has been much too great for avant-garde art or for any kind of art to bear; it seems clearer now than when Chase was writing that it has never been the right sort of responsibility. But what hasn't been seen so clearly, it seems to me, is that the great expectations that have been held out for advanced and continuously advancing literature (to confine myself to that for the moment) haven't been maintained so much by the creators of the modern canon, its central and decisive ones at any rate, as by lesser figures, fervid and narrowly millenarian or acrobatic and ego—ridden workers at the fringes, and by certain critics and pundits for whom it is always difficult to see that art is strangely powerless, that it makes its countergestures to the actual power of the material world, to systems of value that originate in power and to chronologies of progress and myths of impending redemption.

Joyce, Proust, Mann, Eliot, Kafka, Yeats, Stevens, Faulkner, Rilke: none of them seems ever to have thought of himself as a *modernist*, although they were all aware to one degree or another of their peculiarly modern situation in relation to a radically and comparatively suddenly altered general culture, to tradition and the increased pressure toward new forms (a result of the stoppage of literature through its own internal piling up and of the usurpation — without comprehension — by bourgeois culture of the previously new), and to what had recently become expected of literature, its newly prophetic and quasi-religious function. They were conscious, in Stephen Spender's words, of having to "reinvent the world."

Yet they understood, as a great many intellectual critics did not, that these new worlds would remain inventions, imaginative increments (in Blackmur's phrase) or surrogate visions or revelatory structures of language, all of which arose from the most intimate connections with the world of physical events, moral questions and issues of power — what else is art's material? — but would leave all those things intact. And it was in fact the extreme political and often social conservatism — a matter chiefly of distrust of programs and solutions and of a wish, however misguided, to defend the imagination against social reality — of so many of the great figures of twentieth-century literature that disillusioned many of their troubled admirers and set going those great debates of a few decades ago (that have lately been revived in a somewhat less strident form) about the "responsibility of the artist" and on the question of how a radical aesthetic imagination can coexist with a nonhumanist or even an antihumanist politics and social belief.

In the case of the intellectuals we shouldn't be astonished that they have been far more eager that literature bring about recognizable human change and far more troubled by its failure to do it than the great writers have been. Intellectuals have always fought artists for ideal control of the latter's works, for the license to quarry fiction and poetry and drama for meanings and significances that might be brought over into the "real" world to serve as weapons or tools. It is no accident that the best critics have generally been artists themselves, for it's a rare intellectual who can resist the pressure of the wish to be justified in his own right and who has the humility to take works on their own terms.

In his useful if somewhat schematic study *The Theory of the Avant-Garde,* Renato Poggioli has thrown important light on this matter. The intelligentsia, he writes, "has always denied, in a more or less direct and absolute way, the autonomy — even the *raison d'être* — of art. When the intelligentsia turns its attention, or renders homage, to a work of art, it almost always functions in terms of ideological adhesion, that is to say, it attaches itself to content. It tends, in general, to deny any creation in which the purely aesthetic principle seems to dominate. . . ."

The phenomenon Poggioli is describing operates most centrally in literature, with its greater concern with behavior and ideas and its more explicit social origins, and goes beyond political considerations, although it takes on certain of its attributes from them. Right-wing intellectuals or, more relevantly to American experience, radicals who have retrenched, have almost always distrusted the avant-garde; the left intelligentsia (outside Communist countries of course) has almost always theoretically and usually actively supported it. But what unites the majority of intellectuals of any political persuasion is their essential attitude toward the work of art, whether it is experimental or not: that it is there to serve in direct ways, to illuminate and help pave the way, to corroborate or console, to amend or conserve the world.

Alfred Kazin's essay, *The Function of Criticism Today,* written about the same time as Chase's piece on the avant-garde, eloquently expresses the prevailing ideology of the intellectual-critic who, like most other men and women, wants the aesthetic to be a function of something broader and more humanistic than a modality of imagination, wants it to be more useful, too. Criticism, Kazin wrote, should be concerned "explicitly, fightingly, with an ideal of man, with a conception of what man is seeking to become, with what he must become," and such criticism is in accord with "literature's classic function of providing ideas central to social policy and moral behavior."

Kazin has been too sensitive and open a critic ever to have been wholly confined to the implications of this position. Yet its coercions have existed in his own work and, with much more deleterious results, continue to exist in the writings of a number of other critics who came to consciousness in the politicized thirties, as well as in the work of a younger breed who write on films and drama and literature (and even on music) as though these forms were nothing but (aestheticized) statements in the political or moral or social order.

If providing ideas central to social policy and moral behavior was ever the classic function of literature, which is certainly debatable, it hasn't been for a very long time. If it has provided ideas at all, literature in its modern or avant-garde phase has put forward thought (or imaginative structures from which ideas, necessarily paraphrased and so denatured, may be plucked) that has almost always run counter to entrenched social policy and to established or traditional moral behavior. This has in fact been one of the ostensible identifying marks of modernism, one of the qualities that have most commended it to intellectuals.

Of course Kazin might argue that in his definition the word "central" ought not to be understood exclusively as meaning "positive" or as being any sort of endorsement; ideas critical of policy and behavior may surely be central. Yet it seems to me that even such negative ideas — all those notions of inauthenticity and those perceptions of human malfeasance that go to make up what we have called the adversary culture — have in fact been thought of as being useful and thus positive; behind the destructive insights and the indictments lie the elements of a social policy and a moral system for the *world to come,* the world toward which the avant-garde is presumably and by definition moving and bringing civilization in its wake.

I don't think that this is what literature, at its most serious, has taken it on itself to provide, although it is unquestionably what it has been asked to do and even assumed to have done. I believe that as history, the history precisely of social and moral facts and events, has become increasingly irrational and resistant to ordinary sensibility, less and less plausible as the material of a human world, literature has at least partly been created out of an impulse to amend, to fill in the void, to erect existences in the realm of possibility — to reinvent all lost humanness (including the humanness of authentic dismay) and so construct a new and adversary history, something very different from an adversary culture. When Georg Buchner, with whom the modern age of literature begins in the 1830s, composed *Danton's Death* he quite deliberately fashioned a counterstatement to history, proposing nothing for the future, offering no solutions, simply throwing the power of his imagination against the power of the world and so, abstractly, "uselessly," triumphing.

In any case, out of the notion that literature's function is to serve social progress, however broadly defined, and that the critic's is to describe and analyze how this is accomplished, as well as to hold out an ideal of the future for writers, notions against which, as we all know, the so-called new criticism, an enterprise largely of poets, aligned itself. Out of these notions have come all those superbly self-confident exercises in paraphrase and *rewriting* that have made up one source of criticism's contemporary but now moribund prestige.

The Waste Land as map of modern dissociation and fragmentation; *Remembrance of Things Past* as infinitely subtle document of social and psychological analysis; Kafka's tales as parables of modern political tyranny and the cold terrors of bureaucracy; Joyce's fiction as legends and artifacts of the centripetal flight of language, which is in turn a reflection of modern fragmentation — all such readings and exegeses are in fact concerned with establishing how literature reflects and analyzes the age and only incidentally with how it exists in its own right, as increment and as succor from time and facts. And this power of reflection and analysis is seen to be an instrument, a weapon in the struggle toward the future, for through analysis and reflection comes exposure, and to expose the world, to place on exhibition its delinquencies and outrages, has been what intellectuals have wanted from literature as much as they have wanted anything. And that is a very modern note.

The change in attitude toward the avant-garde on the part of its one-time champions is naturally enough presented as having an objective base: present day experimental or advanced writing is simply bad, shapeless, chaotic, nihilistic, above all lacking in that large coherent vision of experience and society that was one of modernism's hallmarks. The two considerations, what we are accustomed to call the thematic and the technical, are intimately related, as is always the case. This humane critical position on modernism held that technical innovation or experiment was in the service of the vision, and as long as there seemed to be a coherence between them, as long as it remained possible to *interpret* new forms, to translate them, that is to say, from the realm of aesthetic imagination to that of ordinary cognition (and of immediate usefulness, I would add) modernism remained exciting and was justified.

But the visions began to fail, the *big* novels and poems were no longer written, the confidence that seemed to characterize the modern masters began to disappear (from Joyce to Beckett). There are many reasons for this, not least important being the fact that literature has perennially to repudiate its own monuments, but the relevant point here is that it hasn't been avant-gardism that has fallen into disrepute so much as avant-gardism with its formal or aesthetic principles, its *literariness* stripped of the epochal and apocalyptic, to the front. The astonishing distaste of American critics for the works of the French New Novelists, the refusal to concede that there could be anything original and valuable in these works, has always seemed to me a glaring instance of our critical provincialism and our demand that literature have "content."

This reduction of scale and renewed grappling with the nature of literature is what I think of as "post-modernist," which in other hands is an epithet to pinion a movement whose sinfulness lies in its failure to remain on the same high plane of "total" accomplishment as the works of the late masters and to possess the same high sense of "responsibility" for civilization' and society and the mind as the latter were presumed to have had. What else can we make of indictments like those of Bellow and Rahv, who in the greatest of ironies inveigh against the current avant-garde (which they refuse to dignify with the term) in the name of the previous one?

Gigantic, immobilized, hieratic, the great modernist works stand in the consciousness of the new conservatives like enormous ice sculptures, filling all space, allowing nothing new to grow or be acknowledged. The disappointment they feel at literature's not having brought the millenium is compensated for by their nostalgia of equal pressure; the works they have enshrined have succeeded in arresting time and they live in this frozen chronology, striking out against the present, which doesn't exist for them.

It doesn't exist because literature, as they conceive of it, isn't being produced; only despicable scribblings, the work of imposters or monstrous adolescents, are. More broadly, art everywhere displays the signs of chaos and decay, is marked by ugliness, a pleasure in outrage, a spirit of the haphazard. It is indeed one of the signs of these times that writers, and painters and other artists, especially the young among them, throwing off the burden of the past — art's recent past — have put new claims on outcast objects (just as was done at the outset of the Dada-Surrealist period), turned away from "high" cultural perspectives and mocked the solemnity of those who still maintain them. "Trash" is a word in aesthetics now; pornography has its intellectual defenders.

Much of the impulse for these phenomena of a culture "lower" than seems ever before to have been granted status comes from a reaction precisely to the oppressions of high culture, of a former seriousness turned to stone. In the preface to his novel *Pornographia* Witold Gombrowicz writes: "We are 'infantalized' by all 'higher' forms. Man, tortured by his mask, fabricates secretly, for his own usage, a sort of 'subculture': a world made out of the refuse of a higher world of culture, a domain of trash, immature myths, indefensible passions . . . a secondary domain of compensation." Not everything erotic or violent or "junky" in our culture arises this way, but the perception is a true one; in the generation after Gombrowicz what has happened is that this secret world has come to make itself public.

That there is something we might call *serious* funk or pop, earnest grotesquerie, is a recognition we have to make, in the face of the abundance of exploitation of the new mood. The Theater of the Ridiculous, for example, has been an enormously serious enterprise, mocking the frozen practices of drama and releasing new energies toward their thaw. Donald Barthelme's prose, made up of all our "polluted" vocabulary, all of what he calls the verbal "dreck" we have piled up, acts powerfully to create a new basis for language's health. So does Barth's writing and that of Peter Handke, whose plays and fiction come to us out of the literary tradition ("the avant-garde is always rediscovering a lost tradition" — Ionesco), but like the work of a mind amazed that language is what it is.

This kind of knowing naiveté, this tactical astonishment, is one condition of innovation. And this is what is lacking in those traditional writers (or those who have become *traditionalized*) who carry on as though all the resources were still at hand, as though language need only be approached with determination and large ideas about mankind in order for it to yield up literature. As though will can do the work of imagination.

The avant-garde is that element in the exercise of the imagination we call art which finds itself unwilling (unable really) to reiterate or refine what has already been created. In this sense there will always be an avant-garde, simply as a matter of the renewal of forms and the effort to make the imagination capable of new actions to meet new experiences. An avant-garde considered as a kind of salvation or one built on belligerence and contempt are historical accidents, not inevitabilities. What we might call the secularization of art, its chastening and the removal from it of the "values" that ought to be obtained elsewhere, are large factors in the apparent decline of the avant-garde. For stripped of its apocalyptic qualities, its competitive aspects and myths of progress — all characteristics that, as I've tried to show, have largely been imposed from outside — art takes on its simple and irreplaceable task of invention, invention in the order of possibility, invention that makes life known to itself.

Yet, it has to be asked, what of life's wanting to know itself directly, without the intervention of imagination or at any rate of imagination organized in the formal, abstract ways that aesthetic reality implies? It's significant that at moments of political confrontation, of seemingly pre-revolutionary situations like the early thirties in this country and more legitimately, those weeks in France in 1968, radical cultural critics and even radical artists are overcome with guilt or at least shame at being avant-garde in the traditional sense. At such times they wish fervidly to move toward "life," which is to say toward everything nonhierarchic and antiaristocratic, toward everything practical and immediately effi-cacious. "Art is dead, let's liberate our day-to-day life," a graffito at the Sorbonne exhorted. And Alain Jouffroy wrote at the time: "I con-sciously and deliberately [ally] the elimination of esthetic values to the necessity and possibility of social revolution," and went on to say that "art is the armchair in which the State sits for its own pleasure."

Art as an impediment to the creation of the new society: this is the latest note. It marks the hundred-and-eighty-degree turn from the all-encompassing radicalism that was to revivify the world through total action (never mind the contempt for the unrevivifiable), when things seemed to hang together and it was a form of treason to the spirit to suggest that such stern choices were there to be made as perfection of the life or of the work. Art as a luxury and worse, art as inhuman, des-tructive, an abdication: the revolt in one quarter is against ideality, transcendence and the absolutism of the aesthetic, its insistence on the need for an alternative to ordinary experience and consciousness. And it's even more passionately against the aristocratic element of avant—garde art, its perfectionism and intolerance of the already accomplished. "Make it new!" and the newness seems to come into existence for its own sake and leave us gasping in abstract realms, disarmed in the struggle against the brutal facts among which we have to live.

Once again, I think this attitude isn't the wave of the future, al-though at the moment it has currency and a certain propulsion. Beneath the surface it represents one more aspect of the process by which art is being demythologized and denuded of its tendency to be a surrogate for the world to come, the one that doesn't come. An avant-garde that is simply art being new, not the world being made new, will go on. "In the long run," Nietzsche wrote, "utility is simply a figment of our imagination and may well be the fatal stupidity by which we shall one day perish." If at the moment it is what some of us think we have to live by, still one protection is precisely that continuing effort of imagina-tion, that risk of the impractical, which may have lost its artificial pres-tige but not its value nor its necessity.

Chapter 5
The Intelligentsia
Arthur Koestler

'Intelligentsia' is one of those terms difficult to define, but easy to associate. It is logically blurred but emotionally vivid, surrounded with a halo, or rather several halos which overlap and vary according to period and place. One may list as examples the romantic salon; the profesional middle classes; terroristic organizations of students and aristocracy in the second half of nineteenth-century Russia; patriotic University Corps in post-Napoleonic Germany; the Bohemians of Montmartre, and so on. There are also evocative geographical names like Bloomsbury, Montparnasse, and Cagnes; and certain typical attitudes to life including clothing, hair-fashion, drink and food. The aura of the intelligentsia changes all the time; its temporary representatives are subdivided into classes and groups, and even its limits are blurred by a host of camp followers and hangers-on: members of the aristocracy, maecenases, tarts, fools, admirers and Earnest Young Men. Hence we won't get far with impressionistic judgements, and had better look up the Oxford dictionary for a solid definition.

There we find:

> 'Intelligentzia, -sia, The part of a nation (esp. the Russian) that aspires to independent thinking.'

Thus the Concise Oxford Dictionary, 3rd edition, 1934.

By 1936, in the climate of the pink decade and the popular front, the definition has undergone a significant change:

> 'The class consisting of the educated portion of the population regarded as capable of forming public opinion.'

(The Shorter Oxford Dictionary, 2nd edition, 1936).

This second version has since obviously been proved too optimistic, and we had better fall back on the first which is excellent.

Historically, it is indeed the 'aspiration to independent thinking' which provides the only valid group characteristic of the intelligentsia.

But how does it happen that an 'aspiration towards independent thinking' arises in a part of a nation? In our class-ridden world this is obviously not a matter of spontaneous association of the gifted – enlightened dukes, plus miners' sons plus General Practitioners. The intelligentsia of a given period and place is of a fairly homogeneous social texture: loose threads only appear on the fringes. Intelligence alone is neither a necessary nor a sufficient condition to become a member of the Intelligentsia. Instead, we have to regard the formation of this particular group as a social process which, as far as modern society is concerned, begins with the French Revolution.

II The Intelligentsia and the Third Estate

Among the upper strata of the Third Estate the aspiration to independent thinking was not a luxury but a dire necessity of survival. The young bourgeoisie, hemmed in by the stultifying feudal structure, had to conquer its historic *lebensraum*, and this conquest was only possible by blowing up the feudal totems and taboos with the dynamite of 'independent thought.' The first modern intellectuals were the Encyclopedists and they entered the historical stage as the great debunkers and iconoclasts. Goethe resurrected is unimaginable in our time, but Voltaire would be within a fortnight acclimatized in Bloomsbury, winning all weekend competitions of the *New Statesman*. For Goethe was the last Renaissance genius, a direct descendant of Leonardo, and his attitude to Society that of a courtier of some enlightened Florentine prince; whereas with Voltaire, the great debunking of feudal values begins.

The intelligentsia in the modern sense thus first appears as that part of a nation which by its social situation not so much 'aspires' but is *driven* to independent thought, that is to a type of group behaviour which debunks the existing hierarchy of values (from which it is excluded) and at the same time tries to replace it with new values of its own. This constructive tendency of the intelligentsia is its second basic feature. The true iconoclasts always had a prophetic streak, and all debunkers have a bashfully hidden pedagogic vein.

But where had these new values of their own come from? This is the point where Marxist analysis ends in over-simplified schemata:

> The bourgeoisie, historically, has played a most revolutionary part . . . Constant revolutionizing of production, uninterrupted disturbance of all social conditions, everlasting uncertainty and agitation distinguish the bourgeois epoch from all earlier ones. All fixed, fast-frozen, relations, with their train of ancient and venerable prejudices and opinions, are swept away, all new-formed ones become antiquated before they can ossify. All that is solid melts into air, all that is holy is profaned, and man is at last compelled to face with sober senses his real conditions of life and his relations with his kind. . . .
> And as in material, so also in intellectual production. The intellectual creations of individual nations become common property. National one-sidedness and narrow-mindedness become more and more impossible, and from the numerous national and local literatures there arises a world literature.
> (Manifesto of the Communist Party, 1848).

The first paragraph quoted shows Marx and Engels at their best; in the second they take the fatal short cut from Economy to "Superstructure": that is culture, art, mass psychology. Marxian society has a basement – production, and an attic – intellectual production; the staircase and the lifts are missing.

For it is not as simple as that: the triumphant class creating its own philosophic superstructure to fit its mode of production like a tailored suit. The Encyclopædia was not commissioned by the National Assembly. Whenever a class or group emerged victorious from its struggles, it found the befitting ideology already waiting for it like a ready made suit in a department store. Thus Marx found Hegel, Feuerbach, and Ricardo, Mussolini had only to pick Sorel and Pareto, Hitler discovered Gobineau, Houston Stuart Chamberlain and Jung; Stalin revived Machiavelli and Peter the Great. This of course, is a mixed bag of examples of progressive and regressive movements which, strictly speaking, should be kept apart. For regressive movements need simply to fall back on superannuated values – not on the last, but on the last-but-one or last-but-two, to perform a romantic revival, and derive a lot of pseudo-revolutionary gusto out of this 'revolution à rebours.' And there is always a part of the intelligentsia which, abandoning its aspiration to independent thought and detaching itself from the main body, lends itself to such romantic revivals. They are the tired and the cynics, the hedonists, the romantic capitulators, who transform their dynamite into Bengal lights, the Juengers, Montherlants, Ezra Pounds.

Discarding these, there still remains the problem of how and why the true, emergent, progressive movements in history, those which led to the Rights of Man and to the founding of the First Workers International, those who have no last-but-one precepts to fall back on, invariably find the right ideology waiting for them at the right moment. I repeat that I do not believe any more that the economic process by itself creates its own superstructure. Orthodox Marxism has never produced the historical evidence for this postulate. Nor, of course, is it a matter of coincidence. It seems rather that political economy and cultural development are merely two aspects of the same basic process, which we are as yet far from being able to define.

Two examples from other spheres may help to bring this vague-sounding assertion into relief. The first is the old mind-body problem where the antithesis between materialistic and idealistic schools was much the same as between historical materialism and historical idealism, until the double-aspect theory brought the quarrel about which is the cause and which the effect, which is the hen and which is the egg, to an at least temporary close. Thus your gastric acid is neither the cause nor the effect of your nervous state, but both are aspects, consequences of your total mode of living. The second example is the relation between physics and mathematics. When Einstein was faced with the contradictory evidence of two perfectly sound physical experiments (Michelson-Morley and Fizeau) he was able to develop the theory of Relativity only because the apparently abstract and useless non-Euclidian mathematical fantasies of Bolyai, Riemann and others were waiting for him just at the right moment, ready-made around the corner. The mathematical and the physical elements of Relativity were developed quite independently, and their coincidence would appear miraculous, without the recognition of a fundamental trend of evolution in scientific thought, of which the various faculties are merely isolated aspects.

The rise of the Third Estate and of the progressive middle classes was thus neither the cause nor the effect of humanistic liberal philosophy. The two phenomena sprang from the same root, they were entwined and correlated like colour and shape in the same object. *The basic function of the Encyclopedists and of all later intelligentsias was this correlating of social and intellectual evolution; they were the self-*

interpreting, introspective organs of the social body; and this function automatically includes both the iconoclastic and the pedagogic, the destructive and the constructive element.

III The Decay of the Third Estate

This function gives a clue to the always peculiar structure of the intelligentsia.

Social behaviour has a much greater inertia than thought. There is always an enormous discrepancy between our collective ways of living and the accumulated data of science, art, technique. We wage wars, go to church, worship kings, eat murderous diets, conform to sexual taboos, make neurotics of our children, miseries of our marriages, oppress and let ourselves be oppressed – whereas in our text-books and art galleries there is embodied the objective knowledge of a way of living which we shall put into practice only in decades or centuries. In everyday life we all behave like creatures in a period piece, anachronistic caricatures of ourselves. The distance between the library and the bedroom is astronomical. However, the body of theoretical knowledge and independent thought is there, only waiting to be picked up, as the Jacobins picked up the Encyclopedists.

This picking up, however, is the function of a special type of people; the liaison agents between the way we live and the way we *could* live according to the contemporary level of objective knowledge. Those who are snugly tucked into the social hierarchy have obviously no strong impulse towards independent thought. Where should it come from? They have no reason to destroy their accepted values nor any desires to build new ones. The thirst for knowledge is mainly confined to situations where the unknown is disquieting; the happy are rarely curious. On the other hand the great majority of the oppressed, the underdogs, lack the opportunity or the objectivity or both, for the pursuit of independent thought. They accept or reject the existing values; both attitudes are inarticulate and unobjective. Thus the function of co-ordination between the two concepts Homo and Sapiens falls to those sandwiched in between two layers, and exposed to the pressure of both. The intelligentsia is a kind of sensitive, porous membrane stretched between media of different properties.

One should not however confound them with the middle classes as such. Sensitivity, searching and groping are attitudes which presuppose a certain amount of frustration – not too much and not too little; a kind of moderate unhappiness, a harmonious disequilibrium. The upper strata which accept the traditional values, lack this frustration; the bottom strata have too much of it – to the degree of being either paralysed or discharging it in convulsive fits. Further, it must be a *specific* frustration – the discontent of the professional man, writer, artist, who rebel not because society has deprived them of every chance, crushed and buried them in pit or workshop, but because they have been given a margin large enough to develop their gifts, but too narrow to make them feel smug and accept the given order of things. For the smug, thinking is a luxury, for the frustrated a necessity. And as long as the chasm between thought and tradition, theoretical insight and practical routine prevails, thinking must necessarily be directed by the two poles of debunking and Utopianism.

All this does not apply any more to the bulk of the middle class. It did as long as their climate was 'Commonwealth' and Jacobinism. Meanwhile the once revolutionary urban bourgeoisie has become a conservative force. No more a sensitive membrane, but an inert sticky glue which holds the social body together. Their frustrations are repressed, their aspirations are not towards new hierarchies of values, but towards climbing to the top of the existing hierarchy. Thus the intelligentsia, once the vanguard of the ascending bourgeoisie, becomes the Lumpen-Bourgeoisie in the age of its decay.

IV The Intelligentsia and the Fourth Estate

As the Third Estate gradually loses its progressive character to become first stagnant then regressive, the intelligentsia becomes more and more detached from it and driven to the quest for more vigorous allies, capable of fulfilling its task of demolition and construction.

The most fascinating example for this quest is nineteenth-century Russia. '. . . Whether they [the revolutionary intelligentsia] spoke of the necessity of political liberty, of the plight of the peasant or of the socialist future of society, it was always their own plight which really moved them. And their plight was not primarily due to material need: it was spiritual' (Borkenau, 'The Communist International').

This spiritual plight of the Russian intelligentsia was yet another form of the duality I mentioned: the contradiction between the inert, stagnant, habit-conditioned form of everyday life on the one hand, and the accumulated data of objective knowledge lying fallow as 'theory' and 'ideology' on the other. For the nineteenth-century Russians this latter principle was embodied in Western European civilization: in British Parliamentarism, French literature, German philosophy. For them, the Western was the incarnation of homo sapiens as opposed to the Barbarians of the steppes; just as, by an ironical turn of history, the Western intelligentsia of the two post-war decades became spell-bound by Russian Communism which seemed to incorporate the truly human Utopia, as opposed to the decay of Capitalism.

There is, however, a fundamental difference between the early Russian revolutionary intelligentsia – the Shelyabows, Sonja Petrovskajas, Bakunins, Nechaews, Kropotkins, and the Bloomsbury of the Pink Decade. It is easy to sneer at the comparison and to contrast the futility of the latter with the heroism of the assassins of Alexander II, the martyrdom of the Siberian exiles and the prisoners of Schluesselburg. Racial comparisons between the undeniably greater endurance and fatalism of the semi-Asiatic Russians and the highly strung Westerners provide one differential factor, but not the basic one. The basic point is that people grow under the burden of their responsibilities and shrink if the burden is taken from them. Nechaew lived for a number of years chained to the wall of a humid cell and when his comrades succeeded in establishing contact and offered to liberate him, refused because he preferred them to concentrate on more important tasks. But later, in the emigré atmosphere of Geneva, he became involved in the most squalid quarrels and died an obscure nobody. The venerable and justly venerated Russian student heroines and martyrs were not less hysterical than any character of Huxley's or Evelyn Waugh's; Lassalle was a snob who got himself killed in a quixotic duel, Marx a pathologically quarrelsome old sponger, Bakunin had an incestuous fixation to a sister, was impotent and died a virgin; Trotsky at a certain period spent all his afternoons and evenings playing chess in the Café Central in Vienna – a typical figure from an Osbert Lancaster Café Royal Landscape; Lenin suffered a traumatic shock when his brother Alexander was hanged – hence his fanatical hatred of the Bourgeoisie of which, in analytical terms, the Russian revolution was merely a 'projection'. Neurosis is inherent in the structure of intelligentsias (I shall come back to this point in a moment): history, however, is not interested in a person's motives, only in his achievements. But why is it that the burden and bliss of responsibility is given to the intelligentsia in certain periods and in others not, condemning the latter to barrenness and futility? This is the question to which the comparison between the early Russians and Bloomsbury boils down; more precisely to the question of the historical constellation which accounts for the sharing-out of responsibilities.

The answer becomes at once obvious by a comparison of the two countries' sociological structure. Nineteenth-century Russia had no Trade Unions, no Labor movement or Co-operatives. Serfdom was only abolished in 1862; in that drowsy, inert giant-country there was no gradual transition from patriarchal feudalism to modern Capitalism; I have spoken to peasants who took aeroplanes for granted, watching them each day fly over their heads but had never seen a railway or motor-car; others who had travelled in a car but wouldn't believe that such a thing as a bicycle existed.

What a paradise for intellectuals with pedagogical yearnings! When the first of them, the martyrs of Narodnaya Volya, started what they called 'going among the people' dressed as peasants, preaching the new gospel, they trod on virgin soil, they found no competition in the shape of Trade Unions and Labor politicians telling them to cast off their masquerade and go back to the Bloomsbury of Petrograd or Moscow. The mushik proved apathetic and did not respond to their appeal; but the crusading intelligentsia was not discouraged because they had no rivals; they changed their tactics from mass-appeal to terrorism, from terrorism to work among the industrial proletariat, the landless peasants, among the soldiers. They quarrelled, they split, they ramified; but all the time they could work in the untouched raw material of History, could project their spiritual plight, their desire to destroy and rebuild on to a gigantic historical plane. Their faith moved rocks because there still were unhewn rocks to move.

In contrast to them, the Western intelligentsia found no virgin fields to plough, no natural allies to realize their aspirations to independent thought. According to Marxist theory the intelligentsia was to join the ranks of the working class and to become their strategists and tacticians. There is no evidence that the intelligentsia lacked the courage or the ability to do so. In 1848 students and workers fought together on the barricades; in the French Commune and in the revolutionary movements after the last war in Germany, Austria, Hungary, Bulgaria, and even in the International Brigades of Spain, they gave an excellent account of themselves. But from the middle of the nineteenth century onward, the workers of Central and Western Europe had rapidly developed their own organizations, parties, trade unions, produced their own leaders and, above all, their own bureaucracy – men with iron wills and wooden heads. In an age of accelerated developments, the organized Fourth Estate had become stagnant much quicker than the Third in its time, and without even ascending to power. The crumbs of material improvements and the shadow of political influence which various Sections of the Second International had wrung from the rulers were enough to paralyse their impetus. Members of the Western Intelligentsia could become Labor members of Parliaments, editors of Left papers, lecturers in dreary evening classes; but there were no rocks to move with the lever of 'independent thought.' Towards the end of the century the Western intelligentsia had only the choice to be either bourgeois decadents or proletarian schoolmasters. Their groups and cliques developed according to these alternative poles, with a spectrum ranging from the French Symbolists through the 'George-Kreis' to the Fabians. Compare Shaw with Voltaire, Leon Blum with St. Just, and you get the difference – not so much in stature as in historical opportunity.

The shake-up of the First World War seemed to create a new opportunity for a general debunking and rebuilding. The whole body of ideas had undergone a radical transformation: Relativity and Quantum mechanics, Hormonology and Psycho-analysis, Leninism and Behaviourism, Aviation and Wireless, Expressionism and Surrealism – a completely new universe had taken shape in the library; and the dazzling light it radiated drove the intelligentsia half crazy by its contrast to the anachronistic, dusty-musty traditions still governing everyday conduct and beliefs. What a historical opportunity for de-bunking and re-building; but where were the allies to carry it out? The sensitive membrane vibrated wildly; but there was no resonance-body attached to it. Utopian striving during those two decades was monopolized by the Third International, whose blue-print for the European revolution was shaped on the conditions of a country with 80 per cent illiterates and a ratio of rural to urban population of ten to one. During the two decades of its existence the revolutionary movement was focussed on and governed by that semi-Asiatic dictatorship. Its European extension needed not intellectuals, but a ruthless and uncritically obedient bureaucracy. The few members of the Western intelligentsia who were accepted into its ranks lost first the right, and soon even the desire for 'independent thought'; they became fanatic sectarians and Party-hacks, while the best among them met a tragic end. Particularly tragic was the fate of the revolutionary intelligentsia in the country where revolution seemed almost within reach, Germany. Liebknecht and Luxembourg were murdered in '18, Paul Levy committed suicide after his expulsion from the C.P., Ruth Fischer, also expelled, vanished into obscurity, Toller hanged himself in New York, Muehsam committed suicide in a Nazi concentration camp, Max Hoelz was drowned under dubious circumstances in Russia, Heinz Neumann, the last survivng C.P. leader who came from the intelligentsia was liquidated.

But the bulk of the Western intelligentsia were never admitted to this bloody Olympus. They were not wanted, had to remain fellow-travellers, the fifth wheel to the cart. The intelligentsia of the Pink Decade was irresponsible, because it was deprived of the privilege of responsibility. Left in the cold, suspended in a vacuum, they became decadents of the bourgeoisie. It was nobody's fault; for they were the mirror, not the light.

I am trying neither to whitewash, nor to accuse. The intelligentsia is part of the social body, its most sensitive part; when the body is ill, the skin develops a rash. The deterioration of the intelligentsia is as much a symptom of disease as the corruption of the ruling class or the sleeping sickness of the proletariat. They are symptoms of the same fundamental process. To sneer at the intelligentsia and, while depriving it of the responsibility of action, shove on to it the responsibility of failure, is either thoughtless stupidity or a manoeuvre with obvious motives. Nazism knew exactly what it was doing when it exterminated the intelligentsia of the European Continent.

V The Intelligentsia and Neurosis

This sensitive membrane not only stretches between heterogeneous social classes, but between the social body as a whole and its environment. It is tempting, and perhaps not entirely futile, to follow up this metaphor for a while. It is the surface, the ectoderm, phylogenetically the rind of the plasmatic bubble, which provides the tissues for the nerves, the spinal cord and the brain in the embryo. The central nervous system is derived not, as one would expect, from the inside, the sheltered parts, the core; but from the exposed surface, permanently submitted to the bombardment of external stimuli, to irritation and excitement, some lust and much pain. Under the influence of this permanent buzzing shower-bath of stimuli the surface-tissue gradually loses its obtuseness and undergoes that strange transformation, that 'burning-through' process which finally gives rise to the elusive, first faint glow of consciousness. The grey matter of the brain-rind was originally skin-tissue, exposed and brow-beaten, transformed by a unique organic metamorphosis. Even Freud, that giant of profanity, became almost lyrical where (in *Beyond the Pleasure Principle*) he dealt with this aspect of the biology of the mind.

However, man developed a skull, in which his precious grey matter is safely packed like caviar in a box. No such casing is provided by society for its nervous tissues. They are rather treated like corns on the toes, a nuisance permanently trampled on and permanently hitting back with mean little stabs.

To return from metaphor to fact: the relation between intelligentsia and neurosis is not accidental, but functional. To think and behave independently puts one automatically into opposition against the majority whose thinking and behaviour is dependent on traditional patterns: and to belong to a minority is in itself a neurosis-forming situation. From the nonconformist to the crank there is only one step; and the hostile pressure of society provides the push.

When a man in a concert hall coughs, everybody will cough, and one feels the physical itching in one's throat. Group-mimicry is a real force; to resist it means getting out of tune with one's social environment, creates neurotic tensions and feelings of guilt. One might in theory be a thousand times in the right, and yet feel guilty for butting against the accepted wrong, sanctioned by a tradition whose roots have sprouted in one's own unconscious self. To quarrel with society means to quarrel with its projections in one's self, and produces the classical neurotic split patterns. Oedipus situation and inferiority complex, timidity and arrogance, over-compensation and introversion are merely descriptive metaphors for deformations which spring from basically the same root. An intelligentsia deprived of the prop of an alliance with an ascending class must turn against itself and develop that hot-house atmosphere, that climate of intellectual masturbation and incest, which characterized it during the last decade.

And it must further develop that morbid attraction for the pseudo-intellectual hangers-on whose primary motive is not the 'aspiration to independent thought' but neurosis pure and simple, and who crowd around the hot-house because the world outside is too cold for them. They infiltrate, and gradually outnumber the legitimate inhabitants, adding to their disrepute, until, in periods of decadence, the camp-followers gradually swallow up the army. It is a sad transformation when social protest dissolves into a-social morbidity.

But even for the 'real' intelligentsia, neurosis is an almost inevitable correlate. Take sex for example. On the one hand we know all about the anachronistic nature of our sex-regulating institutions, their thwarting influence and the constant barrage of unhappiness they shower on society. On the other hand, individual experiments of 'free companionship', marriages with mutual freedom, etc. etc., all end in pitiful failure; the very term of 'free love' has already an embarrassingly Edwardian taint. Reasonable arrangements in an unreasonable society cannot succeed. The pressure of the environment (both from outside and from inside our conditioned selves) is enormous; under its distorting influence the natural becomes cramped, even in writing. You feel it even in such accomplished craftsmen as D. H. Lawrence and Hemingway. You hear, when the critical situation approaches, the author saying to himself: 'Damn it, it is an act of nature and I am going to put it as easily and naturally as if the two of them were having a meal.' And then you watch him, the author, putting his sleeves up and setting himself to the task; sweat pours down his brow, his eyes pop out of his head, the nib of his pen breaks under the pressure of his desperate efforts to be 'easy and natural about it'. The trouble is, of course, that while he writes, his environment (i.e. the potential readers) have closed in around him; he feels their stare and breathless expectancy, and feels paralysed by it. Hence the cramped dialect of Lady Chatterley's lover and that preposterous rabbit in the bag for which no bell would ever toll, in an otherwise masterly novel.

The pressure of the environment cramps art as it cramps behaviour. One may challenge this environment, but one has to pay for it, and the price is neurotic guilt. There never was an intelligentsia without a guilt-complex; it is the income tax one has to pay for wanting to make others richer. An armament manufacturer may have a perfectly clean conscience; but I have never met a pacifist without a guilty look in his eyes.

Those who attack the intelligentsia for its neurotic dispositions might as well attack the miners for their susceptibility to T.B. It is a professional disease and should be recognized as such, without scorn or shame.

VI The Intelligentsia and the Future

The old, liberal and socialist intelligentsia of the Continent is no more; though we still fail to realize how thoroughly Nazism implemented its poet laureate's programme 'When I hear the word culture I fire my pistol.' A new intelligentsia may be growing underground, a new seed beneath the snow; but in spite of newspaper articles, intelligence-digests, radio, etc., we know at present as little about the mental climate of the people beyond the Channel, about how the past, present and future looks, smells, tastes to them, as we know about the planet Mars. Samples of literature which reach us from France do not seem to me very encouraging; but then, I am perhaps prejudiced against what I believe to be the growing French intellectual predilection for melodious bombast. Yet in Italy and the Balkans, in Austria and Norway, a process might already have started which one day will come into the open as a brand-new movement, a fresh attitude to life which will make all of us appear like old Victorian dodderers; and any of us who earn a patronizing pat will have got all the credit which historically we deserve.

This is all speculation; it is easier to prophesy in terms of decades than in terms of years. One may have some ideas as to the historical curve along which we move; but the oscillations and ripples of the curve are completely unpredictable. If, in the long run, Burnham's diagnosis comes to be true (as I believe it well may), and if, after some intermediary oscillations, we are in for an era of managerial super-states, the intelligentsia is bound to become a special sector in the Civil Service. This is less farfetched and fantastic than it sounds; in Russia during the past twenty years this state of affairs has been realized to a very large extent, and Germany during the last ten years was on the way to imitate it. Russian publishing houses, theatres, building trusts, research laboratories, universities and medical services are all owned by the State; the author, actor, architect, scientist, etc., is in fact a civil servant, though the atmosphere is not exactly that of Whitehall. But even the literary movements in Russia – 'Revolutionary Romanticism', 'Socialist Realism', 'Operative Literature', 'New Patriotism' have not spontaneously, organically grown, but were decreed at Party-Congresses and by utterances of government spokesmen; and the same applies, in varying degree, to poetry, drama, architecture, films, not to mention historical research and philosophy. The successive philosophical and artistic movements in the Soviet State look as if they were performed to the pattern 'Left turn – Right turn – As you were.' In the German Reichskulturkammern the transformation of Parnassus into a barrack-square was equally thorough.

In the Anglo-Saxon countries a similar development is difficult, but not altogether impossible to visualize. Above all, a number of different roads may lead to the same goal. Total mobilization during the present war was a kind of dress-rehearsal for the Western version of the bureaucratized state, and during the last two years the intelligentsia has to a large extent been absorbed as temporary civil servants in the M. of I., as P.R.O.s, in the B.B.C., etc. For the time being 'job' and 'private production' are still kept in separate compartments (with the result of the latter becoming more and more atrophied); but it is imaginable that a situation may arise in which the two merge; when, instead of regarding the former as a kind of patriotic hacking and the latter as the real thing, the energies become suddenly canalized into one stream. A few may start the new mode, and the rest follow suit; the individuals concerned may believe that they are following a personal impulse, whereas in reality it would be a process of adaptation to the changed social situation of the managerial state. The danger of this happening is all the greater as conformism is often a form of betrayal which can be carried out with a perfectly clear conscience; and the temptation to exchange the miseries which intellectual honesty entails for the heart-warming satisfactions of managerial efficiency is great. The collapse of the revolutionary movement has put the intelligentsia into a defensive position; the alternative for the next few years is no more 'capitalism or revolution' but to save *some* of the values of democracy and humanism or to lose them all; and to prevent this happening one has to cling more than ever to the ragged banner of 'independent thinking'.

It is, at present, a very popular banner; and unique in this respect, that on its cloth the spittle of derision has clotted together with the blood of our dead.

Chapter Six
Toward a Portrait of the French Intellectual

Victor Brombert

L'intellectuel — rarely has a word inspired more fervor, arrogance, bitter irony and generous anger. Edouard Berth, ardent royalist and sympathizer with the *Action Française,* gave vent to some of these violent feelings in a long-forgotten but significant book, *Les Méfaits des intellectuels* (1914), in which he described the intellectuals as an anti-heroic cast of effeminate, knavish and deceitful weaklings, who strive to impose on the modern world nauseating humanitarian ideals and a morality of cowardice. One recognizes echoes of Barrès' vituperations against the servile mandarins, imbued with Kantian moral principles and determined to emasculate France.

Without even mentioning the hysterical polemics of a Berth or the strident outbursts of a Barrès, it is easy to draw up a catalogue of unfavorable opinions. Paul Valéry inveighed with irony against the megalomaniac, complex-ridden intellectuals; Romain Rolland called them "intolerant maniacs" in love with ideas; Péguy denounced the *"parti intellectuel"*; Julien Benda wrote a series of books about the "treason" of the intellectuals. More recently, Raymond Aron diagnosed their addiction to the ideological opium and their supposed irresponsibility in the face of history.

It is clear that intellectuals themselves, when they are not openly hostile to the term and the concept "intellectual," are secretly disturbed by it. Much of the fictional work of Sartre and of Simone de Beauvoir testifies to this uneasiness. Henri Perron and Robert Dubreuilh, in *Les Mandarins,* proudly affirm that they are intellectuals, but deep in their hearts they are assailed by fears that they may have no function whatsoever, that they are merely sterile windbags or—as Scriassine puts it—guilty of a mental and political "masochism" typical of all intellectuals. Perron is fully aware of the pejorative connotations of the word: "I am an intellectual. I am sick and tired that this word has been made an insult." And is it not one of the functions of petulant Ivich, in Sartre's *L'Age de raison,* to exacerbate the scruples, hesitations and guilt feelings of Matthieu Delarue—a function which Nadine, her counterpart in *Les Mandarins,* fulfills with even more gusto by uttering cruel and occasionally even obscene statements about intellectuals?

The term "intellectual" (that is the substantive *"un intellectuel"*) is a fairly recent word in the French language. One would search in vain for it in the Littré dictionary (1863-1877). To be sure, nineteenth-century writers, groping for the word, made use of certain expressions that vaguely corresponded to this idea. Balzac, for instance, in his *Illusions perdues,* calls Michel Chrestien a *"bohémien de l'intelligence."* Yet quite significantly, when the French delegates to the First Congress of the Workers International in Geneva (1866) asked for the exclusion of all delegates who were intellectuals (a Proudhonian attack on the Blanquists), the appropriate term was still wanting: they were forced to use the clumsy expression "workers of the intellect" (*"les ouvriers de la pensée"*). All the socialist literature of the latter part of the nineteenth century bears witness to the absence of the term. There is talk of the *"professionnels de l'intelligence,"* of the *"travailleurs de la pensée."* Zola, in 1897, still employs the circumlocution *"professionels de l'intelligence"* and Clémenceau, in his articles for *L'Aurore,* refers to the *"hommes de pur labeur intellectuel."* All tends to prove that by 1895, the term was not yet in common usage.

Else why would Karl Kautsky's pamphlet *Der Sozialismus und die Intelligenz* have appeared in *"Le Devenir Social"* (1895), under the title *Le Socialisme et les carrières libérales?* Yet, only a few years later, in the work of Romain Rolland for instance, the term is already familiar. Why the emergence of the term? What occurred in the intervening years?

The answer is spelled out clearly: the Dreyfus case, that "holy hysteria," as Romain Rolland put it. For this ideological war which, eight years after the abortive Boulanger revolution, opposed the two spiritual families of France, was not merely an expression of all the bitterness accumulated since 1789 by a nation with too good a political memory. It marked above all a great moment in the intellectual history of the country, serving as a catalyst for already prevalent tendencies, but also opening a new era which Albert Thibaudet has aptly called the *"République des Professeurs,"* and which, he felt, was brought about by "an insurrection and a victory of intellectuals." The struggle between the two irreconcilable mystiques was probably not followed anywhere with greater intensity than in the little *Librairie Bellais,* the *Revue Blanche,* the editorial rooms of *l'Aurore,* and in the teaching profession (the *"Université"*) which, at a time when even Jaurès' Socialist Party was indifferent (or too prudent), constituted the first professional or social group to throw its weight behind the defenders of Dreyfus.

To the intellectual, "the Dreyfus case is the palladium of history," writes Julien Benda, who was himself deeply marked by the crisis (*La Jeunesse d'un clerc*). Thibaudet sums it all up: "This Dreyfus case . . . this tumult of intellectuals . . . " It is indeed impossible to overestimate the significance of the Dreyfus case to the intellectuals, or the importance of the intellectuals' participation in this uproar. It is difficult to think of the French intellectual in historic terms without situating him first in the passionate climate of a crisis which confirmed unequivocally his vocation of moral responsibility. Indeed, all evidence points to the fact that it is during this ideological battle, and more specifically at its moment of highest dramatic intensity (the Esterhazy and Zola trials), that the word *intellectual* is coined and thrown into circulation. Maurice Paléologue, in his recently published *Journal de l'Affaire Dreyfus* (1955), relates an impassioned evening during which a particularly bellicose Brunetière was battling Paul Hervieu, Gustave Larroumet, Victor Brochard and Gabriel Séailles—all of them ardent revisionists. Paléologue records part of Brunetière's tirade (15 January, 1898—exactly two days after the publication of Zola's sensational letter to the President of the Republic):

As for Mr. Zola, why doesn't he mind his own business? The letter *J'accuse* is a monument of stupidity, presumption and incongruity. The interference of this novelist in a matter of military justice seems to me no less impertinent than, let us say, the intervention of a police captain in a problem of syntax or versification.

As for this petition that is being circulated among the *Intellectuals!* the mere fact that one has recently created this word *Intellectuals* to designate, as though they were an aristocracy, individuals who live in laboratories and libraries, proclaims one of the most ridiculous eccentricities of our time—I mean the pretension of raising writers, scientists, professors and philologists to the rank of supermen. (pp. 90-91)

The faithfulness of Paléologue's transcription cannot be questioned: one need only glance at Brunetière's article in the *Revue des Deux Mondes,* or at his militant public lectures attacking what he termed "the enemies of the French soul," to find the same expressions and the very tone of his harangue in Mme Aubernon's salon.

Paléologue's talent as a memorialist is, however, not in question here. The real interest of these pages is that they testify to the newness of a word which, significantly, appears in italics in this, as well as in most other texts of the period. Brunetière associates the word with the signers of the petitions being circulated. That very day indeed—on January 15th—a protest in favor of a retrial had appeared in *Le Temps* signed by Anatole France, Zola, Emile Duclaux (director of the *Institut*), F. Fénéon (secretary of the *Revue Blanche*), Fernand Gregh, Lugné-Poë, Jacques Bizet, Th. Ruyssen, Daniel Halévy, Gabriel Trarieux, André Baunier, Marcel Proust, Robert de Flers, Victor Bérard, Lucien Herr, Ferdinand Brunot—and many others. If one follows *Le Temps* throughout these first three months of 1898, one is struck by the frequency with which the word "intellectual" appears. On January 25th, an article entitled *"Le prolétariat intellectuel"* complains of the plethora of useless mandarins threatening the social equilibrium. Only a few days later, Jean Psichari, dean of studies at the *Ecole des Hautes Etudes,* sends an open letter in which he demands the right for "intellectuals" to intervene actively in political matters. Rarely has a group become so vehemently aware of itself.

As for the newness of the word, no doubt can subsist. In a pamphlet entitled *Les étapes d'un intellectuel* (1898), Albert Réville proudly proclaims: "Let us use this word, since it has received high consecrations." Clémenceau, in an article dated January 23rd, in *L'Aurore,* employs the word in italics. On April 5th, Anatole France uses it in an article that appears in *L'Echo,* and which is destined to serve as a starting point for the third conversation of *L'Anneau d'Améthyste.* All the while Maurice Barrès affirms (though with considerable bad faith) that it is Clémenceau who invented the term, and that this "neologism" was very "poor French" indeed.[1] Whatever the exact date of the creation of this word (the Hatzfeld and Darm-

---

1. *Scènes et doctrines du nationalisme.* With bad faith, for he himself had used the word some ten years earlier in *Sous l'oeil des Barbares* (1888), though in a somewhat different sense. What Barrès disliked by 1898 was obviously not the word, but what it had come to stand for. As for Paul Bourget, he had used the substantive as early as 1882 (*La Nouvelle Revue,* v. 16, pp. 865-895) in his essay on Flaubert whom he described as a victim of the corrosive poison of "Thought." It is interesting to note, however, that in *Le Disciple* (1889) the word appears only twice, each time in a derogatory sense.

steter dictionary, 1895-1900, is the first, it would seem, to include the substantive), it is evident that the word penetrates into the common language during the winter of 1897-1898. Even in Marxist literature, it is only after this date that one commonly encounters the word in France: the pamphlets by Hubert Lagardelle and Paul Lafargue, respectively entitled *Les Intellectuels devant le socialisme* and *Le socialisme et les intellectuels,* both date from 1900.

Stigma I: Voices without a mandate

But Paléologue's text also tells us much about the affective value, the *color* of the new word. Brunetière pretends to be shocked by the presumptuous interference of Zola. Why doesn't he mind his own business? he asks. The reaction is characteristic, and soon becomes a cliché: here are individuals who should be at work peacefully and modestly in their laboratories and libraries, who suddenly get it into their heads to meddle in affairs totally outside their ken. Brunetière is tireless on the subject. In a resounding article in the *Revue des Deux Mondes* (15 March, 1898), he asseverates that a "first comer" has not the right to insult the French army and French justice, that learned compilers do not know everything, that to have written a treatise on microbiology (an obvious dig at Emile Duclaux) does not entitle one to judge one's fellow men, that scholars are not equipped to understand such "delicate questions" as individual morality and social ethics, and that (the irony is somewhat facile) a professor of Tibetan language may not be the ideal man to govern France. On April 15th, Brunetière is at it again; reviewing Zola's *Paris,* he proposes the following definition of the intellectual: a person who "meddles dogmatically in matters about which he is ignorant." Brunetière is not alone: other voices are heard, and in the same key. "The roster of intellectuals is made up of simpletons," writes Barrès in *Le Journal* (1 February, 1898). And in his *Scènes et doctrines du nationalisme,* after having defined the intellectual as a cultivated individual without any mandate, but who obstinately wants to impose his chimerical ideas on a concrete reality, he recalls the old proverb: *"A chacun son métier et les moutons seront bien gardés."* A member of the French Academy, Emile Gebhart, congratulating Barrès on his article against the professors, turns out to be even more violent, showering insults on what he calls the "battalion of the discontented": virtuosos of Latin metrics, pale paleographers, embittered metaphysicians, microbe hunters and other abstracters of quintessences.[2] Echoes of these reactions will still be felt a few years later in the novels of Romain Rolland: Jean-Christophe is appalled by the number of *littérateurs* who specialize in politics, form leagues, and sign *petitions*. "I do not trust those who speak of what they don't know," he confides to his friend Olivier (*Le buisson ardent*). As for Daniel Halévy, he will recall long after (*Apologie pour notre passé*) how he and his friends were accused of being nothing but bookwormish intellectuals in rebellion against an entire people.

Stigma II: *The death of instinct*

"One is always unfair when one attacks professors," Barrès admits with candor in *Mes Cahiers,* though he does not bother to analyze his brand of unfairness. There is of course the age-old suspicion of the thinker and teacher against whom the social group seeks vengeance by means of a caricature based on the conventional and much-belabored contrast between intelligence and knowledge. ("I'd rather be intelligent than an intellectual," proclaims Barrès.) But more significant still, as far as Barrès and his contemporaries are concerned, the last two decades of the nineteenth century witness a real offensive against the "pernicious professor": novels such as Barrès' *Déracinés,* as well as Bourget's *Le Disciple* and *L'Etape* or Unamuno's *Love*

2. See the letter of February 25, 1898, quoted by Barrès in *Mes Cahiers,* II, pp. 3-5.

and Pedagogy all illustrate the thesis that teachers are directly responsible for the actions and even the crimes committed by their disciples. Trends such as these correspond in fact to a general tendency to devaluate pure intellect. Brunetière maintained that intellectual aptitudes had only a relative value, that he, for one, had infinitely more esteem for will power and force of character. Barrès liked to parade his contempt for intelligence as well. Impressed by some remarks made by the physiologist, Jules Soury, he waxed lyrical about the grandeur of "uncultivated life" (he of all people!) and repeated by heart, like a conscientious school boy: "Intelligence! . . . what a tiny thing at the very surface of our personality!" Behind this attempt to discredit the intelligence of the "simian mammal" (a pet expression of Jules Soury), it is easy to detect a reaction against the rationalist tradition with its faith in science and progress, and its intellectual cosmopolitanism. Had not Brunetière, in a much discussed article, announced the bankruptcy of science?

To be sure, it was better to be intelligent than intellectual —but even that was not the ideal. Barrès preferred *"l'inconscient national"* and complained that the nineteenth century (Hugo, Michelet, Taine, Renan) had been entirely mistaken about the importance of Reason. "The individual! his intelligence, his ability to grasp the laws of the universe—it's time to quell these pretensions. We are not the masters of our thoughts. They do not spring from our intelligence. . . ." (*Scènes et doctrines*). This discrediting of intelligence obviously also corresponded to the affirmation of a nationalistic mystique which, in the decades following the defeat of 1870, called the French back to the cult of their ancestors, exploited the primitive allegiance to the "soil," and praised instinctive solidarity with a carnal France. That, unquestionably, is the significance of Barrès pontifical statement that pseudo-culture "destroys instinct." It is of course this very kind of "betrayal" that Benda had in mind when he later denounced the clerics for having lent themselves to the intellectual organization of political fanaticism. Ironically enough (though not so ironically for a Benda), a similar devaluation of intelligence and culture can be observed in the socialist literature of the period. Karl Kautsky used to call literary bohemians "vain concocters of projects." Hubert Lagardelle attributed to Greco-Latin education the emergence of a group of dissatisfied, ambitious *déclassés* out of touch with the masses, and considered the humanities useless and perhaps even harmful to modern man.[3]

Stigma III: *The hybris of the mandarins*

The same passage from Paléologue's diary points to still another sentiment attached to the new word. Brunetière's remark that the "Intellectuals" claim to constitute an aristocracy of supermen clearly echoes a widespread resentment provoked by the supposed arrogance and boundless pride of the "mandarins" (the word is much used at the time), a thoroughly laughable and unjustified arrogance, according to Brunetière and his friends. Paléologue recalls with what suspicion the judges at the Rennes court-martial listened to the testimony of "intellectuals," these "presumptuous pedants who take themselves for the aristocrats of the mind." Similar sounds are heard from all sides: *"caste nobilière," "aristocrates de l'esprit," "aristocratie intellectuelle," "mandarins des lettres," "aristocrates de la pensée," "élite intellectuelle"*—these are the most common derogatory expressions. President Méline's most admired speech was probably the one delivered in the Chamber of Deputies (28 February, 1898) in which he thundered against the *intellectual élite* with a sarcastic verve that provoked prolonged laughter and unanimous applause. In an article that appears two weeks later, Brunetière repeats that nothing seems to him less bearable than the idea of an intellectual aristocracy.

3. See *Le Socialisme et les carrières libérales* and *Les Intellectuels devant le socialisme*.

In his *"discours de combat,"* he grows even more violent, calling Nietzsche "a professor of Greek, delirious with impotence and pride." As to Barrès, he too, of course, is outraged by these "aristocrats of the mind" who are but "a bunch of people crazy with pride" (*Scènes et doctrines*). Of this supposed arrogance, Paul Bourget had given earlier a' famous fictional example in his Robert Greslou, who believes in an oligarchy of scientists, and who dares to think (and to write) that a man such as he must learn "not to consider as a law for us who think what is and must be a law for those who do not think" (*Le Disciple*).

Many of the anti-rationalistic attitudes of the 90's are in conscious rebellion against the thinking of a Renan who, in *L'Avenir de la science,* had more than toyed with the idea of new spiritual guides for humanity. Even before the publication of *L'Avenir de la science,* it is Renan, no doubt, whom Bourget had in mind when, in the preface to *Le Disciple,* he alluded to the all too eloquent master whose paradoxes and intellectualism had charmed, corrupted and spiritually dried up the typical young Frenchman. Brunetière is more blunt in his denunciation of Renan's "odious dream": he shuddered at Renan's future world, controlled by an elite of scientists "placing unlimited terror at the service of truth."

It is true that in some cases the statements and attitudes of certain "intellectuals" semed to justify accusations of arrogance. Zola, during his trial, clumsily answered the judge: "I do not know the law and I do not want to know it." To a somewhat baffled jury he proudly declared that it was he who was the true defender of France, and that his victories would be more meaningful to posterity than those of any general. Even in the calmer atmosphere of his study, he could not refrain from formulating thoughts that exalted the writer over the statesman: "Our lawmakers seem to me inefficient; I would like to see the task entrusted to moralists, writers, poets" (*La Vérité en marche*). Opinions such as these seemed to corroborate the worst suspicions of a Brunetière!

Here again it is noteworthy that very similar accusations were fired from the extreme Left as well as from the traditional Right. Proudhon, it is well known, resented all "mandarins." The anarchist ex-nobleman Bakunin tirelessly insisted that it would never be possible to convert to socialism the "aristocrats of the intellect," domineering, caste-conscious and filled with contempt for the working classes. French socialists, at the turn of the century, more than ever before express hostile sentiments. In a lecture delivered to a Parisian student group in 1900, Hubert Lagardelle describes the intellectuals as arrogant and thirsty for power.

Paradoxically—as though it were not enough to be caught in the cross-fire of the extreme Right and the militant Left— the intellectuals find themselves in the ambiguous position of being classified simultaneously as an aristocracy and as a pro- letariat. As early as 1860, the brothers Goncourt had noted with a measure of bitterness, in *Charles Demailly*, that the new generation of artists and journalists no longer belonged to the comfortable bourgeoisie as did the generation of 1830, but that instead the new *bohème*, whipped on by economic need, lived, worked and "fought for its soup" with "all the hatreds of a proletariat." At the time of the Dreyfus case, a collective pamphlet appears, *Les Prolétaires intellectuels en France* (among the callaborators are Henry Béranger, Paul Pottier and Pierre Marcel). Barrès is also delighted by the expression (which he attributed to Bismarck): an important chapter of his novel *Les Déracinés* is entitled *"Le Prolétariat des bacheliers."*

Aristocrats and proletarians, élite and proletariat—these "accusations" are contradictory only in appearance: according to a Brunetière the intellectuals are precisely a proletariat of *arrivistes* whose totally insane ambition it is to usurp the privileges of an élite. But the importance of such accusations cannot be limited to the intentions of those who formulate them: obviously, it is precisely such judgments which help situate extistentially the intellectual and define him to himself.

Stigma IV: Enemies of the national "soul"

Paléologue's diary mentions one further sin attributed to the "intellectuals." These "aristocrats of the mind" are also accused of having lost their "national mentality"—of having assumed the function of subverters and corroders of patriotic ideals. According to Brunetière, these "enemies of the French soul" (this is the title of one of his many lectures on the subject) are trying desperately to destroy the traditions of France. As for Emile Gebhart's epigrammatic assertion that teachers of German no longer think often enough in French—it may seem tasteless and excessive, but it was certainly not an isolated opinion. Countless are the bitter remarks provoked by the so-called Kantian invasion of French education. Here again, Barrès's reactions are perhaps most characteristic. Of this subversive *Kantisme* Bouteiller, in *Les Déracinés*, is the living symbol: a "modern sorcerer," uprooted and ambitious, who, by means of the intellectual poison he spreads, succeeds in uprooting entire generations of innocent young Frenchmen.

Much of this explosion of chauvinism at the time of the Dreyfus case can be explained by memories of the recent defeat. Dreams of revenge went hand in hand with a hatred for Germany that was further inflamed by unavowed sentiments of inferiority, and by the awareness that France was lagging behind in the Industrial Revolution. Barrès did not have to invent; there were men like Roemerspacher's grandfather who would not hear of any member of his family studying at a German university. It is against this background that the fictional figure of Professor Bouteiller has to be assessed. Barrès's accusations against intellectuals follow a recognizable and symptomatic pattern: men such as Bouteiller "decerebrate" the nation, they ignore the instinctive faith of the masses, they insist on teaching an "absolute truth" instead of teaching piously

the "French truth" (one can see Benda's grimace of pain!).
The intellectual is an "enemy of society" (*Scènes et doctrines*).

"We must watch the Université," writes Barrès in *Mes
Cahiers*. "It contributes to the destruction of French principles." Such a warning, coming from a cultured writer, may
surprise. Even more surprising, however, is the impassioned
battle cry emitted during a talk to a student group: "Will you
let us be devoured by these people? Lay your hands on your
libraries; to arms, comrades!" That feelings such as these
were quite widespread is proven by André Beaunier's satirical
novel *Les Dupont-Leterrier* (1900). In order to mock this very
brand of militant anti-intellectualism, Beaunier has his Major
Joseph say: "The intellectuals! It was already they who betrayed Constantinople to the Greeks—to some dirty little
Greeks!" Of course, Beaunier's satire has its limitations:
Brunetière, Barrès, Gebhart, Méline and the editorial writers of
Le Temps have little in common with a Major Joseph. Nevertheless, each in his own way expresses what is at the time a
cliché, namely that the "Intellectuals" have all "lost the national
mentality."

Needless to add that what to some is scandalously anti-
patriotic, others interpret as a praiseworthy cosmopolitanism
or a generous internationalism. Barrès calls all intellectuals
déracinés (uprooted). Lucien Herr, in the *Revue Blanche,*
rejoins that they are *désintéressés* (selfless). *Déracinés* or *désintéressés,* uprooted or unbiased—the argument implies nothing
less than a difference of perspective. To the ones, the intellectual
is the sworn enemy of the collective discipline, the enemy of
the established social order. (Did not an article in *Le Temps*
—14 February, 1898—calmly assert that French intellectuals
were discontented trouble makers?) To the others, this supposed
subversive force is but the proof of their moral dynamism, of
the integrity of their critical stand and of their competence to
serve as liaison agents between one culture and another.

A few conclusions and a few ambiguities

Clearly, the word *intellectual* carries, from the moment of its birth, the stigma of derision, contempt, suspicion, and even hatred. Thrown into circulation during the winter 1897-1898, the term implies the intervention in public affairs of supposedly incompetent scholars without a mandate, and suggests a mentality hostile to the mystique of tradition. Intellectuals are held responsible, retrospectively, for all the ills since the French Revolution—and for the worse ills that lie ahead. Hardly a single expression of disparagement or of sarcasm is spared them: envious bookworms, bitter *ratés,* histrionic anarchists, the dregs of society—these are only a few of the colorful expressions used to designate the "impotent" and "cowardly" mandarins! A few nostalgic souls even went so far as to regret the good old days of Sparta when teachers were slaves and kept in a permanent state of inebriety to serve as a lesson to the aristocratic youth.

Occasionally, the "intellectuals" of 1898 themselves display a definite distaste for the term. At the *Revue Blanche*— one of their headquarters—there seems to be some doubt as to whether to rejoice over the appellation. Pierre Guillard, in a pungent reply to one of Brunetière's articles, protests against this "ridiculous title." Léon Blum, reviewing a novel by Paul Adam, establishes an implicit equation between "intellectual" and mental unbalance. As for Zola, he does not hesitate to deride the hairsplitting "silly intellectuals." It is true that Zola especially detested the *Ecole Normale Supérieure* which he sarcastically termed "the school where one knows everything."

But on the whole—and overwhelmingly so—the intellectuals take up the term with pride. Brunetière's accusations do not go unchallenged during that evening in the salon of Mme Aubernon. Hervieu, Séailles, Larroumet, Brochard—all react with fire, pointing out that it is the intellectuals (they are not ashamed of the word) who today incarnate the true traditions of the French conscience. Elsewhere, Emile Duclaux proudly glories in the very accusation: "Yes indeed, it's the intellectuals who made the French Revolution," adding even more categorically: "I don't know what the choice of my country will be. My choice is made: I remain 'an intellectual'" (*Avant le procès*). This militant pride has many echoes. In a letter to *Le Temps* (3 February, 1898), Jean Psichari proclaims that intellectuals are the glory of a country like France.

A triple ambiguity, however, seems to attach itself to the term from its very inception. (1) The apparently contradictory accusation that intellectuals constitute on the one hand a pitiful proletariat and on the other an arrogant, caste-conscious, self-styled élite. (2) The reactions of the intellectuals themselves who oscillate between a feeling of uneasiness (and even of shame) and the most undisguised pride. (3) The fact that the battle cries and utterances of contempt from the traditionalist and nationalistic Right are echoed (and even reinforced) by other bellicose cries coming from the Left, revolutionary, internationalist and equally hostile. This early awareness on the part of intellectuals of being caught in a cross-fire ushers in one of the most serious predicaments of the twentieth century.

The crystallization of a concept

In spite of new historical contingencies, the word *intellectual* continues, throughout the subsequent fifty years, to bear the traces of its ideological origin. The French concept of the intellectual thus remains bound up with the notion of a social, political and moral crisis. Better still: it implies *the notion of a permanent state of crisis*. Given this state of crisis, the intellectual considers it his obligation to intervene. This sense of moral duty may reach a particularly high pitch during certain periods (1930-1950, for instance)—but it constitutes a permanent trait. Passionately committed to political thinking, haunted by dreams of action, he is, according to Benda, a "traitor" to clerical values (*La Trahison des clercs*). But significantly, even Benda fails to live up to his quasi-monastic ideals: not only does he make specific concessions (such as allowing "political speculation," or granting intellectuals the "social mission of truth," or affirming that the "passion for justice" is not a political passion!), but he will quite regularly denounce the traitors of the Right, while tolerating and even admiring the political passion of Leftist intellectuals on the grounds that they, following the dictates of their conscience as true "clercs," protest in the name of justice and out of a pure sense of moral duty. This generous inconsistency in Benda's thinking is symptomatic of a whole climate of ideas.

The intellectual's intervention thus follows a predictable pattern: he considers himself a *voice*. And not merely a voice crying out in protest (Aron calls it the mentality of "permanent opposition"), but a voice that proclaims itself a *conscience*.[4] "To think sincerely, even if it means to think against everybody, still means to think with and for everybody," Romain Rolland was fond of saying. The deep concern here is not with one's private thoughts or suffering, but with the thought and suffering of others, with the need to respond, to declare oneself, to take one's stand whatever the risk—in short, with the impossibility of remaining silent. In his *Apologie pour notre passé*, Daniel Halévy recalls with undisguised emotion that Emile Duclaux was so haunted by the idea of a possible injustice that he literally could not sleep until he had publicly expressed his qualms and so performed what he considered his clear duty. The anecdote is significant: the intellectual's suffering is not a private affair occasioned by some hidden remorse. If he has to speak up, it is because he feels called upon to become the conscience (which often means the guilty conscience) of an entire

4. This has become a cliché. Anatole France, in his panegyric of Emile Zola, called him "a moment of the French conscience." The term is still fashionable. When Camus was awarded the Nobel prize, the *Figaro Littéraire* commented: "The Stockholm Academy undoubtedly wished to honor not merely a writer whom we all admire, but a conscience." Similarly, Mauriac also stated that Camus was "not only a writer, but a conscience."

group, or even—the ambition is not uncommon—of an entire epoch. Half a century later, in Simone de Beauvoir's *Les Mandarins,* professor Dubreuilh asks himself: "What does it mean, the fact that man never ceases talking about himself? And why is it some men decide to speak in the name of others: in other words, what is an intellectual?" But the very question implies the answer: the intellectual is precisely the one who has decided to speak, and speak up, in the name of humanity. This sense of "global responsibility" is one for which intellectuals have been much criticized. But if it is true, as Raymond Aron suggests in *L'Opium des intellectuels,* that this eagerness to think for all humanity does not go without a measure of pride, it must also be added in all honesty that it marks not only moral courage, but a deep and beautiful yearning to reaffirm man's solidarity with man.

Is there a "race" of intellectuals? Vincent Berger, the hero of Malraux's *Les Noyers de l'Altenburg,* observes, during the symposium which brings together philosophers from various countries, that these faces so diversely and profoundly characteristic of the different nations to which they belong, nevertheless resemble each other. "My father discovered to what extent intellectuals constitute a race." But a "race," needless to say, recognizable through moral rather than physical traits.

What are these traits? One hesitates to undertake this moral portrait. Sensibility modeled on thought; faith in the efficiency of ideas as an organizational force in the tangible world; the utilization of culture as an instrument for criticizing tradition; the unselfish, gratuitous pursuit of truth, but simultaneously the pursuit of a humanitarian ideal; the transmission or preaching of moral values; the sensation, now proud, now humiliating, of existing outside the social framework, and yet, on the whole, an obvious sympathy for the laboring groups of the country and a consequent attraction to Leftist political parties; a feeling of "not belonging" and of impotence; jealousy of the men of action; the cult of revolt, sometimes even of anarchy; the nearly obsessive fear of being caught on the side of injustice; nostalgia for the masses coupled with the complexes of a "fils de bourgeois" ashamed of belonging to the privileged classes —these constitute only some of the more permanent traits of the French intellectual.

Toward a literary "type"

Our intellectuals and those of 1898 are of one and the same family. Yet it is also evident that they existed *avant la lettre*. The type-intellectual could not possibly have penetrated so fast and so deeply into literature had he not first slowly emerged and become aware of himself as a social reality. The entire nineteenth century groped for the word.

Is Arthur Koestler right in affirming somewhat peremptorily that the Encyclopedists, entering the historical stage as iconoclasts and debunkers, were the first modern intellectuals, (*The Yogi and the Commissar*)? To limit the Encyclopedists' role to that of iconoclasts and debunkers may seem unfair; it fails to account for their sense of mission and their positive idealism. But Koestler is not alone in pointing to the eighteenth-century *philosophes* as the direct ancestors of modern intellectuals. According to Benda, these *philosophes* with a social conscience and socially involved, were the first traitors to the philosophical spirit. Raymond Aron, for reasons that are also not altogether flattering, sees in these eighteenth-century philosophers the first clear example of the intellectual in the modern sense of the word: using their pens for a living, they assume that they have the right to express generously their critical opinions on any subject.

The danger of such digging for ancestors is that it leads to the alluring game of anachronistic generalizations. Yet it is difficult to deny that there exist parallelisms and even family ties. The *philosophes* of the eighteenth century also considered themselves guides of humanity. They too were slandered and sneered at. The word *philosophe* was also discredited. Accused of fabricating doctrines to cover their narcissistic arrogance, of undermining the highest virtues (such as love of country), they were said to be a threat to the very existence of society. The *philosophes*—especially at the hour of their triumph— sometimes replied with rather excessive statements. In his *Essai sur les règnes de Claude et de Néron,* Diderot defines the role of the philosopher as follows: "The magistrate dispenses justice; the philosopher teaches the magistrate what is just and unjust." Or, even less modestly: "The philosopher teaches the priest what the gods are." Generally, however, the *philosophes* are more measured in their pronouncements on themselves. In the *Encyclopédie,* for instance: "The philosopher does not con- sider himself in exile in this world"—a lapidary but moving statement of human solidarity.

Nothing could be more unfair and more unfounded than to view the nineteenth century as the debaser of these ideals. The Encyclopedists did not degenerate into the ludicrous figures of Homais, Bouvard or Pécuchet. Their true heirs are men such as Hugo, Michelet and Renan—and on a humbler level, the underpaid, undernourished, but dedicated country schoolteachers. Prophets and martyrs for the republican mysti- que, pioneers of the New Regime, these *instituteurs* have shaped generations of French minds, patiently propagating the gospel of progress and civic virtues. Their figure—now already part of a bygone age—has acquired a quasi-mythological stature. "Saints without hope," Brice Parrain calls them in his dense, moving book, *La Mort de Jean Madec.* Charles Péguy was fond of referring to them as "the black hussars of the Republic": one of the *Cahiers de la Quinzaine* he treasured most was that given over to Antonin Lavergne's somber short novel about a pathetic schoolteacher literally asphyxiated by poverty, *Jean Coste.* As for Zola's *Vérité* (a too obvious fictional transcription of the Dreyfus case), it attempted to sum up the virtues of the *instituteur* and raise him to the level of a tragic hero. Dedicated to an apostolate of truth, isolated in his thirst for justice, suffering from all the privations and humiliations of a *déclassé*, Marc Froment is an exalted and frequently naïve portrait of a type that nonetheless did exist in real life.

No less important to literature than the survival of the *esprit encyclopédique* and the emergence of a selflessly devoted body of schoolteachers, is another social phenomenon of far-reaching consequences: the incredible fascination that Paris holds for the young men of the period, the attraction to the metropolis of countless talented and not so talented provincials —in short, the extraordinary intellectual centralization that takes place in the capital. "The French have hoarded all their ideas in one enclosure," complains Paul Valéry's Monsieur Teste, who abhors this paradise of oratory. This centralization is one of the main symptoms of the contagious fever of *arrivisme* racking the young men of the first half of the nineteenth century. This fever spreads through the entire work of Balzac, particularly in *Les Illusions perdues* which describes the flight to Paris of an uprooted generation, losing itself in the sordid mire of journalism, or forming *cénacles* which express the idealism of the epoch. In this urge to conquer Paris, Balzac saw one of the evil results of the Revolution. To some extent, his bitterness can be explained by his own vexatious experiences with the world of Parisian journalism (". . . the journalists in France, the most infamous men I know," he expostulates to Madame Hanska.) Balzac moreover remarked wryly that all sorts of mediocrities were now attracted to literature: "When one does not know how to do anything, one becomes a man with a pen," he writes to Zulma Carraud. But though personal bitterness explains the reaction it does not eliminate the fact that ever increasing numbers of young men of humble birth and without money embark on literary and artistic careers— a phenomenon which can be attributed to political and social changes, the victory of Romanticism, the spread of socialistic ideas, and more generally to the "democratization" of literature.

Many novels since the middle of the nineteenth century—

and some of the finest—testify to this ferment and describe the formation of these groups which so often meant the death of individual talent, of these bohemian *cénacles* of artists, journalists and failures with their ambitions and illusions: Frédéric Moreau and his friends in *L'Education sentimentale*; the group centering around the journal *"Scandale"* in the Goncourts' *Charles Demailly*; the circle of Coriolis, the self-destructive painter in *Manette Salomon*; the youthful and exalted group of young artists dedicated to beauty and suffering in Zola's *L'Oeuvre*; the utopian members of the "Union Tolstoï" in Bourget's *L'Etape*; the young men from Lorraine, Sturel's uprooted fellow students in Barrès' *Les Déracinés*. Similar groups of artists and intellectuals continue to people the novels of the twentieth century: the *"groupe des huit"* in Martin du Gard's early novel *Devenir;* the militant Dreyfusard group of the "Semeurs" in *Jean Barois*; the young "Normaliens" of the Rue d'Ulm in Jules Romains' *Hommes de bonne volonté*; the antibourgeois in search of revolutionary justifications in Paul Nizan's *Conspiration*; the more amenable young bohemians who gather in the *Cour de Rohan* in André Chamson's *La Neige et la fleur*; the frustrated post-war existentialist intellectuals in Simone de Beauvoir's *Les Mandarins*; the less engaging young intellectuals style-Saint-Germain-des-Près in Jean Louis Curtis' ironic novel, *Les Justes Causes*. These "groups"—their evolution during the last hundred years, the changing problems they face, the light they cast on the intellectual and moral preoccupations of successive generations—deserve a serious study.

Finally, the growing prestige of the Universities, and the emergence (especially during the Third Republic) of a *fonctionnarisme universitaire* holding out the promise of a stable though mediocre career, attracting many young men of modest background, created a social phenomenon with far-reaching consequences. The near-obsessive struggle for a diploma became a recognized malady. A growing army of *licenciés,* frequently frustrated in their ambitions, developed side by side with an equally growing white-collar proletariat, and occasionally merged with it. A bitter Vallès, himself the son of a submissive schoolteacher, has drawn the caricature of these pitiful young men, sons of peasants or petty bureaucrats, who find in the teaching profession a life of humiliations and vexations. Needless to say, Vallès' picture is very one-sided: some of the freest minds of France—a Taine in philosophy, a Jaurès in politics, a Romain Rolland in literature—were the products of this very training. The *Ecole Normale Supérieure,* in particular, played an immensely important role in determining the intellectual life of the country. But Vallès is not the only one to complain: at the turn of the century, somber diagnoses are beginning to come in from all quarters. Serious newspapers such as *Le Temps,* scientists, writers, professors, politicians show concern over the growing army of young men with diplomas. Not only Barrès, according to whom all Frenchmen dream of becoming bureaucrats, but men such as Gabriel Monod repeatedly call attention to the dangerous plethora of university graduates and to the "bureaucratic plague" which saps the energies of the country. "The history of the Third Republic," writes a particularly acid critic, "will be marked by the admittance of all to the liberal professions and by the growth of the army of failures."[5] No wonder Marxist propagandists attempted to exploit this situation, for unquestionably, ever since the middle of the nineteenth century, France had been witnessing a steady proletarization of its intelligentsia—which finally led to syndicalist organizations such as the *Confédération Générale des Travailleurs Intellectuels* and the *Compagnons de l'Intelligence.*

It is, therefore, not surprising that, side by side with the intellectuals' idealism and political involvements, the novel should also have mirrored this social phenomenon. From Vallès' pitiful Vingtras *père* to Sartre's Matthieu Delarue, ashamed

5. Jean Rabain, *"Pourquoi trahissent-ils?", Revue Bleue,* November 1929, pp. 657-660.

(among other things) of his *"vie de fonctionnaire,"* French fiction is peopled with these shabby-looking "professor-types," leading apparently colorless lives: Anatole France's hen-pecked but smiling Bergeret, Bourget's monklike, pernicious Adrien Sixte or his utopian Monneron, Barrès's smug and opportunistic Bouteiller, Malègue's worn out Méridier, Louis Guilloux's clumsy but admirable Cripure, Louis de Villefosse's humble, idealistic profoundly unhappy Adrien Bruneau—all types which seem to lean heavily in the direction of conscious pathos or caricature.

This curious tendency toward caricature is hardly a co-incidence: it is probably the most important single key to the emergence of the intellectual as a literary type. For without even insisting on the significance of an anti-intellectual revolt such as the one led in various countries by intellectuals like Unamuno, Péguy or Papini, it is clear that it is the intellectuals themselves who, with a curious lack of solidarity, have in large measure been responsible for this portait of the intellectual. Just as it was the anti-bourgeois son of the bourgeois who invented and exploited the hatred of the philistine in whom he so often still recognized himself, the intellectual, with self-inflicted cruelty, has created in literature the frequently unflattering portrait of the intellectual. The literary climate of the nineteenth century only encouraged such a paradox: with Romanticism man learns to view himself as a "problem," the novelist casts himself as his principal hero, art gradually becomes a meditation on art, and thought the subject of thought. Even a distorting mirror is still a mirror, and, like irony, can be a useful device where there is fear, shame or duplicity. Thus caricature can be ambiguous: the comic figure projected into fiction by the intellectual-novelist may wear another mask, begin to play a more serious role, cease to be awkward or monstrous, and finally be granted the stature and dignity necessary to emerge as the central character in the modern novel of ideas.

Chapter 7
Modernism and Capitalism
Daniel Bell

I

That fabulous polymath Samuel Johnson maintained that no man in his right mind ever read a book through from beginning to end. His own method was to glance rapidly through the pages, read only the parts that interested him, and skip all the rest. This is one way of knowing a book, and for a clever reader it may suffice. But these days, many persons do not read a book but read of it, and usually from reviewers. Given the constraints of the media and the nature of the culture, this knowledge at one remove contains a peril. For one thing, even when a book has a complex argument, most reviewers, busy people they, sprint through a book seeking to catch a few lines to encapsulate the argument and to find a tag which can locate the author into the comfortable niches of the marketable vocabularies of conversation. Since the dominant bias in American culture is a liberal one, an argument that cuts across that liberalism makes some reviewers uncomfortable. And those whose work decries those aspects of contemporary culture which make cheap claims to "liberation," often find themselves labeled as "neo-conservative."

In its own terms, such a designation is meaningless, for it assumes that social views can be aligned along a single dimension. (What is ironic, in fact, is that those who decry the "one-dimensional" society, often hold such a one-dimensional view of politics.) In the larger historical context, the phrase makes no sense because the kind of cultural criticism I make—and I think of similar criticisms by Peter Berger and Philip Rieff—transcends the received categories of liberalism, and seeks to treat the dilemmas of contemporary society within a very different framework.

Since an author's point of view is relevant to the understanding of his intentions, I think it not amiss to say that I am a socialist in economics, a liberal in politics, and a conservative in culture. Many people might find this statement puzzling, assuming that if a person is a radical in one realm, he is a radical in all others; and, conversely, if he is a conservative in one realm, then he must be conservative in the others as well. Such an assumption misreads, both sociologically and morally, the nature of these different realms. I will begin with the values I hold, and deal with the sociological distinctions in the following section.

About economics: The economic realm today is usually thought to be simply instrumental. One of my arguments is that capitalist society, in its emphasis on accumulation, has made that activity an end in itself. But no moral philosopher, from Aristotle and Aquinas, to John Locke and Adam Smith, divorced economics from a set of moral ends or held the production of wealth to be an end in itself; rather it was seen as a means to the realization of virtue, a means of leading a civilized life.

The turning point in modern thought comes with Bentham. Bentham assumed that all men desired happiness, which he described simply as the maximizing of pleasure and the minimizing of pain. In practice this meant that whatever individuals defined as their own good was to be accepted as an "end" to be pursued. Adam Smith had written, besides *The Wealth of Nations*, a book entitled *The Theory of Moral Sentiments*, in which an "impartial spectator" represented the judgment of the community, which all right-thinking men would have to take into account. But for Bentham, in the *Introduction to the Principles of Morals and Legislation*, "the Community is a fictitious body" and the interest of the community is "the sum of the interests of the several members who compose it."

Modern capitalist thought has accepted that argument to its own detriment, for a justification only or largely on the basis of individual interest is a weak moral argument. As my colleague Irving Kristol points out, economics is necessarily bound with normative considerations—the judgments whether the consequences of aggregated individual decisions are just and fair. No society can escape the necessity of making a reasoned judgment about what is proper and desirable, and of assessing the consequences of economic decisions in the light of those standards.

Modern economics has become a positive science in which the ends to be pursued are assumed to be individual and varied, and economics is only a science of "means," or of rational choice in the allocation of resources among competing individual ends. The price system, however, is only a *mechanism* for the relative allocation of goods and services within the framework of the kinds of demands generated. Yet these demands derive from the existing distribution of income. And, what ultimately provides direction for the economy is the value system of the culture in which the economy is embedded. Economic policy can be efficacious as a means; but it can only be as *just* as the cultural value system that shapes it.

It is for that reason that I am a socialist in economics. For me, socialism is not statism, or the collective ownership of the means of production. It is (as Aneurin Bevan once said), a judgment on the priorities of economic policy. It is for that reason that I believe that *in this realm*, the community takes precedence over the individual in the values that legitimate economic policy. The first lien on the resources of a society therefore should be to establish that "social minimum" which would allow individuals to lead a life of self-respect, to be members of the community. This means a set of priorities that ensures work for those who seek it, a degree of adequate security against the hazards of the market, and adequate access to medical care and protection against the ravages of disease and illness.

I accept and reinterpret, the classical distinction between needs and wants. Needs are what all individuals have as members of the "species." Wants are the varied desires of individuals in accordance with their own tastes and idiosyncrasies. I believe that the first obligation of a society is to meet those essential needs; otherwise, individuals cannot be full "citizens" of the society. Admittedly, the word "needs" is ambiguous. Keynes once wrote: ". . . it is true that the needs of human beings may seem to be insatiable. But they fall into two classes—those needs which are absolute in the sense that we feel them whatever the situation of our fellow human beings may be, and those which are relative in the sense that we feel them only if their satisfaction lifts us above, makes us feel superior to, our fellows. Needs of the second class, those which satisfy the desire for superiority, may indeed be insatiable . . . but this is not true of absolute needs.

Unwittingly, modern economics has established its own distinction between needs and wants: the concept of discretionary income. One part of a person's expenditure is relatively fixed—the amount necessary to meet one's self-defined basic (or, in Keynes's sense, absolute) needs. The other portion is variable: it can be postponed, used to satisfy different wants, and is spent quite often in those pursuits that express the signs of status and the desires for superiority.

The social minimum I support is the amount of family income required to meet basic needs. And, since this is also a cultural definition, it will, understandably, change over time. And I am a socialist, also, in that I do not believe wealth should be convertible into undue privilege in realms where it is not relevant. Thus it is unjust, I argue, for wealth to command undue advantage in medical facilities, when these are social rights that should be available to all. In the realms of wealth, status and power, there are principles of just allocation that are distinctive to each realm.

Yet I am a liberal in politics—defining both terms in the Kantian sense. I am a liberal in that, within the polity, I believe the individual should be the primary actor, not the group (be it family or corporation or church, or ethnic or minority group). And the polity, I believe, has to maintain the distinction between the public and the private, so that not all behavior is politicized, as in communist states, or left without restraint, as in the justification of laissez-faire in traditional capitalist societies.

The public realm operates under the rule of law which applies equally to all, and is therefore procedural: it does not specify outcomes between individuals; it treats people equally rather than seeking to "make them" equal. The private realm—in morals and economics—is one where consenting parties make their own decisions, so long as the spillover effects (pornography in one instance, pollution in the other) do not upset the public realm.

I believe in the principle of individual achievement, rather than the inherited, or prescribed allocation of social positions. But I am not an egalitarian in the current, fashionable sense that the law should *make* persons equal—a situation which is not, in fact, equality but representation by numerical quota. One of the reasons that I distinguish between needs and wants is that I do not see how, in the economic realm, one can make incomes equal. The insistence on wage differentials—which is strongest among workers—reflects the moral intuition that differences in skill and effort should be rewarded differently. Once a social minimum is created, then what people do with the remainder of their money (subject to the principle of illegitimate convertibility), is their own business, just as what people do in the realm of morals is equally their own business, so long as it is done privately. And, if universalism prevails in social competition, then the criterion of merit, I believe, is a just principle to reward individual achievement in the society.

I am a conservative in culture because I respect tradition; I believe in reasoned judgments of good and bad about the qualities of a work of art; and I regard as necessary the principle of authority in the judging of the value of experience and art and education. I use the term culture to mean less than the anthropological catchall which defines any "patterned way of life" as a culture, and more than the aristocratic tradition which restricts culture to refinement and to the high arts. Culture, for me, is the effort to provide a coherent set of answers to the existential predicaments that confront all human beings in the passage of their lives. For this reason, tradition becomes essential to the vitality of a culture, for it provides the continuity of memory that teaches how one's forebears met the same existential predicaments. (Which is why the psalmist says: "If I forget thee, o Jerusalem, let my right hand lose its cunning.")

The emphasis on judgment is necessary to fend off that lack of discrimination which regards all "meaningful" experience as good, and which insists that each group's "culture" is as valid as any other. The debasement of modernity is the emphasis on "*self*-expression," and the erasure of the distinction between art and life, so that the acting out of impulse, rather than the reflective discipline of the imagination becomes the touchstone of satisfaction. To have significance, a culture must transcend the present, because it is the recurrent confrontation with those root questions whose answers, through a set of symbols, provide a viable coherence to the meaning of existence. And since the appreciation of tradition in culture, and judgment in art (and a coherent curriculum in education) has to be learned, authority—in the form of scholarship, teaching, and skilled exegesis—is a necessary guide for the perplexed. And such authority can be earned only by study, not by speaking in tongues.

The triune positions I hold do have a consistency in that they unite a belief in the inclusion of all people into citizenship through that economic minimum which allows for self-respect, the principles of individual achievement of social position on the basis of merit, and the continuity of the past and present, in order to shape the future, as the necessary conditions of a civilized order.

II

In the broader sense, my theme is not just the cultural contradictions of capitalism as such, but of bourgeois society: that new world created by the mercantile and fabricating guilds, the middle or bourgeois class that revolutionized modern society after the sixteenth century by making economic activity, rather than military or religious concerns, the central feature of society. Capitalism is a socioeconomic system geared to the production of commodities by a rational calculus of cost and price, and to the consistent accumulation of capital for the purposes of reinvestment. But this singular new mode of operation was fused with a distinctive culture and character structure. In culture, this was the idea of self-realization, the release of the individual from traditional restraints and ascriptive ties (family and birth) so that he could "make" of himself what he willed. In character structure, this was the norm of self-control and delayed gratification, of purposeful behavior in the pursuit of well-defined goals. It is the interrelationship of this economic system, culture, and character structure which comprised bourgeois civilization. It is the unravelling of this unity and its consequence, which are the threads of my argument.

I read the contradictions through two prisms: the first, a synthetic construct, is an "ideal type." It is "ahistorical" and treats the phenomena as a closed system. Thus it can be "hypothetical deductive" and specify the limits of the phenomena. Its virtue as an ideal type is the possibility of identifying the essential lineaments—what I call the axial principles and axial structures—of the circumscribed social realms which the flux of historical change sometimes obscures. Being static, however, the ideal type does not account for origins or future directions. For that, one needs the second prism of history and the detailed empirical complexity which is its content.

Using the ideal type, I see the contradictions of capitalism in the antagonistic principles that underlie the technical-economic, political and cultural structures of the society. The technical-economic realm, which became central in the beginning of capitalism, is, like all industrial society today, based on the axial principle of economizing: the effort to achieve efficiency through the breakdown of all activities into the smallest components of unit cost, as defined by the systems of financial accounting. The axial structure, based on specialization and hierarchy, is one of bureaucratic coordination. Necessarily, individuals are treated not as persons but as "things" (in the sociological jargon their behavior regulated by the role requirements), as instruments to maximize profit. In short, individuals are dissolved into their function.

The political realm, which regulates conflict, is governed by the axial principle of equality: equality before the law, equal civil rights, and, most recently, the claims of equal social and economic rights. Because these claims become translated into entitlements, the political order increasingly intervenes in the economic and social realms (in the affairs of corporations, universities, and hospitals), in order to redress the positions and rewards generated in the society by the economic system. The axial structure of the polity is representation, and, more recently, participation. And the demands for participation, as a principle, now are carried over into all other realms of the society. The tensions between bureaucracy and equality frame the social conflicts of the day.

Finally, the cultural realm is one of self-expression and self-gratification. It is antiinstitutional and antinomian in that the individual is taken to be the measure of satisfaction, and *his* feelings, sentiments and judgments, not some objective standard of quality and value, determine the worth of cultural objects. At its most blatant, this sentiment asks of a poem, a play, or a painting, not whether it is good or meretricious, but "What does it do for *me*?" In this democratization of culture, every individual, understandably, seeks to realize his full "potential," and so the individual "self" comes increasingly into conflict with the role requirements of the technical-economic order.

A number of critics have objected to these formulations on the ground that "power" still lies primarily in the economic realm, principally in the hands of the large corporations, and that the impulses to self-expression in the culture have been "co-opted" by the capitalist system and converted into commodities, i.e., objects for sale.

Such questions are empirical ones that test particular assumptions, not whether this mode of analysis, i.e., the idea of the disjunction between the realms, is useful or not. The answers lie in the court of history, and I shall return to them at the close of my historical exposition, the second thread of my analysis.

III

Much of the prevailing view of capitalism (that of the last thirty years) was shaped by Max Weber through his emphasis on Calvinism and the Protestant ethic—the role of methodical work and the legitimation of the pursuit of wealth—as the doctrines that facilitated the rise of the distinctive Western organization of rational production and exchange. But the origins of capitalism were twofold. If one source was the *asceticism* which Weber emphasized, the other was *acquisitiveness*, a central theme of Werner Sombart whose work was almost completely neglected in that period of time.

Sombart located the main areas of capitalist undertaking not in the Protestant countries, such as Holland, England or the United States, but in the Florentine world, and he argued that the same kind of prudential bourgeois maxims associated with Benjamin Franklin (who in personal life was a *bon viveur*) could be found several hundred years earlier in the writings of Leon Batista Alberti, whose book *Del governo della famiglia* was a classic in its time, and whose views of middle-class virtues, the proper coordination of actions and the profitable employ-ment of time, were adopted by large numbers of bourgeois entrepre-neurs and *commerçants* in Italy and France.

Whatever the exact locations of early capitalism, it is clear that, from the start, the two impulses of asceticism and acquisitiveness were yoked together. One was the bourgeois prudential spirit of calculation; the other, the restless Faustian drive which, as expressed in the modern economy and technology, took as its motto "the endless frontier," and, as its goal, the complete transformation of nature. The intertwining of the two impulses shaped the modern conception of rationality. The tension between the two imposed a moral restraint on the sumptuary display that had characterized earlier periods of conquest. What is also evident is that the ascetic element, and with it one kind of moral legitimation of capitalist behavior, has virtually disappeared.

On the level of philosophical justification, the major attack on asceticism was mounted by Jeremy Bentham, who argued that asceti-cism ("miseries" inflicted by sectarians on unwilling others) violated the "natural" hedonism which rules men—the search for pleasure and the avoidance of pain. Its "mischief" is that, whatever its pure intention, asceticism leads to "despotism" over men. The principle of utility alone could serve as the regulating instrument of men's search to satisfy their diverse ends. Thus the notion of common ends was dissolved into individual preferences.

On the plane of history, the "economic impulse" had been constrained earlier by the rules of custom and tradition, to some extent by the Catholic moral principle of the just price, and later by the Puritan emphasis on frugality. As the religious impulses diminished, a complex history in its own right, so did the restraints. What became distinctive about capitalism—its very dynamic—was its boundlessness. Propelled by the dynamo of technology, there were to be no asymptotes to its exponential growth. No limits. Nothing was sacred. Change became the norm. By the middle of the nineteenth century, this was the trajectory of the economic impulse. It was, as well, the trajectory of the culture.

IV

The realm of culture is the realm of meanings, the effort in some imaginative form to make sense of the world through the expressive-ness of art and ritual, particularly those "incomprehensions" such as tragedy and death that arise out of the existential predicaments which every self-conscious human being must confront at some point in his life. In these encounters, one becomes aware of the fundamental questions—what Goethe called *Urphänomen*—which frame all others. Religion, as the oldest effort to comprehend these "mysteries," has historically been the source of cultural symbols.

If science is the search for the unity of nature, religion has been the quest for the unity of culture in the different historical periods of civilizations. To close that circle, religion has woven tradition as the fabric of meaning and guarded the portals of culture by rejecting those works of art which threatened the moral norms of religion.

The modern movement disrupts that unity. It does so in three ways: by insisting on the autonomy of the aesthetic from moral norms; by valuing more highly the new and experimental; and by taking the self (in its quest for originality and uniqueness) as the touchstone of cultural judgment. The most aggressive outrider of the movement is the self-proclaimed *avant-garde* which calls itself Modernism. I see Modernism as the agency for the dissolution of the bourgeois world view and, in the past half-century, as gaining hegemony in the culture.

The difficulties of defining Modernism are notorious. Schematically, I would specify three different dimensions:

1. Thematically Modernism has been a rage against order, and in particular, bourgeois orderliness. The emphasis is on the self, and the unceasing search for experience. If Terence once said, "Nothing human is alien to me," the Modernist could say with equal fervor, "Nothing inhuman is alien to me." Rationalism is seen as devitalizing; the surge to creativity is propelled by an exploration of the demonic. In that exploration, one cannot set aesthetic limits (or even moral norms) to this protean reach of the imagination. The crucial insistence is that experience is to have no boundaries to its cravings, that there be "nothing sacred."

2. Stylistically, there is a common syntax in what I have called "the eclipse of distance." This is the effort to achieve immediacy impact, simultaneity, and sensation by eliminating aesthetic and psychic distance. In diminishing aesthetic distance, one annihilates contemplation and envelops the spectator in the experience. By eliminating psychic distance, one emphasizes (in Freudian terms) the "primary process" of dream and hallucination, of instinct and impulse. In all this modernism rejects the "rational cosmology" that was introduced into the arts during the Renaissance and codified by Alberti: of foreground and background in pictorial space; of beginning middle, and end, or sequence, in time; and the distinction of genres and the modes of work appropriate to each genre. This eclipse of distance,

as a formal syntax, cuts across all the arts: in literature, the "stream of consciousness"; in painting, the elimination of the "interior distance" within the canvas; in music, the upset of the balance of melody and harmony; in poetry, the disruption of the ordered meter. In the broadest sense, this common syntax repudiates mimesis as a principle of art. (Clearly not all Modernist writers are "anti-bourgeois" in any overt sense. T. S. Eliot was a High-Church Anglican and William Faulkner a traditionalist in his Southern politics. Yet both men were great "experimenters" in poetry and in the novel. Despite their specific political or cultural *beliefs*, one of the effects of their "modernist styles" was to disrupt the "rational cosmology" which underlay the bourgeois world view of an ordered relationship of space and time.)

3. The preoccupation with the medium. In all periods of cultural history, artists have been conscious of the nature and complexity of the medium as a formal problem in transmuting the "pre-figured" into the "figured" result. In the last twenty-five years, we have seen a preoccupation not with the content or form (i.e., style and genre), but with the medium of art itself: with the actual texture of paint and materials in painting, with the abstract "sounds" in music, with phonology or even "breath" in poetry, and with the abstract properties of language in literature—often to the exclusion of anything else. Thus it is the encaustic surface, not the image, that generates excitement in the paintings of Jasper Johns; the aleatory or chance factors in the music of John Cage; the aspirate rather than the syllable, as a measure of line in poetry of Robert Creeley—all of these as expressions of the self, rather than formal explorations of the limits and nature of the medium itself.

Modernism has, beyond dispute, been responsible for one of the great surges of creativity in Western culture. The period from 1850 to 1930 probably saw more varied experiments in literature, poetry, music and painting—if not more great masterpieces—than any previous period we have known. Much of this arose out of the creative tension of culture, with its adversary stance, against the bourgeois social structure. Peter Gay has argued that "the modernist movement was not only an expression of hostility. It was also an act of affirmation . . . modernism was as much an heir as the adversary of liberalism." Certainly this is true, for the essence of liberalism was the emphasis on the self. But Mr. Gay's effort at redress misses the dialectic of tension. What was affirmation for Manet, about whom Mr. Gay is writing, was soured derision later for Apollinaire and Artaud.

There has been a price. One cost has been the loss of coherence in culture, particularly in the spread of an antinomian attitude to moral norms and even to the idea of cultural judgment itself. The greater price was exacted when the distinction between art and life became blurred so that what was once permitted in the *imagination* (the novels of murder, lust, perversity) has often passed over into *fantasy*, and is acted out by individuals who want to make their lives a work of art, and when, with the "democratization" of criticism, the touchstone of judgment is no longer some consensual agreement on standards, but each "self's" judgment as to how art enhances that "self."

Changes in culture interact with a social structure in complicated ways. Where there is a patronage system, the patron—be it prince, or church, or state—commissions a work of art, and the cultural needs of the institution, such as the Church, or the tastes of the prince, or the demands for glorification by the State, will shape the regnant style of the time. But where art is bought and sold, the market is where culture and social structure cross. One would expect that where culture has become a commodity the bourgeois taste would prevail. But in extraordinary historical fact, this has not been the case.

The phrase "cultural hegemony"—identified with the Italian Marxist Antonio Gramsci—signifies the dominance of a single group in shaping the prevailing world view which gives a people an interpretation of the age. There have been many times where a single worldview, growing out of and serving a dominant class, has prevailed. In the twelfth century—the "Age of Faith" symbolized by Innocent III— we see the apotheosis of Church control over society not in the uniformity of devotion, but, as Bryan Wilson has put it, "because the imprint of faith and order demanded by ecclesiastical authority dominated the social framework." The closest analogue today—in the regulation of daily life, the heavy handed control of production and distribution, and the restraint of impulse and the glorification of authority—is the Soviet world, where the Party exercises complete cultural hegemony. It is an ideologically prescribed social order.

Marxists have assumed that under capitalism there has also been a single cultural hegemony—the ideas of the "ruling class." Yet the astonishing fact is that in the past hundred years, if there has been a dominant influence—in the high culture at least—it has been the avowed enemy of that class, Modernism.

At the start the capitalist economic impulse and the cultural drive of modernity shared a common source, the ideas of liberty and liberation, whose embodiments were "rugged individualism" in economic affairs and the "unrestrained self" in culture. Though the two had a common origin in the repudiation of tradition and the authority of the past, an adversary relation between them quickly developed. One can say, as Freud would, that the discipline required by work was threatened by the libidinal energies diverted to culture. This may perhaps be true, but it is abstract. What would seem to be the more likely historical explanation is that the bourgeois attitudes of calculation and methodical restraint came into conflict with the impulsive searchings for sensation and excitement that one found in Romanticism, and which passed over into Modernism. The antagonism deepened as the organization of work and production became bureaucratized and individuals were reduced to roles, so that the norms of the workplace were increasingly at variance with the emphasis on self-exploration and self-gratification. The thread connecting Blake to Byron to Baudelaire—who is the avatar of Modernism—may not be literal, but it is a figurative symbolic lineage.

So long as work and wealth had a religious sanction, they possessed a transcendental justification. But when that ethic eroded, there was a loss of legitimation, for the pursuit of wealth alone is not a calling that justifies itself. As Schumpeter once shrewdly remarked: The stock exchange is a poor substitute for the Holy Grail. The central point is that—at first, for the advanced social groups, the intelligentsia and the educated social classes, and later for the middle class itself—*the legitimations of social behavior passed from religion to modernist culture*. And with it here was a shift in emphasis from "character," which is the unity of moral codes and disciplined purpose, to an emphasis on "personality," which is the enhancement of self through the compulsive search for individual differentiation. In brief, not work but the "life style" became the source of satisfaction and criterion for desirable behavior in the society.

Yet paradoxically, the life style that became the imago of the free self was not that of the businessman, expressing himself through his "dynamic drive," but that of the artist defying the conventions of the society. Increasingly, it is the artist who begins to dominate the audience, and to impose his judgment as to what is to be desired and bought. The paradox is completed when the bourgeois ethic, having collapsed in the society, finds few defenders in the culture (do any writers defend *any* institutions?) and Modernism as an attack on orthodoxy, has triumphed and become the regnant orthodoxy of the day.

V

Any tension creates its own dialectic. Since the market is where social structure and culture cross, what has happened is that in the last fifty years, the economy has been geared to producing the life styles paraded by the culture. Thus, not only has there been a contradiction *between* the realms, but that tension has produced a further contradiction *within* the economic realm itself. In the world of capitalist enterprise, the nominal ethos in the spheres of production and organization is still one of work, delayed gratification, career orientation, devotion to the enterprise. Yet, on the marketing side, the sale of goods, packaged in the glossy images of glamour and sex, promotes a hedonistic way of life whose promise is the voluptuous gratification of the lineaments of desire. The consequence of this contradiction is that a corporation finds its people being straight by day and swingers by night.

What has happened in society in the last fifty years—as a result of the erosion of the religious ethic and the increase in discretionary income—*is that the culture has taken the initiative in promoting change*, and the economy has been geared to meeting these new wants. In this respect, there has been a significant reversal in the historical pattern of social change. During the rise of capitalism—in the "modernization" of any traditional society—one could more readily change the economic structure of a society: by forcing people off the land into factories, by imposing a new rhythm and discipline of work, by using brutal means or incentives (e.g., the theory of interest as the reward for "abstinence" from consumption) to raise capital. But the superstructure—the patterns of family life, the attachments to religion and authority, the received ideas that shaped people's perceptions of a social reality—was more stubbornly resistant to change.

Today, by contrast, it is the economic structure that is the more difficult to change. Within the enterprise, the heavy bureaucratic layers reduce flexible adaptation, while union rules inhibit the power of management to control the assignment of jobs. In the society, the economic enterprise is subject to the challenges of various veto groups (e.g., on the location of plants or the use of the environment) and subject more and more to regulation by government.

But in the culture, fantasy reigns almost unconstrained. The media are geared to feeding new images to people, to unsettling traditional conventions, and the highlighting of aberrant and quirky behavior which becomes imagos for others to imitate. The traditional is stodgy, and the "orthodox" institutions such as family and church are on the defensive about their inability to change. Yet if capitalism has been routinized, Modernism has been trivialized. After all, how often can it continue to shock, if there is nothing shocking left? If experiment is the norm, how original can anything new be? And like all bad history, Modernism has repeated its end, once in the popgun outbursts of Futurism and Dadaism, the second time in the phosphorescent parodies of Pop paintings and the mindless minimalism of conceptual art. The exclamation points that end each sentence of the Manifestoes, have simply become four dots that trail away in the tedium of endless repetition.

In the revelation of wisdom, the Owl of Minerva flies at dusk because life had become gray on gray. In the victorious apocalypse of Modernism, the dawn is a series of gaudy colors whirling in strobismic light. Today, Modernism has become not the work of serious artists but the property of the *culturati*, the "cultural mass," the distribution sector of cultural production, for whom the shock of the old has become the chic of the new. The *culturati* have carried over, in rhetoric, the adversary stance against bourgeois orderliness and sobriety, yet they impose a conformity of their own on those who deviate from its guarded canons.

In the 1960s, one beheld the "new" phenomenon of the counter-culture. Yet the very name was a conceit. The "adversary culture" was concerned with art, the use of the imagination to transfigure recalcitrant memory or intractible materials into a *work* that could, in its power, transcend its time. It existed in the realm of culture. The so-called counter-culture was a children's crusade that sought to eliminate the line between fantasy and reality and act out in life its impulses under a banner of liberation. It claimed to mock bourgeois prudishness, when it was only flaunting the closet behavior of its liberal parents. It claimed to be new and daring when it was only repeating in more raucous form—its rock noise amplified in the electronic echo-chamber of the mass media—the youthful japes of a Greenwich Village bohemia of a half century before. It was less a counter-culture than a counterfeit culture.

In this double contradiction of capitalism, what has been established in the last thirty years has been the tawdry rule of fad and fashion: of "multiples" for the *culturati*, hedonism for the middle classes, and pornotopia for the masses. And in the very nature of fashion, it has trivialized the culture.

VI

Has Modernism been "co-opted," as Herbert Marcuse suggests? In one dimension, yes. It has been converted into a commodity for promotion and profit. But in the deeper transformations of structure, that process can only undermine the foundations of capitalism itself. The sociological truism is that a societal order is shored up by its legitimations, which provide the defenses against its despisers. But the legitimation of the culture, as I have argued, is the quest for self-gratification and the expression of "personality." It attacks established orthodoxy in the name of personal autonomy and heterodoxy. Yet what modern culture has failed to understand is that orthodoxy is not the guardian of an existent order, but is itself a judgment on the adequacy and moral character of beliefs, from the standpoint of "right reason." The paradox is that "heterodoxy" itself has become conformist in liberal circles and exercises that conformity under the banner of an antinomian flag. It is a prescription, in its confusions, for the dissolution of a shared moral order.

Does power still lie in the economic realm, and largely in the hands of the giant corporations? To a considerable extent this is still so in Western society, yet such an argument misreads the nature of societal change today. A capitalist order had historical strength when it fused property with power through a set of ruling families to maintain the continuity of the system. The first deep, internal structural change in capitalism was the divorce of family and property from managerial power and the loss of continuity through the chain of elites. Economic power today lies in institutions whose chiefs cannot pass along their power to their heirs and who, increasingly—since property is not private (but corporate), and technical skill, not property is the basis of managerial positions—no longer have the traditional natural rights, justifications, and legitimacy in the exercise of that power, and feel it keenly. The larger fact is that a modern society multiplies the number of constituencies and given the increasing interdependence of economic and social effects, the political order becomes the place where power is wielded in order to manage the systemic problems arising out of that interdependence and the increasing competition of other, state-directed economies. The major consequence is the expansion of State power, and the fact that the State budget, not the division of profits within the enterprise, becomes the major arbiter of economic decisions (including the formation of capital), and that competition not between capitalist and workers, but between the multiple constituencies (where corporations still exercise a large degree of influence) is the mode of allocating power in the society.

VII

A final word on religion, which for me is the fulcrum of my book. I do not (*pace* Durkheim) see religion as a "functional necessity" for society, or that without religion a society will dissolve. I do not believe in religion as a patch for the unravelled seams of society. Nor do societies "dissolve," though in periods of extreme crises (like times of war) the loss of legitimation may sap the will to resist. Religions cannot be manufactured. Worse, if they were, the results would be spurious and soon vanish in the next whirl of fashion.

As Max Weber bitingly observed more than a half century ago:

> The need of literary, academic, or cafe-society intellectuals to include religious feelings in the inventory of their sources of impressions and sensations, and among the topics for discussion, has never yet given rise to a new religion. Nor can a religious renascence be generated by the need of authors to compose books, or by the far more effective need of clever publishers to sell such books. No matter how much the appearance of a widespread religious interest may be stimulated, no religion has ever resulted from the needs of intellectuals or from their chatter. The whirlgig of fashion will presently remove this subject of conversation and journalism, which fashion has made popular.

Religions grow out of the deepest needs of individuals sharing a common awakening, and are not created by "engineers of the soul."

My concern with religion goes back to what I assume is the constitutive character of culture: the wheel of questions that brings one back to the existential predicaments, the awareness in men of their finiteness and the inexorable limits to their power (the transgression of which is *hamartia*), and the consequent effort to find a coherent answer to reconcile them to the human condition. Since that awareness touches the deepest springs of consciousness, I believe that a culture which has become aware of the limits in exploring the mundane will turn, at some point, to the effort to recover the sacred.

We stand, I believe, with a clearing ahead of us. The exhaustion of Modernism, the aridity of Communist life, the tedium of the unrestrained self, and the meaningless of the monolithic political chants, all indicate that a long era is coming to a slow close. The impulse of Modernism was to leap beyond: beyond nature, beyond culture, beyond tragedy—to explore the *apeiron*, the boundless, driven by the self-infinitizing spirit of the radical self. Bourgeois society sundered economics from moral norms to allow the individual to pursue his own self-defined wants, yet at the same time sought to bend the culture to its restricted moral norms. Modernism was the major effort to break away from those restrictions in the name of experience, the aesthetic and the experimental and, in the end, broke all boundaries. Yet if we now seek to return economics to moral norms, is there not a similar warranty for culture?

We are groping for a new vocabulary whose keyword seems to be limits: a limit to growth, a limit to the spoliation of the environment, a limit to arms, a limit to the tampering with biological nature. Yet if we seek to establish a set of limits in the economy and technology, will we also set a limit to the exploration of those cultural experiences which go beyond moral norms and embrace the demonic in the delusion that all experience is "creative"? Can we set a limit to *hubris*? The answer to that question could resolve the *cultural* contradiction of capitalism and its deceptive double, *semblable et frère*, the culture of modernity. It would leave only the economic and political mundane to be tamed.

Part II

Political Emphases

Introduction

The following essays, though not devoid of theoretical questions, primarily tend to comment on specific conditions and events intellectuals had to confront, and on how they dealt with them.

Dwight Macdonald, in 1941, describes the dilemmas of the independent American left, which found itself caught between backing Stalinism before and after the Soviet Union had become our ally in the war, and coming to terms with its pacifism to combat fascism. Macdonald begins with an attack on *For Whom the Bell Tolls*. Hemingway "lacks the moral and intellectual equipment to handle as complex an event as the Spanish civil war," and by creating a protagonist who renounces thinking, he reduces the central problems of communism, fascism, and democracy and allows for a false antithesis between politics and art. Such an antithesis, in turn, continues Macdonald, gives Hemingway the opportunity to attack Stalinism without really renouncing it, and to remain unaware of "the slow strangling by the Stalino-bourgeois coalition of the revolutionary upsurge of the Spanish masses." But this novel is only one manifestation of political naiveté. The American press, notes Macdonald, is ready to praise any leader, however repressive his regime was in the past, only because he now stands ready to fight the Axis powers; yet all along, the same people had been unaware of the erosion of democracy in order to back, for instance, Latin American dictatorships. (The situation still holds true forty years later.) The use of the press for political ends, of course, was perfected by Hitler, who justified building up his war economy long before 1939, to "systematize the brutalities, contradictions and lunacies of capitalism," and the rationalization of destruction. Thus on all sides of the political spectrum, many intellectuals have become political pawns.

Czeslaw Milosz elaborates on this theme by addressing the

impact of political repression in Soviet satellite countries such as Poland and Czechoslovakia. There, he states, intellectuals accept Murti-Bing pills which make them ignore metaphysical issues, evil and misery. But swallowing such pills, he continues, while inducing outward happiness and serenity, and disguising many symptoms, is lethal to artistic work; for Polish or Czech writers, even when aware that socialist realism is inauthentic, nevertheless are no match for the dialecticians – party organizers who have learned to debate and to persuade. But because the entire society is permeated with their ideology, even the critical intellectual is frequently taken in, or, if a writer, becomes paralyzed. Milosz describes how every writer experiences a crisis, when, after criticizing the real problems caused by capitalism, he must begin to go further – from critical realism to socialist realism, as a matter of survival. If he overcomes his guilt, he can benefit from the system, and Murti-Bing is helpful for his personal survival, though it stifles his talent. Wholesale consumption of this pill, however, makes for "something impalpable and unpleasant in the human climate of such cities as Warsaw and Prague." That Milosz had already left by 1951, and that subsequent events proved his fears to have been justified, would indicate that no system can entirely kill human consciousness, or the emergence of a creative avant-garde.

Whereas Milosz's concern is with the disintegration of Marxism in Communist states, Irving Howe addresses this issue as it relates to America, where "revolutionary mystique" and "a nostalgia for apocalypse" have allowed intellectuals to abdicate politics, or to subordinate it to cultural experience. America lacks a true intellectual community, he finds, so radical criticism remains scattered, as even the welfare state "preserves the essential character of capitalist economy," subject to the free market. Howe suggests that the struggles and issues raised within the welfare state are real, but that American radicals must form a coalition of the major "progressive forces – labor, Negro, liberal, church groups, intellectuals, students – to replace the option of socialism, and to avoid the dangers of class division." For these internal dangers exist side by side with the lack of a coherent American foreign policy, the Vietnam war, the automatism of modern technology with its accompanying alienation, the decay of the party system, and all the problems associated with mass society. But even though socialism failed to transform Western society and became a mockery elsewhere, intellectuals are asked not to abandon the socialist idea – with its "commitment to the values of fraternity, libertarianism, egalitarianism and freedom . . . [and] an envisioned society in which a decisive proportion of the means of production shall be commonly owned and democratically controlled." Chiding the original Marxist movement for having dwelt excessively on political means, Howe suggests that future emphasis must be on long-range questions of changing economic allocation, and on understanding the relationship between social structure and humane values. Thus intellectuals must develop a serious political consciousness, entailing a "power-shakeup" among them all, including the semi-intellectuals, old and new leftists, ex-leftists, etc. Howe, in 1966, predicts a *Kulturkampf* amongst all those who claim to have the "best" radical solution as "successors" to the socialist dream.

It should not be surprising that the insertion of socialist ideals, or their piecemeal application in a constitutional democracy resulted in "neoconservatism," as intellectuals were increasingly co-opted by the "establishment." Edith Kurzweil addresses this issue by reviewing Gouldner's argument in relation to other views on the subject. Intellectuals have come to constitute a New Class which periodically aligns itself with workers and peasants, maintains Gouldner. And because they are employed as technical experts in all the professions, they are in a position to use both "welfare" and "socialist" states for their own ends. By selling their expertise, they are individually linked to power, but also are united amongst each other through what Gouldner calls a "culture of critical discourse." Kurzweil summarizes the major controversies, and questions the possibility that these intellectuals may ever act as a class.

The central concern of all the essays in this section, then, is the fate, or the transformation of the socialist promise – Marx's promise that failed.

Chapter Eight
Reading from Left to Right
Dwight Macdonald

FWTBT Hemingway's publishers advertise his new book as "the novel that has something for everybody." This seems to be an accurate statement. It is the biggest publishing success since *Gone With the Wind*: almost half a million copies have been sold and it is selling at the rate of 50,000 a week; Paramount has bought the movie rights at the highest price yet paid by Hollywood for a novel, and Gary Cooper, at Hemingway's insistence, is to play the hero; the initials FWTBT promise to become as familiar journalistic shorthand as GWTW. At the same time, the book has been extravagantly praised by the critics, from Mr. Mumford Jones of the *Saturday Review of Literature* (who describes Pilar as a "Falstaffian" character and thinks it is "at least possible that *For Whom the Bell Tolls* may become the *Uncle Tom's Cabin* of the Spanish Civil War") to Mr. Edmund Wilson of the *New Republic*. It is seldom that a novelist gathers both riches and reputation from the same book.

In the face of all this enthusiasm, I have to note that my own experience with *For Whom the Bell Tolls* was disappointing.* The opening chapters promised a good deal: they were moving, exciting, wonderfully keen in sensory description. They set the stage for major tragedy. But the stage was never really filled, the promise wasn't kept. The longer I read, the more of a let-down I felt, the more I had a sense that the author was floundering around, uncertain of his values and intentions, unable to come up to the pretensions of his theme. One trouble with the book is that it isn't a novel at all but rather a series of short stories, some of them excellent—Pilar's narratives of the killing of the fascists and of her life with the consumptive bullfighter; the description of Gaylords Hotel; Andres' journey through the Loyalist lines; and the final blowing up of the bridge —imbedded in a mixture of sentimental love scenes, too much talk, rambling narrative sequences, and rather dull interior monologues by Jordan. So, too, with the characters; they are excellent when they are sketched in just enough for the purposes of a short story, as with El Sordo, the dignified Fernando, and the old man Anselmo. But when Hemingway tries to do more, he fails, as with the character of Pilar, which starts off well enough but becomes gaseous when it is expanded.

---

*Elsewhere in this issue, Lionel Trilling reviews *For Whom the Bell Tolls* at length. Here I am concerned primarily with its political rather than its literary significance— as I shall try to show, its shortcomings in both respects are organically connected.

The worst failure is the central character, Robert Jordan. Like previous Hemingway heroes, Jordan is not an objectively rendered character but simply a mouthpiece for the author. The earlier heroes had at least a certain dramatic consistency, but Jordan is a monster, uniting—or trying to—the nihilism and cynicism of the usual Hemingway hero with a rather simpleminded political idealism—a sort of Hemingwayesque scoutmaster leading his little troop of peasants. For the Hemingway who speaks through Jordan is a Hemingway with a hangover, a repentant Hemingway who has been in contact with a revolution and has accepted it enough to be ashamed of his old faith and yet who cannot feel or understand deeply the new values. The result is that Jordan as a character is vague and fuzzy, destroyed by the continual friction of these irreconcilable viewpoints.

"TURN OFF THE THINKING NOW..." Jordan's confusion is shared and not understood by his creator, and this confusion is the root of the failure of the novel. Although Hemingway himself denies it frequently in the course of the book, and although most of the critics take his denial at face value, *For Whom the Bell Tolls* is a political novel, both in that it deals with a great political event, the Spanish civil war, and that its author takes a definite (though largely unconscious) political attitude towards this event. And it is a failure because Hemingway lacks the moral and intellectual equipment to handle such a theme. Instinctively, he tries to cut the subject down to something he can handle by restricting his view of the war to the activities of a small band of peasant guerrillas behind Franco's lines (and hence safely insulated from Loyalist politics) and by making his protagonist—in Karkov's words—"a young American of slight political development but ... a fine partisan record."

But such limitations negate the pretensions of the book. Hemingway's peasants have been so depoliticalized that it seems little more than chance that they are Loyalists rather than Rebels, and so the long novel is reduced to the scale of an adventure story. As for Jordan, on page 17 he admonishes himself: "Turn off the thinking now, old timer, old comrade. You're a bridge-blower now. Not a thinker." But what can be more fruitless than to follow through some five hundred pages the thoughts of a hero who has renounced thought?

I think the novel is a failure for precisely the reason that many critics seem to like it most: because of its rejection of political consciousness. "The *kind* of people people are rather than their social-economic relations is what Hemingway is particularly aware of," writes Edmund Wilson in the *New Republic*, and it is clear from the rest of his review that he conceives of "social-economic relations" as somehow conflicting with "the kind of people people are." This false antithesis, between politics and 'art,' or even between politics and 'life,' attractive enough always to the empirically slanted American consciousness, is doubly seductive today when political creeds have been so discredited by the events of recent years. Mr. Wilson ends his review: "That he should thus go back to his art, after a period of artistic demoralization, and give it a large scope, that in an era of general perplexity and panic, he should dramatize the events of the immediate past in terms, not of partisan journalism, but of the common human instincts that make men both fraternal and combative—is reassuring evidence of the soundness of our intellectual life."

Of course, posing the alternative in these terms, one must agree that *For Whom the Bell Tolls*, is vastly preferable to the "partisan journalism" of *The Fifth Column*. But there is another alternative, namely the treatment of revolutionary struggle as Malraux and Silone have treated it in their novels, on the level of political consciousness. Mr. Wilson describes Hemingway's political understanding as "not so highly developed as it is with a writer like Malraux," adding "but it is here combined with other things that these political novelists often lack." Just what are these "other things"? I find at least as profound an understanding of "the kind of people people are" in Silone and Malraux as in Hemingway. Far from there being an antithesis between these two kinds of understanding, the human and the political, in these European novelists the one illuminates the other and is integrated with it. Politics is simply one category of human behavior—to the novelist who is writing about a revolution, the most important one.

To Mr. Wilson, however, "politics" seems to mean the threadbare, vulgarized formulae, the treacheries and lies of Stalinism. Thus he actually describes the Hemingway of *The Fifth Column* as infused with "the semireligious exaltation of communism," whereas in fact Hemingway in that period expressed the most tepid sort of Popular Frontism. And Mr. Wilson can write of the new novel: "Thus we get down out of the empyrean of Marxist political analysis, where the leaders are pulling the strings for the masses and see the ordinary people as they come." It has never occurred to me that the defects of *The Fifth Column* could be attributed to a too close study of the Marxist classics. And as for the leaders pulling the strings for the masses—Mr. Wilson should read again the passages in *For Whom the Bell Tolls* dealing with the necessity for "discipline," and with the "crazies," the Anarchists.

THE POLITICS OF ANTI-POLITICS

This misconception of the nature of politics leads Mr. Wilson—and many others—to conclude that since Hemingway in *For Whom the Bell Tolls* explicitly rejects the political catchwords of Stalinism, he has therefore liberated himself from 'politics' in general and from Stalinism in particular. Hemingway himself, whose conception of politics is essentially that of Mr. Wilson, may well suffer from the same delusion. But those who see no further into a political program than its catchwords are likely to imagine, when they lose faith in the catchwords, that to reject them is also to free themselves from the program. It may be, however, that they merely become *unconscious* of their political values.

Thus it is precisely that lack of political consciousness which Mr. Wilson finds so admirable that prevents Hemingway from really breaking with Stalinism. Jordan 'turns off the thinking' only to act the more freely in accordance with the very political formulae he has come to distrust so deeply as not to want to think about.

"Here in Spain the Communists offered the best discipline and the soundest and sanest for the prosecution of the war. He accepted their discipline because, in the conduct of the war, they were the only party whose program and discipline he could respect. What were his politics, then? He had none now, he told himself. But do not tell any one else, he thought. . . ." Hemingway tries to write a non-political political novel and Jordan tries to participate in a revolutionary war and yet reject politics. But these are merely *other forms* of political thought and action.

"He would not think himself into any defeatism. The first thing was to win the war. If we did not win the war, everything was lost." Here we see a false antithesis, between thinking and successful action (thought leads to defeatism) similar to that already noted between politics and human reality. This corresponds in turn to the false antithesis made by the Stalinists in Spain between the task of winning the war (a 'practical' matter which must be settled first) and that of creating a new society (a 'theoretical' matter, to be left to the distant future, a sort of dessert to be enjoyed after the war). But there was no real antithesis between the two tasks: the war could have been won only by carrying through the social revolution.

I will be told that Hemingway directly attacks the Stalinists in his portrait of Marty and in his rendering of the cynical atmosphere of Gaylords. It is true that these represent a shift away from Stalinism—but of a superficial nature, like his rejection of the Party catchwords. Hemingway is at pains to indicate that Jordan's first reaction to Gaylords was naive, that war is an ugly business, and that cynicism may be permitted those who are really facing the realities and 'doing the job.' And Marty is presented as literally half-crazy, his lunacy consisting in a passion for shooting Trotskyists and Anarchists—thus attributing the settled and rational (from its viewpoint) policy of the C.P. in Spain as the vagary of an eccentric individual!

It is notable that in his attempts to define to himself why he finds it increasingly harder to believe in the Loyalist cause, Jordan often blames the Spanish national character (which he feels is treacherous, provincial, cruel, etc.) and sometimes even certain disturbing moral characteristics of individual Stalinists. But he never gives a thought to the really disillusioning development: the slow strangling, by the Stalino-bourgeois coalition, of the revolutionary upsurge of the Spanish masses. The most politically revealing thing in the book is Hemingway's vindictive picture of the Anarchists—"the crackpots and romantic revolutionists," "the wild men," or, most often, simply "the crazies." One character thinks of them as "dangerous children; dirty, foul, undisciplined, kind, loving, silly and ignorant but armed." (This character is not Karkov or Jordan but the simple peasant lad, Andres, who might have disliked the Anarchists but would certainly not have disliked them in these drillmaster's terms—a curious example of how Hemingway sometimes violates realism to voice his own prejudices.) What worries Hemingway about the Anarchists is that they were undisciplined and armed, which is a good short description of the masses in process of making a revolution. His counter-prescription is expressed in Jordan's evaluation of the Stalinist generals:

"They were Communists and they were disciplinarians. The discipline that they would enforce would make good troops. Lister was murderous in discipline. . . . But he knew how to forge a division into a fighting unit."

I find it significant that the Communist Party seems to be undecided as to just what line to take towards *For Whom the Bell Tolls*. While the book has been roundly denounced in classic C.P. style in the *Daily Worker*, it is being sold in the Party bookshops. And Alvah C. Bessie in the *New Masses* writes more in sorrow than in anger, taking the line that Hemingway, while still sincerely enlisted in the fight against "our common enemy" (reaction), has been misled so that "at the moment he is found in bad company." The Party has evidently not given up hope of welcoming back the straying sheep into the fold at some future (and happier) date. I should say this is a shrewd political judgment.

•

"A TRIM   "Greeks! We shall now prove whether we are worthy
RECKONING!"   of our ancestors and of the liberty which our fore-
fathers secured for us. . . . The time has come for all Greeks to fight to the death for all they hold dear." Such was the Periclean appeal made by Premier Metaxas on the day the Italians began to invade Greece. The spectacle of the quasi-fascist dictator, Metaxas, calling on the Greek masses to fight to the death for the liberties he himself extinguished five years ago, this is the latest and not the last irony in the world struggle between fascism and "democracy." As the war spreads like a fungus over the globe—the last "world war" was a provincial backyard affair compared to this one—from Danzig to Vyborg to Trondheim to Louvain to Dunkirk to Dakar to Dong Dang to Sidi Barrani to Bahrein to Thailand to Athens, the question becomes ever more urgent and ever more obscure: what is a "democracy"?

A rough empirical definition seems to be: any country that comes into opposition to the Axis powers. The American press stands ready to confer a brevet rank in the army of Democracy on any leader—from Baron Mannerheim to the Royalist general, De Gaulle—or any nation—

from feudal Poland to semifascist Greece—which, for whatever reasons or however reluctantly, finds itself on the side of the angels. The Latin American dictatorships have lately been found to be "democracies," and the *New York Times* has a form editorial standing ready in type, lamenting in pathetic tones the extinction of one more heroic little "democracy," which is printed whenever the Axis invades a new nation. On Greece, the *Times* found it strategic to say more about Pericles than about Metaxas. And doubtless when and if the Reichswehr moves into the Ukraine, the *Times* will see the violation of the Soviet border as one more breach in the citadel of Democracy.

The point is, of course, that just as fascism takes power internally only after bourgeois democracy has strangled in its own economic and social contradictions, so on the international scene the Axis armies overthrow governments already compromised and enfeebled, democratic in form only—or not even in form. The war is constantly exposing the meaninglessness of the concept, "democracy," in the modern capitalist world. So is it, also, with the other terms in the lexicon of bourgeois idealism, which are steadily losing their luster under the corrosive action of events. Think of the millions of noble words which were reduced to so much baled newsprint by the French debacle! *"Be faithful and united. Your sacrifice will not be in vain."* (Weygand to his troops, on assuming command during the Battle of France) *"France enters this war with a pure conscience, which for her is not a word. The world will perhaps soon know that moral forces are also forces."* (Reynaud, on Italy's declaration of war) *"We shall defend every stone, every clod of earth, every lamp-post and every building. We would rather have Paris razed than fall into German hands."* (The French "official spokesman," the day before the Germans entered Paris) *"Tell America that in our fight to save the world from a return to the dark ages, we shall not falter. . . . The morale of the defenders and the people of France has never been higher than at this critical moment. Galvanized by the unprovoked invasion of their soil, steadied by the calm courage of General Weygand, they are determined to win at whatever cost."* (Reynaud, June 10).

The difference between such words and the reality that came to pass must either rouse a people to revolutionary passion or stun it into apathy and cynicism. The latter seems to have resulted in France, whence the survival of the Vichy "government"—a frail shell empty of all social content, which the first stirrings of the French masses will shatter. The quintessence of Vichy is the official report on the recent meeting between Petain and Hitler: "The Marshal was received with the honors due his rank." One recalls Petain's comment on the armistice: "The terms are severe, but our honor is safe." We may be sure that the French people are thinking less in Petain's than in Falstaff's terms about this concept:

"Honor pricks me on. Yea, but how if honor pricks me off when I come on? How then? Can honor set a leg? No. Or an arm? No. Or take away the grief of a wound? No. Honor hath no skill in surgery then?

No. What is honor? A word. What is that word honor? Air. A trim reckoning!"

THE CRISIS OF THE WORD

The almost daily reminders that the fine words of bourgeois ideology, whether in the mouth of a Roosevelt or a Petain, are so much air have naturally had an effect on popular consciousness. The process began long before the war; it has been going on, in fact, since the Great French Revolution, and with unparalleled intensity abroad since 1914 and in this country since 1929. By now, bourgeois democracy has broken down so completely as a social and economic system that increasingly large sections of the population have lost all faith in it. They just don't believe the words any more.

From the viewpoint of the bourgeoisie, this is a very serious matter. "The characteristic of the attitude of the younger generation which most disturbs their elders," said Archibald MacLeish in his famous Association for Adult Education speech last summer, "is their distrust not only of all slogans and tags, but even of all words, their distrust, that is to say, of all statements of principle and conviction, all declarations of moral purpose." MacLeish, who as the Librarian of Congress and the confidante of President Roosevelt is himself not the least securely entrenched of these 'elders,' is quite properly concerned over the impotence today in America of what he calls "The Word." This mystic entity, which he capitalizes throughout, MacLeish seems to conceive of, much as Hitler does, as a sort of medicine man's charm which can *of itself*, regardless of its relationship to reality, sway men to action. To reject The Word as the young men of America are now doing, is "to stand disarmed and helpless before an aggressor whose strength consists precisely in destroying respect for the law, respect for morality and respect for The Word."

Now, of course, Hitler, far from destroying respect for The Word, has exploited it more successfully than any demagogue in history. What MacLeish is really complaining about is that Hitler's Word has shown itself so much more potent than *his* Word as to destroy "respect" for the latter. Hitler has won the youth of Germany, as is well known, by persuading them that fascism offers them what they want from life, that it is worth fighting and dying for. (If respect for The Word is the mark of a healthy society, as MacLeish implies, then Nazi Germany is the high point of civilization.) This is a lie, but it is believed. MacLeish's complaint seems to be that *his*—and Roosevelt's—lies are *not* believed.

●

THESE MAD GERMANS

One way of looking at fascism is as the *systematization* of the brutalities, contradictions and lunacies of monopoly capitalism. (That in the process of systematizing them, the fascists destroy the capitalist system itself—this is another story.) Several years ago, for example, a Nazi economist proposed *planned* depressions: "If there must be crises, then let us have planned and limited crises." He suggested that the disorderly old-fashioned "business cycle" be replaced by "a planned upswing epoch of say thirty years," to be followed by a "sacrificial year" of collapse and ruin. This *annus terribilis* "should be announced at least ten years in advance, to give every one time to prepare for it." His proposal was stillborn, since obviously if the State has enough control over economic forces to *plan* depressions, it can also *prevent* them, which is what seems to have happened in Germany since 1933.

It is significant, however, that such a proposal should have been seriously made. The Nazis are true Germans in this remorseless application of system to the irrational as well as to the rational. Before Hitler and Goebbels went to work, who would have thought that anti-Semitism, crudest and most primitive of cultural hangovers from the middle ages, could become the State doctrine of the most advanced industrial nation of Europe? There is a touch of the paranoiac, with his systematized delusions, in this, and it is not surprising that the unsystematic Anglo-Saxon nations have long regarded the Germans as not wholly sane. When the liberal weeklies depict Hitler as a madman, they are carrying on a long tradition. Disraeli denounced "the fifty mad professors at Frankfurt," Palmerston called Bismarck "the crazy minister at Berlin," and Lord Salisbury was sure that Wilhelm II "must be a little off his head." Actually, the lunacy lies deep in the economic and social system of modern monopoly capitalism, and the Germans are guilty merely of doing consciously and systematically what other imperialist nations do under cover of a smokescreen of hypocrisy. But, of course, every one is shocked when the fig leaf is dropped.

Thus it is with the greatest of all the lunacies of modern capitalism: the fact that its only perspective is mass slaughter and devastation. As every one knows, the Nazis began building their war economy ("wehrwirtschaft") long before the fall of 1939; for the last four years, the one aim of their entire system has been preparation for war. Today, too late, the democracies are coming to understand that efficient warmaking is the only important activity of modern capitalism. The Germans understood this years ago, and proceeded to organize on a vast scale and with the utmost scientific efficiency the apparatus for destruction.

THE RATIONALIZATION OF DESTRUCTION

In their military tactics, also, the Germans, with that method and thoroughness and lack of all taste and proportion which is the maddening thing about them, have simply dared to carry out the logic of imperialist warfare.* The object of warfare, they reasoned in their earnest Teutonic way, is to demoralize and destroy the enemy. Therefore, in addition to the usual technology, the Nazi general staff devised such refinements as air bombs with terrifying sirens attached to them, the use of refugees as an instrument of war (forcing or decoying them onto the roads so as to block enemy troop movements, and often, to insure traffic jams, later machinegunning them from the air), parachute troops who landed dressed as peasants, motorists, enemy officers, even priests and nuns, and the whole fantastic "fifth column" technique of spreading confusion and despair behind the enemy lines.

Such methods were used in the most deliberate, purposeful way. These were no hordes of Mongols, lusting for destruction, but rather the highly trained employees of the firm of A. Hitler & Co., specialists in war. It is significant that there are no atrocity stories in this war, no tales of rape and looting. On the contrary, all reports stress the extraordinarily "correct" behavior of the German soldiery. When the Nazi troops entered Paris, they strolled about the city gaping at the sights, guide book in hand, like so many quiet, sober workmen on a cultural holiday. The "Strength through Joy" organization was ready with maps of Paris and sightseeing tours. Descriptions of the organization and methods of the Reichswehr read like the articles *Fortune* prints on manufacturing technique. Destruction has been rationalized, and the business is gone about with the orderly precision of any large-scale industrial process.

This is especially notable in the air force, where destruction is turned on and off like a water tap. Nazi bombers developed such skill that they were able to destroy every building around the cathedral of Rouen without seriously damaging that historic structure—a feat which there are photographs to prove. It was a commonplace of their bombing technique in the Low Countries to bomb not roads and streets, thus impeding the advance of their own troops later on, but rather objects alongside the roads, so that whole towns would be levelled to dust without a single bomb crater in the streets.

But the showpiece of the *luftwaffe* was the destruction, between the hours of 12 and 2:30 on the afternoon of May 14, of the central district of Rotterdam. The *luftwaffe* demonstrated its virtuosity by localizing all the destruction in a sharply defined area of two and a half square miles. In presenting pictures of the results, *Life* (September 9) states: "By 2:30 some 26,000 buildings were in ruins. The sewer pipes, the water mains, the canal machinery had been smashed. The falling wreckage had trapped

---

*Lest I be accused of overemphasizing racial traits, I hasten to add that the Nazi military triumph is due also to the fact that the Germans had to face the unworkability of democratic capitalism much sooner than did other nations. The Allied democracies won the last war and had vast resources and colonial empires to draw upon, but the Germans had to grapple with problems of class struggle, of huge productive capacity and inadequate markets, of extreme economic instability. Adversity is a great disciplinarian—and teacher. Nations, like individuals, do more thinking in hard times than in prosperity.

great masses of citizens in their bomb shelters. Either they were drowned by the water or they were roasted alive by the fires set by incendiary bombs. The Germans estimated that only 300 Rotterdammers had been killed. The Dutch knew that more than 25,000 were killed. For seven days they kept finding an average of 1800 bodies a day, after the streets had been cleared of dead. . . . The stink of embers, stagnant water and dead flesh hung over the city for a month." No military purpose was served by the destruction, which took place after the Dutch army had surrendered. It was strictly a demonstration of craftsmanship, planned and executed to impress the citizens of Paris . . . and London.

Chapter Nine
Murti-Bing
Czeslaw Milosz

It was only toward the middle of the twentieth century that the inhabitants of many European countries came, in general unpleasantly, to the realization that their fate could be influenced directly by intricate and abstruse books on philosophy. Their bread, their work, their private lives began to depend on this or that decision in disputes on principles to which, until then, they had never paid any attention. In their eyes, the philosopher had always been a sort of dreamer whose divagations had no effect on reality. The average human being, even if he had once been exposed to it, wrote philosophy off as utterly impractical and useless. Therefore the great intellectual work of the Marxists could easily pass as just one more variation on a sterile pastime. Only a few individuals understood the meaning, causes and probable results of this general indifference.

A curious book appeared in Warsaw in 1932. It was a novel, in two volumes, entitled *Insatiability*. Its auther was Stefan Ignacy Witkiewicz, a painter, writer and philosopher, who had constructed an ontological system akin to the monadology of Leibniz. His book, like his earlier novel, *Farewell to Autumn*, could not hope for a large number of readers. The language used by the author was difficult, full of his own neologisms. Brutal descriptions of erotic scenes alternated with whole pages of discussions on Husserl, Carnap and other contemporary ontologists. Besides, one could not always tell whether

Blood flowed freely in Europe during the religious wars; and he who joins the New Faith today is paying off the debt of that European tradition. We are concerned here with more significant questions than mere force.

I shall try to speak of the profound longings in a man as if one really could analyze the essence of his blood and flesh. If I should try to describe the reasons why a man becomes a revolutionary I would be neither eloquent enough nor restrained enough. I admit that I have too much admiration for those who fight evil, whether their choice of ends and means be right or wrong. I draw the line, however, at those intellectuals who *adapt* themselves, although the fact that they are adapted and not genuine revolutionaries in no way diminishes their newly acquired zeal and enthusiasm.

There are, I believe, a few key concepts which may lead us to understand why men accept Murti-Bing.

The society portrayed by Witkiewicz is distinguished by the fact that religion has ceased to exist as a force. Religion long ago lost its hold on men's minds not only in the popular democracies, but elsewhere as well. As long as a society's best minds were occupied by theological questions, it was possible to speak of a given religion as the way of thinking of the whole social organism. All the matters which most actively concerned the people were referred to it and discussed in its terms. But that belongs to a dying era. We have come by easy stages to a lack of a uniform system of thought that could unite the peasant ploughing his field, the student poring over his books, and the mechanic working on an assembly line. Out of this lack arises the painful sense of detachment or abstraction that oppresses those who are the "creators of culture." Religion has been replaced by philosophy, which, however, has strayed into spheres increasingly less accessible to the layman. The discussions of Witkiewicz's heroes about Husserl can scarcely interest a reader of even better than average education; whereas the peasants remained bound to the Church, but only emotionally and traditionally. Music, painting and poetry have become something completely foreign to the great majority of people. To bridge the gap between art and the masses a theory developed that art should become a substitute for religion. "Metaphysical feelings" were to be expressed in the

"compression of pure form"; and so form soon came to dominate content.

The great longing of the "alienated" intellectual is to belong to the masses. It is such a powerful longing that, in trying to appease it, a great many of them who once looked to Germany or Italy for inspiration have now become converted to the New Faith. Actually, the rightist totalitarian program was exceptionally poor. The only gratification it offered came from collective *warmth*: crowds, red faces, shouting, marches, arms outstretched in salute. It was difficult, however, to find rational satisfactions. Neither racist doctrines nor hatred of other nations, nor the glorification of one's own national traditions could efface the feeling that the entire program was improvised to deal with problems of the moment. But Murti-Bing is different. It lays scientific foundations. At the same time, it scraps all vestiges of the past: post-Kantian philosophy, fallen into disrepute because of its remoteness from reality; art designed for those who, having no religion, dare not admit that to seek the "absolute" through a juxtaposition of colors and sounds is cowardly and inconclusive thinking; and the semi-magic, semi-religious mentality of the peasants. All these are replaced by a *single* system, a single language of ideas. The truck driver and elevator operator employed by a publishing firm read the same Marxist classics as its director or staff writers. A day laborer and an historian can reach an understanding on this basis of common reading. Obviously, the difference that may exist between them in mental level is no smaller than that which separated a theologian from a village blacksmith in the Middle Ages. But fundamental principles are universal; the great spiritual schism has been obliterated. Dialectical materialism has united everyone; and philosophy (that is, dialectics) once more determines the patterns of life. It is beginning to be regarded with a respect that one has only for a force on which one's food, happiness and safety depend. The intellectual has once more become *useful*. He, who once devoted himself to his thinking and writing in his free moments away from a paying job in a bank or post office, has now found his rightful place on earth. He has been restored to society. Whereas, the businessmen, aristocrats and tradespeople who once considered him a harmless blunderer have now been dispossessed. They are indeed delighted to find work

as cloak-room attendants and to hold the coat of a former employee of whom they said, in pre-war days, "It seems he writes." We must not oversimplify, however, the gratifications of personal ambition; they are merely the outward and visible signs of social necessity, symbols of a recognition that strengthens the intellectual's feeling of *belonging*.

Even though one seldom speaks about metaphysical motives that can lead to a complete change of one's political opinions, such motives do exist and can be observed in some of the most eminent, most intelligent, and most neurotic people. Let us imagine a spring day in a city situated in some country similar to that described in Witkiewicz's novel. One of his heroes is taking a walk. He is tormented by what we may call the *suction of the absurd*. What is the significance of the lives of the people he passes, of the senseless bustle, the laughter, the pursuit of money, the stupid animal diversions? By using a little intelligence he can easily classify the passers-by according to type; he can guess their social status, their habits and their preoccupations. A fleeting moment reveals their childhood, manhood and old age; and then they vanish. A purely physiological study of one particular passer-by in preference to another is meaningless. Yet if one penetrates into the minds of these people, one discovers utter nonsense. They are totally unaware of the fact that nothing is their own, that everything is part of their historical formation; their occupations, their clothes, their gestures and expressions, their beliefs and ideas. They are the force of inertia personified, victims of the delusion that each individual exists as a self. If at least these were souls, as the Church taught, or the monads of Leibniz! But these beliefs have perished. What remains is an aversion to the domination of the detail, to the mentality that *isolates* every phenomenon, such as eating, drinking, dressing, earning money, fornicating. And what is there beyond these things? Should such a state of affairs continue? Why should it continue? Such questions are almost synonymous with what is known as hatred of the bourgeoisie.

Let a new man arise, one who, instead of submitting to the world, will transform it. Let him create his own historical formation, instead of yielding to its bondage. Only thus can he redeem the absurdity of his physiological existence. Man must be made to understand this, by force and by suffering. Why shouldn't he suffer? He ought to suffer. Why can't he be used as manure, as long as he remains evil and stupid? If the intellectual must know the agony of thought, why should he spare others this pain? Why should he shield those who until now drank, guffawed, gorged themselves, cracked inane jokes and found life beautiful?

The intellectual's eyes twinkle with delight at the persecution of the bourgeois, and of the bourgeois mentality. It is a rich reward for the degradation he felt when he had to be part of the middle class, and when there seemed to be no way out of its cycle of birth and death. Now he has moments of sheer intoxication when he sees the intelligentsia, unaccustomed to rigorously tough thinking, caught in the snare of the revolution. The peasants, burying hoarded gold and listening to foreign broadcasts in the hope that a war will save them from collectivization, certainly have no ally in him. Yet he is warm-hearted and good; he is a friend of mankind. Not mankind as it is, but as it *should* be. He is not unlike the inquisitor of the Middle Ages; but whereas the latter tortured the flesh in the belief that he was saving the individual soul, the intellectual of the New Faith is working for the salvation of the human species in general.

His chief characteristic is his fear of thinking for himself. It is not merely that he is afraid to arrive at dangerous conclusions. His is a fear of sterility, of what Marx called the misery of philosophy. I myself am not entirely free of a like fear as I write these words. Let us admit that a man is no more than an instrument in an orchestra directed by the muse of History. It is only in this context that the notes he produces have any significance. Otherwise even his most brilliant solos become simply a highbrow's diversions. We are not concerned with the question of how one finds the courage to oppose one's self to the majority. It is a much more poignant question that one poses to one's self: can one write well outside that one real stream whose vitality springs from its harmony with historical laws and the dynamics of reality? Rilke's poems may be very good; but if they are good, that means there must have been some reason for them in his day. Contemplative poems, such as his, could never appear in a popular democracy; not only because it would be difficult to publish them, but because the writer's impulse to write them would be destroyed at its very root. The objective conditions for such poetry have disappeared; and the intellectual of whom I speak is not one who believes in writing for the bureau drawer. He curses and despairs over the censorship and demands of the publishing commissions. Yet at the same time, he distrusts profoundly the values of unlicensed literature. The publishing license he himself receives does not mean that the editor appreciates the artistic merits of his book, nor that he expects it to be popular with the public. That license is simply a sign that the author reflects the transformation of reality with scientific exactness. Dialectical materialism in the Stalinist version both reflects and directs this transformation. It creates social and political conditions in which a man ceases to think and write otherwise than as is necessary. He accepts this "must" because nothing worthwhile can exist outside its limits. Herein lie the claws of dialectics. The writer does not surrender to this "must" merely because he fears for his own skin. He fears for something much more precious —the significance of his work. He believes that the by-ways of "philosophizing" lead to a greater or lesser degree of graphomania. Anyone gripped in the claws of dialectics is forced to admit that the thinking of private philosophers, unsupported by citations from authorities, is sheer nonsense. If this is so, then one's total effort must be directed toward following the line, and there is no point at which one can stop. A, which inevitably leads to B, is the first and unnoticed Murti-Bing pill. It is easily swallowed because it comes concealed in the various dishes that constitute the diet of the contemporary intellectual. No untrained mind or barren spirit could ever notice this first, disguised pill. Since I am no philosopher, it is my ambition not to analyze its ingredients, but merely to study its distribution.

The pressure of the state machine is nothing compared with the pressure of a convincing argument. I attended the artists' congresses in Poland in which the theories of Socialist realism were first discussed. The attitude of the audience toward the speakers delivering the required reports was decidedly hostile. Everyone considered Socialist realism to be an officially imposed theory that would have, as Russian art demonstrates, deplorable results. Attempts to provoke discussion failed. The hall remained silent. Usually, however, one daring artist would launch an attack, full of restrained sarcasm, with the silent but obvious support of the entire audience. He would invariably be crushed by superior reasoning plus practicable threats against the future career of an undisciplined individual. Given the conditions of convincing argument plus threats, the necessary conversion will take place. That is mathematically certain.

The faces of the listeners at these congresses were not too legible, for the art of masking one's feelings had already been perfected to a considerable degree. Still one was aware of successive waves of emotion: anger, fear, amazement, distrust, and finally thoughtfulness. I had the impression of participating in a demonstration of mass hypnosis. These people could laugh and joke afterwards in the corridors. But the harpoon had hit its mark; and henceforth wherever they may go, they will always carry it with them. Do I believe that the dialectic of the speakers was unanswerable? Yes, as long as there was no fundamental discussion of methodology. No one among those present was prepared for such a discussion. It would probably have been a debate on Hegel, whose reading public was not made up of painters and writers. Moreover, even if someone had wanted to start such a debate, he would have been silenced. Such discussions are permitted—and even then, fearfully—only in the upper circles of the Party.

These artists' congresses reveal the inequality between the weapons of the dialectician and those of his adversary. A match between the two is like a duel between a foot soldier and a tank. Not that every dialectician is so very intelligent or so very well educated: but all his statements are enriched by the cumulated thought of the masters and their commentators. If every sentence he speaks is compact and precise, that is not due to his own merits, but to those of the classics he has studied. His listeners are defenseless. They could, it is true, resort to arguments derived from their observations of life; but such arguments are just as badly countenanced as any questioning of fundamental methodology. The dialectician rubs up against his public at innumerable meetings of professional organizations and youth groups in clubs, factories, office buildings, and village huts throughout the entire converted area of Europe. And there is no doubt that he emerges the victor in these encounters.

It is no wonder that a writer or painter doubts the wisdom of resistance. If he were sure that art opposed to the official line can have a lasting value, he would not hesitate. He would earn his living through some more menial job within his profession; write or paint in his spare time; and never worry about publishing or exhibiting his work. He believes, however, that in most cases such work would be artistically poor; and he is not too far wrong. As we have already said, the objective conditions he once knew have disappeared. The objective conditions necessary to the realization of a work of art are, as we know, a highly complex phenomenon, involving one's public, the possibility of contact with it, the general atmosphere, and above all freedom from involuntary subjective control.

I can't write as I would like to [a young Polish poet admitted to me]. My own stream of thought has so many tributaries, that I barely succeed in damming off one, when a second, third or fourth overflows. I get halfway through a phrase, and already I submit it to Marxist criticism. I imagine what X or Y will say about it, and I change the ending.

Paradoxical as it may seem, it is this subjective impotence that convinces the intellectual that the one method is right. Everything proves it is right. Dialectics: I predict the house will burn; then I pour gasoline over the stove. The house burns; my prediction is fulfilled. Dialectics: I predict that a work of art incompatible with Socialist realism will be worthless. Then I place the artist in conditions in which such a work *is* worthless. My prediction is fulfilled.

Let us take poetry as an example. Obviously there is poetry of political significance. Lyric poetry is permitted to exist on certain conditions. It must be: (1) serene; (2) free of any elements of thought that might trespass against the universally accepted principles (in practice, this comes down to descriptions of nature and of one's own feelings for friends and family); (3) understandable. Since a poet who is not allowed to *think* automatically tends to perfect his form, he is accused of formalism.

It is not only the literature and painting of the popular democracies that prove to the intellectual that *things cannot be different*. He is strengthened in this belief by the news that seeps through from the West. The Western world is the world of Witkiewicz's novel. The number of its aesthetic and philosophical aberrations is myriad. Disciples imitate disciples; the past imitates the past. This world lives as if there had never been a second World War. Eastern

Europe knows this life; but knows it as a stage of the past that isn't worth looking back on. Even if the new problems are so oppressive that they can break a great many people, at least they are contemporary. And mental discipline and the obligation to be clear are undoubtedly precious. The work of really fine Western scholars and artists escapes notice. The only new names that are known are those of "democrats"—a delicate circumlocution that means one is not dealing with a pagan. In short, the recompense for all pain is the certainty that one belongs to the new and conquering world as its propaganda would have one think.

Mystery shrouds the political moves determined on high, in the distant Center. People speak about prominent figures in hushed voices. In the vast expanses of Euro-Asia, whole nations can vanish without leaving a trace. Armies number into millions. Terror becomes socially useful and effective. Philosophers rule the state—obviously not philosophers in the traditional sense of the word, but dialecticians. The conviction grows that the whole world will be conquered. Great hordes of followers appear on all the continents. Lies are born from seeds of truth. The philosophically uneducated, bourgeois enemy is despised for his inherited inability to think. (Classes condemned by the laws of history perish because their minds are paralyzed.) The boundaries of the Empire move steadily and systematically westward. Unparalleled sums of money are spent on scientific research. One prepares to rule all the people of the earth. Is all this too little? Surely this is enough to fascinate the intellectual. As he beholds these things, historical fatalism takes root in him. In a rare moment of sincerity he may confess cynically, "I bet on this horse. He's good. He'll carry me far."

A delinquent has a hard time, however, when the moment comes for him to swallow Murti-Bing in its *entirety*. He becomes such a nervous wreck, that he may actually fall ill. He knows it means a definite parting with his former self, his former ties and habits. If he is a writer, he cannot hold a pencil in his hand. The whole world seems dark and hopeless. Until now, he paid a minimal tribute: in his articles and novels, he described the evils of capitalist society. But after all, it isn't difficult to criticize capitalism; and it can be done absolutely honestly. The charlatans of the stock exchange, feudal barons, self-deluding artists, and the instigators of nationalistic wars are figures who lend themselves readily to his pen. But now he must begin to *approve*. (In official terminology this is known as a transition from the stage of critical realism to that of Socialist realism. It occurred in the newly established popular democracies about the year 1950.) The operation he must perform on himself is one that some of his friends have already undergone, more or less painfully. They shake their heads sympathetically, knowing the process and its outcome. "I have passed the crisis," they say serenely. "But how he is suffering. He sits at home all day with his head in his hands."

The hardest thing to conquer is his feeling of *guilt*. No matter what his convictions, every man in the countries of which I speak is a part of an ancient civilization. His parents were attached to religion, or at least regarded it with respect. In school, much attention was devoted to his religious upbringing. Some emotional traces of this early training necessarily remain. In any case, he believes that injury to one's fellow man, lies, murder, and the encouragement of hatred are evil, even if they serve to accomplish one's ends. Obviously, too, he studied the history of his country. He read its former poets and philosophers with pleasure and pride. He was proud of its century-long battle to defend its frontiers and of its struggle for independence in the dark periods of foreign occupation. Consciously or unconsciously, he feels a certain loyalty to this history of toil and sacrifice on the part of his forefathers. Moreover, from earliest childhood, he has been taught that his country belongs to a civilization that has been derived from Rome. He has been imbued with the concept that his native land is bound to Europe by ties he should cherish and cultivate. He once parsed Vergil's poetry, learned the history of Dante's life, and laughed at Rabelais' jokes. He tended to consider the centers of this ancient tradition—France, England, Italy—as culturally linked with his own country.

Now, knowing that he must enter a gate through which he can never return, he feels he is doing *something wrong*. He explains to himself that he must destroy this irrational and childish feeling. Only by weeding out the roots of what is irretrievably past, can he become free. Still the battle wages on. A cruel battle—a battle between an angel and a demon. True, but which is the angel; and which, the demon? One has a bright face he has known since his childhood; this must be the angel. No, for this face bears certain hideous scars. It is the face of the old order, of stupid college fraternities, of the senile imbecility of politicians, of the decrepitude of Western Europe. This is death and decadence. The other face is strong and self-contained, the face of a tomorrow that beckons. Angelic? This is doubtful.

There is a great deal of talk about patriotism; about fine, progressive, national traditions; about veneration of the past. But no one is so naive as to take such talk seriously. The reconstruction of a few historical monuments, or the re-edition of the works of former writers cannot change certain revealing and important facts. The country has become a province of the Empire, ruled by edicts from the Center. It retains some autonomy, but to an ever-diminishing degree. Perhaps the era of independent states is over; perhaps they are no more than museum pieces. Yet it is saddening to say good-by to one's dreams of a federation of equal nations, of a United States of Europe in which differing languages and differing cultures would have equal status. It isn't pleasant to surrender to the hegemony of a nation which is still wild and primitive, and to concede the absolute superiority of its customs and institutions, science and technology, literature and art. Must one sacrifice so much in the name of the unity of mankind? The nations of Western Europe will pass through this phase of integration later, and perhaps more gently. It is possible that they will be more successful in preserving their native language and culture. By that time, however, all of Eastern Europe will be using the one universal tongue, Russian. And the principle of a "culture that is national in form, socialist in content" will be consummated in a culture of monolithic uniformity. Everything will be shaped by the Center; though individual countries will retain a few local ornaments in the way of folklore. The Universal City will be realized when a son of the Kirghiz steppes waters his horses in the Loire, and a Sicilian peasant plants cotton in Turkomen valleys. Small wonder the writer smiles at propaganda that cries for a freeing of colonies from the grasp of imperialistic powers. O how cunning dialectics can be, and how artfully it can accomplish its ends, degree by degree!

How bitter all this is. But what about the harbinger of the

Springtime of Nations; and Karl Marx; and the visions of the brotherhood of mankind? After all, nothing can be accomplished without the iron rule of a single Master. And what about this Master? A great Polish poet, describing his journey to the East—where he went in 1824 as a political prisoner of the Tsar—compared the soul of the Russian nation to a chrysalis. He wondered anxiously what would emerge when the sun of freedom shone: "Then will a shining butterfly take flight, or a moth, a somber creature of the night?" So far, nothing prophesies a joyous butterfly.

The writer, in his fury and frustration, turns his thought to Western Communists. What fools they are. He can forgive their oratory if it is necessary as propaganda. But they believe most of what they proclaim about the sacred Center; and that is unforgivable. Nothing can compare to the contempt he feels for these sentimental fools.

Nevertheless, despite his resistance and despair, the crisis approaches. It can come in the middle of the night, at his breakfast table, or on the street. It comes with a metallic click as of engaged gears. *But there is no other way.* That much is clear. There is no other salvation on the face of the earth. This revelation lasts a second; but from that second on the patient begins to recover. For the first time in a long while he eats with relish; his movements take on vigor; his color returns. He sits down and writes a "positive" article, marveling at the ease with which he writes it. In the last analysis there was no reason for raising such a fuss. Everything is in order. He is past the "crisis."

He does not emerge unscathed, however. The after-effects manifest themselves in a particular kind of extinguishment, that is often perceptible in the twist of his lips. His face expresses the peaceful sadness of one who has tasted the fruit from the tree of the knowledge of good and evil; of one who knows he lies; of one who feels compassion for those who have been spared full knowledge. He has already gone through what still awaits so many others.

In 1945, an eminent Soviet journalist came to Poland. He was an elderly gentleman, who looked like a middle-class lawyer. That he was an extremely clever and completely unscrupulous person was evidenced by the tenacity with which he had maintained his position—and by his advanced years. After his return to Warsaw from a tour of several provincial Polish towns, he laughingly recounted an incident that had occurred in Silesia. Someone had spread the report that a delegation of foreigners from the West had arrived. The journalist (whose round belly and honest expression were inducive to such effusive manifestations of confidence) was seized and embraced on the street by a man crying "The English have come!" "That's just how it was in the Ukraine in 1919" was his comment on the incident. This recurrence of sterile hopes amused him and he was flattered to be the representative of a country ruled according to infallible predictions; for nation after nation had indeed become part of its Empire, according to schedule. I am not sure that there wasn't in his smile something of the compassionate *superiority* that a housewife feels for a mouse caught in her trap.

The "post-crisis" writer may well expect one day to be sent on a similar journalistic mission to some newly acquired western country. Such a prospect is not altogether distasteful. To observe people who know nothing, who still have everything to learn, must undoubtedly afford moments of unadulterated sweetness. The master knows that the trap in which the mouse has been caught is not an entirely agreeable place in which to live. For the moment, however, the citizens of these newly converted countries will understand little of their new situation. They will be exhilarated at first by the flutter of national banners, the blare of marching bands, and the proclamations of long-awaited reforms. Only he, the observer, will see into the future like a god, and know it to be hard, necessarily hard, for such are the laws of History.

In the epilogue of Witkiewicz's novel, his heroes, who have gone over to the service of Murti-Bing, become schizophrenics. The events of today bear out his vision, even in this detail. One can survive the "crisis" and function perfectly, writing or painting as one must; but the old moral and aesthetic standards continue to exist on some deep inner plane. Out of this arises a split within the individual that makes for many difficulties in the daily life of popular democracies. It facilitates the task of ferreting out heretical thoughts and inclinations; for, thanks to it, the Murti-Bingist can feel himself into his opponent with great acuteness. *The new phase and the old phase* are co-existent in him; and together they render him an experienced psychologist, a keeper of his brother's conscience.

One can expect that the new generation, raised from the start in the new society, will be free of this split. But that cannot be brought about quickly. One would have to rid one's self completely of the Church, which is a difficult matter, and one that demands patience and tact. And even if one could eliminate this reverenced mainstay of irrational impulses, national literatures would remain to exert their malignant influence. For example, the works of the greatest Polish poets are marked by a dislike of Russia; and the dose of Catholic philosophy one finds in them is alarming. Yet the state must publish certain of these poets and must teach them in its schools for they are the classics, the creators of the literary language, and are considered to be the forerunners of the Revolution. To place them on the index would be to think non-dialectically and to fall into the sin of "leftism." It is a difficult dilemma, more difficult in the converted countries than in the Center, where the identification of national culture with the interests of humanity has been achieved to a much greater degree. (But trouble exists even there, for its youth, despite sensible persuasion, insists upon reading Dostoevsky.) Probably, therefore, the schizophrenic as a type will not disappear in the near future.

Someone might contend that Murti-Bing is a medicine that is incompatible with human nature. That is not a very strong argument. The Aztecs' custom of offering human sacrifices to their gods or the mortification of their own flesh practiced by the hermits in the early centuries of Christianity scarcely seem praiseworthy. Yet they were practiced successfully. The worship of gold has become a motive power second to none in its brutality. Seen from this perspective, Murti-Bing does not violate the nature of human kind.

Whether a man who has taken the Murti-Bing cure attains internal peace and harmony is another question. He attains a relative degree of harmony, just enough to render him active. It is preferable to the torment of pointless rebellion and groundless hope. The peasants, who are incorrigible in their petty-bourgeois attachments, assert that "a change must come, because *this can't go on.*" This is an amusing belief in the natural order of things. A tourist, as an anecdote tells us, wanted to go up into the mountains; but it had been raining for a week. He met a mountaineer walking by a stream, and asked him if it would continue to pour. The mountaineer looked at the swelling stream and voiced the opinion that it would not. When asked on what basis he had made his prediction, he said "Because it would overflow." Murti-Bing holds such magic judgments to be fossil remains of a past era. The "new" is striving to overcome the "old," but the "old" cannot be eliminated all at once.

The one thing that seems to deny the flawlessness of Murti-Bing is the apathy that is born in people, and that continues to live in spite of their feverish activity. It is hard to define; and at times one might suppose it to be a mere optical illusion. In the last analysis, people bestir themselves, work, go to the theater, applaud speakers, take excursions, fall in love, and have children. Yet there is something impalpable and unpleasant in the human climate of such cities as Warsaw or Prague. The collective atmosphere, resulting from an exchange and a re-combination of individual elements, is bad. It is an aura of strength and unhappiness, of internal paralysis and external mobility. Whatever we may call it, this much is certain: if Hell should guarantee its lodgers magnificent quarters, beautiful clothes, the tastiest food and all possible amusements, but condemn them to breathe in this aura forever, that would be punishment enough. No propaganda, either pro or con, can capture so elusive and little-known a phenomenon. It escapes all calculations. It cannot exist on paper. Admitting, in a whispered conversation, that something of the sort does exist, one must seek a rational explanation for it. Undoubtedly the "old," fearful and oppressed, is taking its vengeance by spilling forth its inky fluid like a wounded octopus. But surely the Socialist organism, in its growth toward a future of guaranteed prosperity, is already strong enough to counteract this poison; or perhaps it is too early for that. When the younger generation, free from the malevolent influence of the "old," arises, everything will change. Only, whoever has observed the younger generation in the Center is reluctant to cast such a horoscope. Then we must postpone our hopes to the remote future, to a time when the Center and every dependent state will supply its citizens with refrigerators and automobiles, with white bread and a handsome ration of butter. Maybe then, at last, they will be satisfied.

Why won't the equation work out as it should, when every step is logical? Do we have to use non-Euclidean geometry on material as adaptable and plastic as a human being? Won't the ordinary variety satisfy them? What in the hell does a man need?

(Translated by Jane Zielonko)

Radical Questions and the American Intellectual: Introductory Note

It is now just about fifteen years since the following essay was written and, of course, in some respects and at certain points it has "dated." How could it not? I have never thought of myself as someone who writes for the ages; it is hard enough to write for one's moment. Since this essay first appeared in *Partisan Review* in 1966 we have had the partial breakup, certainly a serious crisis, of the welfare state and, to mention a more paltry matter, the rise of neoconservative ideology among American intellectuals. Reading this essay over again, I felt tempted to note an amendment here, a change there, and of course the usual reconsiderations which time prompts. But that would be foolish. I must let it stand, as testimony, for whatever it may be worth, to its own moment.

Irving Howe

Chapter Ten
Radical Questions
and the American Intellectual
Irving Howe

Suppose we were to ask ourselves, "What have been the decisive trends in American intellectual life these past few decades?" The answer, I think, would have to include some of the following:

The disintegration of Marxism as a frequently accepted mode of social analysis and subsequent efforts to patch together surrogate ideologies or, finding virtue in necessity, to dispense with ideology entirely.

Even those intellectuals who were never under the sway of Marxism have been strongly affected by its crisis and collapse, both as a system of politics and an encompassing Weltanschauung. At least part of what has happened among our intellectuals these past twenty-five years can be regarded as the result of the loss or abandonment of a powerful sustaining belief: one that, in its psychological dynamics, operated as a variety of religious experience. Future historians of ideas are likely to see this experience as similar in consequence—in pain, disorientation and a series of brilliant reactive improvisations— to the experience of those mid-nineteenth-century English writers who broke away from orthodox Christianity yet could not rid themselves of a yearning for transcendence. A whole generation has been marked, often marred, by the deflation of the revolutionary mystique. Some intellectuals have, in fact, been so thoroughly captive to a nostalgia for apocalypse that they have failed to respond to the urgencies of political life today. Others have conducted a frantic search for a substitute "proletariat," ranging from hipsters to the alienated underclass, that might provide a new motor for social energy. Still others have settled into political empiricism, content to work within the limits of "the given."

While it seems to me almost impossible for a man of critical intelligence to retain belief in such crucial aspects of political Marxism as the "revolutionary potential" of the working class, the "withering away" of the state and the "dictatorship of the proletariat," we must acknowledge that the Marxist heritage, no doubt shaping our thought in more ways than we know, remains powerful, and that the Marxist method, especially if it becomes absorbed with a minimum of self-consciousness into a larger style of thought, can still be valuable in sharpening the issues of political debate.

A considerable change in the social status, economic condition and prestige ranking of the intellectuals as a group.

The intellectuals can no longer be said to live beyond the margin or within the crevices of society. Those who continue in bohemian poverty must often choose to remain there. The honorific role accorded the intellectuals under the Kennedy administration was merely a symbolic climax to a process long under way—a process bringing to a virtual end that condition of psychic displacement and political estrangement which had first begun in the early or mid-nineteenth century. Today the intellectuals are, as a rule, firmly entrenched within the society: as academicians in a growing university system; as middlemen whose skills are exploited, while their tastes are violated, in the industries of cultural entertainment; as members of a slowly cohering elite within or near the government. The term "Establishment" has been used with a comic recklessness in the last few years, mostly as a "put down" of those unfortunate enough to be over thirty, regularly employed and addicted to suits and shaving; but for the first time we are perhaps beginning to have in the United States the kind of coherent and influential formation of intellectuals which in England is called "the Establishment."

The Cold War has shaped—I would say, mostly mis-shaped—intellectual life to a very large, though unmeasured, extent.

It requires an effort to remember the atmosphere in this country during the early fifties. A good many intellectuals formerly on the Left were engaged in a flight to conservatism that was as ungainly as it was premature. Seriously entertained, conservatism can be a respectable point of view; but the sour hostility toward their own past, the frantic pursuit of intellectual "novelties," the barely disguised contempt for freedom which some ex-radical intellectuals showed in their devotion to the Cold War—all this was a good deal worse than conservatism. Do I exaggerate in saying that for the ex-radical intellectuals there was a steady need to depreciate the menace of Senator McCarthy's hooliganism, and that what really mattered was a kind of *union sacrée* in behalf of "anti-Communism"? Or that under the tranquilizing influence of a new affection for the American system, social problems were regarded as largely solved or, in more exalted moments, as symptoms of that impulse toward evil forever lodged in the human soul?

An increasing tendency toward and an implicit acceptance of intellectual specialization, what might be called the "privatization of work," so that the very idea of the intellectual vocation has come into question.

We are all familiar with the troubled inquiries as to whether the intellectual as a distinct type is likely to survive in an increasingly managerial and technological society. We are also familiar with privately voiced complaints—some may reflect no more than the sourness of people getting older, but some are a recognition of painful truth—that among younger writers these days there is no shortage of talent, energy or ambition, but rarely evidence of that freewheeling and "dilettantish" concern with general ideas which we take to be characteristic of the intellectual life. No one supposes that in any future society intellectual work can possibly cease; what is at stake is whether such work can be broken down into a series of discrete and specialized functions, so that the larger animating concerns with values and ideals may gradually (or at least sooner than the state) wither away. What in some accounts is said to have happened to modern philosophy, seems a possible terminus for the life of the intellectual as an historical type.

Criticism of social institutions has in the last few decades been increasingly appropriated by journalists who combine useful exposé with a lack of fundamental theory and/or values.

Much of the muckraking—the attack upon specific deformations and failures of the welfare state which appeared during the fifties and early sixties—was composed by journalists with little grasp of what their material signified and with an inclination to transform their exposures into mere amusements for middlebrow readers. The intellectuals, having virtually ceded this area of work, largely confined themselves to criticizing the superficiality and vulgarity of such journalism, without recognizing that their own abdication was in part responsible for its influence.

Moods and theories of political resignation, and sometimes assertions as to the inherent recalcitrance of social problems, became frequent among the older or more sophisticated intellectuals.

The welfare society throws up certain kinds of social troubles which cannot be as precisely delineated—nor can solutions be as confidently proposed—as we felt it possible to do for the economic problems of a few decades ago. These new social troubles seem so endemic and pervasive, so much a matter of tone, atmosphere and malaise, that an impression grows up that neither revolution nor reform, and not even social engineering, can significantly affect them. And some intellectuals proclaimed during the fifties what was presumably never known before: that solutions to problems engender further problems; there is no end to the chain. All of this reflected a decrease of confidence in the powers of human reason, and a growing doubt as to the uses of human will.

One of the main avenues for intellectual activity and self-assertiveness—our common opposition to the products, the very idea of "mass culture"—has recently been little taken.

Not that intellectuals became noticeably slacker in their critical standards or less contemptuous of popular trash. The problem is rather that, almost unwittingly, they resigned themselves to the supposedly intractable evils of "mass culture," just as some have learned to resign themselves to the supposedly intractable evils of society in general—or (in a response to which I am more sympathetic) they became weary with the Sisyphean task of cultural hygiene. The once numerous and, up to a point, fruitful discussions of "mass culture" have by now almost disappeared from the serious journals. And in truth the problems connected with "mass culture" have become more slippery than they were, or seemed, a few decades ago. It is increasingly difficult, in that no-man's-land where the middlebrow abuts upon the serious, to draw a line between the authentic and a skillful simulation of the authentic. The theoretical analyses of "mass culture" begun in the thirties and forties have run into a dead end, and none of them seems fully applicable at the present moment. The militant zeal of the critics of "mass culture" has cooled; a few find themselves quite at home in the atmosphere and institutions they were among the first to attack. And meanwhile, perhaps in consequence, there has arisen a new school of sensibility which denies the relevance of esthetic discrimination, insisting that the Beatles are as "good" or "important" as Stravinsky, and priding itself upon a capacity to submit to every variety of cultural or pseudo-cultural experience.

The last few decades have been characterized by a quick, often facile, sometimes exciting shift in cultural fashions; by a quantity of stylistic and temperamental display; and by a drive toward personal distinction as an end in itself, such as must surely always be present in intellectual life but has seemed especially strong since the end of the war.

At no point in the life of American intellectuals during the twentieth century has the *idea* of an intellectual community been weaker than it is today. Yet at no point has the life of the intellectuals been more clearly or fully structured into a compact, miniature society than it is today.

The picture is bleak, but in the last few years there have been changes, though not yet changes strong enough to reverse the general drift of American intellectual life. People seem more inclined to question and speculate than they were ten years ago; radicalism, as a mood if not a movement, is beginning to revive; at the very least, we are done with the suffocating complacency of the fifties. Poverty was then mentioned nowhere but in the radical press; today it has become a theme for national discussion, if not yet sufficient national action. A decade ago, merely to suggest that there was a problem of power in the United States—a concentration of resources, wealth and "decision-making" which undercuts the formal claims of democracy—would call down scorn for clinging to "Marxist clichés"; today the matter is seriously discussed even among moderate analysts. In the fifties American foreign policy met with little sustained criticism; now a portion of the academic world is pressing its criticisms with great vigor. Why this shift in political and intellectual attitudes? A few reasons can be suggested:

• The Cold War has largely run its course. That Western Europe has been stabilized on a more or less democratic basis is certainly a major achievement; otherwise, the record of the West in the Cold War is largely one of sterility. The inadequacies of Western power, especially in regard to areas like Latin America, have become clear; and it will not do simply to keep repeating the anti-Communist catchwords of a decade ago.

• It seems likely that we shall not soon be plunged into a nuclear war through the deliberate choice of one or both of the major powers. At least a partial relaxation can therefore begin, as a result of which new problems, not accessible to Cold War politics, can come to the forefront.

• It is increasingly hard to maintain that American society has reached a state of health so complete that little more than marginal problems remain to be solved—and those (as Arthur Schlesinger, Jr. suggested a few years ago) having less to do with gross exploitations than with psychological disturbances and esthetic needs.

• While a sharp distinction between democratic and totalitarian values remains a moral imperative, the view of the world as polarized between extremes of good and evil, "we" and "they," becomes increasingly tiresome.

• In the United States the civil rights movement has had a substantial liberating effect, not merely in gaining victories for the Negroes and in providing the idealistic young with opportunities for activity and sacrifice, but also in opening up the country to fresh moods and sentiments.

• The Kennedy administration, more through its civilized tone than actual achievements, helped clear the air of McCarthyite fumes and brought to national consciousness at least the possibility of further social advance.

• The ideological, or what may come to the same thing, the anti-ideological zealousness characterizing a good part of the intellectual world in the early fifties was bound to exhaust itself. Just as after the crude Marxism of the thirties, there has followed a period of sobering second thoughts.

Nevertheless, the truth is that radical criticism remains scattered, limited in impact, uncertain as to intention, ill-developed in program and confined to a very few writers. Suppose, however, there were or could be such a criticism. To what order of problems would it address itself?

The Function of Criticism in the Welfare State

The welfare state preserves the essential character of capitalist economy, in that the interplay of private or corporate owners in the free market remains dominant; but it modifies the workings of that economy, in that the powers of free disposal by property owners are regulated and controlled by political organs. A more detailed description of the welfare state as a static "model" is provided by Henry Pachter:

> The welfare state is a capitalistic economy which largely depends on the free market but in which the countervailing powers have been politicized and are consciously employed to balance the economy, to develop the national resources or to pursue fixed goals of social policy. . . . The fully developed welfare state has at its disposal a wide range of economic instruments, classical as well as Keynesian and statist. . . . The welfare state may achieve techniques of industry-wide planning, price-fixing and over-all control of development, but though it will nationalize the coal industry in France and England, erect a TVA in the United States and build a government steel mill for India, it stops short of expropriation. On the contrary, its proclaimed aim is to preserve the structure of property and to protect the formation of a free market. Whatever expropriating is to be done must come through the free play of the market, as is being done, e.g. in our farm economy despite price supports. The basic relationships of buyer and seller, employer and employee, owner and non-owner are no different from those prevailing under pure capitalism, but they are supplemented by state interference in two important areas: where classical capitalism is indifferent to the distribution of income, the welfare state at least tries to make income differentials less steep; also, whereas under pure capitalism the development of resources is but an accidental by-product of the profit incentive, the welfare state sets itself definite goals of developing public and private facilities. . . .

> . . . We should not be misled by its efforts to plan, regulate and control production, to redistribute income and to curb the un-

inhibited use of private property. At the hub of its mechanics, it is different from socialism. Though some prices and wages are determined politically, on the whole they are still determined by the market, and that is true even of the public enterprises; the regime of property prevails throughout, with the dead weight of past investments burdening the calculation of profit and the decisions on future investments, with at least a theoretical obligation to balance all budgets, and with remuneration still tightly ruled by a man's contribution to the value of the product. Public projects still need to be justified in terms of national policy rather than human needs, and expenditure for defense and similar competitive purposes still exceeds the welfare expenditure.

What this excellent description does not claim to provide is any sense of the way in which the welfare state tends to be open-ended at both sides, the way—within limits that need not be rigidly fixed in advance—the welfare state is an algebraic container that can be filled with the arithmetic of varying socio-political contents. Nor does it provide a sense of the welfare state as the outcome, not necessarily a "final" one, of prolonged social struggle to modulate and humanize capitalist society. It would be hard, perhaps impossible, to say to what extent the welfare state is the result of a deliberate intent to stabilize capitalist society from above, so that it will avoid breakdown and revolutionary crises; to what extent it is the outcome of relatively autonomous economic processes; and to what extent it is the partially realized triumph in the struggle of masses of men to satisfy their desires. As against those intellectuals who feel the major need for the immediate future to be a benevolent social engineering and those who see the welfare state as a device for maintaining, through diversions and concessions, the traditional forms of economic power, I would stress the idea that welfarism represents, both in achievements and potential, a conquest that has been *wrested* by the labor, socialist and liberal movements.

For radical intellectuals the welfare state presents a set of new difficulties. The bulk of the intellectuals, to be sure, have adapted only too easily to its comforts and inducements; a society with an enormously expanded need for administrators, teachers and cultural agents can offer position and prestige to intellectuals. But for those of us who wish to preserve a stance of criticism while avoiding the sterility of total estrangement, the welfare state has been an unsettling experience. Here are some of the characteristic responses of leftist intellectuals in the past few decades:

• *A feeling that the high drama (actually, the vicarious excitement) of earlier Marxist or "revolutionary" politics has been lost, and that in the relatively trivial struggles for a division of social wealth and power within a stable order there is neither much room nor need for intellectual activity.* By now, this response is simply tiresome. The snobbism of nostalgia can easily decline into a snobbism of abstention; but those who care to act within history as it is, no matter in how modest a way, must accept the possibilities of today in order to transform those of tomorrow.

• *A belief that the welfare state will, in effect, remain stable and basically unchanged into the indefinite future; that conflict will be contained within the limits prescribed by the welfare state; and that the problems of technique (e.g., how to administer a poverty program, how to retrain workers left jobless by automation) will supersede the "irresponsible" tradition of fundamental criticism.* By accepting the "givenness" not merely of the welfare state but also of its present forms and boundaries, this view underestimates the value of basic moral-political criticism. To cite a simple example: is the shameful failure to tear down the vast slum called Harlem due to difficulties in technique and administration or is it due to moral indifference, social timidity and racial meanness? Another example: whether poverty can be entirely abolished within the present society is not so much a matter for analysis or speculation as for experiment and action. Such an effort might well require a radical restructuring of the welfare state to include a large program of public works, a degree of economic planning and a new allotment of social resources; and what keeps it from being enacted is not so much difficulties in execution as a failure of social will, responsibility and imagination. If I am right in saying this, the traditional responses of the intellectual—even if these are dismissed in certain quarters as utopian, impractical, etc.—remain quite as necessary as in the past. It might be maintained that even for new proposals to alleviate social troubles within the present society a degree of utopian perspective and intellectual distance is required. For essential to such alleviation is a continued extension of the idea of the practical. One need not agree with Paul Goodman's general outlook or his schemes for social improvement in order to recognize that his recent utopian writings may have a more practical effect than the routinism and blundering of the practical men—and precisely because his writings are, in the current sense of things, less "practical."

• *A belief that the welfare state is characteristic of all forms of advanced industrial society; that it offers bread and television, palliatives and opiates, to disarm all potential opposition; and that it thereby perpetuates, more subtly but more insidiously than in the past, class domination.* Such views have recently become popular in academic circles which in part are profiting from those struggles of yesterday that made possible the advantages of today. Despite their seeming intransigence, these views strike me as essentially conservative—they lead to passivity, not action—and inhumane—they ignore, or minimize, the improvements in the immediate life-conditions of millions of human beings. Ignore or minimize, above all, the fact that the welfare state has meant that large numbers of working-class people are no longer ill-fed, ill-clothed and insecure, certainly not to the extent they once were. That automobile workers in Detroit can today earn a modest, if insufficient, income; that through union intervention they have some, if not enough, control over their work conditions; that they can expect pensions which are inadequate yet far better than anything they could have expected twenty years ago—all this is *good*: politically, socially, in the simplest human terms. To dismiss or minimize this enormous achievement on the lordly grounds that such workers remain "alienated" and show little awareness of their plight, is to allow ideology to destroy human sympathy.

Concerning these matters I want to quote some cogent remarks from the English writer Alisdair MacIntyre:

> It was only gradually that people in Britain became conscious of themselves as living in a society where a right to minimal standards of welfare was presupposed. . . . Even a modern affluent working class, even a working class with a socialist tradition . . . has to learn that the welfare state is *essentially a realm of conflict* in which the real benefits of welfare are always in danger of being undermined by defense spending, by the encroachments of private interests, or simply by inflation, and thus a realm in which it needs a good deal of running even to keep standing in the same place. So a working-class political

self-consciousness about welfare as a point at which elementary rights have continually to be reclaimed seems to be one of the preconditions of the maintenance of welfare in an advanced capitalist society. . . .

The problem of a politics that goes further than this is partly the problem of a working class that sixty years ago had to set itself the goals of welfare and now has to find for itself new political goals. . . .

In contrast to these three attitudes toward the welfare state, let me suggest the following position. The struggles and issues raised within the welfare state are real, not mere diversionary shadow plays or trivial squabbles. They matter. They affect the lives of millions. Regardless of how mundane or inadequate the "level of consciousness" at which they are conducted, the struggles for social betterment within the welfare state merit our concern and involvement.

No magical solution is available for the problems faced by American radicals; if there were, someone would by now have discovered it. I am myself committed to the "coalition" approach suggested by Bayard Rustin and Michael Harrington: it proposes a loose and intermittent association of the major "progressive" forces in the country—labor, Negro, liberal, church groups, intellectuals, students—in order to work for current and intermediate goals. Socialism not being an immediate option, it is necessary for radicals, while continuing to speak for their views in full, also to try to energize those forces that are prepared to stretch the limits of the welfare state. Such a dynamic once set in motion, there may be possibilities for going still further; but any political approach that dismisses movements embodying the hard-won victories of yesterday, must doom itself to sectarian isolation today.

This strategy has many difficulties, not the least being that it isn't very dramatic. For young people who have just "made it" into radicalism, it sometimes seems insufficiently radical. But radicalism is neither a quantity nor a measure of purity and rectitude; it is a political outlook, and if a rough adaptation of Fabianism is a possibility, then we must seize upon it.

One reason for this political stress has been suggested by Meyer Schapiro: that American society is now significantly different from what it was thirty years ago, in that it formally accepts the values of social welfare, yet frequently does not work to realize those values. Among the consequences of this disparity between norm and reality are: the more complacent liberals feel, though they do not quite say, that there really are not many short-range goals still to be reached; the left-liberals have not succeeded, nor perhaps tried, to work out a clear program of immediate objectives such as they had a few decades ago; and the impression grows that problems are insoluble, or that those who claim to be solving them are mere hypocrites, etc.

Carey McWilliams has listed immediate problems for which the answer is *more* (welfare measures) and those for which the answer is *new* (automation, allocating national resources); his catalog is worth noticing if only to remind ourselves of the urgency of the obvious:

> Is a "great society" one that, on an ever larger scale, continues to despoil the environment? Are present budget priorities really designed to produce a "great society" or a caricature of one? Can we continue to guide our foreign policy with compulsive slogans: "anti-communism," "containment," "the free world"? How is the scale of the military budget to be determined? How is a policy of reconversion to be brought about? How should resources be allocated? Should we plan and for what? How do we propose to cope with the consequences of the scientific-technological revolution?

Now there is in our society an occasional effort, more often a half-effort, and sometimes a mere pretense of coping with such problems; but increasingly the result is to blur the issues and discredit the very idea of rational action. What happens more often than not has been pungently described, perhaps overstated a little, by Paul Goodman:

> "Education" means subsidizing schools to train National Science Foundation grade-getters for higher status and salaries in Research and Development, and as professional institutional personnel. "Urban Reconstruction" is the cabal of Washington, city party-bosses, real-estate promoters and automobile manufacturers to destroy neighborhoods and communities. . . . "Agriculture" is the underwriting of chain-grocers and *latifundia*,

pesticides, the eradication of farmers, and the enclosure of the countryside for motels. . . . "Political Economy" is the galloping Gross National Product, stepping up TV advertising, the unchecked aggrandizing of the broadcasting networks . . . and more highways when there are already too many cars. . . .

. . . In the teeth of this magnitude of bucks, one cannot seriously point to the minimum wage of $1.25 (excluding many categories) or 10,000 in the Peace Corps (after three years and $300 million) or the anti-discrimination housing order (applied to a minority of cases). Indeed a good synonym for Liberalism is Tokenism. But where are good neighborhoods, or clean rivers, or rural reconstruction, or liberating education, or an effort to improve the quality of the standard of living, to countervail regimenting and brainwashing? . . . It is insulting to hear these people talk of a Great Society.

Old problems fester and new ones appear, threatening the precarious equilibrium of the welfare state. For the great temptation in thinking about the welfare state is to assume *in effect* what we deny in theory; that it is stable and static. The inner motions of economic development, the heavy impact of technology, the complicating effects of international politics—all disturb, if not dissolve, the seeming fixity of the welfare state. Perhaps the most immediately threatening force is the cybernetic revolution which cuts through technique, management and economy, with some of the following possible repercussions:

• We face the danger of drifting into a society in which there will appear new and fierce class divisions: not so much between owners and workers or even rich and poor, though these will persist, but between various skilled elites living in affluence and a stratum of permanent unemployables, an "underclass" consisting mainly of older workers, the young and the Negroes.

• The power and size of the trade unions seems certain to decline, even if they undertake—which they probably will not—bold steps to meet the new conditions.

• The problem of government intervention in economic life will become a sharper political issue than it has been these past several years.

That such problems, inherently difficult enough, should come to the forefront simultaneously with the upsurge of the American Negroes is something of a tragedy. For automation threatens most severely the jobs that have been traditionally open to Negroes; it intensifies difficulties which, under the best of circumstances, would have been severe enough. (The recently fashionable "leftist" counter-position of "revolution" against "integration" as strategies for the Negro movement fails to take into account the context in which the movement must act: it fails to recognize that to achieve integration, even in the presumably limited terms proposed by Martin Luther King, would indeed *be* a revolution, probably greater in consequence and impact than that effected by the rise of industrial unionism in the thirties.) Bayard Rustin, the most perceptive of the Negro leaders, has remarked upon this problem:

> The civil rights movement, because of its limited success, is now confronted with the problem that major Negro demands cannot be met within the context of the civil rights struggle. The frustration in the Negro community is not merely the result of difficulties in the struggle, but also of the fact that these demands are made in a context where *the Negro alone* is in motion. So that the major problem before us is how to relieve the Negro of this isolation. If there were a democratic left in this country, the Negro movement would be in it along with labor, liberals, and intellectuals and people from the churches.

> But now the Negroes have to deal not only with discrimination but also the problems of the whole society. While many Negroes would not so analyze it, they know in a visceral way that this is true. They know there is really no way to get jobs for Negroes unless something else happens. And they also know, and I know, that the labor movement, affected by automation, is itself unable to provide jobs for the people already enrolled in the unions; that the only way labor can handle this problem is if it allies with the Negro in a bigger struggle in which it can then afford to be an ally because its problems are being simultaneously met. . . . Such an alliance should be programmatic-political: that is, around questions like total employment, limited planning, work training within planning and a public-works program.

There is no easy solution to the dilemma Rustin describes: that the Negro movement is, at least intermittently, more active and alive than its potential allies, but that the socio-economic situation makes it impossible for the movement to achieve its aims short of stirring those potential allies into a bolder action they may resist or refuse. Consequently, within the Negro movement there will be sharper internal strains and factionalism than during the past few years, with some following Rustin's policy, others exhausting themselves in an increasingly desperate activism, and still others straying into an apocalyptic, semi-nationalist "radicalism." For through the very intensity of its work and the defined limits of its success, the civil rights movement dramatizes its own insufficiency. It is a movement desperately in need of political-intellectual help; yet the very situation giving rise to that need also creates intense resistance to any efforts that might satisfy it. Nor, for that matter, is the Negro movement a movement in the traditional sense. It is a loose alliance of organizations, some of them large and with nominal demands upon their members, others composed of full-time elite activists; and, as a result, there are special difficulties in working out programs and strategies. One can barely speak of a Negro political intelligentsia attached to or associated with the movement, who might provide some intellectual substance; indeed, given the kind of advice offered by certain Negro writers, it is perhaps just as well that they are detached from the movement. And it is a further difficulty that the most active, though not necessarily most representative, sectors of the Negro movement are often hostile to liberals and intellectuals, partly for reasons that can be understood if not accepted, but also for perfectly sound reasons: too many liberals and intellectuals, still sunk in the apolitical moods of the fifties, have shown little inclination toward active participation or help.

That the Negro protest movement will emerge from its present state of uncertainty—a condition at least partly the result of its notable victories these past several years—seems quite certain. The very magnitude of the tasks still facing it will be a powerful stimulus to strategic innovation and tactical ingenuity. But the hopes of a few years ago that as a direct consequence of the civil rights struggle there might emerge a larger movement for social radicalism seem unlikely to be fulfilled. Though it has already had a profoundly refreshing and valuable impact upon American society, the Negro movement cannot, by itself, be expected to do what more powerful and numerous segments of the society have neither cared nor been able to.

The alignment of forces within the United States which makes possible a moderate if insufficient progress in domestic affairs simply breaks down when it has to confront foreign policy. For here the issues are ambiguous, complex and charged with emotion, certainly more so than in regard to, say, an education bill; here the psychic smog of the Cold War still hangs across the national horizon. The loose coalition of labor, liberal, Negro, church and minority groups which usually supports welfare measures has no consensus within itself regarding foreign policy— or, perhaps more accurately, a large part of this coalition tends unreflectively to go along with the Johnson administration. Except for a tiny fringe emotionally caught up with charismatic figures abroad, the Negro movement has little to say about Vietnam and the Dominican Republic, and its constituency cares even less. In regard to foreign policy the trade unions are quiescent, ritualistically liberal in one or two instances, and sometimes merely reactionary. Sustained dissent on foreign policy comes only from minority segments of the academic world, small groups of pacifists and some liberals. The result is more impressive for articulateness than mass support.

Yet if one remembers how narrowly based this dissent actually is within the academic and intellectual worlds, one is struck by the moderating effect it has had upon the formation of foreign policy. Certain academics, hand-wringers of alienation, complain that no one listens; I, aware of how few people are complaining, am astonished that anyone does listen. Perhaps this is due to the fact that in a mass society, which may necessarily mean a society in which large portions of the population are politically indifferent and passive, there is always the possibility for aggressive minority groups to exert a disproportionate influence: a fact, if it is one, that should not lead to dancing in the streets, since the results could be quite as disturbing as they are momentarily pleasing. Still another reason may be that the intellectuals occupy a more important place in American politics than they did thirty or forty years ago; they shape opinion in the universities; and the universities, in turn, serve as the training school for the American political elite. From a persistent and thoughtful criticism in the universities there may follow a crisis in morale among sections of this political elite, especially if the country stumbles deeper and deeper into the Vietnam disaster while preparing for itself still greater disasters in Latin America tomorrow.

But let us not delude ourselves. On the issue of foreign policy even these modest hopes for a progressive coalition may be dashed, and on this issue the new academic dissidence may be driven—or may drive itself—into a hopeless isolation. In principle there is no reason why those who oppose the Vietnam war and at least some of those who support it should not be able to cooperate for desirable legislation and action in domestic politics. Between opponents of the war and *some* of its supporters there exists a common interest in not allowing the war to become a pretext for cutting back or refusing to initiate necessary domestic measures. Yet if the war in Vietnam drags on for months and years, with one probable consequence a growing embitterment in political and intellectual life at home, radicals will find it difficult to maintain a balance between coalition on the domestic front and criticism of foreign policy. For in the actuality of experience it is hard to keep clear the distinctions that seem persuasive in the logic of discourse. Whatever hope there is for a new political upsurge in the United States —and by this I mean something more substantial than the outbursts of student rebellion—largely depends on a quick solution to the problem of Vietnam. That is hardly the main reason for wanting to see the war end, but it is a reason.

Otherwise, the consequences could be disastrous, both for the political life of the entire nation, perhaps again infected with a low-charged version of the McCarthyite sickness, and for the still very weak and insecure radicalism that has begun to appear on the campus. There is already a tendency among academic protestors to fall back upon postures of rectitude instead of trying to engage in the far more difficult business of influencing the shape of politics, just as there is a destructive and at times nihilistic fringe in the essentially healthy student protests. But if the war in Vietnam continues, there may in conscience be nothing left for its critics except postures of rectitude and declarations of conscience—partly because of a tightening in the political atmosphere, partly because of righteous misdirection in the protest movement itself. What would then happen? Locked into isolation, academic protest would risk the danger of becoming merely shrill, righteously impotent and foolishly "anti-American"; some would be tempted—disastrously, I think —to see themselves as shock troops of the campus waging a battle of advertisements against U.S. imperialism in a way parallel to the war of bullets waged by Castroite guerrillas in Latin America. And one consequence of such a development could well be a wave of anti-intellectualism in this country, a new attack upon the academy as the reservoir (*the last reservoir*) of sedition. It is a frightful prospect.

There is nevertheless, a growing sentiment of moralistic radicalism, attached to visions of apocalypse and the theory of mass society, which accepts this prospect as virtually inevitable. Among sections of the student Left there also flourish feelings that call into question the viability of politics in the various senses that have been traditional to the Western world. If, as these academic radicals increasingly feel, the major social classes and institutions have, through comfort or corruption, become utterly absorbed into the existing society, then there seems to be no significant social force that can be expected to work toward major change. There follows a desperate search for a "substitute proletariat," located by some among the hipsters, by others among the middle-class students, by still others among the underclass of poverty. And the consequence can only be a strategy of raids, dramatic in character but dubious in impact.

Mass Society, Technology and the Specter of Contentment

The sentiments and feelings to which I have just referred are attached to a political outlook of great importance; its most distinguished spokesman is probably Herbert Marcuse. This theory seems so opposed in tone and spirit to everything I have been saying that if I now suggest that both perspectives—the politics of democratic radicalism I have outlined and the vision of "mass society" I shall now describe—need to be kept in some sort of uneasy and uneven balance, I may open myself to the charge of intellectual schizophrenia. I cheerfully (or, given the subject, gloomily) accept the risk. For there are sharply opposing tendencies and potentialities in Western society; we cannot yet know which will prevail. To say that for a grasp of American society one must simultaneously employ the traditional Marxist analysis of class conflict, the approach I will label "mass society," and a study of competing power groups within a more or less balanced pluralist system—to say this is not necessarily to lapse into an easy eclecticism. It is rather to acknowledge the mixed character of the present reality, and that the various theories, none complete or satisfactory by itself, point to different elements within that reality.

The school of political-social thought associated with the idea of "mass society" singles out the potential in modern industrialism for a drift toward a bureaucratic, non-terrorist and prosperous authoritarianism. Whatever our wish to qualify this kind of theorizing, and whatever our impatience with the grisly fascination some of its proponents seem to take in envisioning a universal passivity, there can be no question that it points to significant realities. Such theories rest upon a number of related assumptions:

• *The alleged automatism of technology.* Jacques Ellul writes as an extreme reductionist:

. . . Because of its proliferation, the technical phenomenon has assumed an independent character quite apart from economic considerations, and . . . it develops according to its own intrinsic laws. Technique has become man's new milieu, replacing his former natural milieu. And just as man's natural environment obeys its own physical, chemical and other laws, our artificial, technical environment is now so constituted that it has also its own laws of organization, development and reproduction. . . .
. . . This view of technique leads me to think that modifications in economic structure, a *detente* in international relations, and improved cooperation among nations will cause practically no change in the technical phenomenon.

And on a somewhat wider plane, Herbert Marcuse writes:

The world tends to become the stuff of total administration, which absorbs even the administrators themselves.

• *The decay of the Western party system.* Though touched upon in many studies, this theme has, to my knowledge, not yet received a definitive statement. It is clear that in most of the Western countries the party system has been steadily drained of content. It survives, in some places, as mere ritual or anachronism, and sometimes as a mechanism for the efficient division of power and spoils among an elite; it no longer reflects, certainly not to the extent that it once did, basic differences of class interest, political allegiance or moral value. Even in those countries where the apparatus of representative democracy survives, it tends to become vestigial, confined to a minority of professionals and of decreasing interest to the mass of citizens. Yet for democrats this party system, even in decline, remains precious, a concrete embodiment of freedoms for which, thus far, no substitute nearly as satisfactory has been found.

• *The satisfaction of material wants tends to undercut the possibility for social transcendence.* Herbert Marcuse writes:

Technical progress, extended to a whole system of domination and coordination, creates forms of life (and of power) which appear to reconcile the forces opposing the system and to defeat or refute all protest in the name of the historical prospects of freedom from toil and domination.

• *There develops, partly in consequence of the above-listed elements, a new kind of society, what we call "mass society."* It is a relatively comfortable, half-welfare and half-garrison society in which the population grows passive, indifferent and atomized; in which "primary groups" tend to disintegrate; in which traditional loyalties, ties and associations become lax or dissolve entirely; in which coherent publics based on definite interests and opinions gradually fall apart; and in which man becomes a consumer, himself mass-produced like the products, diversions and values he absorbs.

When one is involved in concrete political analysis that involves firm and immediate choices, it seems to me both intellectually facile and morally disastrous to affirm an identity between the societies of East and West. Though there is a tendency for the two to move closer together in certain ways, the differences remain enormous and crucial. But if one turns from the immediate political struggle to a kind of speculation about the indefinite future, there may be some reason for anticipating a society ruled by benevolent and modernized Grand Inquisitors, an efficient political-technical elite that will avoid terror and the grosser aspects of totalitarianism, that will perhaps even go through the motions of democracy but in its essential character be thoroughly authoritarian. It would be a society in regard to which Huxley's prophecy would seem more accurate than Orwell's.

If there will not be a war within the next period and a way is found for controlling the birth rate, it becomes possible to envisage a world, at least the part of it that has been industrialized, in which material wants will be moderately satisfied. This possibility arises, not, as radicals once thought, because there is an immediate likelihood that the race will create for itself a free and humane order, but largely because of the sheer cascading growth of technology.

To advance such a speculation at a time when the majority of human beings on our planet still suffer from terrible poverty may seem irrelevant and heartless. It is a speculation which rests on grossly simplified ideas, partly on a technological determinism that cannot be accepted by a sophisticated mind. But I offer it *not* as a prediction, only as a possibility. That this possibility will not be realized in the next several decades seems certain. But it remains worth considering in its own right.

Suppose, then, that the goal of moderate material satisfaction is reached after the next several decades in large areas of the world and in societies that are not socialist and often not democratic. What would the intellectuals say? We may assume that large numbers of ordinary people, fed regularly and diverted by the mass media, would be satisfied. But the intellectuals? Would they still remember or care about the vision of human freedom?

In our time the Grand Inquisitor is no longer a withered Churchman: stern, ascetic, undeluded. He is now a skilled executive who knows how to manage large-scale enterprises and sustain the morale of his employees. In the West he is a corporation official, in the East he is on the Central Committee. He is friendly. And he feeds the hungry. What, then, can one say about this mode of speculation?

• Its main value is as a corrective to the ameliorative optimism (the twentieth-century version of the supposedly discredited nineteenth-century theory of "progress") held by conventional liberals. By this I mean not merely something as obvious yet basic as the fact that our welfarism is deeply tied in with a steadily burgeoning militarism and would face a severe crisis if the prop of "defense spending" were removed. I mean also the fact that a serious radical politics must seek not merely for the extension of welfarism but for controls to check the accompanying bureaucratic expansion; must concern itself not merely with what happens to or is done for people, but with their capacities toward self-assertion and autonomy.

• That there have been in recent years outbursts of political activity on the campus and in the civil rights movement does not in itself invalidate the "mass society" prognosis. The Negro demands are, after all, largely concerned with the kinds of issues that could and should have been settled before "mass society" was imagined. The student rebelliousness may be no more than the futile effort of a small minority to diverge from a dominant pattern. We do not yet know.

• The central difficulty with the "mass society" style of thought is that, pushed hard enough, it posits a virtual end or blockage of history. Now much modernist literature, as Georg Lukács has shrewdly noted, does exactly the same thing: it abandons the idea of historicity, falls back upon notions of a universal *condition humaine* or a rhythm of eternal recurrence, even as it is committed within its own realm to change, turmoil, ceaseless re-creation. Powerful as this vision is in the modernist novel, it will not suffice for political analysis. In studying the novel we must explain the vision of a historical blockage in essentially historical terms, and thus posit, at some point, an end to modernism. In social life itself, however, all experience points to the certainty of change. We should profit here from the fate of Hannah Arendt's brilliant theory of totalitarianism: it lacked a sense of the dynamic that might lead to disintegration from within or transformation from without. And what the experience of the postwar years strongly impresses upon one is that even institutions seemingly invulnerable crack under the pressure of internal conflict (*including conflicts we cannot foresee*) and thereby call into question the nightmare vision of stasis.

• One of the things that today distinguishes a radical from a liberal is not merely that the radical holds to a vision of social transformation going beyond the limits of the welfare state while the liberal acts within those limits; it is also that the radical sees the possibility that from, or with, the evolution of the welfare state there may arise the kind of appalling "double" signified by the idea of the "mass society," while the liberal is not as a rule disturbed by speculations of this kind. The radical is both more optimistic and more pessimistic. Yet he has no choice but to act as if the mass society can indeed be averted; otherwise, he may doom himself to a self-confirming prophecy. And meanwhile there is surely enough evidence of continued social conflict and change to warrant the assumption that history will continue, that we have by no means reached the end of major social transformations and that the impulse to a secular transcendence remains a living force.

The Problem of Socialism, Again

About this complex and entangled subject I want to say only one thing: the one thing that indicates the central difficulty of a radical criticism that would go beyond "the given."

Does a great historical movement ever get a second chance? Suppose Saul of Tarsus and the rest of the original "cadre" had been destroyed, or had committed some incredible blunder: could Christianity have regained its momentum after an interval of isolation and despair? For socialism, it is clear, the great historical opportunity came in the first quarter of this century, and for a variety of reasons—the Social Democrats and Leninists were keen enough in their criticism of each other—the chance was not taken.

Historical mission and idealism cannot be whipped up at demand; once a generation becomes exhausted or an idea contaminated, it takes a long time before new efforts can be made, if they can be made at all. Meanwhile history does not stand still. Socialism having failed to transform Western society in the first quarter of the century, part of what it had supposed to be its "historical missions" was now appropriated by the existing society. Where that did not happen, as in the backward countries, there arose a corrupt mockery of socialism, a total state (I quote Proudhon's uncanny anticipation)

> having the appearance of being founded on the dictatorship of the masses, but in which the masses have no more power than is necessary to ensure a general serfdom in accordance with the precepts and principles borrowed from the old absolutism; indivisibility of public power, all-consuming centralization, systematic destruction of all individual, corporative and regional thought, and inquisitorial police.

Whether socialism as a movement—I leave aside the European Social Democracy, which has mostly a formal relation to the idea of socialism—can be revived, or whether it will have served historically as a bridge toward some new radical humanism, I do not know.

Socialists remain: a few. They are people devoted to a problem, or a memory that gives rise to a problem. The socialist idea signifies, first, a commitment to the values of fraternity, libertarianism, egalitarianism and freedom. It means, secondly, commitment to an envisioned society in which a decisive proportion of the means of production shall be commonly owned and democratically controlled. What, however, is the relation between these two commitments?

One great failing of the socialist movement in the past was that it did not recognize, or recognize sufficiently, the inherent tension between the values it claimed to embody and the social scheme it proposed to enact. Traditionally, it was assumed that a particular change in property forms and relations would be adequate to, or at least largely prepare for, the desired change in the quality of life. (At its most Bourbon-like level, this meant the notion that mere state ownership or nationalization of the means of production would be a sufficient criterion for bestowing the label "workers state.") Now we know from sad experience that the transformation of economy from private to public ownership is not necessarily "progressive," and such transformations seem, in any case, to be part of a general worldwide drift.

The dominant stress of the Marxist movements has been upon political means (strategy, tactics, propaganda) concerning which it often had sophisticated theories; but in regard to the society it envisaged, the content of its hope, it had surprisingly little to say, sometimes no more than the threadbare claim that once "we" take power, "we" will work things out. Martin Buber is right in saying:

> To the questions of the elements of social re-structure, Marx and Engels never gave a positive answer, because they had no inner relation to this idea. . . . The political act remained the one thing worth striving for. . . .

By now the more reflective socialists feel differently, but as often happens in human affairs, a growth in awareness does not necessarily facilitate confidence in action. If today we are asked what we mean or envision by socialism, our first instinctive response—even if it never reaches our lips—is likely to be in negative terms: "we don't mean such and such . . . we don't mean simply nationalization of industry. . . ." Our first response, that is, rests upon a deviation from a previously-held norm, and thereby constitutes a kind of self-criticism. (That listeners may not even know the tradition from which we are deviating is one of the perils of the passage of time and American ahistoricism.)

We now try to describe our vision of the good society in terms of qualities, sentiments of freedom and fraternity, norms of conduct and value, priorities of social allocation; whereas, by and large, the tradition of socialism has been to speak in terms of changing institutions and power relationships. Yet in undertaking this shift of emphasis we cannot but admit the cogency of a certain kind of, criticism: "A society, even one envisaged in the future, cannot be described simply by specifying desired qualities. You may hope to infuse a future society with those qualities; you may expect that a new social structure will promote or encourage those qualities. But a society must also, perhaps even primarily, be described or foreseen in structural terms."

For most of the European Social Democratic parties, this problem barely exists, since they have decided, usually in practice and sometimes in program, to abandon the idea of socialization of the economy. In doing so, they become little more than liberal welfarist parties. Arguing against Anthony Crossland's theoretical defense of such a course, George Lichtheim properly remarks:

> . . . The Conservative party could in principle accept all his reform demands and still retain control of the country. What would really undermine its hold—a major shift in the ownership of property—is precisely the thing he regards as unnecessary. The residual demand for it is, he thinks, a vestige of Marxism. In that case the Tories must be regarded as full-blooded Marxists, for the one thing they seem determined to prevent is a drastic change in the social balance which would transfer the power of decision-making from private firms to public authorities.

If, then, we do retain the perspective of a long-range socializations of economy, the problem becomes how to reconcile the traditional socialist emphasis upon property forms—an emphasis necessary but not sufficient—with a more sophisticated understanding of the relationship between social structure and humane values. In any case, we neither can nor should wish to recapture the innocence of traditional socialism. We may try to develop schemes for autonomous and pluralistic social institutions within a collectivist economy. We may wish to place a decisive stress upon the idea of democratic participation. We may argue that the trend toward economic collectivism is historically unavoidable and the only choice facing men is whether it should be allowed to drift into bureaucratic authoritarianism or brought under the sponsorship of a democratic policy. But in the end we know that "history" guarantees us nothing: everything is now a question of human will.

Perhaps another way of saying all this is to insist that the vision of utopia remains a genuine option, a profound need. (Could one imagine the survival of the intellectuals as a distinct group if that vision were extinguished?) It is the sense of a possible good society that provides a guiding norm for our day-to-day political life. Without such an assumption, radical criticism runs the danger of declining into mere complaint or veering into elitist manipulation. Perhaps, then, the accumulation of defeats suffered by socialism can yet provide a premise for new beginnings.

Finally, The Intellectuals

It is tempting to end with a call for greater political involvement. But what, in the present circumstances, would that mean? The American intellectual world, except in regard to an occasional issue or figure arousing strong emotions, is not greatly interested in politics. Things have, to be sure, improved a little since the fifties: one encounters less frequently the smugness of literary people who regard politics as a sign of vulgarity. But the idea of a sustained political involvement seems abstract or unlikely to most American intellectuals. Some of the reasons for this are not at all admirable: narcissism, lucrative busy-work, exhibitionism, competitiveness, all related to an affluent but insecure culture. Other reasons deserve to be taken seriously: a genuine doubt as to what intellectuals can achieve, uncertainty as to how to act. That there is no party or movement to which radical intellectuals can attach themselves does not bother me as much as certain intellectuals claim it bothers them. I am more concerned with the development of a serious political consciousness within the arena in which intellectuals live and work. Concerning which, three concluding remarks:

• The American university has recently become more alive, more concerned politically, than it had been for several decades. This, on the whole, is a cheering development, but some aspects are also disturbing. There are available on the American campus—which, as it grows at an astonishing rate, becomes one of the major centers of national life—far more spokesmen for a democratic radicalism than are now making themselves heard. To the extent that they fail to speak out and establish relations with the aroused students, to that extent will the rising campus rebelliousness be diverted and entangled. Silence, abstention, indifference may not have mattered very much in university life these past few decades; now they matter enormously. To carry the moods of the fifties into the sixties will have bitter consequences.

• A major shift or shakeup of "power relations" seems in prospect for the intellectual world. For the first time in several decades, the generation of intellectuals associated with the thirties—a generation bound together by common problems, experiences and quarrels—seems in danger of losing its dominant position in American intellectual life. That it has kept that position for so long and through such a bewildering series of political-intellectual changes is itself extraordinary. But now there is beginning to appear in the graduate schools, and near the student and civil rights movements a younger generation of intellectuals and semi-intellectuals, perhaps not as well-equipped dialectically as the older leftists, semi-leftists and ex-leftists, and certainly not as wide-ranging in interest or accomplished in style, yet endowed with a self-assurance, a lust for power, a contempt for and readiness to swallow up their elders which is at once amusing, admirable and disturbing. Thinking of themselves as "new radicals," these young people see as one of their major tasks the dislodgment of the old ones; and they are not inclined to make precise distinctions as to differences of opinion among the old ones. It seems clear to them that a good many radicals of the thirties have grown tired, or dropped out, or in some instances, sold out. They encounter teachers who, on ceremonial occasions, like to proclaim old socialist affiliations, but who really have little or no sympathy with the rebelliousness of today. They are very shrewd at sensing how a profuse nostalgia for radical youth can serve to cloak acquiescence in the status quo. They are also very quick on the draw in dismissing those with whom they disagree as "middle class" or "establishment" or "fink." A *Kulturkampf* seems in prospect, and one in which, I must confess, my own sympathies would be mixed.

• For radical intellectuals one theme should stand out above all others: the articulation of democratic values. In the American academy today, as in our intellectual life, there is a considerable fallout of authoritarianism, that major blight of the twentieth century. (A significant study could be undertaken of the way American political scientists and sociologists, in their recent passion for hardheaded "realism," have provided rationales for authoritarian societies and outlooks.) It is a blight spread across the entire political spectrum: conservative, liberal, radical. It fits the age only too well. It rides the wave of the future— perhaps. To speak out in behalf of the ideal of democracy; to resist all rationalizations for authoritarian rulers and movements; to proclaim our pleasure in the appearance of the "revisionist" intellectuals in eastern Europe who also insist that without freedom there can be no good society, no life worth living: that would be a task which could again make the calling of intellectual a reason for pride.

Chapter 11
Old and New Classes
Edith Kurzweil

A review of *The Future of Intellectuals and the Rise of the New Class*, by Alvin W. Gouldner, Seabury Press, 1979.

Nearly as old as the notion of the class struggle, the role of a New Class of intellectuals has been discussed by every self-respecting political thinker since Marx. Joseph Schumpeter, for instance, saw intellectuals as undermining the capitalist system, as adversaries, as staffers of political offices, speech writers, and newspeople; F. A. Hayek maintained that the move towards socialism was governed by intellectual leadership in corporate managers; and Milovan Djilas talked of party leaders and bureaucrats after a revolution as the New Ruling Class. Most New Class hypotheses about the West denied an impending class conflict between bourgeoisie and proletariat, and those about the East proved that even the revolution cannot abolish classes. But currently, in America, some have used the term "New Class" as a catchall designation for neoconservatives, for former liberal and socialist thinkers such as Daniel Bell, Irving Kristol, Seymour Martin Lipset, Daniel Patrick Moynihan, and Norman Podhoretz – most of whom not only theorize about the existence or nonexistence of this New Class but are also close to power.

In this company, Alvin Gouldner's *The Future of Intellectuals and the Rise of the New Class* represents a departure: he takes on all these theorists and also steps outside the fray to argue that the New Class is composed of two major segments – intellectuals and a technical intelligentsia – and that the radical components of their ideas, though badly flawed, eventually will revolutionize our society. Gouldner supports this position with sixteen closely reasoned theses, beginning with the defects in the Marxist scenario which forgot to account for the vanguard position of the peasants in Russia and

China, for the revolutionary theorists in a revolution, and for the transition from the old state apparatus to a new and nonrepressive one. But Gouldner's "end of ideology" bypasses the ritual indictment of communism and the glorification of the status quo (however qualified), if only because he perceives technocratic consciousness and scientism as ideologies shared by both Marxists and their opponents. And he does not consider the New Left and the counterculturists of the late 1960s as a dangerous political force. Some of them, however, he argues, may belong to the Vanguard of the New Class, having become politically radicalized – not through economic deprivation but through *political* suffering. They overcome alienation by doing political work, subverting conservative ideology, and mediating the radical political practices of the New Class.

In sweeping Hegelian fashion, Gouldner proceeds to show how the New Class in advanced industrial societies, where production increasingly depends on technical skills, at times is politically revolutionary yet constantly helps improve the mode of production (this enhances their importance); how it simultaneously accepts and resists subordination to the old moneyed class; how it pursues its own aggrandizement; and how it progressively arrogates more and more decisional, legal, and administrative competence to itself. Gouldner illustrates – in broad strokes – how some members of the New Class harass the old class, periodically ally themselves with the working masses or peasants, or use the "welfare" or "socialist" state strategically for their own ends. Arenas of controversy include issues of academic freedom, consumer rights, scientific management, unionization of civil service employees, honesty in government, ecology, nuclear energy, and many more. But this class does not seek struggle for its own sake: it is concerned with securing more of its own ideal and material interests with a minimum of effort.

Trained either in the enterprises controlled by the old class, or, increasingly, through specialized systems of public education, the New Class values autonomy and professionalism; its power and privilege are grounded in the individual control of special cultures, language, and techniques; and the New Class's fundamental objective is to increase its own share of the national product, so that it can afford to be egalitarian about old class capital (rent, stocks, profits, etc.), but antiegalitarian in its wish for special guild advantages based on the possession of cultural capital. Gouldner defines such capital as produced by the New Class, as knowledge rather than as "natural" raw material or even inborn talent; it is a "product of both human labor and culture whose income claims are socially enforce-able and culturally recognized."

Inserted in many spheres of activities, Gouldner's New Class is linked through its speech, through its culture of careful and critical discourse (CCD) which suspects all authority, questions even its own methods, and provides a common ideology based on the importance of modes of justification, of expression, of impersonal speech. This discourse also serves as a bond between humanistic intellectuals and the technical intelligentisa. Versed in all the "two culture" arguments, Gouldner refutes opposing views: Shils, for instance, by postulating several cultural sources for modern intellec-tuals as foundation is said to neglect the impress of their own status group, that is, of contemporary intellectual ideology; Parsons is alleged to revitalize the foundering of the old class by uniting it with the New Class and professionalizing it. And Chomsky, who, unlike Shils, is said to overemphasize the alienating disposition of intellec-tuals, overstresses their subservience to power. By perceiving even opposition to the system as an integrative mechanism, Gouldner questions whether this renders Chomsky's politics useless, or places him at the very Vanguard of the New Class.

It is impossible even to name all the issues Gouldner touches – on education and the reproduction and subversion of the New Class through education, on old line bureaucrats and new staff intel-ligentsia, on elitism, Maoism, Cuba, revolutionary intellectuals, Cambodia, Marx and Engels. Nor is it feasible to show how carefully he argues the cultural contradictions of both capitalism and com-munism. Since the capital of Gouldner's New Class is expertise – the most important commodity to improve economic production and political organization – in both capitalist and communist systems, all those who possess it can be thought, ultimately, to share power. And this, I believe, is precisely where definitions of the New Class, and of its location, and its potential for action, impinge on politics. If the neoconservatives alone are defined as the New Class, this would not only point to the fact that *they* are the intellectuals who wield political power, but would also disenfranchise critical or revolutionary thought. If, however, the New Class, as Gouldner maintains, encom-passes all those who share a common language and culture, then the current neoconservatives' closeness to power would be incidental, a passing phenomenon. For the real issue underlying *all* the New Class theories is power.

Even though most of these theories now reject "traditional"

Marxism, they accept the notion of the revolutionary Vanguard or at least the idea that intellectuals influence politics. Thus Daniel Bell's perception, for example, of the New Class as a new cultural stratum and attitude that lacks class unity, reaffirms his conservative biases and politics. And Andrew Hacker's focus on salaried managers who are part of a growing upper middle class of bit players rather than potential rulers, or Irving Louis Horowitz's rejection of class analysis in favor of a theory of privilege also play down the New Class's potential to induce radical change. Yet Gouldner might consider Michael Harrington's call to the New Class to participate in a new democratic Left as too ideological, though helpful to New Class radicalization. Grounded in the belief in the power of the words of Vanguard intellectuals, he is critical of all dogmatism.

Gouldner, too, rejects the possibility of a revolutionary struggle (his reformism has been coming for some time), declaring Marx the last of the Utopians instead of the first scientific Marxist. Inevitably, Marxists tend to lump him with the other defectors. But Gouldner, ever eager to perfect a theory of theories (his most recent book shows how each theory, and particularly Marxism, contains the seeds of its own destruction), is concerned with the Vanguard position of the theorist, and/or the maintenance of this position. Yet his conception of the New Class as dynamic, and as busily undermining the system which pushed it to the top, assumes that the growing numbers of educated and technically trained experts will mobilize against their increasing alienation; that they will organize around their lack of autonomy and their discontent, using their own progressive potential and ethics to supersede the old class. Gouldner "overcomes" utopian implications by maintaining the tension between the New Class's fight for goodness and morality for all, and its propensity to push the advantage of its own culture. Such an assumption, I think, expects critical discourse to remain strong enough to withstand political repression and cooptation. It also expects that the Vanguard will be of the Left rather than the Right – a notion Daniel Bell has recently attacked by showing that in the past right-leaning intellectuals frequently used to lead. In addition, Gouldner assumes that intellectuals and the technical intelligentsia have the potential eventually to act as a class – an assumption the Right dismisses as utopian and the Left as reformist. We would, of course, prefer his crystal ball to be more clairvoyant than Bell's. But whatever happens, he has worked out the most comprehensive and lucid theory to help us understand our very confused class structure.

Part III

Emphasis on Literature and Art

Introduction

The essays in this section have different foci, and could just as easily be classified as "theory" or "politics." But this illustrates only one of our points, namely that writers and artists reflect the politics of their day in their work even when they do not reflect on them.

William Phillips, in 1941, comments on the intellectual traditions of writers, primarily in America, and we are reminded at once of his role as founder of *Partisan Review*, that is, of his dedication to remain on the left while fighting against Soviet communism. This conviction leads him to question Marxist interpretations of, for instance, Balzac's concerns with status and intrigue or Poe's experiments in sensations and articulations of class, as well as those interpretations which focus on art as experience. Instead, he observes that artistic works, always, resonate the immediate moods and interests of the intellectuals – a distinct group conscious of its elite status which "thrives on its own anxiety over survival." The individual artist, even when rejecting all social and artistic conventions, also shares a sustaining tradition of convention and experiment: a variety of traditional memories and associations are part of the artist's reality. Phillips describes how American writers, largely because of American history and politics, have lacked the literary community Europeans take for granted, so that each of them tended to work in isolation, or to start from scratch. They had no organized bohemia until the twentieth century, and then, argues Phillips, its inspiration was for the most part European. Distrusting ideological fiction and influenced by populism, American writers did not create the intellectual heroes Victor Brombert finds "populating" French (and English) novels. Regional nostalgia, the rebellion of the twenties against provincialism, and the bent for self-portraiture – unconnected though they were – are shown to be manifestations of nationalism, militant provincialism, and the self-abnegation of the intelligentsia. Consequently, concludes Phillips, American intellectuals seem to accept the official voice of society as their own.

Those who rebelled, such as Eliot and Pound, Stephen Spender states, "left what they regarded as barbarous America to come to civilized Europe." But Europe is not of a piece, and distinctions have to be made between the English and the French, and again between the older and the younger Bloomsbury generations. Whereas to "the ethos of literary Bloomsbury political action seemed vulgar," their children's primary concern was to defeat fascism, although they too were unsympathetic to mixing art with politics. Spender's essay centers around the lives of Julian Bell and John Cornford, who chose to fight in Spain, and who – in different fashion – had given up writing and embraced communism – to save liberal traditions. Spender explores all the nuances of taking political positions and relates them to their milieu. In England and America, where writers take up causes and depict these in dazzling moral contrasts, intellectuals are only part-time "politicians." "In France, [however], the intellectuals are, as it were, more or less in continual session," and their shifts in position over time always correspond to political events such as the Algerian War, or the twentieth congress of the Communist party. This allows the French to develop "respect-worthy opinions about politics," argues Spender, so that both right and left literary interventions are more trustworthy.

Spender, himself a poet, is particularly enlightening on the poet's temptation to replace politics by metaphor, to subordinate them "to the creative and critical attempt." The right tends to do this by glorifying the past, the left by counting on the coming revolution. In the 1930s, ends Spender, "the reactionaries wrote out of their tragic sense of modern life. The Cornfords and Bells lived and died the tragedy." And many years later, we might add, we reinterpret their lives and works as texts, although the problems they faced remain with us.

Though Barbara Rose's essay is about visual artists, it raises questions common to painters, sculptors, and writers. Her focus is on the element of protest in art works – aesthetic, political, economic or social – which during Dadaism and neo-Dadaism was "an aesthetic phenomenon stripped of critical content." But during the 1960s, when the media became infatuated with novelty, American society began to take note of artists, and to buy their works. This in itself spurred artistic creation. Increasingly, *épater le bourgeois* was no longer enough, all sorts of previously forbidden or taboo themes were explored, and especially the propensity to shock. Rose argues that artists, originally, had not intended to equate the disruption of the social order with the disruption of culture, but that the existence of a mass audience itself seems to have inspired them continually to exceed previously existing limits. Acts of self-mutilation and masochistic practices came to be "ordinary" as artists turned against themselves rather than against society.

Rose states that in this situation "society appropriates to itself the artist's license to remain a child, perpetually at play, knowing no limits." Thus art cannot be taken seriously, even if the official rhetoric exalts creativity and sets up funds and endowments – where decisions are made by bureaucrats and cultural experts, further infantilizing the artist. What happens, then, is that all activities begin to be interpreted as games, and to destroy art-life boundaries. The danger, for Rose, is the confusion between the two spheres – confusion that reaches from the aesthetic to the moral, to contaminate the entire society.

Whereas Phillips noted that until World War II, the lack of an organized artistic community worked against American artists, Rose's observations would indicate that the artists' acceptance by society did too. For neither total integration nor total isolation provides the bohemia which allows for an in-group experimenting within specific traditions. Bloomsbury, as Spender demonstrates, was such a group – united but feeding on its internal conflicts.

Chapter Twelve
The Intellectuals' Tradition
William Phillips

1.

IT IS GENERALLY RECOGNIZED that in the course of its alienation from society modern art has developed a highly organized regime of its own; yet the implications of this fact have hardly been explored in critical writing. Traditional criticism, at least of the more formal variety, has tended to fetishize the idea of detachment to the point of regarding the individual writer, rather than the creative grouping, as a whole, as the unit of alienation. While, at the other extreme, the historical—or Marxist—school of criticism fixed the meanings and mutations of art in the social pattern; and though it granted a separate status to intellectual activity, its emphasis was almost completely on historical determination.

The Marxist approach was, of course, primarily concerned with the political and ideological origins of esthetic movements. And its doctrine of art as one of the modes by which society becomes conscious of itself—class conscious in the present system— was undoubtedly an advance over such traditional mystifications as the idea that a work of art amounts to the sum of its parts. Yet the Marxist theory, it seems to me, is a kind of half-truth, overstressing the correspondences between the historical context and the work itself, and leading to endless theoretical maneuvers as its exponents attempted to hold on to the autonomous values of literature in the very act of denying them. The apparent contradiction was never resolved.

For, surely, the art of the past is too full of ambiguities and obsessive designs to be regarded simply as an articulation of class needs—unless, of course, one is ready to accept the doctrinaire principle that anything short of a revolutionary view is an instrument of conservative opinion. What class is served, for example, by Balzac's research into the patterns of status and intrigue, or by Poe's experiments in sensation? Considered as a whole, modern literature is a continual recoil from the practices and values of society toward some form of self-sufficiency, be it moral, or physical, or merely historical, with repeated fresh starts from the bohemian underground as each new movement runs itself out; yet no major class exhibits any such compulsion to withdraw from the conditions of its existence. Nor has modern art taken for its subject the common denominator of experience. On the contrary, its great protagonist has been the figure of the artist, himself, through his successive phases of assertion, alienation, and survival. And more recently, in a kind of reversal of the process, he has been loaded by Thomas Mann with the burdens of civilization, while novelists like Joyce and Kafka have recast him in the role of mankind—as an estranged human abstract. In the work of Joyce, as in the contemporary tendency to make painting itself the actual content of painting, this result is achieved largely by an identification of the subject with the medium.

2.

It would be more accurate, I believe, to locate the immediate sources of art in the intelligentsia, which, since the renaissance at least, has made up a distinct occupational grouping within society. For the special properties of modern literature, as well as the other arts, are readily associated with the characteristic moods and interests of the intellectuals. True enough, they are, themselves, outgrowths of the historic process, their social position depending, ultimately, on the relative power and prestige of the contending classes; even their illusion of spiritual freedom can be explained as a sublimation of their material bondage. And their literary efforts, do in a measure generalize our full social experience, insofar as that is, after all, the reality that creates the need as well as the possibilities of the artists's estrangement, and it is to this experience that he turns for his parables of frustration and fulfillment. But modern art, with its highly complicated techniques, its plaintive egotism, its messianic desperation, could not have come into being except through the formation by the intelligentsia of a distinct group culture, thriving on its very anxiety over survival and its consciousness of being an elite. In no other way could it have been able to resist being absorbed by the norms of belief and behavior; and society, for its part, while it could tolerate an enduring cult of intellectual abnormality, would certainly have had little patience with outbursts of non-conformity in esthetic matters by individuals who in every other respect remained within the fold. Nor is it at all likely that any other mode of art, springing more directly from the people as a whole, should have developed in our social order, since most of the existing modern equivalents of folk-art, which some populist critics still exalt as the true voice of the masses, are little more than the remains of earlier esthetic movements adapted to the needs of popular taste. In fact, all new and genuinely creative impulses in our time, as Trotsky once observed in a study of the Russian symbolists, tend to take the form of bohemianism, as the *avant-garde* in a kind of permanent mutiny against the regime of utility and conformity, proclaims its faith in the freedom, the irresponsibility, and the higher integrity of art.

Now, the complexion of the intelligentsia has undergone many changes—their extremities of belief being a fairly late development—but throughout their history, and despite their growing tendencies toward atomization, they have maintained the kind of institutional stability vital to the production of art. Obviously, it was through such a unified and self-perpetuating group that our cultural continuity has been preserved, and the individual artist has been provided with a sustaining tradition of convention and experiment, without which he could never hope to be more than a gifted eccentric. In addition, however, as society lost its earlier unity of belief, which the artist shared and took as his starting point, the very plight of the intelligentsia and the more or less homogeneous outlook it had acquired served as a philosophic mooring for the modern artist. Thus, even today, while their bent is entirely against any kind of social authority or discipline, nevertheless the intelligentsia, in their role of intellectual conservation and in their tightly knit traditions, perform for modern times a function that an institution like the church, for instance, had in the medieval period. And, in an historical sense, the church was actually the organized body of intellectuals in the middle ages, for at the height of its dominion it was the conveyor of all secular, as well as spiritual, culture, and it was set apart from the laity as much by its intellectual as by its hierarchical distinction. The church, like its modern successors, tried jealously to maintain its cultivated and inbred esthetic traditions by absorbing, sometimes through actual physical possession, the more-popular forms of folk-art at the time. In opposition to such spontaneous performances as the sword plays, for example, which arose in the primitive agricultural community much the same way as the early dramatic rites of the Greeks, the church used all its powers to keep art primarily a vehicle for its own myth.

If the secular intellectuals who came to the fore with the rise of a bourgeois society in Europe were not bound by any common creed, still they managed through the years to build what might be called a tradition of approach or perspective. In the realm of literature this tradition amounted to a highly elaborate sense of its achievements and its tasks, thus providing the creative imagination with a fund of literary experiences—a kind of style of work—to draw on. For the old-world writer, from about the seventeenth century on, had to mediate between the great scramble of the new order and the authority of the past, between the boundless perspectives for the individual personality and the material forces tending more and more to confine it, between scepticism and faith, between the city and the country. . . . And he was able to do so to the extent that he shared the generalized vision of the intelligentsia as a whole; or where any great divergence of belief existed, he simply took his cue from the collective opinion of some dissident group. The fact is that European literature made little headway in the smaller, marginal countries—or appeared late in a backward region like Russia—that, on the contrary, it enjoyed the greatest success in those nations that set the social and intellectual pace for the rest of the continent. (It was, after all, in Italy, the original home of the new mercantilism, that the beginnings of humanist theory and renaissance art first appeared.) Not only did most of the problems and crises of European expansion come to a head in France and England (and in Germany somewhat later), but, in addition, these countries were sufficiently prosperous and were becoming sufficiently urbanized to support a scientific and literary intelligentsia. Hence they were able to rationalize the general European predicament and to provide a tentative equilibrium of opinion for all political and intellectual pursuits. While the lagging industrial nations had to be content with sporadic cultural expressions, which were largely an adaptation of the more advanced currents to the local ethos, the great tradition of French and English art maintained itself at the crest of the upheavals and large-scale movements that marked the growth of bourgeois society. One can hardly conceive of a Julien Sorel, balancing himself on the contradictions between ambition and personality, in, say, Warsaw or Madrid—or the domestic drama of the eighteenth century being born outside the boom of British trade at the time and the plebian sentimentality that accompanied it.

It is plain that we have here more than a coincidence of geographical and social factors. Indeed, the major impulses of European art can be traced in practically every instance to the existence of an active intelligentsia, crucially involved in its contemporary history, and sufficiently self-conscious to be able to assimilate some new experience to the norms of its past. One might almost put down as an esthetic law that continuity is the condition for creative invention. Thus the dream of fulfillment released by the French revolution lingered on in the modern mind: disengaged from its social frame and turned inward, it served, at one pole, as a basis for the series of movements dedicated to the primacy of art; while at the other extreme, stripped of its critical and tendencious spirit, it lay behind the celebrations of progress that appeared toward the end of the last century. In fact, the increasing complexity of contemporary literature is at least partially to be accounted for by the variety of traditional memories and associations that fill the consciousness of the writer today. And in such works as *The Wasteland* and *Finnegans Wake*, where this natural tendency has been converted into a deliberate method, both Joyce and, to a less extent, Eliot have actually set out to dissolve their immediate perceptions in the timeless reality of the past.

3.

Now, in the case of American literature, unlike that of the old world, we have a kind of negative illustration of the relation of the intelligentsia to art. For the outstanding features—not to speak of the failures—of our national culture can be largely explained by the inability of our native intelligentsia to achieve a detached and self-sufficient group existence that would permit it to sustain its traditions through succeeding epochs, and to keep abreast of European intellectual production. One need hardly stress such symptoms in American writing as shallowness, paucity of values, a statistical approach to reality, and the compensatory qualities of forthrightness, plebianism, and a kind of matter-of-fact humanism: they have been noted in a number of historical studies; and, to be sure, our cultural innocence has been practically a standing complaint of American criticism. As Howells had Bromfield Corey remark in *The Rise of Silas Lapham:* "A Greek got his civilization by talking and looking, and in some measure a

Parisian may still do it. But we, who live remote from history and monuments, we must read or we must barbarize."

Obviously, our history has been too rapid and too expansive for the American mind to settle down and take stock of itself. Moreover, the city, as the symbol of modern civilization, did not fully emerge until after the Civil War, with the result that our intellectual life, in its formative years, could not escape the atomizing influence of ruralism. And, what is perhaps more important, the lusty pioneer motif running through American letters, with its strong tinge of hinterland philosophy, exerted a constant regional pull on the intelligentsia and tended to sanction an individual rather than a group solution of the cultural problem.

Our early literary expressions were, of course, little more than British amenities feeling their way through strange, primitive surroundings. Nor could the Puritan outlook serve as the groundwork for a tradition. Essentially prohibitive and regional, it was a kind of frontier Calvinism, destined to be superseded by a more materialist creed—in keeping with the rough-and-tumble spirit of aggrandizement that was possessing the country as a whole. Hawthorne, of course, whose imagination was tortured by the Puritan demons of guilt and decay, was the prime literary beneficiary of the Puritan mind; but, on the whole, it entered into later writing mainly as a negative factor, a repressed strain, as in Melville, where it was in a sense a purged element; and through the nineteenth century it persisted largely as a characteristic moral wholesomeness.

The Concord school may be said to mark the first appearance, in full intellectual dress, of an American intelligentsia. Revolting against the all-absorbing commercialism of the day and against the bleakness of the Puritan heritage, they set out quite consciously to form, as Emerson put it, "a learned class," and to assimilate the culture of Europe into a native tradition. Yet, just as they had no established past to draw on, so they were unable to transmit a full-blown literary mentality to succeeding generations. Emerson was, of course, intoxicated with the pioneer spirit, with the hardbitten realism of the plain people, and his bias was strongly agrarian in its emphasis on bare hands and the self-reliant mind. He was essentially a transcendental commoner, and for all his cultural yearnings, his philosophy was at bottom an affirmation of individual fulfillment in a boundless American expansion. Thus, in later years he turned upon New England, the seat of his own cultural development, to cast a loving eye on the turbulent settlements of the West, where he found the dawn of our native genius. No wonder, then, that the entire tendency, of which Emerson was, perhaps, the most representative figure, was soon reabsorbed, in the main, by the life and philosophy of the general mass, whose premises it accepted, and to whom it made its prime appeal.

This, in essence, is the story of American letters: momentary efforts by solitary writers or by intellectual groups to differentiate themselves and to set a new current in motion, with the inevitable petering out, and the necessity for a fresh start over again. Hence our unusual number of literary sports. By the time Whitman, for example, was ready to affirm again the democratic ethos and the frontier excitements of the new cities, he had to start from scratch, with the result that his vision was largely a matter of itemized experience, devoid of those central symbols and values that are handed down by a creative tradition. The case of Poe is even more striking: he was the first truly bohemian writer in America (if we except the peculiar rustic bohemianism of Thoreau), and throughout his life practically the only one. Hence he lacked those professional resources of esthetic and social subversion that are normally provided by an organized bohemia. In only a negative, escapist sense, did his poetry have a characteristically bohemian content; although it gave the lead to Baudelaire, his poetry fell short of the programmatic experimentalism of his French contemporaries; even his essays, as Henry James once remarked, were excessively amateurish and provincial; and his verse constantly tended, in an over-felicitous fashion, toward a lovelorn provincialism. What saved Poe, I suppose, was a happy coincidence of talent, morbidity, and the capacity for absorbing those literary strains that served the needs of his sensibility.

Not until the last two or three decades did any literary "schools," promoted by an active literary intelligentsia, make their appearance here. But their inspiration was largely European, and, in a basic sense, they never really succeeded in lifting themselves above the conceptual plane of American writing as a whole. Consider the Marxist or proletarian school; perhaps the most confident, aggressive, and most thoroughly international of recent trends. One might have expected that a movement so completely regulated by an organized body of left-wing intellectuals, committed to an all-embracing philosophy and to the principle that literature must serve as a vehicle for revolutionary ideas—that such a movement would have been able to grasp the effects of our social experience on our national mythology in more significant terms than the simple rites of awakening and conversion. As it was, radical novelists in this country took the short cut to integration by substituting data for values and the specious unity of the narrative for the interplay of historical meanings. Sharing the general aversion and distrust of ideological fiction, they failed to create a single intellectual character—either revolutionary or conservative—thus depriving themselves of their very medium of understanding, for it is only through the consciousness of such a character that it is possible, it seems to me, to depict the modulations and tensions of belief that make up the political movement.

If any one figure can be said to be a symbol of our entire culture, it is Henry Adams, whose active life covered almost the entire phase of our modern development and whose work sounded its principal themes. In its spiritual bafflements, its peculiarly native mixture of materialism and religious feeling, its desperate search for some central tradition, his *Education* reads like a diary of our speculative conscience. A product of the New England mind, he was soon cast adrift by what he called the "multiplicity" of the world—his repeated use of the word suggests a morbid fondness for it—and he began his life-long probe into history for some principle of unity, some contemporary equivalent of the ideal unity he believed to have existed in the thirteenth century. In a measure, he thought he discovered this principle in a dynamic law of history, but it served only to confirm his dilemma, for the law merely proved all over again the increasing complexity and disintegration of society; and, besides, his experimental bent led him to distrust theoretical constructions because they tend to "falsify the facts." He turned to science. But he could not overcome his feeling that its authority was limited to purely secular matters; and even in this sphere the prevailing chaos all but defied the efforts to create order, or, as Adams put it, "the multiplicity baffling science." Finally, there was God, the supreme and infallible synthesizing force; yet he could derive no conclusive satisfaction from his faith because his Calvinist leanings toward a personal creed precluded any belief in a single unifying system. What was left?—nothing but to return, after completing the cycle of his researches, to a kind of methodological groping for a common denominator of belief. "The old formulas had failed, and a new one had to be made. . . . One sought no absolute truth. One sought only a spool on which to wind the thread of history without breaking it."

In a sense, this has been our persistent tradition—this periodic striving for a unified outlook and the inevitable return to a clean slate all over again—though one hesitates to describe it as such because it is exactly this discontinuity that is the mark of our inability to form a complex, intellectual tradition. In this respect, the American intelligentsia exhibits a kind of ambivalent psyche, torn between the urge toward some degree of autonomy and an equally strong tendency to self-effacement, for it is largely its natural inclination to merge with the popular mind that has prevented any such lasting intellectual differentiation as has been achieved in European art and thought. Generally, these dual impulses have found expression in the repetitive cycle of our literary history, but on occasion they have also appeared side by side—in figures like Emerson and Whitman, and, to some extent, Dreiser,—as a combination of populist sensibility with some broad cultural vision. And, is not the predilection for the real, the fatal attraction for the overwhelming minutiae of every-day life, that characterizes so much of American writing, but the creative equivalent of the instability of the intelligentsia?

In the last few decades, we have run the gamut of three important trends, and we are at present in the midst of one more movement to stir the embers of the past, to discover once more the secrets of the national spirit. Yet, except for the natural persistence of certain states of mind, one cannot discern any organic linkage between these successive currents. The regional nostalgia that appeared in such writers as Masters or Frost, which, incidentally, can hardly be said to be a direct outgrowth of the earlier expansive naturalism, was literally brushed aside by the great rebellion of the twenties against provincialism, gentility, and the native bent for minute self-portraiture. At one pole, were the provocations of modernism, with their libertarian effects in the social sphere; at the other stood figures like Mencken and Lewis, attacking the moral and intellectual proprieties. As for the Marxist school, which held sway in the following decade, and whose demise was as sudden and mechanical as its birth, it could scarcely have been expected to establish a line of continuity, since, in addition to the strong resistance it naturally encountered, it believed one of its chief historical assignments to be the task of erasing the traces of the bourgeois past. But it is surely ironic that the current appeal to immerse ourselves in the splendors of the American tradition should ignore the critical acquisitions and revaluations of these last decades.

In a typically compulsive way, this effort to frame a new cultural myth has not only made a clean break with the Marxist outlook, but in its special concern with the indigenous, it is patently a negation of everything the twenties stood for. Thus we have the astonishing phenomenon of a writer like Van Wyck Brooks now forsaking his earlier studies in creative frustration for a gayer—and more successful—version of the literary life in America. One cannot find, it seems to me, a surer sign of the lack of a *felt* tradition—of one that can be assumed—than in such a wilful endeavor to invoke it into being. In a recent address Brooks, who is apparently intent on carrying the quest for a native heritage to the most comic and painful extremes, called for a purge of such figures as Joyce and Eliot—of the truly characteristic works of the modern tradition. As for a "usable past"—Brooks has finally discovered it in the humanitarian pieties of none other than Whittier.

Our concern at the moment, however, is not with the career or the latest views of Van Wyck Brooks, but with the current epidemic of literary nationalism in which Brooks is simply an advanced case. And what is this nationalist revival—this militant provincialism—if not a new phase of self-abnegation on the part of the intelligentsia? Once again they are renouncing the values of group-detachment as they permit themselves to be drawn into the tides of prevailing opinion. In a complete reversal of role, they have come to echo all the stock objections to the complex and ambiguous symbolization of modern writing: and the improvised tradition they now offer in its place—is it not the popular, Sunday version of our history? The immediate effect is bound to be some kind of creative disorientation. But even more important, from the viewpoint of our culture as a whole, it is evident that this constant fluctuation between dissidence and conformity, this endless game of hide-and-seek with the past, cannot but thwart the production of a mature and sustained literature. And the intelligentsia in America, for all its efforts to preserve its intellectual identity, seems to have a deep-seated need to accept as its own—if only periodically—the official voice of society.

Chapter 13
Writers and Politics
Stephen Spender

In England, the circumstances giving rise to poets interfering in politics are special. In their study of Julian Bell's and John Cornford's tragically broken off lives, Peter Stansky and William Abrahams[1] inevitably devote much space to explaining the family background and the personal psychological and intellectual problems which led these young men to anti-Fascism and their deaths in Spain.

If they had been French critics writing about the young Malraux, Aragon or Eluard, there would not have been need of so much explanation. For in France the nineteen thirties was only a recent episode in the long involvement of the French intellectuals with politics since before the French Revolution. As David Caute has pointed out, writers like Romain Rolland, Henri Barbusse, Georges Duhamel and André Gide publicly discussed their attitudes to the Russian Revolution, the League of Nations, war, disarmament, after 1918.

The rightist as well as the leftist French intellectual had centers, organizations, reviews, newspapers, platforms. They regarded imagination and critical intelligence as instruments which could be applied to social problems. In taking sides, the intellectual exploited the legend

1 JOURNEY TO THE FRONTIER. By Peter Stansky and William Abrahams. Constable.

that, *qua* intellectual, he represented detached intelligence. Stooping from his exalted height, the "clerk" made objective, disinterested judgments.

It is true of course that sometimes a Romain Rolland or a Henri Barbusse, infected with the virus of the International disguised as Internationalism, looked across the channel and appealed to a Shaw or a Wells to attend some international conference or sign some declaration of Human Rights. But if and when they responded, the English "great writers" did not descend as radiant messengers from the realms of pure imagination and impartial intellect. Wells, although priding himself on being a social prophet, cultivated the manner of a traveling salesman for the scientific culture, when he made his public "interventions." Like Shaw, Bennett and Galsworthy he thought of his public personality as antiesthetic, lowbrow. He was forever explaining that he was a journalist who breathed a different air from that in the novels of Henry James.

Eliot, Virginia Woolf, even D. H. Lawrence saw to it that Wells and Bennett should never forget their public streak. When during the thirties E. M. Forster appeared on *"front populaire"* platforms he did so because the time demanded that he should assume a role in which he had no confidence and for which he felt little enthusiasm. His presence at Congresses of the Intellectuals during the anti-Fascist period, and that of young English poets, was extraordinary—like lions walking the streets of Rome on the night preceding the Ides of March, a sign that the artist had become denatured from his function by apocalyptic events.

Until the thirties the younger generation of Oxford and Cambridge were infected by the antipolitics of their parents' generation. Stansky and Abrahams mention that the famous society of Cambridge intellectual undergraduates—the Apostles—which had such a close connection with literary Bloomsbury, agreed in the twenties that "practical politics were beneath discussion." Even more striking, in the early thirties, the Apostles ceased for some years to exist, as the result of the pressure of "too many conflicting political beliefs" among their members. Yet so different was the atmosphere by then that to Julian Bell, no longer then an undergraduate, and to John Cornford, who was one, this must have seemed like saying that having at last something to discuss, the Apostles had decided to discuss nothing.

To the Cambridge and Bloomsbury generation of their parents Bell and Cornford were ducklings hatched out from supposititious hen's eggs, swimming out on to those dirty choppy political waters. Not that

Clive and Vanessa Bell and the Cornford parents disagreed with the younger generation's anti-Fascist politics (they sympathized with them). But they regarded politicians as philistine and the artist in politics as betraying the pure cause of individualist art. Leftish political sympathies were almost a part of the ethos of literary Bloomsbury, but political action seemed vulgar. Art had no connection with political action, nor with the good life of personal relations and refined sensations which could only be enjoyed by the individual in isolation or among friends. J. M. Keynes and Leonard Woolf were, of course, in their different ways, politically involved and influential but they were so without lowering their intellectual values or sacrificing personal relationships.

These attitudes are reflected in Forster's novels, in which the good characters have liberal values but realize them only through the medium of personal relations. Business, power, government for Forster belong to the world of "telegrams and anger." That Margaret or Helen Schlegel should carry their socialism further than a few committees, and those personal relations with Henry Wilcox and Leonard Bast which test their principles, seems unthinkable. And although Fielding, Aziz and the other characters who fight on the side of the angels are opposed to the British Raj, it is difficult to think of them taking any effective political action: they attempt to resolve their problems through personal relations between British and Indians. One of their chief grievances against the British occupiers is that they have made relations perhaps impossible.

Forster's antipolitics, antipower, antibusiness attitude is implicit also in the novels of D. H. Lawrence, Virginia Woolf and Aldous Huxley, which have so little else in common. The fact is that the separation of the world of private values imagined in art from the world of the public values of business, science, politics was an essential part of the victory of the generation for whom "the world changed in 1910" against their elders Shaw, Wells, Bennett and Galsworthy. The accusation leveled against the "Georgian" novelists was that they depicted characters who were the social average of the material circumstances in which they lived. They interpreted human beings as walking functions of the society that conditioned them with body, soul, sensibility and sex, common denominators of the general gritty smog, stabbed through with steely rays of scientific materialist social progress. The aim of D. H. Lawrence and Virginia Woolf was to create characters who were isolated creatures of unique awareness with sensibility transcending their material circumstances.

Of course I do not mean that Lawrence had no political sympathies: still less that he had views in common with the liberal ones of Virginia Woolf and E. M. Forster. In his novels those characters like Birkin and Aaron who are representative of the politically searching Lawrence shop around in the contemporary world of action looking for lords of life who are passional, violent and antidemocratic. Bertrand Russell, after some dealings with him during a few months toward the end of the First World War—when Lawrence toyed with the idea of founding some kind of brain (Bertrand Russell) – and – blood (D. H. Lawrence) political movement—came to the conclusion (stated thirty years afterward) that Lawrence's blood-and-soil view of life was later realized in the horrors of Nazism. My point is though that, apart from this one disastrous attempt to get together with Russell and the Cambridge intelligentsia, and apart from his general sympathy with what might be termed bloody-bodiedness (in Germany, Italy or Mexico), Lawrence found the world of public affairs, business and any kind of social cooperation, utterly antipathetic. He even went so far as to write a letter to Forster (in September, 1922) charging him with "a nearly deadly mistake [in] glorifying those *business* people in *Howards End*," and adding that "business is no good"—a conclusion with which he might have found his correspondent concurred, had he bothered to read Forster's novel.

Different as E. M. Forster, Virginia Woolf and D. H. Lawrence were, they all agreed that the novel should be concerned with awareness of life deeper than the conscious mind of the "old novelistic character" and the computable human social unit. Lawrence in his essay on Galsworthy, and Virginia Woolf in her lecture on Arnold Bennett ("Mr. Bennett and Mrs. Brown") attack Galsworthy and Bennett on similar grounds: that the characters in their books are "social units."

Thus, although the 1910 generation (I call them this to make them immediately distinguishable) sympathized with the anti-Fascism of Julian Bell and John Cornford, they were also horrified at the idea of literature being compromised by politics. Virginia Woolf's *Letter to a Young Poet* (1935) is a subdued but troubled protest at the spectacle of sensitive and talented young Oxford and Cambridge poets echoing public matters with a public voice and not writing out of a Wordsworthian isolation, solitary among the solitary reapers. And E. M. Forster, with politeness and forbearance, indicated the underlying grief of Cambridge friends, when he wrote that the future probably lay with Communism but that he did not want to belong to it.

John Cornford was seven years younger than Julian Bell, who was almost contemporaneous with Auden, Day Lewis, MacNeice and myself. In our speeded-up century, perhaps even those few years marked still another "new generation." For our earlier Oxford and Cambridge one secretly sided with the personalist generation old enough to be our parents. We had, written on our hearts, the motto from *The Orators*:

> *Private faces in public places*
> *Are wiser and nicer*
> *Than public faces in private places.*

But John Cornford's generation of anti-Fascist undergraduate agitators at Cambridge, and of the Oxford October Club, did not cherish our sense of the supreme importance of maintaining the distinction between public and private worlds. This difference of generations comes between Julian Bell and John Cornford.

For Bell, to have to choose between personal loyalties and the public cause was always agonizing. By upbringing antipolitical, his choice would always have been for personal values, if he had not come to think of anti-Fascism as a burning loyalty beyond mere politics. But even so he remained conscious of having to make choices in which one set of loyalties had nearly always to be sacrificed to another. He came to think that the private ones of poetry and of love for his family had to submit to the public ones of anti-Fascism. Yet when he went to Spain, in joining an ambulance unit rather than the International Brigade, he sacrificed his interest in war and strategy to his parents' pacifism.

For Cornford, however, there was no question that personal values had to be sacrificed to the public cause. All that mattered was to defeat Fascism. For him, and for his already "new generation," all choices had to be decided by the Marxist interpretation of history. Subjective motives did not count.

In the jargon of the new activist generation (only five years younger than ours) all our generation's scruples about personal relations and subjective feelings could be consigned to the dustbin of liberal inhibitions. Cornford's conviction of the superiority of the Marxist objective reason over personal consideration is indeed the dominating theme of most of his poetry. Leaving the girl who is mother to his child, the objective reason becomes the image of the surgeon's knife cutting away the soft rot of compassion:

Though parting's as cruel as the surgeon's knife,
It's better than ingrown canker, the rotten leaf.
All that I know is I have got to leave.
There's new life fighting in me to get at the air,
And I can't stop its mouth with the rags of old love.
Clean wounds are easiest to bear.

The adroitness with which he establishes the superiority of the ideological "new life" struggling in him to the real new life—a child—
struggling in her, tells a lot about young human nature dominated by
an ideology.

To say that Julian Bell could not, except through a distortion
of his nature, have discovered such impersonal grounds for apparent
callousness is not to say that he might not have behaved just as
egotistically to any of his mistresses (whom Stansky and Abrahams list
as A, B, C, D, etc., far down the alphabet). The difference is that
Bell would have found a personal reason for justifying conduct that
Cornford justified by an "objective" one.

To most literary-minded readers, Bell will seem more interesting
than Cornford because he is the more self-searching and Hamletian
and literary character. Certainly his personality and his relations with
his relations make fascinating reading. It is part of the excellence of
their book that the authors, having put the reader in possession of
some of the facts, often leave him wondering. For instance, when Bell
wrote that dissertation *The Good and All That* which, it was hoped,
would get him a fellowship at Kings, there were plenty of psychological
reasons why he should make a hash of it. On the one hand he wished
to please his Cambridge mentors by writing an essay on good and evil
in the manner of the discussions of the Apostles, but on the other
hand "more perhaps than he himself realized, Julian was in full revolt
against his Bloomsbury philosophical background, and its static conception of 'states of mind' as values in themselves, or consequences that
might ensue from them." The confusedness was perhaps in part the
result of a naïve desire not to shock Roger Fry, to whom the dissertation was sent for a report. This was of course a model of tolerance and
fair-mindedness. How *liberal*!

Anna Russell in her famous burlesque exposé of Wagner's operas
points out (rightly or wrongly) that Siegfried had the misfortune never
to have met a lady who was not his aunt. There was something of such
a burlesque Siegfried about the young Julian Bell, who gives one the
impression of always encountering very understanding Bloomsbury aunts.
He certainly developed something of an anti-aunt complex. But, as

with the other Siegfried, we are also left with a further question on our hands—wasn't this Siegfried after all a bit stupid?

John Cornford was priggish but not at all stupid, and it is this which in the end makes him more interesting than Bell. He was a Greek hero rather than a confused Wagnerian one, his specialty being the cutting through of Gordian knots. He dealt with family, school, Cambridge, love affairs, the problems dividing the poet from the man of action, all in the same way—cut right through them with the steel blade of objective action. As between poetry and fighting in Spain, he decidedly chose the latter, after he left Cambridge:

> Poetry had become a marginal activity, and a private one. He never discussed his work with his friends in the party; most of them did not even know until after his death that he had been a poet. . . . In the rare moments when he was free to do so, he wrote both personal and political poems. The latter represents a conscious effort to "objectify" his ideas and attitudes as a revolutionary participator, and to transform them into revolutionary poetry.

Instead of being, like Julian Bell, a poet partly stifled in his work by his need to take action in circumstances which cried out for it, he put poetry aside and immersed himself in the war, but from this, and out of the ideology with which he tempered his will and determination, a hard clear new poetry of the objective will began to emerge. He writes sketchily, tentatively but effectively, as someone dominated by the Communist idea of transforming the dialectic into history—hammered out of his mind and body occupied at the given moment in doing just this:

> The past, a glacier, gripped the mountain wall,
> And time was inches, dark was all.
> But here it scales the end of the range,
> The dialectic's point of change,
> Crashes in light and minutes to its fall.
>
> Time present is a cataract whose force
> Breaks down the banks even at its source
> And history forming in our hands
> Not plasticine but roaring sands,
> Yet we must swing it to its final course.

The attempt here is to write a secular Communist poetry corresponding to religious metaphysical poetry. It is blurred perhaps because Marxism, in common with other analytic and scientific systems, cannot be taken outside its own method and terms, and interpreted imagistically, or converted into a mystique, without appearing to lose its own kind of precision. Here the Marxist poet is only encountering the difficulty of other modern poets in a secular world. The precision of science resists being interpreted into the precision of poetry. But if one sees beyond the poem, as through a transparent screen, the structure of the dialectic, it is clear that this is an attempt to write Communist poetry. If one does not see this, then one might agree with Stansky and Abrahams that "the abstractions and metaphors proliferate, taking us still further from reality and deeper into the visionary world of the seer." Having lived through the thirties, I can only rub my eyes reading this. Still—from the Marxist standpoint—all that is wrong is thinking that "abstractions" (if they are "correct") lead away from reality instead of penetrating deeper into it. The point is that Cornford was trying here to be a Marxist visionary and seer. And, but for Stalin and the Marxists, the attempt would not be a contradiction in terms.

What does seem strange is that the idea of literary Bloomsbury that literature should be untainted by politics seems to have derived from France, or rather, from Roger Fry's and Clive Bell's idea of a France of complete esthetic purism. Probably this went back to de Nerval, Gautier, Baudelaire, Mallarmé and Flaubert—and to the eighteen-nineties, reviled and disowned, yet such an influence up till 1930. Art for art's sake looks sophisticated when metamorphosized into "significant form," and Oscar Wilde walks again, but unrecognized, through G. E. Moore's doctrine of the value above all other things of "certain states of consciousness, which may roughly be described as the pleasures of human intercourse and the enjoyment of beautiful objects."

But to hold up post-1918 France as the country of pure esthetic aims is rather as though the French were to point to the work of Edgar Allen Poe in Baudelaire's translations as the type of recent American literature.

A young English writer going with eyes unprejudiced by Bloomsbury's view of France to Paris in the late twenties or early thirties soon discovered that the newspapers and reviews had national parks freely ranged over by French novelists and poets offering their opinions on social topics. When Julian Bell was sent in 1927 to Paris, to learn French at the home of a teacher, he found that his host, as well as knowing much about French literature and art was a theoretical Communist though "there was nothing of the modern party line about him."

Just as English good taste is often modeled on an idea that France is the country of perfect elegance (one has only to travel a little in the provinces to see that the real strength of France lies in its bourgeois bad taste) so Bloomsbury estheticism was modeled on the idea of French writers and artists devoted to nothing but their art. But France is pre-eminently the country of the *deuxième métier*, of the writer who is also a teacher or journalist, the writer who, though he may be "pure" in his poetry or fiction, yet lives by selling his opinions. Even Paul Valéry wrote about politics in the modern world.

It is, indeed, the English who are the real esthetes, failing perhaps to be as pure as they would like to be, but nevertheless upholding a standard of art for art's sake. One has only to mention the names of Kipling, Wells and Shaw to see that these writers, because they published undisguised opinions about politics, damaged their reputations as artists here more than they would have in any other country. And today the writers of the thirties suffer from the odium of their early work being tainted with politics.

All the English or American writer may do with his politics, if he is not to be labeled journalist, is cultivate convictions which show through his work, attitudes basically political, but implicit, not vulgarly declared. The anglicized Americans, Henry James and T. S. Eliot, adapting chameleon-like to England, acquired a traditionalist coloration that, on the rare occasions when it is developed to the point of crude statement, is conservative. But in fact they hardly ever do come into the open.

A point which Mr. John Harrison rather misses in his book *The Reactionaries*,[2] in adding up the sum of Eliot's anti-Semitic and politically reactionary observations, is that they are not in character with the Eliot who after all became an English poet. They come rather from another Eliot character, a somberly jaunty young American in Paris, a figure in a cape, almost eighteen-ninetyish. The famous pronouncement about being a royalist would do better as a bouquet thrown to the Comte de Paris, than to George V.

The characteristic of the special kind of crisis which persuades the young English or American poet (yesterday Spain, today Vietnam) to take the plunge into politics is one of conscience among sensitive and intelligent young members of the ruling class caused by what they regard as a betrayal of principle on the part of their fathers' generation. The failure is the failure to act according to principles when interests are threatened. Since the principles of democratic and "free" societies are basically liberal and since liberal values are always open to the challenge that those who profess them have refused to pay the

2 THE REACTIONARIES. By John Harrison. Golancz.

price which they demand, the crisis is one of the liberal conscience. At the time of the French Revolution and in the early nineteenth century the fury of the Romantic poets was against an English governing class which refused to support freedom when revolution threatened English interests. Byron and Shelley were never more the young English aristocrats than in supporting the overthrowers of kings and priests, and in reviling Castlereagh as though he were their delinquent lackey. Their attitude has something in common with that of Robert Lowell to President Johnson.

Likewise in the thirties anti-Fascism was predominantly a reaction of middle-class young men brought up in a liberal atmosphere against the old men in power, of the same class, who while talking about freedom and democracy, were not prepared to denounce Hitler or defend the Spanish Republic. They feared that as the price of doing so they would find themselves on the same side as the Communists. That the old who professed liberal principles should not see the threat of Fascism or, if they did see it, that they did not take action, seemed to the young a betrayal of basic liberal principles by liberals. Cornford and Bell were not just young Oedipuses subconsciously wishing to destroy their father's image. They had conscious reasons for attacking it: Laius was a liberal.

It is only in the circumstances of a moral power vacuum that the English or American writer can justify, to his conscience as an artist, his taking a political stand. But he does so not without qualms. The anti-Fascist writers of the thirties conducted debates, not only in reviews or at meetings, but in their own hearts, between public and isolated artistic conscience. Indeed, ever since the nineteenth century (Shelley, Arnold, Clough, Ruskin, Morris) it has been the case that the English poet mixed up in politics may spend a lifetime divided between two voices: that of social, and that of esthetic, conscience: Shelley calling on the world to dethrone kings, and Keats claiming that his poetry is unshadowed by any trace of public thought.

There is a good deal to be said in support of the English poets' mistrust of overtly taking sides. Only in exceptional historical circumstances do writers here attend the "boring meeting" or read or write the "flat ephemeral pamphlet." Very rarely do they find themselves involved in "the conscious acceptance of guilt in the fact of murder."

The "disgrace" attaching to the "low dishonest decade" of the thirties in England was not the same as that in France of some surrealist turned Communist and currying favor with Stalin by accusing André Gide of being a Fascist because he was critical of the Russia of the Moscow trials. We had the humility to believe that for writers to be involved in politics was itself a fall from grace. To us part of the hideousness of Fascism was that it produced anti-Fascism, involving disinterested artists in interested politics. Reading Auden's poem on the death of Yeats, in 1939, "Intellectual disgrace/Stares from every human face," I think of the whole politically involved intellectual life of that decade, disgraced with ideologies.

However, our English and American idea that the intellectuals should only take political sides in situations providing moral contrasts of inky black and dazzling white has its disadvantages. For one thing there is something unserious about a seriousness which is made conditional on things being so serious.

After all, the shining emergent Causes—Spain, the Bomb, Vietnam—do have chains of further causality stretching before and after. That the intellectuals only have time for them when they have become moral scandals might seem to indicate that they do not have time anyway. The English and American political-unpolitical intellectuals sometime have the look of the gadarene swine hurling themselves down the steepest slope: the gadarene swine being of course in the latest apocalyptic fashion. The cause evaporates when the crisis in its immediate emanation has passed. The long term causes of the Cause find few among the English and American intellectuals to interest them.

In France the intellectuals are, as it were, more or less in continual session like the British House of Lords. They are sometimes irresponsible, nearly always narrowly legalistic in their interpretations of a political line (with that deceptive French "logic") but their concern with politics is sustained and (despite Clive Bell and Roger Fry) not thought to dishonor their art. They do not have to prove that in attending a conference about peace or freedom, they are being serious, whereas the English and Americans are under pressure to show that when they do take up a cause, they do more about it than travel to nice places. His biographers note that Julian Bell dismissed "in a few satirical phrases" the International Writers' Congress which was held in Madrid in the summer of 1937, while he was driving an ambulance on the Brunete front. I happened to attend the Congress of Intellectuals myself and also to have described it satirically (in *World within World*) though without Bell's justification that I was carrying a gun or driving an ambulance. But I don't think any but English and Americans would have thought that a meeting of writers in Madrid when shells were falling was a despicable exercise. The French would have seen it as a useful part of a larger strategy of help for the Republican cause, as useful, in its way, as being at the front, though not so courageous and praiseworthy. They also serve who only sit and talk.

The authors of two books which I have been reading recently seem to me to take the difference between the situation of the French and the Anglo-American intellectuals insufficiently into account: *The Reactionaries* by John Harrison, to which I have already referred, and *Writers and Politics* by Conor Cruise O'Brien.[3]

O'Brien is at his brilliant best when he is discussing French writers: e.g., the shift in Camus' earlier revolutionary position to the resigned pessimism of *La Chute,* written when he refused to take sides over the Algerian War. O'Brien analyzes the relations of Camus with the general current of French-intellectual life with a precision which reads like a description of the modifications caused to some receiving instrument by the electrical impulses passing through it.

O'Brien quite rightly derides those critics who discovered Camus to be "objectively revolutionary," employing what he calls "the convenient principle: 'I know what he thinks: it doesn't matter what he thinks he thinks.'"

Since he has such insight into the fallaciousness of this principle, it seems strange that, on occasion, he employs it himself. In the essay on Dwight Macdonald (*A New Yorker Critic*) he argues that Mr. Macdonald in giving up his "socialist past" and writing about "masscult," "midcult" and the rest for *The New Yorker* in effect (and regardless of what Macdonald may think he thinks) subscribes to the policy of that magazine, which is a projection of the views of its advertisers. This is the "objective" argument squared. *The New Yorker* is as object to its backers, and Dwight Macdonald is as object to *The New Yorker.*

The insidious nonpolitical policy of *The New Yorker* as it operates subliminally on the mind of Dwight Macdonald works like this:

> you could say *almost* anything about Mark Twain, James Joyce, James Agee, Ernest Hemingway, James Cozzens, Colin Wilson, the English or revised Bibles, or Webster's *New International Dictionary*—to list most of Mr. Macdonald's subjects—without causing a *New Yorker* reader or advertiser to wince. If, however, your favourite author happened to be Mao Tse-tung and Fidel Castro and you tried to say so in *The New Yorker,* then you would be going "against the American grain" and you would not be likely to go very far.

3 WRITERS AND POLITICS. By Conor Cruise O'Brien. Alfred A. Knopf.

This is really a variant of the "objective" argument: *The New Yorker* is not filled with articles in praise of Mao Tse-tung because of the invisible thought-control of the advertisers. But supposing, after all, that *New Yorker* writers don't admire the prose of the Chinese and Cuban dictators? Should *The New Yorker* nevertheless contain a quota of opinions praising it just to prove to Dr. O'Brien that *The New Yorker* is free from the pressures to which he thinks it is subject? Or supposing that Dr. O'Brien had suggested some different writers whom *New Yorker* writers would praise if they were free agents—say Hitler and Trujillo? One only has to suggest this to see the bias of the argument. Dr. O'Brien is playing on the reader's secret guilt about China and Cuba. There are I think false steps in O'Brien's attack on Dwight Macdonald. In the first place, Macdonald was never a party line socialist revolutionary, he was just a lone rebel all by himself. He was a highly individualist rebel against American capitalism who sought allies among Anarchists, Communists, Trotskyites. In discussing him as though he had reneged from revolutionary socialism (perhaps—because he is such a nice fellow—without realizing he was doing so), Dr. O'Brien fails to mention the important statements made by Macdonald when he gave up his magazine *Politics*, that in the complexity of the postwar situation he no longer found it possible to take up clear positions. He found, as did many other survivors from the simplicist world of the thirties, that politics had become extremely complicated and that it was no longer possible to see them in black and white.

O'Brien's case against Camus seems stronger than that against Macdonald, because the early Camus wrote within the context of the ideas of the left-wing French intellectuals. Camus' attitude toward Algeria certainly separated him from Sartre and his followers. It is plausible then to regard him as abandoning a path followed by leftist French writers. With Macdonald though, all one can say is that an independent thinker whose thoughts when he was young were anarchistic later had other thoughts about other things. The new thoughts were about culture and not about politics. One may or may not agree with them, one may or may not regret that Macdonald stopped having things to say about politics, but to say that he changed the content and the direction of his thinking to suit *The New Yorker* is misleading.

Mr. John Harrison's reactionaries are W. B. Yeats, Wyndham Lewis, Ezra Pound and D. H. Lawrence. Mr. Harrison knows that to prove that they are really reactionary, it is not enough to show that they occasionally labeled themselves so. However he does not altogether avoid the dangers implicit in compiling lists of their reactionary pronouncements without asking how far these really correspond to ideas in their best creative work. His problem is to relate their expressed opinions to convictions of which they themselves may not have been wholly aware, but which do have political implications, in their best writing.

The extent to which we should take a writer's expressed opinions seriously is difficult to ascertain. What I have been suggesting here is that in France it is not so difficult to do this, because there is a tradition of intellectually respect-worthy opinion about politics to which the writer can relate his own views. But in England and America there is no such tradition of the writer in politics. Therefore his interventions tend to be sporadic and occasional and perhaps not consistent with his truest, that is his most imaginative, insights.

This is even more true of the Right than of the Left. For the Left, after all, even in England and America, can merge into the traditions of the French and American Revolutions, the internationalism of nine-teenth-century liberals, Marxism, mingling, for the time being, with a world river of continuous thought and energy. During the decade of the Popular Front the English anti-Fascist writers became, as it were, honorary French intellectuals. And this was not altogether absurd be-cause of the international character of the Left. But Fascism, and indeed the European right, so diverse in its manifestations in different coun-tries, although potentially an international threat, was nationalist and local in ideas and performance. Therefore there was something much more esoteric and perverse about the intermittent support which Mr. Harrison's reactionaries gave to right-wing and Fascist movements than about the corresponding political involvements of the anti-Fascists.

The traditionalism which appealed so much to Yeats, Pound, Eliot, Wyndham Lewis and others doubtless had political implications, and given the crucial nature of the period, it was not dishonorable of traditionalists to want to realize these by supporting rightist parties. But a big leap into the near dark had to be made in order to convert the poetic traditionalism of Yeats, Pound or Eliot into support of General O'Duffy, Mussolini or the *Action Française*.

The political attitudes of Yeats, Eliot, Pound, Lewis, Lawrence, consist largely of gestures toward some movement, idea, leadership which *seems* to correspond to the writer's deeply held traditionalism. Such gestures and attitudes are largely rhetorical. For the politics of these writers are secondary effects of their thoughts about the tragedy of culture in modern industrial societies. They are sometimes conscientious, sometimes irresponsible attempts to translate their traditionalist standpoint into programs of action.

Whereas the leftist anti-Fascist writers—believing that the overthrow of Fascism was the most important task of their generation—tended to think that their writing should perhaps be the instrument of the overriding public cause, the reactionaries thought that politics should be the servant of their vision of the high tradition. Wyndham Lewis, for example, never supposed that he should become the mouthpiece of Hitler. What he thought was that as the living representative in the contemporary world of renaissance "genius" perhaps a few renaissance thugs would be helpful to the cause of his art: if this was the role that Hitler and Mussolini had unknowingly cast for themselves, maybe they should be encouraged. Yeats had a not very different attitude toward the soldiers of the Right who could perhaps be given orders by Art, and who also were useful in providing sound effects for the end of a civilization.

The most important thing common to the reactionaries was that they had a kind of shared vision of the greatness of the European past which implied hatred and contempt for the present. It might be said that all their most important work was an attempt to relate their experiences to this central vision. On the secondary level of their attempts to carry forward the vision into action and propaganda there is a good deal of peripheral mess, resulting from their search for political approximations to their love of past intellect, art, discipline and order. Often their politics only shows that they care less for politics than for literature.

Mr. John Harrison takes some remarks of Orwell as his text which he sets out to illustrate with examples drawn from his authors. This text is worth examining:

> The relationship between fascism and the literary intelligentsia badly needs investigating, and Yeats might well be the starting point. He is best studied by someone like Mr. Menon who knows that a writer's politics and religious beliefs are not excrescences to be laughed away, but something that will leave their mark even on the smallest detail of his work.

This sounds sensible enough though it is perhaps too offhand to bear the weight of Mr. Harrison's thesis. Certain objections occur to one. For example, if it were true that a writer's politics and religious beliefs extend from a center outward into every smallest detail of his work, then the converse would also be true that one could deduce his party or creed from an analysis of any smallest detail, whether or not the writer thought that he supported such a party or a creed.

This leads back into the objectivist fallacy of the writer holding certain views whether he thinks he does or not.

What is wrong is Orwell's loose bracketing of religious and political beliefs, and his assumption that it is a comparatively simple matter to know what a writer believes. But it is not simple, since he is writing out of his imagination, his vision of life, and not according to labels which he or others may stick on to him. Orwell appears to think that Yeats's symbolism, mythology, imagery—his poetry in a word— are projections onto the plane of the imagination of his declared political and religious beliefs. It is really the other way round. Yeats's religion and politics are the results of numerous inconsistent attempts to rationalize his central poetic vision, as dogma, politics, action. Whether or not they should be "laughed off," Yeats's Fascism was an excrescence. It grew rather approximately and grossly from the center of his poetic imagination which was neither approximate nor gross. To any- one who reads *A Vision* or his journals and prose, it must be quite clear that his opinions are attempts to systematize the intuitions of his imagination.

Add to this that even when they are stated as prose, one cannot discuss Yeats's beliefs without making many qualifications. Outside of be- lieving in art and in some universe of the spirit in which the visions of art are realistic truth, Yeats himself was extremely approximate about what he believed. He was candid in admitting that he cultivated be- liefs and attitudes in himself for the purpose of propping up the sym- bolism of his poetry. He also had a sharp picture of a materialist world which undermined his world of the poetic imagination: this was Bernard Shaw's Fabian philosophy and belief in material progress. That which to Shaw was superstition and reaction recommended itself as dogma and practice to Yeats.

Dr. O'Brien has drawn up a formidable list of Yeats's pro-Fascist statements, including one or two sympathetic to Hitler. But to the reader who thinks that Yeats's poems and not his opinions matter, it will seem, I think, that he used the political stage properties of the thirties in the same way as he used the assertions of his esoteric system set out in *A Vision*—as a scenario stocked with symbols and metaphors which he could draw on for his poetry. To Yeats writing the tragic-gay poetry of his old age, Hitler had the seductive charm of an apocalyptic cat.

What is distressing about the reactionaries is not that they were occasionally betrayed by intoxication with their own ideas and fantasies into supporting dictators who would, given the opportunity, certainly have disposed very quickly of them, but that in the excess of their hatred of the present and their love of the past, they developed a certain cult of inhumanity. One has to ask though—was not their renaissance vision enormously valuable to us, and could it have been stated without dramatizing the statuesque figures of a visionary past against the twittering ghosts of the disintegrated present?

Eliot's political views, like those of Yeats, are a defense system hastily thrown out with the intention of defending a spiritual world deriving strength from the past, against modern materialism. One suspects that Eliot was convinced intellectually, as a critic, and not with his imagination, as a poet, of the necessity of rationalizing poetic values as politics. Without the example of T. E. Hulme and without some cheer-leading from Ezra Pound and some satiric pushing from Wyndham Lewis, Eliot would scarcely have made those remarks about liberalism and progress, which seem casual asides, and which yet set him up as an authority, defender of the monarchy and the faith. In his role of political commentator in *The Criterion* he must have baffled readers who did not realize that his mind was moving along lines laid down by Charles Maurras. There is also something cloak-and-dagger about the anti-Semitic passages in the Sweeney poems which Mr. Harrison inevitably relies on to demonstrate his thesis:

> *The smoky candle end of time*
> *Declines. On the Rialto once.*
> *The rats are underneath the piles.*
> *The jew is underneath the lot.*
> *Money in furs.*

Of course this was distasteful caricature even when it was written. In the light of later developments it seems almost criminal. Nevertheless what seems wrong about the Sweeney poems is not that they are reactionary-political but that they use a tawdry view of a conspiratorial capitalism to construct a rather cardboard background to the poetry.

That Eliot, Yeats, Pound and Lawrence were all exiles (and Wyndham Lewis a self-declared outsider—"the Enemy") has a bearing on their politics. The exile is particularly apt to dramatize himself as a metaphor moving through a world of metaphors. Pound and Eliot left what they regarded as barbarous America to come to civilized Europe, where they found, in the First World War:

There died a myriad,
And of the best among them,
For an old bitch gone in the teeth,
For a botched civilisation.

Their poetry exalted the past which they had sought among the Georgian poets and found only embalmed in museums, and it derided the present, the decay of standards. They were, politically, Don Quixotes of the new world armed to rescue the Dulcinea of the old— an old hag. The aim of their polemical criticism was to reinvent the past, shining and modern, and use it as a modern weapon against the arsenals of the dead men stuffed with straw.

Their politics were secondary to the creative and critical attempt. In them, they were drawn to whatever points of view presented social and economic problems as metaphors for their idea of the state of civilization. The appeal of politics in the guise of metaphor is curiously shown in the great attraction—which can only be compared with that of Donne's ideas about time—of Social Credit theories for a number of writers, including not only Eliot and Pound but also Edwin Muir— during the late twenties and thirties. Social Credit is easy to visualize. One sees objects of value being produced on one side of a chart and on the other side money—credit—being printed equal to the value of the objects. Since Schacht and Mussolini actually made adjustments to the German and Italian economies along similar lines, Social Credit seemed to be an idea which could be abstracted from the rest of Fascism and applied to other systems. For reactionaries who could not swallow violence, it was a kind of Fascism without tears.

Students of Ezra Pound's *Cantos* will observe how metaphors of this kind drawn from a reading of economics imagized and then applied to describe the state of the civilization are used by Pound, sometimes to justify inhuman attitudes. A famous example is the passage about usury in which Pound explains that the introduction of usury into the economic system falsifies the line drawn by the painter, causes his hand to err. This justifies a massacre of Jews.

The Left also of course had their metaphors, which by making history appear a poetic act tended to regard human beings as words to be acted upon, deleted if necessary, so that the poem might come right.

In fact, on a level of false rhetoric, so far from there being a separation of politics from poetry, there is a dangerous convergence. Marxism, because it regards history as malleable material to be manipulated by the creative will of the Marxist, is rich in this kind of raw material poetic thinking.

The temptation for the poet is to take over the rhetoric of political will and action and translate it into the rhetoric of poetry without confronting the public rhetoric of politics with the private values of poetry. If there is a sin common to poetry such as Auden's *Spain*, the anti-Semitic passages in Eliot's Sweeney poems, the political passages in Pound's cantos, Wyndham Lewis' adulation of what he calls "the party of genius" (meaning Michelangelo and Wyndham Lewis), Lawrence's worship of the dynamic will of nature's aristocrats (in *The Plumed Serpent*), certain of my own lines, it is that the poet has— if only for a few moments—allowed his scrupulous poet's rhetoric of the study of "minute particulars" to be overwhelmed by his secret yearning for a heroic public rhetoric. Sensibility has surrendered to will, the Keatsian concept of poetic personality to the dominating mode of character.

In a period when poets seemed imprisoned in their private worlds, their occasional acts of surrender to the excitement of a public world of action in the service of what they could pretend to themselves was a civilizing cause is understandable. But the reactionariness of the "reactionaries" is the weakness, not the strength, of their work. William Empson writes in his curious, sympathetic preface to Mr. Harrison's book that he doubts whether the political issues of "their weakness for Fascism" was "the central one." He adds:

> Now that everything is so dismal we should look back with reverence on the great age of poets and fundamental thinkers, who were so ready to consider heroic remedies. Perhaps their gloomy prophecies have simply come true.

We (and here by "we" I mean the thirties' writers) not only look back on them with reverence, but we also revered them at the time. It is important to understand that we thought of them as a greater generation of more devoted artists. That we did so made us reflect that we were a generation less single-minded in our art, but which had perhaps found a new subject—the social situation. We did not think this could lead to better work than theirs, but on the other hand we saw that young poets could not go on writing esoteric poetry about the end of civilization. Yet their endgames were our beginnings. Our generation reacted against the same conventions of Georgian poetry and the novel as did the generation of T. S. Eliot, Virginia Woolf, D. H. Lawrence and E. M. Forster. They were indeed our heroes.

Pound, Wyndham Lewis and Roy Campbell were the only reactionaries whose public attitudes we sometimes attacked: with the mental reservation that we thought them zanies anyway. As for Eliot, Yeats and Lawrence, if one minimized their statements about politics, there was much in their deepest political insights with which we agreed.

> *Things fall apart: the centre cannot hold;*
> *Mere anarchy is loosed upon the world.*

This described our situation. By comparison the fact that Yeats went out and supported General O'Duffy seemed singularly irrelevant. No poem could show better than *The Second Coming* how wrong Orwell was to approach Yeats's poetry as a function of his Fascism. To us, his Fascism seemed a misconception arising from his deep political (and here the word seems quite inadequate) insight.

It is a pity that Mr. Harrison, instead of accepting at their face value labels like "left" and "reactionary," did not compare at a deeper level than that of political parties the social vision of the poets of the thirties and the older generation. He might have found then that the two generations often agreed in their diagnoses: they came to opposite conclusions with regard to remedies. He might also have found that the younger generation, in coming to their revolutionary conclusions, owed their view that we were living in a revolutionary situation to the insights of the reactionaries.

His biographers point out that John Cornford, while he was still a schoolboy, was led to Communism by reading *The Waste Land*. "He believed it to be a great poem, read it not as a religious allegory . . . but as an anatomy of capitalist society in decay; it shaped his style, but more important, it was a preface to his politics."

To the imagination the poetry does not preach party matters. It penetrates into the depths of an external situation and shows what is strange and terrible. Eliot drew conclusions from his own poetic insight with his intellect, with which Cornford disagreed when he wrote:

> *The Waste Land* . . . is of great importance not for the pleasure it gives, but for its perfect picture of the disintegration of a civilisation. . . . But something more than description, some analysis of the situation is needed. And it is here that Eliot breaks down. He refuses to answer the question that he has so perfectly formulated. He retreats into the familiar triangle—Classicism, Royalism, Ango-Catholicism. He has not found an answer to the question of resignation. Rather he has resigned himself to finding no answer.

Here the imagination which can give the "perfect picture of dis-integration" is dramatized as posing the question to which the intellect gives the answer—the wrong answer, according to Cornford, but even he, the convinced Communist undergraduate about to go to Spain, cares more that the question should have been posed than that the answer should be "correct," for the question suggests what was to him the "correct" answer.

What was common to modern poets between 1910 and 1930 was their condemnation of a society which they saw as the disintegra-tion of civilization. Given this agreed on line, it was possible to be on the reactionary or the socialist side of it. The reactionaries, on their side asked: "What of the past can be saved?" The socialists, on their side, asked: "How can there be new life?" The awesome achievement of the earlier generation was to have created for their contemporaries a vision of the whole past tradition which had a poignant immediacy: giving shattered contemporary civilization consciousness of its own past greatness, like the legendary glimpse of every act of his life in the eyes of a man drowning. Without the awareness of drowning, of the end of the long game, the apprehended moment could not have been so vivid. Thus the gloomy prophecies of the future, and the consequent weakness for reactionary politics, were the dark side of an intensely burning vision.

The liberals, the progressives, the anti-Fascists could not invest their future with a vision of the values of present civilization as great as the reactionaries' vision of past values. Perhaps though they agreed with the reactionaries that the genius of our civilization which had flickered on since the Renaissance was soon to be extinguished. E. M. Forster, whose work stands midway between the idea of past and present, sees the greatness of England and Europe as over. The past commands his love, though the causes which should ultimately make people better off—freedom of the peoples of the world from the old imperialisms, greater social justice, etc.—command his loyalty. But his loyalty in-spires him with little love, and he has no enthusiasm for the liberated materially better world which he felt bound to support.

The anti-Fascists in the end accepted or were influenced by the idea that the struggle for the future meant abandoning nostalgia for a past civilization. They had now to emphasize "new life," a new culture not obsessed with the past. Julian Bell and John Cornford came to feel that in putting the cause before everything they must be pre-pared even to jettison their own poetry. And they found themselves quite glad to do so. In 1932, when he started becoming interested in politics, John Cornford wrote to his mother: "I have found it a great relief to stop pretending to be an artist" and in the same letter he told her that he had bought "*Kapital* and a good deal of commentary, which I hope to find time to tackle this term. Also *The Communist Manifesto.*" In renouncing being an artist he is also turning back on the world of his mother, Frances Cornford, the poet. Julian Bell experienced an immense sense of relief when he decided to turn away from literature and go to Spain. If Auden and Isherwood had written a play on the theme of Bell and Cornford one can well imagine that their deaths on the battlefield would have been seen as the finale of a dialogue with their art-loving mothers.

Feelings and motives involved here are extremely complex. Uncertainty about their vocations, rebellion against their mothers and against the values of the literary world of Cambridge, Oxford and London, a suppressed anti-intellectualism and an expression of the tendency of the young in that decade to interpret all current issues as a conflict between principles of "life" and "death," the "real" and the "unreal," all enter in. The reader of Stansky and Abrahams cannot help noting that in a decade when people were always being reproached for "escapism" the immersion into the life of action and political choice filled Bell and Cornford with an elation remarkably like that of escape —escape from having to be poets. Escape is wrong only if it means an escape from high standards to lower or more relaxed ones. In their renunciation of those standards of their parents which were, perhaps, too esthetic, Cornford and Bell shared a tendency to escape into accepting means which were perilously close to Fascist ones. Thus Cornford writes:

> The disgraceful part of the German business is not that the Nazis kill and torture their enemies; it is that Socialists and Communists let themselves be made prisoners instead of first killing as many Nazis as they can.

Julian Bell states still more strongly the objection to the liberals. His reaction is all the more striking because it is so much a renunciation of that pacifism which was one of his deepest ties with his parents:

> Most of my friends are utterly squeamish about means; they feel that it would be terrible to use force or fraud against anyone. . . . Even most Communists seem to me to have only a hysterical and quite unrealistic notion about violent methods . . . I can't imagine anyone of the *New Statesman*

> doing anything "unfair" to an opponent. . . . Whereas for my own part . . . I can't feel the slightest qualms about the notion of doing anything effective, however ungentlemanly and unchristian, nor about admitting to myself that certain actions would be very unfair indeed. . . .

and he ends the same letter with a sentence that is surely very revealing:

> I don't feel, myself, as if I could ever be satisfied to do anything but produce works of art, or even nothing but leading a private life and producing works in the intervals.

I do not quote these passages because I think them characteristic of Cornford and Bell (in fact they are hysterical outbursts out of character) but because of the light which—paradoxically—they throw on the relationship of the thirties generation with an older one. This balances the violence of the reactionaries supporting Fascism in the name of art, against the violence of the leftists prepared to sacrifice art to the cause of anti-Fascism.

The reactionaries cared passionately for past values. Their nostalgia misled them into sympathizing with whatever jack-booted corporal or demagogue set himself up in defense of order. As the history of Ezra Pound shows, the results of this could be tragic. But they did put literature before politics, and their first concern was to preserve the civilization without which, as they thought, neither past nor future literature could survive. They did not, as the anti-Fascist writers did, abandon or postpone their literary tasks. For the anti-Fascists allowed themselves, rightly or wrongly, to be persuaded that civilization could only be saved by action: the logical consequence of this attitude was to put writing at the service of necessity as dictated by political leaders.

There was, then, the paradox that the reactionaries who were on the side of the past, the dead, had to live for the sake of literature, whereas circumstances drove the most sincere anti-Fascists—men like Cornford, Bell, Fox and Caudwell—to death as absolution in a cause which they had made absolute. The reactionaries wrote out of their tragic sense of modern life. The Cornfords and Bells lived and died the tragedy.

Chapter Fourteen
Protest in Art
Barbara Rose

Puerilism we shall call the attitude of a community whose behaviour is more immature than the state of its intellectual and critical faculties would warrant, which instead of making the boy into the man adapts its conduct to that of the adolescent age. — J. Huizanga, *Salmagundi,* 1972

Because Dada reacted against bourgeois society and its culture in the period just preceding, during, and after World War I, various antiauthoritarian styles of behavior in America in the late fifties and sixties have been variously labeled neo-Dada. Undoubtedly direct connections between happenings, environments, ephemeral art, and the like characteristics of the American avant-garde and Dada manifestations exist. There are, however, crucial dissimilarities, especially with regard to the role of antiauthoritarian behavior as an act of protest.

Recent interest in Dada dates back as far as the publication of Robert Motherwell's anthology *The Dada Painters and Poets* in 1951, which introduced a new generation of American artists including Robert Rauschenberg, Jasper Johns, Allan Kaprow, Claes Oldenburg, Robert Whitman, George Brecht, and Red Grooms to a tradition of antiformalist art. The presence of Marcel Duchamp in New York also provided a continuous bond with the Dada past. Interestingly enough, New York had crystallized as a Dada center before Zurich, Paris, Hannover, or Berlin. One might say Dada — especially the sceptical satiric Dada of Duchamp — came naturally to Americans, who saw themselves not as the heirs of a great cultural tradition but as the inhabitants of "god's junkyard." In fact the negative assessment of American culture by its own avant-garde has its origin in New York Dada. The critics of the Stieglitz circle who wrote for *Camera Work* and *291*, Picabia's Dada publication, heaped abuse on American philistinism and materialism, and John Sloan suggested that Hieronymous Bosch was the only painter capable of capturing the American scene.

Although the publication of *The Dada Painters and Poets* reintroduced Dada concepts in America, crucial transformations had already taken place in American society which meant that the interest in Dada was not at all in its spirit of protest, but rather in its antiformal aesthetic attitudes. Art historians have taken the purported political content of Dada far too seriously. The Dadaists by self-admission were politically naive; their "political" protests were non-specific. Bourgeois *culture* not capitalist politics was the main target. Dada's strategy was to challenge the bourgeois ideology of progress by rupturing continuity with historical tradition. The art of environments, happenings, and concepts and the ironic use of popular imagery in pop art that flourished in New York around 1960 was tied to Dada in that it also challenged the ivory tower idealism of pure art. But Dada *attacked* — its aggression was turned outward toward the world. It insulted, shocked, subverted, and threw into question the entire apparatus of bourgeois culture. What was called neo-Dada in New York attacked nothing, not even art. Dada techniques and experiments were used only as devices to initiate new forms; Dada, in other words, was appreciated as a purely aesthetic phenomenon, stripped of critical content.

To a degree, the lack of interest in the social protest element of Dada in American neo-Dada had to do with the strength of the identity of the New York School as an independent avant-garde. Dada forms and antiforms were used as a means of reacting against Abstract Expressionism and abstract art generally, but there was no question of protesting politics, economics, ethics, or any other social concerns because the artist stood so firmly *outside* society. During the sixties, however, American society began to take notice of artistic activities, largely as a result of the media obsession with news. And as long as art directed itself toward newness, the media infatuation with novelty assured its intrusion into the American consciousness.

Suddenly the American artist found himself within instead of outside society. This created a bewildering situation. Lacking any previous interaction with that society, these artists had developed no means or tradition of protest: the American avant-garde had never protested because there had been no context within which to protest. The abrasive relationship that had developed between bourgeois society and the avant-garde in Europe simply did not exist. In fact Duchamp had always maintained he lived in America because it was the only place that as an artist he could remain completely anonymous.

Beginning in the sixties the existence of an audience created a whole set of new problems. Even initially, it was obvious that the permissive attitude of this audience was evidence of bad faith. Thus by the time the American avant-garde was forced into direct commerce, so to speak, with an audience that was not itself, the original Dada impulse to *épater le bourgeois* was no longer viable as a strategy of protest. For one thing, the notion of shock is predicated on an idea of what normative behavior might be, and even that standard was lacking in America. Something is shocking only in relation to an accepted system of values. Here a system of decorum had never been firmly enough established to create a code of behavior with regard to which certain kinds of activities could be considered shocking. There was of course one notable exception, and that was the vestiges of sexual prudery left over even as late in 1960 from American puritanism. Whether American art helped inspire the sexual revolution, or whether it simply ran along side it is a difficult question to answer. At any rate, we do see suddenly around 1960 a preponderance of forbidden and taboo themes in American art. Lucas Samaras's plaster dolls (recently seen at the Whitney Museum) miming the positions of the Kama Sutra, George Segal's plaster copulating couple, Ed Kienholz's bordello, Oldenburg's overt sexual imagery, Wesselman's mammary fantasies (with their clear juxtaposition of female genitalia, breasts, and food) generated a certain excitement when they were originally exhibited. Today they seem almost prudish, reticent in comparison with ordinary popular entertainment. Porno movies, massage parlors, topless clubs, and the rest have forced the artists to look for categories other than the erotic for forbidden themes which might challenge conventional norms.

It was only natural in this situation to turn to anti-social Dada behavior in areas beyond the erotic. However, Dada's negation and nihilism were rejected. American artists did not connect with Dada's protest because their view of Dada had been filtered through John Cage, who altered the Dada aesthetic in a number of significant ways. For Cage was influenced not only by Satie, Duchamp, and Dada, but also by the oriental philosophy of Zen. And it was this odd mix of Dada and Zen that Cage handed on to his disciples and followers who were so numerous it is difficult to think of an important artist of the sixties unaffected by his thought. The crucial difference is that where Dada says attack, Zen says accept. It is this oriental passivity we remark among younger Americans that strikes us as so foreign to the aggressive Dada spirit. There was, however, an area in which Zen and Dada coincided. That was in the attitude toward chance, which became an extremely important element for American art in the sixties. But the use of chance itself as a method to form creation implies a large degree of passivity toward the external world.

The irrelevancy of overt protest was accepted by the generation of American artists who grew up in the Eisenhower years, lived through McCarthy, and went to war in Korea. Nor could you scandalize an audience whose public morals became increasingly lax as the decade wore on. You could, however, bore them or irritate them. Cage prescribed both. For a time boredom seemed an effective way to irritate — that is, until the public began enjoying sitting through eight hours of Andy Warhol's *Sleep* and queing up for marathon viewing of an immobile camera recording the *Empire State Building* lighting up hours of close-ups of people engaged in the most mundane occupations. When boredom ultimately was found to have an aesthetic dimension, another strategy of alienating the audience was exhausted.

Inevitably the nature of the relationship of the avant-garde to its audience defines the types of protest available at any given time. When the audience has become as excessively permissive as the current American audience, there is no longer any act of aggression the artist can direct toward it, since these actions will not be interpretated as aggression but as more diversion. The system of signaling has therefore broken down, largely as a result of the communications revolution which neutralizes information and deprives both art and criticism of a role antagonistic to established culture. Through the media, aggression is transformed into harmless entertainment.

On one level, every stylistic change in the history of art may be viewed as an Oedipal confrontation. However, as the ruptures between generations become greater, and entire systems of values are at variance, the generational confrontation takes on a more and more violent character. All forms of rebellion are revolts against authority; but the degree to which this authority is held to be illegitimate becomes critical. The initial rebellion of the avant-garde in the nineteenth century took place within the context of a specific and generally understood discipline. How much classical academicism reflected the values of an entire social structure, its investment in ideals of hierarchical order, is revealed by the violence with which the questioners of these values were attacked by the public. They were jeered at, mocked, deprived of honors and status, deliberately impoverished, and forced to live as classless bohemians. When we read Manet's and Degas's letters, we realize how ill-prepared the artist was for such rejection, and how much he continued to crave society's acceptance. For no mere stylistic change in the past had ever evoked such hostility from society at large. Therefore something greater than stylistic change must have been at stake in these first manifestations of the modern spirit.

The equation of a disruption of the social order with a disruption of the cultural order was not the intention of the artists who originally caused these disruptions. Once cast out from society, however, they had no choice but to play the role of pariah which society had assigned them. Yet they never ceased suffering from rejection, for their goals were highly idealistic. It is at this stage of rejection, for example, that we get figures like Van Gogh and Gauguin, tortured by guilt because of the discrepancy between the idealism of their intentions and the reception of their art by society.

Van Gogh's career as a missionary and evangelist testifies to the extreme idealism of his personality; as does Gauguin's religious iconography. Yet both ended as martyrs — Van Gogh a suicide, Gauguin an exile. Both were haunted by masochistic guilt feelings expressing the conflict between their own conception of the good and society's values. Gauguin's self-portrait in the National Gallery in Washington, for example, illustrates this conflict, for he shows himself with both angelic and diabolic attributes — a celestial halo as well as the devil's pronged tail.

The artist's self-identification with martyrs provides a fascinating art historical category. At first he paints himself as martyred religious figures — Dürer sees himself as Christ, Rembrandt as the apostle Paul. Beginning in the late nineteenth century, however, the theme of the artist as society's martyr goes beyond his identification with religious figures or saviors. In one of his best known essays, the playwright, poet, and essayist Artaud writes of Van Gogh as "the man suicided by society." Society's rejection of the artist forces him to accept the role of martyr as opposed to his intended role of savior. A work by Claes Oldenburg illustrates the contemporary artist's feeling that the public is eating him alive: it is a jello mold in the image of the artist. Andy Warhol finally attracted so much violence to himself that it was inevitable that he should be shot — martyred by a society that literally endangers any artists that dares come into direct contact with its chaos.

By the late sixties, the artist's feelings of rejection, self-hatred, and guilt have crystallized to new dimensions in a form called Body Art. The success of Body Art depends on the degree to which the artist can mutilate his own body. We have had many recent examples, all exhibited in galleries and museums to a public no longer shocked but titillated into a sadomasochistic identification with the act of self-mutilation. One may cite as examples Dennis Oppenheim methodically ripping off a toenail, Vito Accounci rubbing cockroaches out into his bare chest, and Chris Burden's suspending himself between buckets of water and live electric currents which presumably would electrocute him if one of the buckets were tipped over.

The *ne plus ultra* of Body Art, however, was the self-castration of Rudolph Schwarzkogler, a German artist who cut off slices of his penis until he finally bled to death. The photographs recording this process were exhibited at Documanta 5 last summer in Kassel, West Germany. The examples of self-mutilation and masochistic practices among artists today are so numerous that it becomes simply repetitious to catalogue them. What is significant is that protest is no longer directed outward as an aggression toward society — as in Dada — but turned in against the self. As the potential for protest is gradually eradictated by the ability of technological culture to coopt any form of criticism toward its own ends, the artist turns against himself.

Although conceptual art presumably sought to destroy the status of the art object as a medium of exchange, its strategies too were proved pointless as the artists began exhibiting "documents" — photographs, videotapes, prints, etc., of their works in commercial galleries and museums. The permissiveness of dealers, curators, and the public seemingly had no end. Dada's testing of limits was demonstrated as ridiculous in the present context, which admits of no limits. The result is that in its current confusion, society has abdicated the parental authoritorian rule vis-à-vis the rebellious artist adopted in the formative years of the avant-garde. In other words, society in general no longer wishes to perpetuate the traditional relationship between itself and the avant-garde: the society appropriates to itself the artist's license to remain a child, perpetually at play, knowing no limits.

Dada exalted play as a form of artistic activity: now Dada has become the activity of the masses reflected in its films and rock concerts. And conversely, the artist can no longer practice Dada if he wishes to remain in a critical role. This has produced an enormous crisis, polarizing artistic protest into forms on the one hand more infantile and, on the other, more mature than those of Dada, whose adolescent attitudes no longer seem opposite to the current situation.

For the key to Dada from a psychological point of view is to understand how closely its interests and activities conform to those of the adolescent. In *En Avant Dada,* the Dadaist Richard Hülsenbeck speaks of "The New Man — armed with the Weapons of Doubt and Defiance." To speak of the "new man," and call doubt and defiance weapons, is to speak in a sense as an adolescent, who doubts and defies the old order, envisioning himself as the new man who will replace his father, the old man. The adolescent sees that the old generation with its dead values, hypocrisy, and corruption must be replaced with new values. He is optimistic; he has hopes that he can transform the world. Current despair, on the other hand, is predicated on the understanding that society will no longer assume its traditional role of parental opposition. In this case, the hope of transforming the world — making it new again dwindles with each manifestation of permissiveness — the signal that the parent does not care.

Dada seems to us now a delightful episode, its despair a combination of adolescent *weltschmerz* and romantic self-pity, in contrast to the present moment of harsh truths and dead-ends. Adolescence is the period of preparing for something else, preparing for a future without precisely knowing what the future might be. It is a period of testing, experimentation. Above all, it is a period of fantasies. "For a while," Hülsenbeck reminisced, "my dream had been to make literature with a gun in my pocket." The gun, however, the means to true revolution, remains safely in his pocket. Rebellion is fantasy, a dream of revolution.

For the Dadaists, the revolution is made only in art, that is, only in fantasy. Politics for the Dadaists was merely an aspect of the old order, not its essence. It was still presumed that the cultural revolution could proceed without or, in more elaborately constructed fantasies, in advance of, the political revolution. Today no artist can make any move without entertaining the public; no stance is sufficiently alienating not to be retrieved for the purpose of diversion. The Dadaists lived in a more innocent time when they might scandalize others by entertaining only themselves. How much their performances, manifestations, and theater events resemble traditional adolescent revues — even in terms of structure, acts and vaudeville overtones — has not been noticed. Although the programs at the Cabaret Voltaire may have been a bit more daring than those at the Princeton Triangle Club or Harvard's Hasty Pudding, the impulse to get together and perform for friends and the initiated, to satirize the inanity of the older generation, in a gathering of peers sharing a common language often unintelligible to the elders being ridiculed is a feature common to all types of adolescent theater.

In discussing Dada psychology, I do not use the term adolescent in a pejorative but in a descriptive sense to distinguish Dada modes of rebellion from current forms of antiauthoritarian behavior. The Dada artist had the good fortune to be permitted to act as an adolescent with regard to his relationship to a society that still conceived of itself as paternalistic and authoritarian, a society in which there were still boundaries and standards of behavior. In such a society, the hope of growing up, of finally replacing the old order, was not yet dead. In the face of so many additional defeats of the idealistic utopian spirit subsequent to Dada, that hope is all but extinguished in the current generation of artists. Present forms of antiauthoritorian behavior can no longer conform to the model of adolescence, nor even in most instances to any classical generational conflicts, which presuppose the possibility of vanquishing the father.

"Dada holds war and peace in its toga but prefers to have a cherry brandy flip," Hülsenbeck wrote in a passage that perfectly evokes the fashionable nihilism of the twenties. Even pop art had a little of the fun-loving aspect of Dada. But the irony had grown cold, cruel, and finally vicious by the time today's super-realists began to paint the horrors of the American tinsel and neon nightmare in photographic *trompe l'oeil.* The shopping centers and luncheonettes are vacant, devoid of any human presence. The motorcycles gleam with vicious coldness, the precise mechanical style in which they are painted an analogue of total depersonalization. There is no more mocking irony, only cynical passive acceptance. There are no expressionist distortions to spell out a point of view; the artist is reduced to mute witnessing of a horror that is the more nightmarish for its reality.

The attitude is not of protest but of infantile passivity, and even those acts of protest which continue are couched in infantile terms. Thus the late Italian neo-Dadaist Manzoni exhibits his own canned feces in the gallery. Blood and filth are smeared over performers in ritualistic happenings. Galleries are filled with heaps of junk, garbage, and dirt as the artist resorts to more and more infantile strategies to attract the attention of the unloving uninterested parent. Infantile feelings of omnipotence are expressed in earth works — grandiose projects to change the world — giant sandpiles financed by a bored public. Eventually every kind of pathology is hailed as art: Exhibitionism (Vito Acconci masturbating in public); Autism (the "living sculpture" of Gilbert and George impersonating singing automata); Narcissism (Lucas Samaras using double exposure Polaroids to create the image of sodomizing himself); Necrophilia (Paul Thek's life-size replica of himself entombed); all are common fare. Alienation becomes a favored subject. The body itself is conceived of as a foreign object. Bruce Nauman paints his testicles black and Wolfgang Stoerkle animates his penis in rhythmic patterns on videotape. Images of castration and dismemberment are everywhere, from Jim Dine's headless bathrobes (one with ax attached) to Jasper Johns's scattered parts of the human anatomy to Robert Morris's brain covered with dollar bills to Ed Kienholz's recent tableau *5 Car Stud,* depicting castration of a black by four whites. The Images of masochism, self-mutilation, and self-destruction multiply, as the artist, deprived of his capacity to protest, or sensing the inadequacy of protest, turns against himself.

Part of the artist's sense of impotence derives from his recognition that society affords him no possibilities for responsible action. All decisions regarding the artist's life and work are made by others — bureaucrats, government functionaries, trustees, dealers, collectors, institutions, etc. Artists are rarely if ever consulted in a decision-making capacity because society sees them as irresponsible infants — whose antics are considered cute or bad, depending on how much mess they make. Given this situation, the type of personality who chooses to be an artist at this juncture in history is frequently dysfunctional to the point of pathology, infantile and desperate.

Do we need any more proof that this society does not take art seriously? It exalts creativity in official rhetoric, sets up funds and council and endowments in which the artist is not permitted a decision–making role. The artist realizes he is no longer even an ornament, but an expendable entertainer. Within such a context, the Dada attitude has no place. The freedom to experiment coupled with the sense, characteristic of adolescence, of looking forward to a new world is not a possible option. The present situation permits only passive infantilism, or as a more difficult alternative, a higher state of consciousness and a more developed sense of responsibility. But moral responsibility cannot express itself in art, but only in the artist's conduct. Artists for example were among the first openly to oppose the war. In 1966 a peace tower was built in Los Angeles by Mark di Suvero; works were donated by many leading artists to raise funds for the peace movement. Irving Petlin was injured defending the tower. As a protest against the war, di Suvero left this country and works in Europe. In 1970 artists organized the Art Strike and refused to associate themselves with official exhibitions of the government. A group of artists formed an Emergency Cultural Government and went to Washington to speak with government leaders. They were told that since they were artists no one would take them seriously; but if they had been doctors their plea might have been heard.

One cannot speak of artists like Andy Warhol and Claes Oldenburg as protesting in Dada terms. However, they are effective mirrors of the role and function we have assigned art. Warhol presents himself as an art-making machine, a prostitute to the capitalist system of profit-taking. Oldenburg mocks the absurdity of inflated official rhethoric with his grandiose forms. His art resembles giant toys — a constant reminder of the infantilism of the society in which the artist is forced to function. The ineffectuality of protest today creates a more profound crisis than that experienced prior to the present.

Conceptual art aims to deprive the public of art as commodity. Depriving the parent of the desired object is the typical infantile strategy; and the infantilism of conceptual art should be evident. It is also a strategy doomed to failure, because it presumes that society is still acting *in loco parentis* with regard to its wayward artists: that it in fact feels the absence of the art object as a deprivation. Yet there is no evidence to cause us to believe art is missed: what is missed is the amusement provided by art.

We are confronted now with artistic attitudes formulated not in terms of the disgust of Brecht, but the disgust of Beckett. In the world of Dada and Brecht, the world is garbage. But garbage for an artist like Schwitters is imbued with charming nostalgia — the past is in pieces, but nevertheless we may still reconstruct the fragments. In the world of Beckett, the garbage cans of *Endgame* are filled not with the Merz scraps of dead civilizations, but with empty human beings. Humanity, not merely its cultural artifacts, has become garbage. This is the deepest pessimism, an eschatalogical view no longer relieved by the possibilities of millenarian fantasies of redemption. In these circumstances art is conceived not as a form of protest, but as a form of pathology.

In this case, the emphasis on the play element, on the ephemeral as opposed to the experimental, leads to a redefinition of art not as a specific kind of object but as non-goal-oriented behavior. In these terms, art is no longer involved with any fixed objective, but with acting out various antiauthoritarian strategies. New categories of the forbidden must be located, not in protest against institutions or value systems, but in terms of overtly pathological behavior. The following description of a performance of the Viennese artist Hermann Nitch's Orgies-Mysteries Theatre at The Kitchen last December advertises the worth of Mr. Nitch's work on the basis that "his abreaction theatre was cause for trial and prison sentences for offending the public and for blasphemy." Mr. Nitch, according to his publicist, "is' working with very essential materials, like flesh, and blood and brains.

In his theatre he wants to sublimate the excessive, sado-masochistic 'abreaction' (dilacerating of meat, disembowlement of slaughtered animals, trampling on the entrails). . . . The means of this theatre to achieve its goal are the sado-masochistic dispute with meat and 'abreactive' events which lead to a cathartic climax."

Such a description indicates that increasing permissiveness has created a state of desperation in the minds of artists whose principal tactic for engagement has been shock. Moreover, when all activities — war, art, and human relations included — begin to be interpreted as games, as forms of behavior not tied to value systems, pathological activity more obviously attracts attention. One of the most alarming aspects of neo-Dada theory is its embrace of the play ethic, if one may use this for a call to destroy art-life boundaries, which is implied in the view that all events are theater and all art is an extension of the real world to the exclusion of boundaries previously separating the two. In the essay on "Puerlism" quoted, J. Huizinga the Dutch historian noted for his study of play (*Homo Ludens*), comments: "The most fundamental characteristic of true play, whether it be a cult, a performance, a contest or a festivity, is that at a certain moment it is *over*. The spectators go home, the players take off their masks, the performance has ended. And here the evil of our time shows itself. For nowadays play in many cases never ends and hence is not true play. A far-reaching contamination of play and serious activity has taken place. The two spheres are getting mixed." Here exactly is the danger of a kind of moral confusion beyond any aesthetic confusions that current strategies of antiauthoritarian behavior imply.

Part IV

Writers' Political Documents

Introduction

Each article in this section addresses a specific moment of writers' political involvement, and each of them also speaks to the larger context – the freedom to write without governmental reprisal, to publish, and to criticize. But whereas in the Western countries writers tend to be situated both on the right and the left side of the political fence, writers living in the Soviet orbit are more concerned with being allowed to write, and with finding a metaphorical language adapted to their situation.

Nicola Chiaromonte reports on the by now famous quarrel between Sartre and Camus, about intellectuals' responsibility in relation to political commitment. Because in *L'homme révolté*, in 1951, Camus had attacked all ideologies as being murderous, he drew fire from Sartre and other former friends. For by "placing himself outside history," that is, by attacking socialism as practiced in the Soviet Union and by the Communist party, he had challenged Sartre's existential politics, which, of course, had to do with the idea of communism rather than with its practice behind the iron curtain. Sartre, according to Chiaromonte, rather than being in any way helpful to the party itself, or a fellow traveller, was only an amateur Communist "interested in the defeat of the bourgeoisie and the victory of the proletariat." This view, itself a reflection of French politics in the 1950s, indicates once more the importance of milieu for intellectual concerns. Edmund Wilson, for example, who had been immersed in "American" Marxism in the 1930s, already wrote in 1940 of the "eclipse of Marxism" as the "end of an era."

By 1966, when Susan Sontag attended the PEN writers' congress in Yugoslavia, the conditions under which writers work had become more visibly polarized. Sontag, who originally had gone to the meeting for frivolous reasons, commented on the complacency of Western intellectuals who talk about the writer's privilege to espouse or decline *serving* a particular moral or social cause – unaware that their Eastern colleagues try preserving "the values of liberal individualism in a collectivist society." Sontag left the congress, convinced that PEN actions, or even the threat of unpleasant worldwide publicity, were of some help to dissident intellectuals, although at the time this term was not in use, and almost none of the larger figures had yet left the Soviet Union. PEN was becoming more "political" than literary, observed Sontag, as she suggested how the literary end could be better upheld, but as we know, its political arm, by now, has become extremely effective.

With Morris Dickstein's retrospective on the 1950s we get to the American scene, particularly to the "Cold War anti-Communism" dominating this period, and to the emergence of the Jewish novel in American fiction. Before then, argues Dickstein, Jewish intellectuals had been more evenhandedly on the left, attacking both Soviet communism and capitalism, while by the 1950s they had become more patriotic, "singing the virtues of American life, with its pluralism and pragmatism, its procedure by consensus and its presumed freedom from ideology and moralism." Dickstein's radical 1960s perspective, of course, colors his politics, as he revives the issues raised by the Rosenberg and Hiss trials, and reexamines the question of their guilt along with the commentary of their intellectual contemporaries. The literary works of the new Jewish novelists as well, he finds, are laden with American politics, mostly by omission, and by creating heroes who "recoil" from political engagement, and others who are *schlemiel* figures – too busy with their small lives to look beyond their narrow environments. Dickstein perceives some of the writing of the period, for instance, as "one kind of response to the frozen and quietly fear-ridden political atmosphere of the McCarthy and Eisenhower years." We do not quite agree that this is only an extension of the predominating 1950s mentality which glorified home and family, getting and spending, and cultivating one's own garden, because the literary mind is not such a direct expression of events, although innumerable sociological studies about the politics of American writers show that the connections between writing and its context are strong – in the 1950s, the 1960s, and at all other times.

William Barrett, in a comment on the political and economic crisis in the 1970s, underlines such connections. "The overshadowing difference between then and now," he states, "is in the relative positions of the United States and the Soviet Union," especially after Vietnam and Watergate. Were the United States to go under, he maintains, liberty would disappear because the Soviet bloc would take over. Barrett has no illusion that Stalin's successors might be able to induce liberalization, if only because their own power base depends upon expansionism and repression. Still, Barrett thinks the way the United States responded to the Cold War was stupid, as was the Vietnam War, which helped the Communists. He is not only aware of the naiveté of American government officials, but links them to the rest of society, including intellectuals, who equate the imperfections of American democracy with those of dictatorships. Park Avenue Stalinists were superseded by Park Avenue Maoists – symbolic politics of fellow travellers that only increase the confusion. To Barrett, "fellow-travelling appears to be a permanent part of modern life, . . . [an] 'aesthetic' politics, 'literary' Marxism, the lure of utopian thinking on the part of those who feel secure enough in their liberty to play around with it." Barrett fears that this might help enslave ourselves, and that the Russian dissidents seem to be the only ones really interested in liberty. Moving to the cultural scene, Barrett reminisces about the good old days when art was more serious, less "tricky," and when the great Modern movement was in full swing, when experimentation had not given way to "experiencing." Because we have learned to take experimentation in our stride, we have lost the ability to be shocked, and also the ability to be taken in. This insight leads Barrett to conclude that we live in a time of transition – a time when we must reassess and rediscover both our political and cultural values in order to preserve the future of true liberty.

William Phillips replies that Barrett may be correct in alleging that Europe needs America to help defend itself, but does not perceive either of them as stable entities with the defined interests and commitments Barrett assumes. Simply to argue, he says, that America is the "bulwark of democracy" fails to describe the real powers of the country and the situation of the rest of the world, and ignores the fact that we have suffered from poor leadership. Hence Phillips would evaluate American policies and motives rather than focus on a static conception of liberty inevitably bound up with America's future. And he would examine whether there is a national interest that surmounts class interest, and what this means in the actual and changing political context. As for the cultural anarchy, from pop to the popular distortions of modernism, Phillips sees them as triumphs of the market, which, in turn, cannot save our values or our freedoms. He accuses Barrett of "lumping fashionable versions of the avant-garde . . . with genuine talent by writers and painters who have resisted the pressures of their time." That Barrett forgets about these makes him paint a more static picture, and in that sense he is more conservative than Phillips.

By 1980, notions of conservatism, radicalism, and even of socialism, had again changed, and we now address neoconservatism – a catchall label applied to many former socialist intellectuals who have achieved a certain stature and who tend to be listened to by governmental officials. Still, as Nathan Glazer says, "there is something denigrating about the 'neo.'" But he concedes that all the "neos" share common assumptions insofar as they all "focus on facts," in such fields as social welfare or housing, whereas those on the left, allegedly, are less well informed and more interested in "doing good," that is, in reallocating the social benefits more equitably. Glazer disagrees with the socialists and all the others on the left, because they are not involved in the real world, in the world of public policy Glazer knows, and thus don't realize that their ideas, however good they may be, cannot work. Peter Steinfels argues on the other side of this fence, although he says that because the neoconservatives have no unified policy suggestions – on energy, unemployment or inflation – they are not easily lumped. Still, he finds neoconservatism important, because its selective views shape public discussions, and because it plays an important role in the so-called "new class" of intellectual leaders. Precisely for the reasons Glazer states, that is, because this class does not know about policy issues and is listened to by a government having to deal with the halt of economic growth for the first time in American history, the mobilization of this "new class" will "reinforce rather than counterbalance the power of corporate wealth." Clearly, the underlying division, once again, is between political assumptions. As the commentators and the audience in this symposium noted, the crucial issues have to do with the fate of liberalism, with the renewal of common intellectual premises about central problems which cannot be solved by slogans, rhetoric, and promises. Insofar as this symposium itself was meant to provide a forum for opposing views it was successful, even though no conclusions were reached.

In looking at these "documents," however, we recognize the increasing specialization of concerns, and the ever more national focus of the questions. Although *Partisan Review* always has tried to overcome such biases – at times through the selection of pieces – the effort is increasingly arduous. At a recent conference honoring

Andrei Sakharov's birthday, we were, at first, surprised that American scientists completely misinterpreted his message for "mutual disarmament." But we soon realized that his use of metaphor addresses his own existential situation – a situation no longer comprehensible to most of the people in societies where free speech prevails.

Chapter Fifteen

Sartre versus Camus: A Political Quarrel
Nicola Chiaromonte

The news in Paris is the public break between Albert Camus and Jean-Paul Sartre on the issue of Communism. I hope PR readers will not think the fact that these two famous Parisian intellectuals could be aroused by such an issue to the point of ending a ten-year-old friendship is another sign of European belatedness. This polemic and this break are in fact a sign that in France ideas still count, and, more particularly, that French intellectuals cannot easily reconcile themselves to the divorce between principles and political life which has been the mark of the postwar years all over Europe. Moreover, the arguments exchanged between Camus and Sartre touch upon questions of general intellectual import. Finally, the Communist issue will be a live and significant one in Europe as long as the Communist parties retain their strength. The fact that they are still strong is not the fault of the intellectuals. And while the Communist issue is alive, it is worth the trouble to study its phenomenology.

At the origin of the Sartre-Camus clash, which occupies a good part of the August issue of *Les Temps Modernes,* there is *L'Homme Révolté.* With this book, Albert Camus attempted to do something that Jean-Paul Sartre has never found the time to do, namely to give an account of the reasons which led him to take the position he has taken with regard to the political ideologies of our time, and more particularly Communism. Camus had taken part in the resistance as a writer and a journalist, he had been the editor of a daily paper after the liberation; during this period he played a public role, and took political stands. Having withdrawn from public life in order to devote himself to his writing, he felt that he was under the obligation of thinking through the ideas that he had been expressing in articles and speeches. In other words, he felt intellectually responsible for his political commitments, and attempted to live up to this responsibility. For this, if for nothing else, he deserves credit.

In the author's own words, *L'Homme Révolté* is intended to be "a study of the *ideological* aspect of revolutions." This has to be stressed because, as we shall see, the attack launched upon the book by *Les*

Temps Modernes is all based on the assumption that Camus had meant his work to be primarily a political manifesto, if not a new *Das Kapital*. Briefly summarized, the main thesis of *L'Homme Révolté* runs as follows: (1) Nihilism, already implicit in the Jacobin myth of terroristic violence, has been brought to its extreme consequences by contemporary Communism. But nihilism is not exclusively a political phenomenon. It is rooted in the history of modern consciousness, and its origins can be traced back to such strange "revolts" against reality as Sade's, Lautréamont's, and Rimbaud's. Philosophically, the Hegelian notion of reality as "history," and of human action as a dialectical series of "historical tasks" knowing of no other law than their realization is one of the main sources of ideological nihilism. From Hegel, in fact, Marxist prophecy is derived, with the vision of a "happy end" of history for the sake of which, in Goethe's words, "everything that exists deserves to be annihilated." This is the aspect of Marx emphasized by Communist fanaticism at the expense of Marx's critical thought, simply because apocalyptic prophecy, being as it is beyond the pale of proof, is the surest foundation of a ruthless orthodoxy. (2) At this point, the revolutionary myth finds itself in absolute contradiction with man's impulse to revolt against oppression, leading to systematic enslavement rather than liberation. (3) By denying that human life can have a meaning aside from the "historical task" to which it must be made subservient, the "nihilist" must inevitably bring about and justify systematic murder. The contradiction between the revolutionist who accepts such a logic and the man who revolts against injustice in the name of the absolute value of human life is radical. And the very absurdity of this contradiction should convince the man who insists on acting for the sake of real humanity that he cannot escape the classical question of the "limit." To begin with, the limit of the idea of "revolt" is, according to Camus, the point where the idea becomes murderous. Contemporary ideologies, the revolutionary as well as the reactionary ones, are essentially murderous. Hence they must be refused once and for all, at the cost of one's being forced into what the ideologists call "inaction," but which, in fact (except for the self-satisfied and the philistine), is a refusal of automatic action and an insistence on choice, real commitments, and the freedom to act according to authentic convictions on the basis of definite situations, rather than follow ideological deductions and organizational discipline.

This is a rather crude simplification of Camus' thesis. It should, however, be sufficient to indicate that, no matter how debatable the arguments and the conclusions, the question raised by Camus is a serious one, and deserves to be discussed seriously at least by those people today who, while not pretending to have at their disposal any new systematic certainty, are aware of the sterility of the old political dogmas. Let's notice in passing that until recently Jean-Paul Sartre was not unwilling to recognize that he belonged in the company of these people. As a matter of fact, he went so far as to write that the biggest party in France was that of those who abstained from voting, which proved how deep among the people was the disgust with the old parties, their methods and their ideologies; a new Left, he added, should try to reach those masses.

An attentive reader of *L'Homme Révolté* will not fail to notice that, in his own peculiar language, and in terms of general ideas rather than of specific moral problems, Camus formulates against the modern world the same indictment as Tolstoy. For Camus, as for Tolstoy, modern society does not recognize any other norm than violence and the accomplished fact, hence it can legitimately be said that it is founded on murder. Which is tantamount to saying that human life in it has become a senseless affair. Tolstoy, however, believed that, besides retaining an "eternal" value, Christianity was still alive in the depths of our society among the humble; hence he thought that a radical Christian morality: non-violence, could offer a way out. Camus is not religious, and much more skeptical than Tolstoy as to the moral resources of the modern world. He does not advocate non-violence. He simply points out the reappearance, through nihilistic reduction to absurdity, of the need for a new sense of limit and of "nature."

No matter how uncertain one might consider Camus' conclusions, his attack on the modern ideological craze appears both strong and eloquent. Of course, if one believes in progress, one might still maintain that Nazism and Stalinism were the result of contingencies, factual errors, and residual wickedness. But progressive optimism is precisely the notion that Camus vigorously questions. His arguments cannot be easily dismissed by a philosophy like existentialism, which stresses so resolutely the discontinuity between human consciousness and any "process" whatsoever, and which in any case makes it very difficult to go back to the notion that man's ethical task is to "change the world" through historical action. This not only because the idea of "changing the world" is a radically optimistic one in that it presupposes precisely that fundamental harmony between man and the world which existentialism denies; but because only if man is "historical" through and through (as Hegel and Marx assumed) is the definition of a "historical task" possible at all. Now, the main existentialist claim was the rediscovery of an essential structure of human consciousness beyond historical contingencies. From this, going back to Hegel and Marx seems a rather difficult enterprise, one, in any case, that requires a lot of explaining.

Yet, lo and behold, in the first attack against *L'Homme Révolté* launched in the June issue of *Les Temps Modernes* by one of Sartre's faithful disciples, Francis Jeanson, this critic found no better line of attack than to accuse Camus of "anti-historicism." His argun.ents can be summarized as follows: (1) by rejecting the cult of History which seems to him characteristic of the nihilistic revolutions of our time, Camus places himself "outside of history," in the position of the Hegelian "beautiful Soul," which wants to remain pure of all contact with reality, and is satisfied with the reiteration of an abstract Idea void of all dialectical energy; (2) by criticizing Marxism and Stalinism, Camus accomplishes an "objectively" reactionary task, as proved by the favorable reviews of his book in the bourgeois press; (3) intellectual disquisitions are a fine thing, but the task (the "choice") of the moment makes it imperative to struggle in favor of the emancipation of the Indo-Chinese and the Tunisians, as well as in defense of peace; this cannot be done effectively if one attacks the CP, which, at this particular moment, is the only force capable of mobilizing the masses behind such a struggle.

This was bad enough. Much worse, and much sadder, is the fact that, in his answer to Camus' "Letter to the Editor of *Les Temps Modernes*," Sartre himself did little more than restate his disciples's arguments.

In his "Letter," Albert Camus had addressed the following remarks, among others, to Sartre: "To legitimate the position he takes toward my book, your critic should demonstrate, against the whole collection of *Les Temps Modernes*, that history has a necessary meaning and a final outcome; that the frightful and disorderly aspect that it offers us today is sheer appearance, and that, on the contrary, in spite of its ups and downs, progress toward that moment of final reconciliation which will be the jump into ultimate freedom, is inevitable. . . . Only prophetic Marxism (or a philosophy of eternity) could justify the pure and simple rejection of my thesis. But how can such views be upheld in your magazine without contradiction? Because, after all, if there is no human end that can be made into a norm of value, how can history have a definable meaning? On the other hand, if history has meaning why shouldn't man make of it his end? If he did that, however, how could he remain in the state of frightful and unceasing freedom of which you speak? . . . The truth is that your contributor would like us to revolt against everything but the Communist Party and the Communist State. He is, in fact, in favor of revolt, which is as it should be, in the condition (of absolute freedom) described by his philosophy. However, he is tempted by the kind of revolt which takes the most despotic historical form, and how could it be otherwise, since for the time being his philosophy does not give either form or name to this wild independence? If he wants to revolt, he must do it in the name of the same nature which existentialism denies. Hence, he must do it theoretically in the name of history. But since one cannot revolt in the name of an abstraction, his history must be endowed with a global meaning. As soon as this is accepted, history becomes a sort of God, and, while he revolts, man must abdicate before those who pretend to be the priests and the Church of such a God. Existential freedom and adventure is by the same token denied. As long as you have not clarified or eliminated this contradiction, defined your notion of history, assimilated Marxism, or rejected it, how can we be deprived of the right to contend that, no matter what you do, you remain within the boundaries of nihilism?"

This is a stringent argument. Sartre did not answer it, except by insisting that "our freedom today is nothing but the free choice to struggle in order to become free . . . ," and that if Camus really wanted "to prevent a popular movement from degenerating into tyranny," he should not "start by condemning it without appeal." "In order to deserve the right to influence men who struggle," Sartre admonished, "one must start by participating in their battle. One must start by accepting a lot of things, if one wants to attempt to change a few." Which is, among other things, a theory of conformism, or at least of reformism, not of revolution and drastic change. Because if one "must start by accepting a lot of things" in order to change "a few," then why not begin by giving up wholesale notions such as "capitalism," "communism," the "masses," etcetera? If he had cared to answer further, Camus could easily have retorted that it was precisely the awareness that "one must start by accepting a lot of things" if one wants to obtain real changes that had persuaded him to give up ideological radicalism. While Sartre, for the sake of changing "a few things," is ready to swallow a totalitarian ideology plus a totalitarian organization.

One thing is certain: Sartre is more intelligent than that, and knows much better. How can he then, in polemic with a man like Camus, imagine that he can get away with taking over the most ordinary kind of journalistic arguments?

The answer, I believe, must be found in the phenomenology of the amateur Communist, a type widespread in Europe today, especially among the intellectuals.

The first thing to say about the amateur Communist is that he is by no means a "fellow traveler." He does not receive either orders or suggestions from the Party; he does not belong to any "front organization," and, except for an occasional signature, he does not give any particular help to the Communist cause. What he is interested in is the defeat of the bourgeoisie and the victory of the proletariat. A truly independent Communist, and, within the framework of the Communist *ideal,* a liberal, that is what he is. His points of contact with official Communism are two: (1) he considers it obvious that the Soviet Union is a socialist, that is, a fundamentally just state; (2) for him, it is self-evident that the CP, being the party of the "masses," is also at bottom the party of social justice and peace. Hence, he supports both these institutions in principle, but by no means on all counts. The totalitarian mentality is utterly foreign to him. As for the difficulties and ambiguities of his position, he is perfectly aware of them. But, precisely, "one must accept a lot of things, if one wants to change a few."

One would surmise that, being neither a Communist nor an anti-Communist, neither a totalitarian nor a liberal, and insisting as he does on the difficulty, if not the illegitimacy, of a resolute political stand, the amateur Communist should be a rather hamletic character. At this point, however, we witness a remarkable phenomenon: the fact of participating (at a variable distance) in the massive intellectual universe of Communism (of being able, i.e., to use Communist arguments without subjecting himself to the rigid rules by which the militant Communist must abide) gives the amateur Communist a singular kind of assurance. Far from feeling uncertain, he feels very certain, and behaves as if his position were not only politically sound, but also guaranteed by the laws of logic, ethics, and philosophy in general, not to speak of history. Which amounts to saying that he enjoys both the prestige of the Communist uniform which he shuns and the advantages of the civilian clothes which he ostensibly wears. He considers himself "objectively" a Communist insofar as he embraces the proletarian cause, but "subjectively" a free man, since he does not obey any order from above. The last, and most refined, touch of such a character is the conviction he often expresses that, in case of a Communist victory, he will be among the first to be "liquidated." His heretical orthodoxy will thus receive even the crown of the martyrs. In what substantial way these refinements can further the cause of the oppressed is, on the other hand, a question that should not be asked. The important thing here is that the unhappy consciousness of this believer without faith should continue to feed on contradictions, since contradictions are to him *the* sign that he has a firm grip on real life.

A man of Sartre's talent cannot be forced into a "type." But the fact is that, since 1945, every time they took a stand on contemporary politics, he and his friends have been behaving more and more like amateur Communists. Worse still, they have been more and more satisfied with taking over the usual arguments of the Communist catechism, and this with an arrogant refusal to justify their position in terms of the philosophical tenets with which they fare so well. They have been behaving, that is, as if, once they had declared themselves in favor of the Proletariat, the consistency of their ideas was a matter of automatic adjustment of which no account was due to "others." By so behaving, these philosophers have obviously fallen victim to the most intolerably dogmatic aspect of Communist mentality: the idea that being a resolute partisan can make short work of all questions.

The crudeness of the arguments used by Sartre against Camus cannot be explained if one does not assume that, having established an intellectual connection with the Marxist-Leninist-Stalinist mentality, he is intellectually dominated by it. Personally, of course, he remains independent. That is precisely why he, an intellectual, can be a victim of the delusion that intellectual assent has no intellectual consequences. But, having reached the conclusion that "participation" in the Communist system is the most effective way to pacify his political conscience, it follows that the philosopher of "anguished freedom" participates in the moral smugness which the system guarantees to its proselytes. From moral smugness to intellectual arrogance the step is short indeed. Once one has adopted a certain logical system, it is of course absurd not to avail oneself of the arguments that, from such a point of view, are the most effective.

It remains that Jean-Paul Sartre has not answered Albert Camus.

The latest news has it that *Lettres Françaises* has offered the excommunicated Sartre a political alliance. It is unlikely that the editor of *Les Temps Modernes* will accept such an offer. He prizes independence too much. He will not give any direct help and comfort to the Communist Party. He will simply continue to spread the intellectual confusion by which the Communist Party benefits.

Chapter Sixteen
Yugoslav Report
Susan Sontag

I came to the PEN congress in Bled last summer with a well why not attitude, easy to adopt if one is going, all expenses paid, to one's first literary congress (curiosity), and it's taking place by a lake at the foot of the Julian Alps in northern Yugoslavia (vacation-lust). It was almost too easy to be cynical. The official theme of the congress was that venerable catch-all "The Writer and Contemporary Society," and, as W. H. Auden (who was invited and didn't come) is reported to have written to Stephen Spender (who did come), surely in the last thirty years everything that can be said on *that* subject has been said. Of course. Yes, the writer has the right to absolute freedom of expression, protected by the law, and access to publication; his right to be politically disengaged, asocial, morally heretical, or just plain irresponsible must be zealously defended. Yes, writing and writers flourish when they have some sense of responsible connection with the life of their societies; writers are also citizens, educators, guardians of language, etc. What more could be done than to recite truisms, to glance fondly from "on the one hand" to "on the other"? And PEN? What was that? In New York: a joke, a bore, something to be polite to. Monthly postcards announcing cocktail parties at the Hotel Pierre on which one might be improbably promised the chance to meet at one fell swoop Virginia Kirkus, William Burroughs, and Isaac Bashevis Singer? Expensive dinners at the Overseas Press Club with dessert a lecture on how to write articles for travel magazines, or a panel discussion on whether the modern novel is going "too far"? And if the activities of the American PEN are rather remote from literature as an art, what would an international PEN congress do but compound the distance?

The truth is, the recent PEN congress did have little to do with literature. And how could it have been otherwise? One does not become a member of PEN because one is a good writer, but simply because one is a writer. Everyone there ("*Poets, Essayists, Novelists*") was a writer. There were top drawer personages like Stephen Spender, Arthur Miller, Ignazio Silone, Pablo Neruda, Richard Hughes, Ivo Andric, and Rosamond Lehmann. (Ionesco promised but failed to show up; Charles Olson came on the last day.) But what one noticed was the absence of all the star novelists, poets, and playwrights who had been invited and had turned PEN down. Of those who did come there seemed to be a disproportionate number of critics and of writers who are regularly connected to institutions, inured to the professional reasonableness of committees. Spender is an editor of *Encounter*, and currently at the Library of Congress; Vladimir Dedijer is not only Vladimir Dedijer but has also taught at the University of Manchester and several American universities; Jean Blot (from France) and José Angel Valente (from Spain) both work for UNESCO; Pablo Fernández (from Cuba) is his country's cultural attaché in London; and there were also Roger Caillois, editor of *Diogenes*, Norman Podhoretz, editor of *Commentary*, Jean Bloch-Michel, literary editor of *Preuves*, Robie Macauley, editor of *Kenyon Review*, Ivan Boldizsár, editor of *The New Hungarian Quarterly* (an excellent magazine, printed in English, which more American intellectuals should read), and university-based critics like Jan Kott, of the University of Warsaw, and Roger Shattuck, of the University of Texas. And then there were the PEN masses, legions of obscure toilers, busy on their eighth novel, their travel articles, their childrens' books, their mystery stories. These were the "lady writers" (the celebrity-writers' throwaway label for all of them, male and female), invariably middle-aged or elderly, who filled the plenary sessions held in the large hall, adjusting their plastic earphones to tune in the speeches translated into English and French (the official languages of the congress), collecting autographs from the celebrity-writers, dutifully taking all the tours and consuming the endless food and drink provided by the Slovene PEN center, lavishly generous hosts to the congress. A writer is a writer.

Discussions about literature useful to writers as poets, essayists and novelists were, then, conspicuously absent; their surrogates were speeches about "The Importance of Literature Today" and "Mass Communication." Sharing few assumptions about their art, particularly the level at which it was to be practiced, the writers were called on to consider themselves as diagnosticians of culture. And a pretty amateurish lot in this role they proved to be. Early on during the congress, the members found in their hotel mail slots the following questionnaire—which I am quoting verbatim—made up by two Yugoslav weekly magazines, *TT* of Ljubljana and *Svet* of Belgrade:

1. What are the most important ideological and philosophical trends of the world at present (Marxism, Buddhism, Existentialism, etc.) and which is the strongest integrative force?
2. What is the real root of the East-West conflict, and what of the North-South conflict?

3. How do you conceive of the involvement of the artist in the modern world?

4. Does the march of civilization (automation, affluence) cause the crisis of culture or merely the crisis of traditional forms of culture?

5. Two thousand years ago a philosopher said that the fate of the world depended on the marriage of the mind and the power. Is this philosopher's thought still walid today?

6. Which thought or idea, whether expressed by yourself or somebody else at Bled, did most appeal to you, and which one you thought the most objectionable?

To be sure, the speeches were not quite on this ambitious Hyman Kaplan level. But many did not lag behind, even if their high-minded rhetoric was supplemented by a lot of mysterious cultural information. One learned that Sartre has lost favor with Polish intellectual youth for what they take to be his over-politicized reaction to the Nobel award, but that Camus and Kafka remain idols, with Salinger bringing up the rear; that Sartre remains extremely influential in Brazil; that Kafka is *démodé* in Hungary; that John Updike is coming up strong among young Russian readers; and that in Holland there are many novels on "the Jewish problem" but plays are taken more seriously than novels.

But what is really worth reporting about the congress is something else that took place, something which had unexpectedly (for me, at least) its extraordinary moments. Human beings from many countries came together as men of good will, because as writers they are self-appointed citizens of that hypothetical civilized world order that seems farther than ever from being realized, despite all the predictions that were fashionable twenty, even ten years ago about the imminent demise of the era of nation-states. And the spirit of fraternity at the Bled congress, however flimsily based on the pretext of a common vocation, was extremely moving. That spirit was, perhaps, a mixture of conscientious tact, of curiosity—and wonder, wonder and relief that we were talking to each other and that nothing awful or unpleasant was happening. For most of us *have* been sold a bill of goods—by our governments, by our prejudices, or by our own sophistication. When one was able to repress the easy smile that such verbal doings as I've described above induced in those of us assembled at Bled who are too sophisticated to be so solemn, one had a chance to discover one's own provincialism and complacency.

Can a regularly published American writer, busy with his own work, really imagine what it's like to run the risk of exile, persecution, imprisonment for what he writes? Probably not, until he goes abroad, meets such a writer in the flesh, and stays up with him talking until four in the morning. In New York one could never anticipate the pleasure and dismay one feels lingering over coffee to answer ardent, naïve, very well-informed questions about the history of *Partisan Review* or recent off-Broadway theater put to one by a young writer from Belgrade or Sofia who has never been further west than Bled. Not until one sees it going on at the next table can one grasp what it means for writers from West and East Germany, who have no other chance of meeting, to sit together and talk; after the first such impromptu gathering, one East German writer is reported to have been close to tears. No matter that a writer's club is, at best, a diversion, at worst an irrelevance, in the permissive quarrelsome literary capitals of New York, London and Paris. It does mean, in many cases has meant or could mean, a great deal in Warsaw, Montevideo, Accra, Havana, Tunis, Vientiane, Karachi. During the fifties, at the height of the Cold War, PEN was the only instrument for any regular dialogue between intellectuals of Communist and non-Communist countries. This dialogue is scarcely less useful during the perilous *détente* of the sixties, to them and to us. The comfortable certainty with which "Western" liberals espouse the writer's privilege to decline to serve as a spokesman for any particular moral or social point of view reveals, in many cases, a lack of imagination. Only change the verb: what if the writer is not "serving" but "preserving"? One of the congress' more instructive moments came when a Czech writer arose to argue for the writer's duty as a moralist and educator—not, as one immediately expected, because writers should help build socialism or work for world peace, but because they are needed to uphold the values of liberal individualism in a collectivist society.

PEN has always had the reputation of being "outside politics," which accounts for its strength and survival in Eastern Europe. Yet there is no doubt the function, purpose, *raison d'être* of PEN—whether it's admitted or not—*is* a political one: to liberalize the writer's situation. Since its founding in the early twenties by a wealthy Englishwoman, Mrs. C. A. Dawson-Scott, on the model of the new international parliaments that came into being after World War I, PEN has been dominated by its English center (John Galsworthy was the first international president) and devoted to discreet pressure on less liberty-loving countries to leave their writers alone. Resolutions passed at the annual congresses are one technique. The most memorable of these was at the 1933 congress in Dubrovnik when, under the international presidency of H. G. Wells, the assembled members debated, then formally denounced the new Nazi government for book-burning and racism and the Berlin PEN center for expelling its Communist members, and part of the German delegation walked out. In recent years, Spain and Portugal have come in for a ritual drubbing. At this congress, the usual resolution was passed condemning censorship in these two countries, and particularly singling out the Spanish government's suppression of outlets for Catalan writers and refusal to permit one of its dissident writers and a guest of honor at the congress, José Bergamin, to make the trip to Yugoslavia. But most of PEN's effective work, one gathers, takes place behind the scenes. David Carver, the organization's international secretary for the last fifteen years (the only full-time salaried official of PEN) and president of the English center as well, is credited with getting out of prison and, in a number of cases, saving the lives of eighteen Hungarian writers in 1956. He is also said to have been instrumental, through communication with Alexei Surkov, head of the Soviet Writers Union, in securing the release from prison of Olga Ivinskaya, Pasternak's former secretary, and her daughter, soon after they were sentenced to seven years for currency offenses. And to cite only one more instance, among many that are reliably reported, he tried to do something about the editor and two assistant editors of a South Korean newspaper who were sentenced to *death* for publishing an editorial advocating cultural, not political, contacts with North Korea. (The American PEN tried to get Washington to intervene; the editor was executed, the two assistant editors are still in jail.)

The specter that hung over the PEN congress this time was, of course, the case of Mihajlo Mihajlov, the young Yugoslav academic who had been sentenced to nine months in jail for his outspoken account of the Stalin era and the not exactly impetuous progress of de-Stalinization, "Moscow Summer 1964." I imagine a good many delegates to PEN came to Yugoslavia prepared to raise a row over Mihajlov, but just a few days before the congress opened the appeals court acquitted Mihajlov of one of the two charges, and suspended his sentence. It was scarcely as complete a victory as one would have liked, not only because Mihajlov was not wholly cleared but, more important, because no firm precedent was established. Yet I met no Yugoslav literary bureaucrat, of which there were many at the congress, who did not deplore the persecution of Mihajlov. And there seems no doubt that the verdict of the appeals court was partly, or even mainly, due to the imminent arrival of PEN, and to the quiet pre-congress negotiations between Carver and Matej Bor, head of the Slovene PEN center; Bor is said to have intervened decisively on Mihajlov's behalf.

Of course, one can cite plenty of distressing instances where PEN has been silent. Where was the PEN resolution in the fifties when Arthur Miller's passport was taken away for six years, when Lillian Hellman was threatened with jail, when Dashiell Hammett and a number of other writers actually were imprisoned? Where are the PEN resolutions protesting the insulting and inhuman treatment of Soviet writers of the stature of Anna Akhmatova? I can't fathom why PEN didn't speak out for the American writers. But as for its not raising a storm over the plight of the writers in Communist countries, the answer again seems to be that PEN is a political organization. It pushes where it can hope to accomplish something. In the case of the Russians, wholesale denunciation would accomplish little except make the denouncers feel more virtuous, but, say, the establishment of PEN centers in the Soviet Union might indeed lead to an easing of conditions there. And this prospect, which seems close to realization, supplied the principal drama of the recent congress. For the first time, the Soviet Union sent a delegation of "observers," a big step toward joining PEN, setting up centers in the largest Russian cities, and participating as regular members in next year's congress.

It was not simply the presence of the seven Russian observers that augured well, but the fact that the delegation agreed, after much soul-searching, to split up, and participate singly, each out of the watchful surveillance of the others, at the five *tables rondes,* or seminars, organized by Keith Botsford, which took place in a small building near the congress hall and overlapped with the large speechifying plenary sessions. (These seminars were a new feature of PEN congresses, and had many veteran members angrily complaining that PEN was being divided into first- and second-class citizens—which it was—and that the small rooms and the scheduling of the seminars made it virtually impossible for other PEN members even to audit—which it did. Each seminar had about ten participants. Their composition rotated among a specially invited fifty out of the more than four hundred PEN members who came to Bled, and included virtually all the famous writers at the congress.) And take part the Russians did, at first shyly and watchfully, and eventually gaining the full confidence of their clichés. For PEN didn't get Anna Akhmatova or Andrey Voznesensky or Aleksandr Solzhenitzyn, who were invited. We got Surkov himself, some critics and professors, and only one writer of some note, the novelist Leonid Leonov. These were big bulky elderly men, full of exhausting affability, who turned out a kind of endless verbal bubble gum. The other members, including those from Eastern Europe, generally treated them with an eager and slightly guilty politeness that made one think of upper-middle-class white children in a newly integrated liberal private school welcoming and trying to put at ease a small troupe of mentally defective children from Harlem. The way the Russians talked—all that they did not respond to or jovially evaded—was terribly depressing. Yet they were there. That was what mattered. And if we did nothing to excite their paranoia, maybe next time they would send us their real writers.

Anyone, then, who came to Bled looking for a high-level exchange among professionals must judge the congress a flop. The only exacting literary paper was one on Robbe-Grillet given by Jean Bloch-Michel, an excellent piece of work which had nothing to do with anything else that was going on; the first day of the congress, Stephen Spender made an unexpected and warmly received plea for daily readings of poetry, which were tried but never really got off the ground. However, if one suc-cumbed to the idea that being a writer creates strategic occasions for being a valuable amateur—at world citizenship? at self-transcendence?—the congress was elating, troubling, funny, touching, worthwhile. I, for one, having arrived at the congress as a surreptitious tourist to Yugoslavia, left an ardent PENnik.

Yet, the ambiguities of PEN's role remain—and with respect to these, PEN seems to be at a turning point. Arthur Miller, the new inter-national president, elected at this congress, offers PEN the prospect of new life—which it badly needs after the disastrous absentee-presidency of Alberto Moravia, during which period PEN almost foundered, and the caretaker-presidency of Victor van Vriesland. (International presidents serve three years.) But the life that Miller wants to infuse into PEN may dilute the organization. It is clearly Miller's intention to do two things. (1) Revive the American PEN, which is, for all serious purposes, an emp-ty shell. (2) Increase the representation of the Asians and Africans. Up to now, PEN has been largely a European affair—plus the United States and a few Latin American countries and Japan, with only a token representation from other continents. Something of the coming de-Europeanization is evident from the site of the future congresses. The one this year will take place in New York (June 12-17); the 1967 one in Bangalore; Senegal and the Ivory Coast are vying to play host to the one after that. PEN congresses are expensive—the one in London in 1956 cost about ten thousand pounds—and just about all the European capitals have had one. (Since its founding, only four congresses have taken place outside of Europe: in New York in 1924, in Buenos Aires in 1936, in Tokyo in 1957, and in Rio de Janeiro in 1960). And it is idle to pretend that the de-Europeanization of PEN will not have profound consequences.

As it becomes more and more truly an international parliament, PEN seems bound to become more "political" and even less a forum for discussion about literature. In all honesty, how much writing of high quality is there in Asia and Africa? How far can the notion of a writer be stretched? One disgruntled English writer told me in Bled that the PEN center in British Guiana is made up mainly of local newspapermen; the good West Indian writers, he says, are all in London. And, that question aside (for the difficulty may be just our insularity and ignorance), it still remains true that the kinds of things European writers can say to African and Asian writers must be vaguer, less concretely about literature, than those European, American and Latin American writers can say to each other. As the artistic assumptions shared by PEN members are diluted even further by stepped-up internationalization, there is the danger that discourse at the congresses will sink into Basic Esperanto, with the same words meaning different things to everyone there.

This is a problem that won't be solved, say, by having more regional congresses. PEN has to find a way to remain reliably and respectably literary—to become that far more so than it is—if it is also to play, on a still wider stage, its half-quixotic, half-eminently practical "political" role. But the problem is not, I think, insoluble. A strong start on it could be made by pruning some of the dead branches and twigs among the individual PEN members, and by encouraging local centers to set standards for admission beyond that of mere appearance in print. As the extremely promising inauguration of the *tables rondes* at the Bled congress indicates, some such search for a more aristocratic constitution of PEN is already underway.

Chapter Seventeen
Cold War Blues: Notes on the Culture of the Fifties
Morris Dickstein

I.

The recurrent flurries of nostalgia for the 1950s —— and the hovering threat that we might yet *become* the 1950s —— have not yet issued in any deep interest in what actually happened then; I don't mean the names and dates but what life felt like to those who were there. As the sixties recede and go out of fashion, the fifties have become the blank screen on which many project fantasies of an alternative, as the thirties were then to some who cared about alternatives.

But such nostalgia works only by distortion and historical invention, whose effect can be perverse and self-destructive. If rock music seems to have its innovative edge, if it seems to founder in a decadent sophistication, we look back to the banal but energetic simplicities of fifties rock 'n' roll. If our poetry has gone too far toward free form and undisciplined subjectivity we reach for a hair shirt, as Robert Lowell did in his immense sonnet sequence *Notebook* (1970), which has gone through numberless versions without ever becoming a poem. If our political life becomes too violent and problematic we grasp at something more orderly, as a writer in *Commentary,* John Mander, did, when he eulogized the fifties as "the happiest, most stable, most rational period the Western world has known since 1914."

This is perhaps a more exact analogy than Mander would care to acknowledge. The "long summer's day" of the Edwardian peace was also the frozen smile of countless social and political hierarchies. Nearly all of Europe welcomed the war with a sense of release, as long as the thrill of letting go obscured the accumulated debt. In retrospect the explosive conflicts of the sixties, agonizing as they often were, unmasked another Old Regime whose convenient symbol was Eisenhower, whose substance was the increasingly decayed and irrelevant traditions of rural or small-town America, and whose stability was grounded in a suppression of grievances and new energies that could be suppressed no longer.

The political atmosphere of that time is hard to recall today. The period was shadowed by the fear of thermonuclear war yet suffused by a mood of business-as-usual, everyone in his niche. Its legislative monument was the interstate highway system, which helped transport an ever more rootless population from the farms to the cities, from the cities to the suburbs, from the South to the ghettoes, from the Midwest to California. While hymning the praise of traditional values people were learning to live without a past, on a roller coaster of technological novelty that had already begun to Americanize the world.

This whirl of social movement found no echo in the political arena. The hallmark of both foreign and domestic policy was the extremely narrow range of permissible debate. Formal democracy thrived while the real issues of the day were excluded from the domain of choice. When Adlai Stevenson raised questions about the draft and about nuclear testing in the 1956 campaign he was said to have exceeded the bounds of mainstream opinion. Obviously he was not a serious candidate. High school students could debate ad nauseam whether Red China should be admitted to the UN but no one in public life would dare take similar liberties. Allied to this was the mania of national security which ruined the lives of some, touched many others with the cold hand of fear and conformity, and helped foreclose the political options of all. Much later, the domestic achievements of Johnson's Great Society and the dramatic coups of Nixon's foreign policy were but the thawed-out imperatives of this twenty-year freeze in the political process.

I enumerate these things not to close off the question of the fifties but to underline its importance. The fifties were the seedbed of our present cultural situation and the ground against which the upheavals of the sixties sought to define themselves. The challenge of these upheavals has yet to be met and we are still living with the consequences. The lure of the fifties hints that history moves like a pendulum; it speaks to our wish to have done with these problems; it tells us we can return unscathed to an idealized time before life grew complicated and we grew older. What happened in the fifties really matters, not only for what it gave rise to but for what it seems to offer us, for the way we shall choose to live.

For that reason it is impossible to limit one's evidence, as John Mander does in his *Commentary* article, to the often unreal world of foreign affairs. My own alternative, "what life felt like," is precarious but essential, for the culture gives our lives a tone and quality which may not be reflected by diplomats and presidents, which may be more truly expressed in the work of artists and intellectuals. Despite the interminable bloodbath of Vietnam, and because of it, the great changes of the past decade were ones of sensibility, awareness, attitude, not of institutions. For all the alarm of entrenched liberals and conservatives, the political changes of the sixties — as opposed to shifts of rhetoric and mood — were nothing if not gradual and melioristic.

The cataclysms of the moral landscape are quite another story, harder to discern because changes in sensibility resist ready generalization. What is at stake is a network of assumptions and feelings that link the individual to the wider public realities of his time. Artists and intellectuals, for all their supposed alienation from prevailing social values, often articulate these assumptions most subtly. They are daily awash in a medium of feeling and opinion, and where they do take dissident positions their resistance to the age may turn out to be crucially *of* the age. Even the formal concerns of the artist, which, like the quarrels of the intellectuals, often seem parochial to the world at large, usually reflect that world in intense miniature. The culture of an age is a unified thing, whatever its apparent contradictions. Touch it anywhere and it can reveal its secrets: the texture exposed, the part betrays the whole.

One example I'll use extensively here is the Cold War anti–Communism that predominated among intellectuals of the late forties and fifties, which weirdly refracted the political tenor of the nation at large. Later on in 1967 in the wake of revelations that leading periodicals and cultural organizations of the postwar period had been secretly funded by the CIA, apparently as instruments of the Cold War, *Commentary,* itself in the last throes of its newfound sixties liberalism, invited some of the best-known intellectuals of the fifties to rethink their past political behavior in a symposium on "Liberal Anti-Communism Revisited." The result was a revealing lesson in the varieties of self-exculpation. Some were penitent, some impenitent; some seemed desperately embarrassed while others were indignant at being asked to reconsider, as if the Vietnam war and the CIA exposure could have any effect on the timeless truths of political philosophy.

What nearly all shared, however, was a tendency to minimize the scope and effect of their past opinions, and to make distinctions which few had been so precise about in the previous period. We were anti-Stalinist, they insisted, not antiradical or anti–Communist. Nothing disgusted us more than the garden variety of Red-baiting that followed both world wars. We were libertarians and free minds, not witch-hunters or kept men. Our independent position made us a small dissident group with little influence either on national policy in the fifties or on the climate of opinion that later made the Vietnam war possible. (At least no one bothered to add, Some of my best friends were blacklisted.)

Yet for all these protestations what future historian who examines the vagaries of intellectuals during the period will fail to observe the correspondence between the views published in *Encounter* and the government policies that made the support of *Encounter* a good investment? Nor should our historian fail to note that at a low ebb of American civil liberties Mary McCarthy wrote a novel about a faculty Machiavel who tries to save his job by *posing* as a victim of political persecution; that Robert Warshow and Leslie Fiedler wrote essays attacking the Rosenbergs and their sympathizers rather than the government which had just executed them; that Irving Kristol and others minimized the importance of McCarthy while criticizing liberals and intellectuals who were alarmed by him; that an influential group of social scientists antipathetic to McCarthy tried to blame him, in a sense, on the Left rather than the Right by associating his demagoguery with populism and the presumed dangers of ideology;[1] that Sidney Hook supported the firing of supposed Communists from schools and universities *on libertarian grounds*, since such centers of independent thought had no room for those whose minds were *by definition* unfree; that teachers and academics everywhere stood by quietly while some of their colleagues became unpersons; that Elia Kazan and others went before the House Un-American Activities Committee to beat their breasts, swear fealty, name names, tell all —— the "all" being mainly trivial gossip many years old, the detritus of left-wing political life of the thirties. These episodes but skim the surface and isolate a few conspicuous individuals, yet they tell us enough to know that our future historian may abridge certain fine distinctions intellectuals love to make, especially when they are in bad faith. Hindsight will not fail to connect their opinions with certain gross actualities of the time, including blacklists, union purges, jail terms, university firings, McCarran and Smith Acts, supinely cooperative Supreme Court decisions, to say nothing of a much wider range of political intimidation that these events helped to enforce, as the range of public policy and private opinion grew ever more narrow.

II.

The details of these Cold War episodes are hardly new and despite their maleficence I don't wish to belabor them, though I'll soon return to some of them in greater detail. My other field of evidence is not political but literary: the curious emergence of the Jewish novel into a central position in American fiction. This is not to say there was a purely Wasp hegemony over American letters before the fifties, but earlier Jewish writers like Henry Roth, Daniel Fuchs, and even Nathanael West did not gain substantial recognition until they were republished in the wake of the Jewish-American renaissance of the fifties (championed by an aggressive new generation of Jewish critics like Howe, Fiedler, and Kazin, themselves no mean flowers of that awakening).

1. See the essays in *The Radical Right*, edited by Daniel Bell (1955, 1963) and a critique by Michael Paul Rogin in *The Intellectuals and McCarthy* (1967).

If the Jewish writers of the thirties, as writers, failed even to survive the decade, the generation of the forties remained in its own way *maudit* and unfulfilled —— and hardly acknowledged today except for its star performers. In a sense they were writers too talented but also too restless and unconfident to pursue a single line of work. Like many of their non-Jewish contemporaries —— Randall Jarrell comes to mind —— they were intellectuals and men of letters rather than novelists and poets. Several —— including Delmore Schwartz, Paul Goodman, and Isaac Rosenfeld —— made their mark as critics and essayists, and in fiction they tend to assume a no-nonsense tone of plain talk which, despite a leaven of whimsy and fantasy, reveals a distrust of the imaginative process when it gets too far from "real life." They gravitate toward small forms and big ideas, which they sometimes manipulate so brilliantly that they overwhelm the fictional context. They distrust eloquence and Art but remain beautifully close to the vital facts of experience, especially the experience of intellectuals caught in a wild, unsettling rush of acculturation, a crazy quilt of America. For all their attraction to ideas they never forget that intellectuals have mothers and fathers, friends and lovers, and that ideas are hatched by people, who can be elated, changed, or even destroyed by them.

Bellow is a characteristic member of this generation, its only survivor, its only "success" as a novelist. His friend Isaac Rosenfeld is its fallen soldier, but Delmore Schwartz remains its most fascinating and least-appreciated prophet. A *wunderkind* who never fulfilled his matchless promise, he descended increasingly into paranoia and isolation during the latter part of his life. By the time of his terrible, anonymous death in a shabby hotel in 1966 he had entirely faded from public view. The ripples of interest that followed first his death and then the publication of a thick volume of selected essays in 1970 consisted mainly of testimony from old friends to his extraordinarily vital personal presence.

As a writer he is hard to characterize or pin down, and few have tried. Younger readers seem not to have heard of him, though his work is one long brooding adolescence, and a scholar like Allen Guttman, whose book *The Jewish Writer in America* aims at a certain comprehensiveness, gives him no space at all. The finale of

Guttman's work is a long section on "Mr. Bellow's America," with chapters on every one of Bellow's novels, but Schwartz's great stories "America! America!" and "In Dreams Begin Responsibilities" evidently don't belong to the semiofficial canon of explicity "Jewish" writing. Yet, as much as Bellow's first book, *Dangling Man* (1944), they do introduce themes that would become decisive in the Jewish literary renaissance of the fifties.

Yet even a background has its background: behind the awkward new sensibility of the 1940s lay not only the disruptions of the war but the adventures and sorrows of Marxism. "Marxism is in relative eclipse," wrote Edmund Wilson in 1940, after nearly a decade of immersion in it. "An era in its history has ended." Nowhere is that eclipse more visible than in the work of the young writers. The introspective diarist whose mask Bellow wears in *Dangling Man* begins by attacking his age as "an era of hardboiled-dom" dominated by a belief in action rather than self-knowledge. He writes in 1942 when the obligations of wartime patriotism had replaced the pressures of social activism but the thrust is broadly aimed. In keeping a journal and keeping to his room, Joseph —— whose name recalls Kafka's antihero —— announces a new turn in the direction of the novel, away from Hemingway and from the proletarian writers who had appropriated his tight-lipped manner to their own ideological purpose. *Dangling Man* is the strangest, most claustral of war novels, a late, mild flower of the Underground Man tradition, morosely ideological in its refusal of all ideology.

Dangling Man would probably be forgotten today if Bellow's later work had not kept it in view. *The World is a Wedding* (1948), which collects Delmore Schwartz's stories of a decade, *is* forgotten, perhaps *the* neglected gem of the fiction of the forties. Schwartz received recognition mainly as a poet but neither his poetry nor his criticism have worn well —— which is to say, survived the period of uncritical adulation of the great modernist writers. Everything he wrote shows a good deal of stiffness and self-consciousness, but when the hermetic, elliptical intensities of Rilke, Eliot, and the symbolists merged with the gauche poeticism of his own language and sensibility the results could be disastrous. Where his poetry is alternately hermetic and "sincere" his critical

manner is uniformly earnest and labored. Except for a few first-
rate pieces like "The Duchess' Red Shoes" (a critique of Lionel
Trilling) his longer essays offer access to his mind more than they
illuminate the object. Only in his stories does that mind become
conscious of itself, for only there does his strange ruminative voice
work dramatically. Instead of donning the robes of abstract cultural authority he makes his style and personality part of his
subject, part of the problem.

I can't resist quoting an example of this style from "New
Year's Eve," one of three stories that concern "a youthful author
of promise" with a name —— Shenandoah Fish —— even more
improbable than the author's own: "Shenandoah and Nicholas
travelled crosstown in a street-car, standing up in the press and
brushing against human beings they would never see again. They
continued their argument which on the surface concerned the
question, should Nicholas go to a party where he would for the
most part be a stranger? This was a type of the academic argument, since the street-car slowly went crosstown, bearing the
young men to the argument's conclusion." The awkward, chiselled
quality of Schwartz's critical prose is on view here but the tone is
wry rather than earnest, a volatile mixture of irony and affection.
A moment later the argument deepens and we see the other pas-
sengers "listening in amazement to their virtually ontological discussions of character." Schwartz's own boyish mind is just the sort
that bears down on experience in an "ontological" way, risking
absurdity in an effort to both express and overcome its own sense
of isolation, its singular intensity. His stories are populated by
images of himself, named like himself, who become both the meat
of his satire and the vehicles of his aspiration to art, genius, and
fame. Such stories as "New Year's Eve" and "The World is a
Wedding" dwell lovingly on the preciosities of urban intellectuals
and artists *manqués* whose quasi-bohemianism is enforced by the
depression rather than founded on talent or creative energy. Contemptuous of a middle class which refuses to bow down to them,
cut off from their origins yet without much inward direction, they
devolve into a brittle cynicism and cliquishness that leaves them
cut off from "real life," trapped in their own anxious feelings of
superiority.

Delmore Schwartz's attitude toward these characters is complicated: there must be a great deal of himself and his friends in them, yet he lays bare their weaknesses with a scalpel. Surely *he* is the "youthful author of promise" whose name betrays his own divided soul. Ironically, the stories as a whole are hobbled by the same sort of claustral self-involvement for which he tellingly indicts his characters, as if the Hemingway code of action had been replaced by a cult of sensitivity so stringent that no action whatever is possible. Taken by themselves these stories would seem to confirm Irving Howe's suggestion that the sensibility of the New York intellectuals was too nervous and special for major creative work.

The major action of the stories is conversation: despite his irony Schwartz lovingly orchestrates his characters' talk. We are told of Rudyard Bell, who presides over a circle of would-be geniuses in "The World is a Wedding," that "the volley of the conversation, as at a tennis match, was all he took [away] with him. For what he wanted and what satisfied him was the activity of his own mind. This need and satisfaction kept him from becoming truly interested in other human beings, though he sought them out all the time." Surely Delmore Schwartz is exposing himself as well as Rudyard, for in his own talk he too "was like a travelling virtuoso who performs brilliant set-pieces," but in his self-diagnosis the author becomes a Rudyard who knows and transcends himself. Like Rudyard, Delmore is an Artist and talker but his bohemian contempt for the middle class is superseded by a fascination with his origins and identity. After Schwartz's death Dwight Macdonald, with his usual amiable obtuseness, wrote that he could never understand his friend Delmore's "obsession with his Jewish childhood." Paradoxically then, his self-involvement forced him to become truly interested in other human beings. Only they could help him decode his own secret, and it's precisely this obsession that propels his fiction from random satire and self-dramatization to an entirely different order of material.

In "America! America!" (his best story) and "In Dreams Begin Responsibilities" (his most famous one) Schwartz turns from the narrow circle of his contemporaries to the enigma of the previous generation. Both stories focus on the formative bonds between parents and children and the infinite abyss that separates them, that especially separates the immigrant generation from its "American" offspring. "America! America!" is about the declining fortunes of the Baumann family, which devolve from the father's prosperous importance in the immigrant social world to the chronic failures of the clever, maladaptive, ne'er-do-well sons. As in Joseph Conrad's novels, however, half the interest of the story comes from its teller, in this case Mrs. Fish, Shenandoah's mother, to whom he seems to be listening for the first time, thunderstruck by the complex world from which he came (and which lies accusingly outside his ken as an artist), struck too by the sensitivity of the speaker, whose intuitive insight into "the difficulties of life" shames him for his arrogance and self-importance. "Shenandoah was exhausted by his mother's story. He was sick of the mood in which he had listened, the irony and contempt which had taken hold of each new event. He had listened from such a distance that what he saw was an outline, a caricature, and an abstraction. How different it might seem, if he had been able to see these lives from the inside, looking out."

The whole story is brilliantly punctuated by such notations, by the undulations of self-awareness in this writer as he is flooded by the past and by the alien world of the middle class. "He reflected on his separation from these people, and he reflected that in every sense he was removed from them by thousands of miles, or by a generation, or by the Atlantic Ocean. . . . Whatever he wrote as an author did not enter into the lives of these people, who should have been his genuine relatives and friends, for he had been surrounded by their lives since the day of his birth, and in an important sense, even before then. . . . The lower middle-class of Shenandoah's parents had engendered perversions of its own nature, children full of contempt for every thing important to their parents."[2]

2. Compare the following reminiscence by Alfred Kazin: "It was not for myself that I was expected to shine, but for them — — to redeem the constant anxiety of their existence. I was the first American child, their offering to the strange new God; I was to be the monument of their liberation from the shame of being — — what they were. . . . Our families and teachers seemed tacitly agreed to be a little ashamed of what we were." — — *A Walker in the City*

Schwartz's theme has more than a personal dimension. He is sounding a note that goes back 150 years to the first stirrings of romanticism in Europe: the alienation of the artist from middle-class society. This was an especial dogma in the wake of the modernist movement of the 1920s, whose difficult art, addressed to a purified elite, was sometimes built on an attack on modern life in toto, and in the wake of the radicalism of the thirties, which identified the middle class as the special villain of contemporary society. A staggering number of contemporary writers were strangers in a strange land: Americans in Europe, Poles writing in English, Anglo-Irishmen living by their wits, self-exiled questers like Lawrence, hunting for a new spiritual home. Such deracination could be a source of strength. As Isaac Rosenfeld argued in 1944, "marginal men" could have a perspective on modern society unavailable to the insider. Delmore Schwartz echoes this theme in an essay on Eliot: "Modern life may be compared to a foreign country in which a foreign language is spoken. Eliot is the international hero because he made the journey to the foreign country."

Where this view of modern life prevails the Jew, especially the secular Jewish intellectual, becomes the quintessential modern man: doubly alienated, from the prevailing national culture and from his own traditional culture, uprooted from the European pale and yet cut off from his own uprooted parents. But the artist who is truly interested in other human beings —— and has some concern for his own sanity —— soon comes to the limits of alienation as a viable ground for his work. (This is why so many modernists, like Eliot and Yeats, like Lawrence in Mexico, fell eventually into eccentric nostrums of pseudotradition in religion or politics.) This is what Shenandoah recognizes as he hears his mother telling the story of the Baumanns, and surely no writer has inserted a more crushing insight into the strengths and limitations of his own work: "Shenandoah had thought of this gulf and perversion before, and he had shrugged away his unease by assuring himself that this separation had nothing to do with the important thing, which was the work itself. But now as he listened, as he felt uneasy and sought to dismiss the emotion, he began to feel that he was wrong to suppose that the separation, the contempt, and the gulf had nothing to do with his work; perhaps, on the contrary, it was the center; or perhaps it was the starting-point and compelled the innermost motion of the work to be flight, or criticism, or denial, or rejection."

Delmore Schwartz's best stories move away from this starting-point, toward an empathy for other lives, but they never fully evade these limitations. They are exquisitely wrought but excruciatingly self-conscious. No one would call them expansive. Their main theme remains that of the isolated self and the mysteries of identity that can never be solved but never evaded. For the author himself the final paranoia and anonymity, the trail of broken friendships and brilliant memories, to say nothing of the deterioration of his work, were the final seal of the same failure.

III.

The very title of Saul Bellow's first novel suggests its kinship with Delmore Schwartz's work, almost more than the book itself. As William Phillips has aptly remarked, Bellow's Joseph dangles "with both feet on the ground." (His resemblance to the Underground Man is skin-deep.) Not until *Herzog* (1964), his retrospective summation of the cultural life of the postwar period, would Bellow fully convey the glory and anguish of the deracinated Jewish intellectual of that time. What makes *Dangling Man* prophetic of a new literature and sensibility is its intent focus on the theme of the isolated self. Where Herzog and Tommy Wilhelm (in *Seize the Day*) will desperately reach out to people to overcome their almost unbearable sense of disconnection, Joseph attenuates all human connection in order to experiment on himself, to sound every inward note. *Dangling Man* is literally a book about a man who keeps a journal ("to talk to myself"): "and if I had as many mouths as Siva has arms and kept them going all the time, I still could not do myself justice." Severed from his job, not yet in the army, out of touch with wife, friends, and family, scarcely able to read, Joseph is performing an ontological experiment on the self, acting out a dream of absolute freedom that is the flip-side of the coin of alienation. In its small and weightless way *Dangling Man* foreshadows the metaphysics of the self, the elusive mysteries of personality, that would dominate the fiction of the fifties —— the legion of small novels which would recoil from the Promethean extremes of modernism and naturalism to take refuge in craft, psychology, and moral allegory.

One ingredient of these new novels of sensibility would be the abandonment of the public world that had provided much of the terrain of the great novels —— to say nothing of the terrain of Jewish millennial aspirations —— politics, class, manners and mores, even the very feel of the streets. In a shrewd and ambivalent review of Bernard Malamud's extraordinary collection of stories, *The Magic Barrel* (1958), Alfred Kazin commented that "his world is all too much an inner world —— one in which the city streets, the houses, the stores, seem, along with the people who broodingly stand about like skeletons, some with flesh, always just about to fold up, to disappear into the sky. . . . People flit in and out of each other's lives like bad dreams."

How different from this or from any other Jewish fiction of the forties and fifties is a book like Daniel Fuchs's *Summer in Williamsburg*, first published in 1934, ten years before *Dangling Man*. When Fuchs's novels were reissued in the early sixties much was made of the fabulistic, "poetic" side, as if they could only be appreciated in the wake of a moral allegorist like Malamud. Actually, the great strength of the books is their feeling for the life of the streets, the Runyonesque "low company" of youthful gangs in Williamsburg and Jewish mobsters in the Catskills, a chapter of social history quickly forgotten when the Jews became more respectable and the Jewish novel more morally austere. In Fuchs the moral temperature is low —— he is notably ham-handed in portraying the religious life of his Jews, a more inward subject. He is a folklorist, an anthropologist of street life rather than a purveyor of moral parables. For all his freedom from the cant of proletarian writing he remains in essence a 1930s realist; for him life is with the people.

Well, Daniel Fuchs folded up shop after three novels and went off to make his fortune in the great world —— Hollywood. Delmore Schwartz's characters need have no truck with the world because they are Artists, too pure to be responsible, or responsive. Bellow never allows his characters that exit. His Joseph is explicitly *not* an artist, despite his diary writing; he claims no higher moral license to drop out, adheres to no adversary community of the alienated, finds no salvation in "acts of the imagination": "I have no talent at all for that sort of thing. My talent, if I have one at all, is for being a citizen, or what is today called, most apologetically, a good man. Is there some sort of personal effort I can substitute for the imagination?" But this is precisely the talent Joseph never uses, the effort he can never make. Compared with Fuchs Bellow is deeply involved in the moral and communitarian strain of the Jewish tradition. Joseph claims to seek a social equivalent for the profound commitment of the artist. But the final gesture by which he abolishes his alienation is ominous: he puts himself up for induction. Of course this is no Vietnam but a "just" war, one Joseph says he believes in, but the satisfaction he expects is quite different from that of defeating the Germans. The bittersweet last lines of the book make clear that the dream of freedom has given way to an equally absolute dream of adhesion: "I am in other hands, relieved of self-determination, freedom cancelled. Hurray for regular hours! And for the supervision of the spirit! Long live regimentation!"

There is a good deal of self-irony in these lines, and Bellow could hardly be said to endorse their vision of the good life. But I call them ominous for they anticipate a great deal in Bellow's later work, from Augie March's opening chant that "I am an American, Chicago bred," to Herzog's polemics against "the Wasteland outlook, the cheap mental stimulants of Alienation," to Mr. Sammler's tract against the moral and political radicalism of the sixties, his defense of "civilization" against the "petted intellectuals" who attack it "in the name of perfect instantaneous freedom." Bellow's turn in the fifties toward accommodation with American society and his increasing hostility toward intellectuals who criticized it are quite well known, though few have noticed that the pattern of self-immolation goes back as far as his first book. This would be of little importance except to students of Bellow's development were it not representative of the whole intellectual climate of the fifties. The Partisan Review symposium on "Our Country and Our Culture" in 1952 is only the most famous indication of this new mood, which spread at just the time our country was prosecuting its most dubious adventures: the Cold War and its domestic correlative, the mania of internal security.

It's true that some intellectuals, especially literary intellectuals, did try to maintain an adversary stance. Delmore Schwartz, for example, ever faithful to the modernist mentality, contributed to the symposium a defense of "critical nonconformism" as against the new spirit of accommodation. But the whole brief, like the term itself, is lamentably abstract and typically confined to the cultural sphere: a defense of highbrow values against the incursions of mass and middlebrow taste. This was the usual tack of "adversary" intellectuals of that day; it suggested a strict hierarchy of cultural values with you-know-who at the top. (Even Harold Rosenberg accused sociologists of "mass culture" of secretly *liking* the stuff! Gasp!) Only the smallest handful of independent intellectuals effectively focused their criticism where it was most needed: on political decisions, on aggregations of social and economic power, on questions of civil liberties which then affected so many lives.

Thus it would be fair to say that the residual intransigence of some (mostly literary) intellectuals and the newfound Americanism of other (mostly political) intellectuals amounted to the same thing. The political intellectuals sang the virtues of American life, with its pluralism and pragmatism, its procedure by consensus and its presumed freedom from ideology and moralism —— this in the age of John Foster Dulles! —— and excoriated the illusions of liberals, radicals, Popular Front types, and strict constructionists of the Bill of Rights (like Justices Black and Douglas). The literary intellectuals, while maintaining the cult of alienation, simply abandoned politics to pursue private myths and fantasies, to devote their work to the closet intensities of the isolated self or isolated personal relationships. The concept of alienation lost its social content and took on an increasingly religious and metaphysical cast. European existentialism and crisis theology became an incalculably great influence on the mood of the fifties —— shorn, however, of their political matrix. The moral and psychological Sartre of the forties was admitted. The political Sartre of the fifties was ignored or ridiculed —— then replaced by Camus, whose emphasis on the absurdity of the human condition and nostalgia for a lost simplicity of being were more painlessly assimilated, and answered to the dominant mood.

IV.

What makes all this heartbreaking is the simple fact: though the intellectuals lost interest in politics, politics itself went marching on, shamefully —— desperately in need of critical scrutiny and principled antagonism. In exploring the climate of opinion of the fifties I don't mean to blame America alone for the Cold War or to slight the terror of the Stalinist monolith and the fatuity of its American apologists. I don't mean to suggest that intellectuals should have made common cause with the Party, as Sartre did for a brief period in France, a party that was at once servile and manipulative, philistine and morally and politically bankrupt. Yet, as the historian Allen J. Matusow has written, "the great irony of McCarthyism is that it developed in the absence of any real internal Communist menace; for by 1950 Communism in America had lost whatever influence it once possessed."

However true this may be for the country at large it does not quite apply to the intellectuals. For them the internal menace was real, within the culture, within themselves, like their Jewishness, always threatening a return of the repressed. This fear helps explain the vengeful confessional tone of some political writing during the period ("couch liberalism," as Harold Rosenberg dubbed it). Behind the guilt and animosity looms a burning memory of the thirties, the inculpation in a Great Lie. Even those who were still in knee-pants then felt that they had somehow been taken in, that all radicalism, all politics, had been tainted irrevocably by Stalinism, and that all intellectuals were potential dupes unless ideology gave way to "realism" and complicity were absolved by confession.

It would be hard to find more vicious examples of serious political writing than the first three essays in Leslie Fiedler's *An End to Innocence* (1955), devoted in turn to the Hiss case, the Rosenberg case, and to "McCarthy and the Intellectuals." Fiedler's involvement in the political life of the thirties was practically nil,[3] yet he endlessly harries his subjects with their failure to confess

3. Though in a later book, *Being Busted* (1969), written in a different political climate, after he himself had fallen victim to an official frame-up, he fondly wheels out some schoolboy adventures in radicalism.

and takes a confessional tone himself but has nothing to reveal except some "illusions," which quickly turn out to be the illusions of others. Joseph K. in Kafka's *Trial* is charged with no crime but rather stands "accused of guilt"; Fiedler is not content to malign the guilty: he indicts a whole generation for its "innocence."

What lies behind this puzzling assault on language and sense is a psychodrama on the theme of "growing up," in which radicalism and social hope equal childishness, while maturity demands the acceptance of middle-class values, society as it is, the tragic ambiguity of all worldly commitment, all action.[4] This coming to maturity for the once-alienated intellectual requires the traumatic *rite de passage* of public repentance. Thus Whittaker Chambers qualifies as a tragic figure, the "scorned squealer" who deserves our empathy since he suffers for all of us. Alger Hiss, on the other hand, is a "hopeless liar," "the Popular Front mind at bay." Why? Not simply because he is guilty, though Fiedler hasn't the faintest doubt of that, but because he refuses to put away childish things: unwilling to "speak aloud a common recognition of complicity," he cuts himself off from "the great privilege of confession."

The religious (and markedly Christian) tone and fervor of these bizarre comments is even more intense in the essay on the Rosenbergs, which after twenty pages of vituperation concludes that "we should have offered them grace," yes grace —— not mercy or clemency but grace, "even to those who most blasphemously deny their own humanity" (that is, by refusing to confess). The Rosenbergs should have been spared not for *their* sake but to ratify our own godlike virtue and superiority. America! America! indeed.

---

4. A glance through the back volumes of *Commentary* or *Encounter* would disclose many curious playlets on this theme, for instance Alan Westin, "Libertarian Precepts and Subversive Realities: Some Lessons Learned in the School of Experience," *Commentary* (January 1955), an article whose very title speaks volumes. Many civil liberties, it suggests, are fine abstractions, but must bend to meet the hard realities of subversion. Libertarians, however well intentioned, who insist on "an absolutist framework," who are "unwilling to make the necessary compromises," risk leaving society "without the means of *making necessary judgments and distinctions* in coping with the formidable problem offered by the agents, *conscious or otherwise*, of a hostile foreign power." (my italics)

Fiedler refuses even to entertain the possibility that Hiss or the Rosenbergs might not have all that much to confess. 'Twere to consider too curiously to consider so. To consider it would shatter his faith in American institutions: "One would have to believe the judges and public officials of the United States to be not merely the Fascists the Rosenbergs called them, but monsters, insensate beasts." But the record, even the record available when Fiedler wrote, provides abundant evidence for the most extreme judgment. There is no more horrifying document of Cold War hysteria than Judge Kaufman's notorious remarks as he sentenced the couple to death. Full of inflamed rhetoric about the deadly struggle with Communism, the "challenge to our very existence," he accused them of "devoting themselves to the Russian ideology of denial of God, denial of the sanctity of the individual and aggression against free men everywhere instead of serving the cause of liberty and freedom."

> I consider your crime worse than murder. . . . I believe your conduct in putting into the hands of the Russians the A-bomb years before our best scientists predicted Russia would perfect the bomb has already caused, in my opinion, the Communist aggression in Korea, with the resultant casualties exceeding fifty thousand and who knows but that millions more of innocent people may pay the price of your treason. Indeed, by your betrayal you undoubtedly have altered the course of history to the disadvantage of our country.

Never mind that scientists then and since have labeled the A-bomb charge simplistic nonsense. All the frustrations of postwar foreign policy, all our fantasies of an enemy within to which this nation of immigrants has proved especially vulnerable, demanded a scapegoat. President Eisenhower went even further in his last-minute refusal of clemency: "I can only say that, by immeasurably increasing the chances of atomic war, the Rosenbergs may have condemned to death tens of millions of innocent people."[5] Who can establish innocence for what has not yet happened? Who dare ask mercy for the destruction of the world?

What these judges and public officials do so grossly, what

5. I take these quotations from Walter and Miriam Schneir's excellent brief on the case, *Invitation to an Inquest* (1965).

Fiedler and Robert Warshow —— whose essay on the Rosenbergs is a companion piece to Fiedler's —— do more ingeniously, is to completely dehumanize the Rosenbergs and turn their execution into an impersonal act, almost a merciful one. (This casts a rather sickly glow on Judge Kaufman's banner of "the sanctity of the individual." As individuals the Rosenbergs were accorded not much more sanctity than the defendants in the Moscow purge trials.) In line with the strategy of blaming the victim, they accuse the Rosenbergs of having destroyed themselves —— by adhering to ideology, by becoming a "case." Both Fiedler and Warshow analyze the published prison letters of the couple to demonstrate their vulgarity of mind, "the awkwardness and falsity," says Warshow, "of the Rosenbergs' relations to culture, to sports, and to themselves." The supposed meaning is that "almost nothing really belonged to them, not even their own experience." The implicit moral is that they were so empty, so crude, so bereft of style that there was nothing for the electric chair to kill. It takes Fiedler with his talent for blatant absurdity to announce this message clearly: "They failed in the end to become martyrs or heroes, or even men. *What was there left to die?*" (my italics)

What all this postmortem textual criticism with its vengefulness and personal animosity tells us about the issues in the case is hard to fathom, but from our vantage point it tells us much about the Cold War mentality of 1953 (especially as expressed in the two leading journals of intellectual anti-Communism, *Commentary* and *Encounter,* where the articles first appeared). For all their political, even propagandistic intent, both essays show an eerie displacement of politics into aesthetics: issues of power and justice —— indeed, of human life itself —— get argued in terms of taste and style. For these two clever critics the Rosenberg letters are a godsend, a text, life in an orderly bundle. In their mixture of high-minded platitudes about politics and middlebrow cultural opinions the letters provide an ideal foil for the myopic fifties highbrow with an axe to grind, for the literary mentality with a tendentious cult of style. The unity of personality —— in this case the Popular Front personality —— that E.L. Doctorow would grasp so beautifully in his novel about the case (*The Book of Daniel*) completely eluded Fiedler and Warshow, or proved too threatening for them. The strange synthesis of Communism, Judaism, idealism, and Americanism, so characteristic of the Popular Front period (with its stress on Communism as "twentieth-century Americanism"), they could only read as proof of mendacity, though it's familiar enough to anyone who grew up with an uncle in the Party or a parent in a CIO union.

For Fiedler and Warshow the vulgar middlebrow Jew is a cultural embarrassment who must be exorcised, so that the high-brow critic can confirm his place in the kingdom of art. The Jewish radical, the quaint Popular Front "progressive," will be sacrificed so that the children of immigrants, the despised intellectuals with their foreign ideas, can become full-fledged Americans.

Years earlier Warshow himself had criticized a novel by Lionel Trilling for its failure to portray the "deep psychological drives" involved in the Stalinist experience and its aftermath, and for suppressing the dominant Jewish involvement in the radical politics of the thirties. That was in 1947. By 1953 when the Rosenbergs were finally killed that Jewish element had been trumpeted for years in the world's headlines. The deep psychological drives of a Warshow or a Fiedler are as understandable, however unforgivable, as the quiet terror of many ordinary Jews that a pogrom was in the works (despite the thoughtfulness of the courts in providing the Rosenbergs with a Jewish judge and Jewish prosecutors). What was buried with the Rosenbergs, a few months after Eisenhower took office, was two decades of American (and Jewish) Marxism, and two centuries of a different innocence from the kind Fiedler attacks: the innocence of a nation convinced it could play the world's good citizen and moral arbiter. "Watch out!" wrote Sartre the day after the executions. "America has the rabies!" If the substance of idealism was shattered, however, the rhetoric and its illusions lived on to fight another day. It took the Vietnam war to expose the emperor's clothes and shake his righteous self-assurance.

V.

I have put such emphasis on the Rosenberg case because of its magnitude but also because by the early fifties the Jew was well on his way to becoming the American Everyman, as the black would be in the early sixties. In the wake of the Holocaust the fate of the Jew, to many, had become a parable of the human condition —— a drama of pointless, horrendous suffering which revealed the modern dimensions of terror and evil. Now, in the postwar period, the relentless hunt for traces of Communism in American life was bound to have an inordinate effect on the Jews, who had been as deeply implicated as any group in the radicalism of the thirties and the fellow-traveling of the forties. In the essays of Fiedler and Warshow, as in the fiction of Bellow and Delmore Schwartz, we feel the impact of these new shocks: we see evidence of the Jewish psyche taking stock of itself, revising itself, recoiling from its recent historical role.

Red-baiting did not begin with Senator McCarthy, a late-comer who appeared when some of the battles had already been fought. The forgetting of the thirties and of the wartime Russian alliance had been in full swing in American society since 1946, with liberals like Humphrey vying with right-wingers for initiative on the issue. It was President Truman who created a massive loyalty–review apparatus for government employees early in 1947, though this probably affected Jews less than the purge of left-wing unions in the CIO and the hearings of the House Un-American Activities Committee on the entertainment industry. By 1949 the leaders of the Communist Party had already been prosecuted under the dubious terms of the Smith Act, which had been passed with Communist support in 1940 as an instrument against Fascism.[6] When McCarthy made his famous list-waving debut as a Red–hunter in Wheeling, West Virginia, in February 1950, he was seizing and exploiting —— and soon personifying —— a situation years in the making and especially ripe for a right-wing dema-gogue.

It happens that 1950 was also the year that Bernard Malamud began publishing the stories that were eventually collected in *The Magic Barrel*. Nowhere do we see the revised version of the Jewish psyche more clearly expressed, more poignantly imagined, than in his work. Needless to say his books show no trace of the McCarthy period, no trace of politics of any sort (at least until the flawed historical novel *The Fixer* in 1966); this is one thing that helps

---

6. On this point and others see the spirited and generally fair-minded history of the American Communist Party by Irving Howe and Lewis Coser, published in 1957.

make him one of the quintessential writers of the fifties. "Revised" is an odd word to apply to him since he is the most deeply traditional of the Jewish novelists, traditional in his unrivaled grasp of the Jewish imagination of disaster, traditional in his authentic stock of immigrant and second-generation characters, traditional above all in the very feel of his stories —— his preference for moral fables and realistic storytelling over modernist experiments in technique and narrative consciousness. In fact it is Malamud's genius in *The Magic Barrel* and in his best novel, *The Assistant* (1957), to combine a distilled accuracy of urban Jewish speech and scene with a mode of poetic parable reminiscent of Hawthorne, or of his older Yiddish contemporary, I. B. Singer. But this succeeds only within a narrow imaginative range. Malamud's best work is built around a few obsessive metaphors and situations. From the pathetic little grocery store in *The Assistant* to the actual prison in *The Fixer* to the abandoned tenement in *The Tenants* (1971) he sees the world in Pascal's terms as a prisonhouse from which we are led off one by one to die. His protagonists, whose names are as similar as his titles, are all rooted in the *schlemiel* figure of the Jewish folk tradition: antiheroes thwarted at every turn, sometimes comically, sometimes horrifyingly —— ordinary souls with a rare talent for catastrophe. To be a Jew is to suffer —— this is the simple moral equation at the heart of *The Assistant* —— and the only proper response to suffering is quiet stoicism and stubborn if hopeless decency. Morris Bober, the grocer, is a Good Man, for all the good that does him.

If the prisonhouse metaphor suggests the influence of existentialism (or a parallel development), the theme of suffering and endurance is more authentically Jewish, distilling as it does much of the grimmest of Jewish historical experience, so apocalyptically renewed in this century with the destruction of the European communities. But it is one thing —— though perhaps too limited —— to convey the experience of suffering, to capture the banal, grinding agony of the small shopkeeper eking out a marginal living; this is a heartrending achievement (though I feel that, intent on an allegory of Man Alone, he screens out the compensatory joys of religious, communal, or family life). But it is quite another thing to put a high moral valuation on this agony; there is a strain in

Malamud's work that is more Christian than Jewish, an emphasis on bearing the cross, on suffering-for-others, on salvation through suffering. When Frank Alpine, the Italian assistant, asks the old storekeeper, "Why do you suffer, Morris?" he calmly answers, "I suffer for you." At the heart of Malamud's work is a quasi-religious theme of salvation, as when Alpine finally becomes a Jew and takes on his back the same wretched store, the same wretched life, that had crushed his dead employer.

What do these timeless patterns of suffering and redemption have to do with the 1950s when they were conceived? There is little sense of specific historical time in *The Assistant*. Though nominally set in the 1930s its historical matrix is as shadowy as its New York milieu is claustral and specterlike. Yet I believe this tells us a great deal about the period when it was written. As Ruth Wisse shows in her fine study *The Schlemiel as Modern Hero*, the schlemiel character became dear to Jewish folklore as a vehicle of spiritual transcendence amid constrained and sometimes desperate social circumstances. As in farce, where the most extreme violence is rendered harmless and absurd, the schlemiel, usually a comic figure, provides a catharsis of catastrophe and pain, a way of coping. Sholom Aleichem, in adapting this folk motif, Wisse says, "conceived of his writing as a solace for people whose situation was so ineluctably unpleasant that they might as well laugh. The Jews of his works are a kind of schlemiel people, powerless and unlucky, but psychologically, or, as one used to say, spiritually, the victors in defeat." Maurice Samuel makes a similar point about Sholom Aleichem's "application of a fantastic technique that the Jews had developed over the ages. . . . a technique of avoidance and sublimation. . . . They had found the trick of converting disaster into a verbal triumph, applying a sort of Talmudic ingenuity of interpretation to events they could not handle in their reality." The schlemiel (or the schlemiel people) achieves a victory of mind or heart, even in the shadow of the iron fist.

Yet such a strategy can be deeply quietistic and evasive —— quite literally "fantastic," as Samuel says —— especially in circumstances less constricting than the Russian Pale or the Polish ghetto. Even there, as currents of socialism, Zionism, and the Hebrew Enlightenment spread among the people, some of Sholom Aleichem's contemporaries were scornful of these folk attitudes and psychological habits. Wisse suggests that the most famous schlemiel story in Yiddish literature, Y. L. Peretz's "Bontshe the Silent," which is "now widely regarded as a study of sainthood, is actually a socialist's exposure of the grotesquerie of suffering silence; Chaim Nachman Bialik's response to the infamous Kishinev pogrom was outrage against the *victims* who flee or hide, pretending that vengeance will come from God." The controversy that has flared repeatedly over Jewish behavior under Nazi occupation and in the death-camps is an extension of the same quarrel, the same anguish, on an immensely more terrible scale.

In its own way then, Bernard Malamud's work can be seen as one kind of response to the frozen and quietly fear-ridden political atmosphere of the McCarthy and Eisenhower years. This is not to say that it's not deeply imagined, with profound roots in the Jewish psyche and the Jewish moral tradition. Yet that tradition has many branches —— not simply its line of Jacob, sensitive, wily, domestic, passive, fed by mother love, but also its thwarted line of Esau, hairy hunter, "activist," doomed favorite of the father. The Jewish novel of the 1950s is a reversion to the line of Jacob, *an atonement for Jewish radicalism* that is also perfectly in tune with the wider currents of the age: ruminative, private, morally austere and self-conscious, apolitical.

Finally, the literature and politics of the period are one. There is no special "key" to the sensibility of the age: almost anything works if we turn it right and press it hard. But the Jewish novel works especially well. The fifties were a great period for home and family, for getting and spending, for cultivating one's garden. All that is reflected in its writing. But its spokesmen also call it an Age of Anxiety; behind its material growth hovers a quiet despair, whose symbols are the Bomb and the still-vivid death-camps and a fear of Armageddon that rings true even in the monstrous phrases of a Judge Kaufman. But this anxiety is metaphysical and hermetic, closed in upon itself: the Bomb evokes despair rather than anger or opposition. The Jewish novel reflects this spirit and ministers to it, for it is literally overwrought —— anguish hemmed in by form —— offering finally the uneasy absolution of art for a torment whose origin it cannot know and whose course it cannot alter.

Chapter Eighteen
While America Burns
William Barrett and William Phillips

EDITOR'S NOTE: *Mr. Barrett's letter and William Phillips's reply are part of a continuing series of comments on the political and economic crisis in America and Western Europe.*

William Phillips
Editor, Partisan Review

Dear William:

In trying to collect my thoughts on the present situation, I found myself persistently going back to the time more than twenty-five years ago when I was connected with the magazine. A great deal has happened in between; but it seems to me that the situation then, or the situation as *Partisan Review* then faced it, might serve as a channel-marker against the present turbulent currents. You were then both mentor and friend; and as my mind turns back in that direction, it seems only natural that I should be addressing my thoughts to you.

The great and overshadowing difference between then and now, it seems to me, is in the relative positions of power of the United States and the Soviet Union. America has become much weaker, markedly so after Vietnam and Watergate; and Russia much stronger. Everything else in the contemporary scene comes under the shadow of this shifting balance of power. If the United States were to go under, liberty would disappear for mankind. I don't say this out of any patriotic conviction of America's messianic destiny. History has simply dealt the cards in this way. If the American presence were to disappear, western Europe would slide quickly into the Soviet bloc. Britain would be left an isolated island with a faltering economy and severe class conflicts; and Japan would be similarly isolated, with mounting internal pressures of its own. Anything, then, that weakens the strength of the United States weakens the cause of liberty.

In the past we had always nursed the hope, silently at least, that the Soviet regime might eventually liberalize itself. We were socialists, after all, and in some sense it was a socialist state. Perhaps we fixed too much on the person of Stalin as the evil figure responsible for the dictatorship. But now any such hope of liberalization is illusory. The iron law of a Communist regime is that its bureaucracy must not only perpetuate itself but expand its power as well. The permanent revolution is the permanent dictatorship. Security from external attack doesn't lead to any relaxation of its grip. We should have known this as early as 1946. At the end of the War, Russia had secured its borders and accumulated a fund of good will on the part of the Allies as a residue of wartime partnership—and it chose to launch the Cold War. One has to emphasize this point now against the distortions of our various revisionists. In 1946, when I joined you on *PR*, I found you already engaged in the Cold War, which I promptly joined. You were politically avant-garde then, ahead of the rest of the country. *PR* was engaged in trying to point out to liberals their illusions about Russia and Russian expansionism. The response of the American government, which seemed to us so tardy and faltering, often left us feeling like climbing the walls out of frustration. That's the way it is to be politically avant-garde. The evil is not that the United States eventually responded to the Cold War, which it had not initiated, but that it carried it on so stupidly during the McCarthy era.

The Vietnam War was another stupidity on America's part. It could not have waged a more pro-Communist war if it had deliberately set out to do so. The struggle against Communism, which is bound to be long and protracted, and will go on Détente or no Détente, has to be a matter of much more limited commitments.

One thing that remains constant now as then is the presence of the Fellow Traveller, though he has now changed his colors. Usually he professes to be thoroughly disabused and cynical about Russia, but the cynicism ends by equating the imperfections of American democracy with dictatorship. It's as if we were back with Orwell and Koestler arguing against the fellow-travellers of the late forties. China, or Cuba, is now the utopian and fair-haired darling. We have Park Avenue Maoists as we once had Park Avenue Stalinists. (The hostess, at one fashionable party I attended, wore a Chinese gown just to set the right tone.) Apparently we'll have to wait another generation until the Chinese dissenters begin to appear in order to change this attitude.

Fellow-travelling appears to be a permanent part of modern life, a condition of the modern spirit. It is "aesthetic" politics, "literary" Marxism, the lure of utopian thinking on the part of those who feel secure enough in their liberty to play around with it; a surrogate for the religion they have lost. In a back-handed way, Dostoevski was right: the socialist question is above all the religious question.

Anyway, everybody else seems to be doing the old-fashioned fellow traveller's work for him. The democracies are going through an orgy of self-destruction just as the Greek historians and philosophers described the process in the ancient world. We seem to have lost the sense of liberty as something connected with the continuing life of liberal institutions, which we have all been engaged in undermining in recent years. At this turn of history mankind (the intellectual most of all) seems hell-bent on enslaving itself. Sometimes I get the impression that nobody is really interested in liberty today except the Russian dissidents.

On the cultural scene: there is an awful lot of talent knocking around, but much of it, I'm afraid, goes to waste on the trivial and aimless. We've been in the midst of a cultural inflation for some time, worse in its way than the economic one. When we first knew De-Kooning, he hadn't yet had his first one-man show, and was just scraping along. It was you—just to get the record straight on this—who opened the pages of *PR* for Clement Greenberg to push the Abstract Impressionists (the name didn't exist then). That was a first step in what later turned out to be a whole revolution in the artist's financial status. The artists who formerly had trouble getting galleries began to have income-tax problems. It's nice that with all the money flowing around, some of it should drain off to the artists. Still, affluence has brought other problems—the commercial conniving of dealers, the bandwagons of taste, public relations promotions, etc., etc. In short, a cultural inflation, with its consequent debasing of real values. It's nice that Pollock's estate should have been able to get two million dollars for "Blue Poles," but is the picture really worth that much?

The more inflation the less seriousness about the art itself. The kinds of ambition for the individual work that the movement—and DeKooning particularly—had back in the late forties would seem strange nowadays. There is more trifling with the tricks of the medium, non-art as art, nihilism toward art—in a word, camp. As the substance becomes more minimal the rhetoric about it becomes more inflated. A recent ad in *PR* (I don't of course hold the magazine responsible for its advertisements) announced a collection of stories under the title *Superfiction.* Isn't it enough for the writer to aim at a good piece of fiction, which becomes all the harder as literary history accumulates, without seeking some new and inflated genre? ''Supercolossal'' used to be Hollywoodese, but the literary seem now to be aping that style.

In the history of art the great movements—the Renaissance (which was really two different movements), the Baroque, etc.—ran their course in less than a century. Their followers couldn't see, or didn't want to see, when the original wave had run out. As the imitations got more elaborate they became emptier, more inflated as they became more contrived. Similarly, nobody seems to want to face up to the fact that the great Modern movement has by now come to an end.

That should be an opportunity for the critics to reexamine that movement and find out what was really happening. They might be surprised to discover the traditional values that were always present in it. Art is, after all, one of the most traditional of human enterprises. Thus modern art taught us to see primitive art. Now that the superficial novelties have worn off, how Proust resembles Balzac, or Joyce, Dickens, begins to interest us as much as the differences. Once DeKooning was trying to do the same thing as Giotto—to impart as much movement and tension to the pictorial surface as possible.

One great legacy of the Modern movement could be that it taught us to take experimentation in our stride. We're no longer shocked by it, but we're no longer taken in by it either. We allow the artist all the gimmicks he pleases; but when we have looked past them, we have to put to him the simple and central question: Does he have anything to say? We may discover he is empty. That might be enlightening. We might discover we are empty, too. That could be a beginning.

In short, we are caught in a difficult period of transition, of reassessment and rediscovery of values. That is bound to be painful, but it could be challenging work, a new world to discover, as we go about constructing the postmodern period. Unfortunately, this adventure has to take place under the shadow of the awful and brutal political reality we cannot allow ourselves to forget: that we live in the time when the future of liberty may be decided for the whole of mankind.

Many years ago, William, you kidded me that I was "paranoid about the future." You could always beat me in an argument, but I've waited a quarter of a century to make this snappy retort: "Was I wrong?"

WILLIAM BARRETT

Dear Will:

It was always a pleasure to argue with you, regardless of who won, because both of us were interested in the truth almost as much as we were in arguing. And if you were paranoid about the future, still, as Delmore used to say, and he was an expert on this subject, one could be paranoid and right. Anyway, the future has not turned out so well, and it may be better to be paranoid than to be schizoid, as I am. I seem to have mixed feelings about almost every political question facing us, particularly the question of the role of America in the coming period. But I think my own uncertainties reflect the complexities of the situation.

One of the complications is the politically polarized atmosphere, which makes it difficult even to discuss the issue of American versus Russian power, and the related issues of the preservation of freedom and the future of socialism. If one is anti-Communist, even from the left, one is tagged as a conservative; and if one is critical of America, he or she is lumped with fellow travellers and apologists for Soviet policies. It has been particularly difficult to maintain a radical, socialist perspective—or conscience—in a time when a vocal part of the Left confuses progress with backwardness, while the Right has cast itself in the role of defending democracy.

Obviously, there are no simple answers. And though I agree with much of what you say, I think your argument is too syllogistic and hence leaves out many factors. Essentially, your point is that if America became so weak that it could not resist Soviet, or Communist, expansion anywhere, then the kind of freedom that we identify with Western democracy would almost surely disappear—unless communism, itself, in these circumstances would develop into the free society that Marx envisaged. As things now stand, I believe you are right. If America could not defend Western Europe, no doubt it would go communist and come under the Russian sphere of influence—again, unless it was strong enough to defy the Soviet Union. But what is assumed in this line of reasoning, is that America and Europe are stable entities with well defined interests, democratic commitments, and predictable developments.

The fact is that America cannot be counted on to defend even limited forms of democracy, as we have seen in Spain, Portugal, and Greece, for example, and as we can now see in the Mid-East. If America is so dedicated to the defense of Western democracy, how can we explain the games being played with Israel and the Arabs? I need hardly remind you that in many, if not all, situations, the love of money is stronger than the love of liberty.

Besides, the strength and stability of Europe and America depend partly on the ability to solve their political and economic problems. The power of the Communist parties on the continent is not due simply to their clever propaganda or the craving of the intellectuals as well as the masses for political illusions.

And all this talk about America being the bulwark of democracy does nothing to ameliorate the conditions that deny it that role. On the home front, the notion of America's global mission, like most patriotic rhetoric, is actually a substitute for enlightened thinking and action. The truth is that the country has become a jungle of competing interests and pressure groups, corrupt and anarchic, unable to plan its economy, its ecology, its traffic, its control of crime, its foreign policy, its race problems, its urban decay. This state of affairs used to be rationalized by the myth that these contradictions were essential to democracy.

What I am saying is that the proposition that the decline of America will lead to the decline of political and intellectual freedom is a half-truth. It does not take into account all the other factors that create totalitarian parties and regimes. And it ignores the fact that the affairs of the country have been in the hands of those who seem least capable of dealing with them. Unless one has some alternative politics, one is simply putting one's faith in the people and ideas one never trusted much in the past. And if, as you imply, your position is that of critical support of the policy of the lesser evil—a position taken by liberals and radicals when their ideal, long-range program did not appear to be viable—then it seems to me your critical attitude should be both stronger and clearer.

But aside from the practical and immediate implications of an argument which is basically an appeal to Realpolitic, I think one must have some larger vision, if only for intellectual reasons, some idea of a better social order, which would provide a perspective from which to criticize both the communist and our own societies. Otherwise one's political identity is dissolved in that jumble of opinions that can never extricate themselves from the assumptions of the status quo. Even if it is true that America is now the guardian of freedom, this is at best a reassuring observation, perhaps a fact, but scarcely a theory, and hardly distinguishable from the ready-made opinions of all the stalwarts of·the popular media. No politics, other than support for America, follows from such an attitude, support, that is, in the event of a confrontation with Russia, which in any case few people would question. Obviously, your own knowledge and insight, for which I have great respect, are incomparably greater, but they are not given an adequate outlet in a statement that confines the future of freedom to the limits of American power.

Hence, the real question is not whether liberty is bound up with the American future, but how to evaluate American policies and motives. Obviously, reactionaries would have widely different estimates and programs from those of socialists, for example.

You speak of the change in the ratio of American to Soviet power, but of the persistence of the "fellow-travelling" mind as a constant. Here, too, I think you are right. However, I believe you are wrong in your assessment of its importance and its influence. In the thirties and forties, it seemed necessary to dispel the illusions about Russia and the Communists because so many people who should have known better were taken in. Now, on the other hand, with the exception of those who cling to a half-baked idealism, the whole country has no illusions about the Communists. Also, at that time, the unmasking of Stalinism was part of the struggle on the Left, to educate honest but mistaken radicals and liberals, and to free the Left from the corrupting effects of its association with the Communists. Today, however, people may be muddle-headed, but no serious person on the Left is pro-Communist. Neither on the Right nor on the Left can the problem now be said to be the failure to recognize the nature of communism.

The problem for the country is not whether it understands the aims of the Communists, but whether there is a national interest and if so what its relation is to this understanding—in other words, whether the support of democracy is always in the national interest. As you know, Marxists have usually claimed that there is no national interest, that there are only class interests, and that the so-called national interest in this country is only a mask for the interests of the dominant economic class. This is probably too schematic and reductive a view of national motives. Nevertheless, many recent American policies certainly seem to suggest that the government has tried very hard to prove that Marx and Lenin were right. True, there have been instances when the country did not appear to act either in the interests of the nation as a whole or of any one class. I must confess that I see no explanation for this but stupidity—the kind of myopic stupidity that comes from the national addiction to empirical, day-to-day thinking. And I do think stupidity has been underestimated as a factor in history by Right as well as Left ideologues.

When you talk about the cultural decline, it is not clear whether you think this is connected with our political predicament and therefore with the question of freedom. If so, then what you take to be the signs of cultural decline must be seen as part of the political situation. For what are the cultural anarchy, the reign of pop, the popular distortions of modernism—what are these triumphs of the market if not products of the system of advertising and packaging. And this is the system that is supposed to save our freedoms and preserve our cultural values. I need not remind you that the serious art of this period has been critical and detached.

And in your dismissal of the art scene today I think you make the mistake of lumping fashionable versions of the avant-garde, tailored to the popular market, with work of genuine talent by writers and painters who have resisted the pressures of the time. Most poets, for example, perhaps because of the intractability of the medium, have kept their distance from pop taste. And a number of novelists might even be said to have become too eccentric in their effort to stay out of the entertainment business. Thus, in failing to distinguish between the conformist and noncomformist part of the culture, you are confusing the cure with the disease. I am sure you have no such political motives, but you must be aware that a favorite gambit of conservative critics is to blame the cultural slump on the radical sensibility, that is, on the sensibility that is opposed to all the things you are against.

What more can I say—except to deplore the situation in which people who have the same values and goals find themselves on opposite sides of the fence. In the "old days," which you refer to apparently with some nostalgia, there was plenty of nonsense, but one felt closer to those one was able to argue with. One can argue fruitfully only with those who share one's assumptions, but in the fragmentation and confusion of thinking today differences become barricades.

W.P.

Chapter Nineteen
Neoconservatism: Pro and Con*
Nathan Glazer, Peter Steinfels,
James Q. Wilson, and Norman Birnbaum

William Phillips: Welcome to tonight's discussion of neoconservatism, one of a series of meetings conducted under the auspices of
Partisan Review and Boston University. This evening has been
partially funded by the Massachusetts Foundation for the Humanities and Public Policy, and of course we're very appreciative of that.

Conservatism, which used to be a dirty word in intellectual
circles, has now become quite popular and even respectable. For the
first time in this country, there has arisen a new conservative
movement led by intellectuals and addressed to the educated public.
It has been advanced by such well known writers as Irving Kristol,
Nathan Glazer, Martin Lipset, Robert Nisbet, Daniel Bell, James Q.
Wilson, and Norman Podhoretz, and is promoted by such publica-
tions as *Commentary*, *Public Interest*, and *The American Scholar*.
Nevertheless, the fact that many conservatives, or neoconservatives,
still deny that they are conservatives would suggest some uneasiness
in accepting their success. In fact, one of the strategies of conservatism is to deny that the old categories of conservative, liberal, radical
have much meaning today because there have been some crossovers
and reversals of positions. *Commentary* magazine had two symposia
on some aspects of this question. In the first, known conservatives
argued that the term "conservatism" had no meaning. Without
going into the merits of the argument, I might simply say that
common sense tells us that there are conservatives, liberals, and
radicals in the world today even though, through the perversions of
contemporary politics, many liberals hold some conservative positions and vice versa. The second symposium in *Commentary*, aimed
mostly at discrediting the idea of liberalism, asked whether liberalism is good for the Jews. That is like asking whether jogging or
wholewheat bread is good for the Jews. This is indeed an age of
specialization, especially when we remember that we used to ask
whether a social movement or outlook was good for humanity, not
for the Jews or the Catholics. Generally, neoconservatives have

---

*This discussion took place last April [1980].

different views from liberals and radicals on such issues as the communist threat, the Third World, welfare, feminism, affirmative action, the role of the state, the quality of existing society, crime, etc. There are also cultural differences on the question of authority, elitism, mass culture, and modernism. And *Commentary* has even reviewed fiction ideologically. I suppose too, some of the speakers will want to talk about the relation of neoconservatism to old-fashioned, traditional conservatism.

The main question, however, is whether the views of neoconservatism are helpful in solving the enormous domestic and foreign problems this country faces. This is what I expect will be explored this evening. Nathan Glazer will begin.

NATHAN GLAZER

This is only the second time in my life I've stood in front of an audience to defend or expound neoconservatism, both times reluctantly, because while I am happy to defend my own positions, and attack those I disagree with, I am allergic to all-embracing labels, whether applied to me, or others. Nevertheless, I am here to talk about neoconservatism because I have the feeling that I would be considered evasive if I didn't rise to this occasion. They are after all talking about me and my friends when they say "neoconservatism," even though we didn't invent the term. Pat Moynihan says it was Michael Harrington who did. There is hardly one of us who has written an article explaining what neoconservatism is. We do squirm a bit, but it's not because of the conservatism—actually I rather like that word—it's the "neo" part. There is something denigrating about "neo." Think for example of a neoliberal, who is not really a liberal. I find it hard to label the people I disagree with, and I reject most of the labels people try to pin on me.

This began with socialism. I was a socialist in my youth—as who was not?—but after a while all possible meaning disappeared from it. Despite that, people who continue to call themselves socialists maintain an air of superiority over those of us who no longer do, and expect suitable moral obeisance, even though the fact that Sidney Hook is still sticking to the term hardly helps him. I find it more and more mysterious to understand why socialists feel superior, for it seems to be the case that socialists and nonsocialists agree on more and more. Neither of us think that nationalizing industry, which used to mean socialism in my youth, is a good idea anymore. Neither of us think the states that call themselves socialist are models of either justice or equality or freedom. Neither of us—of course—believes in imperialism or colonialism. It is very hard for us to define what it is that divides us, in any centrally principled way. We might, depending on which socialists, and which neoconservatives are arguing, disagree about the details or the scope of health insurance plans; or about the level of taxation that should be imposed upon corporations; or how much should be going into social security; or whether unemployment insurance contributes to unemployment and how much. But where are the principles that separate us? On the socialist side of such arguments, we will hear that Germany—that model of socialism!—provides a much higher replacement of wages and unemployment insurance than we do, and imposes a much heavier tax burden for social purposes. And these may be very good things to do, and there may be very good arguments for us in the United States to follow Germany in this respect.

But to me the issues appear pragmatic, while to others they are ideological. The arguments with socialists have more or less come down to the question, "Why aren't we more like West Germany or Sweden or Denmark?" They used to be, "Why aren't we more like England?" Well I wish we were more like West Germany in some respects, with a higher and a more rapidly growing per capita income, a higher rate of productivity, better social services, less crime. But I don't think the difference has anything to do with socialism or capitalism.

The issue, of course, is not Soviet Russia or Cuba or even China. Most of the socialists we argue with or are denounced by, for example, the editors and writers of *Dissent*, don't think any better of these dictatorships or whatever they are called than we do. I don't think I have any distinctly neoconservate positions in that area.

Thus our disagreements do not have anything to do with deep underlying philosophical positions. They have to do with facts and common sense. Very often the people we disagree with, or who disagree with us, don't seem to have the facts. I've worked my way through many fields of domestic social policy over the last twenty years, and again and again found that if I've disagreed with people who are on the left, it was simply because they didn't know enough.

Now I know that sounds terribly arrogant, and I will simply have to expose myself to that charge. But let me give you a few examples. Take welfare. People thinking themselves on the left and on the right have for a long time been talking of welfare reform. The left wants to raise welfare benefits, sometimes the right does, too. Welfare as you know goes primarily to mothers and children, children whose fathers have either died—that's not too common—or left. The details of welfare reform have gotten complicated, but mostly the proposals consist of raising the benefits, nationalizing them so they are the same in Mississippi as in New York, making them more a matter of right, reducing the aspect of detailed investigation insofar as it still exists, and introducing some element of incentive to work or to get off welfare by reducing benefits only gradually as the recipients earn income, so that earned income does not simply substitute for welfare. If it does do that, if your welfare goes down a thousand dollars every time you earn a thousand dollars—which is called a hundred percent tax rate—what are you getting? And so all agree, whether fervent advocates of the expansion of welfare benefits, or their opponents, that the one hundred percent tax is not a good idea.

Now the problem with welfare reform is that it raises benefits in many states above what poorly skilled workers can earn. If going on welfare is a rational response to a situation in which if you work or stay with your husband you get x, and if you don't, you get x plus y in addition, that's not a very good reform. The problem is that in the argument over welfare reform, the left thought that it was not enough to provide x plus y, but that we should provide x plus 2y.

Ideologies seem to become relevant to the problems of welfare only insofar as they prevent people from looking at the facts. Another, and local, example—subsidized housing. We have an area in Boston, the South End, of red brick townhouses which people with sufficient energy or money are rehabilitating. It also has many housing projects; another is planned. I was asked by a lawyer who represents those who opposed the new housing project—the rehabilitating home owners—to testify against it before a federal judge. I asked on what grounds. They told me that the federal government requires an environmental impact statement for each federally funded program, and there had been no such statement for this project. I said that I thought the law was to protect us against smoke, noise, and dirt, and not against low-income tenants. They told me that a federal judge in New York had already ruled that it could be so used, and was required for low-rent housing projects. But standing by one of my few modest principles, that is, that judges should not expand the law and take it into their own hands, I said I would not testify on that ground. Then they said it also destroys historic buildings. Well, that interested me more. But when I saw the few survivors of urban destruction in that area, I didn't think that was a very good reason to prevent public housing there. But then I looked at the figures for the project, and this is what I mean by a fact, and it turned out that each unit in this project was going to be subsidized by the federal government to the tune of $5,500 a year. There is nothing exceptional about that subsidy. This is not what the low income family would pay; they pay additional rent, depending on their circumstances.

These projects also provide tax shelters to investors and thus reduce their tax liability; and Boston foregoes the higher property taxes it could get if it continued to allow middle-class rehabilitators to invest their money in improving the area. The simple irrationality of this kind of expenditure to subsidize housing would have been enough to persuade me, but I thought further. This project is organized by an Hispanic community group. So I wondered whether the project would help Hispanics. They were probably living in the three deckers, the typical working class housing of Boston in which the Irish and the Jews and others had lived before them. Hispanics were probably doing the same, living in one unit, renting out the others. What was the point of this entire enterprise, I asked myself. It seemed an irrational form of public policy, whose end effect was to spend a lot of public money to hurt those few Hispanics who were buying and renting out housing, and replace them with those few other Hispanics who would be better off by running this housing project on federal money.

My problem is that theory is short—that is, simple, principled, ideological—social policy is long—that is, complicated, and even dull. It's not that I think the profit motive is great and noble, but it does seem to impose a modest economy and efficiency. A private landlord, if you look at all of the figures, does a better job with old housing, better for the tenants in terms of the resources being put in, than the public landlords do. He might do even better if he had part of those subsidies that we give to public landlords.

I began by saying my views have come out of experience with public policy. Those I disagree with, socialists and others on the left, seem to have inherited their views along with a pristine distance from these grubby issues. I have ended up, alas, generalizing, and I suppose this makes me conservative, and if people add neo I'll have to suffer it. This brings me to one definition of the term: a neoconservative is someone who wasn't born that way or didn't start that way. He stumbled upon the principles of conservatism when he became involved in the real world.

Now there are two other broad policy areas—and I'll say almost nothing about them—that are spoken about in articles and books that take us to task for being neoconservatives. One is economic policy. There I'm even more innocent of theory than in social policy. But there too I have reluctantly come around to the position, as so many people have, even *The New Republic* in recent editorials, that Keynesianism, which I once took to be gospel, is badly flawed, and that the economists who emphasize the need for investment in productive resources to control inflation, have a great deal going for them. It is not economic theory which has convinced me of all of this, but the examples of Japan and Germany, and the recent figures on how little we save in this country for investment. In the third area in which a neoconservative position has been discerned and attacked, foreign policy, I remain skeptical of many of the positions of my friends. But here I will follow the advice I would give to our State Department: Don't issue a report on the state of the world or on the state of human rights in each of the 150 countries in the world—it will make too many enemies.

William Phillips: There is one question I want to ask you, and I hope you will answer when it's your turn to speak again. You seem to say that the left got the facts all wrong. Does the left have a monopoly on ignorance and does the right always get the facts right? Peter Steinfels is the next speaker.

PETER STEINFELS

Having arrived late, I did not hear Nathan Glazer's definition, or I suspect nondefinition, of neoconservatism. Almost everybody claims that he or she is following the facts rather than bringing their preestablished ideas to interpret the facts. And I certainly don't have Nathan Glazer's experience or knowledge about social policy to challenge him on those grounds. I do know, however, that when I was reading for my book on neoconservatism, although I did not find what might be called a strict ideology, I did find a school of opinion possessing certain common themes. One of them was the need for stability—in no way was social instability regarded as an opportunity for useful change. Second was the theme of a cultural crisis, a crisis of authority and legitimacy. Unlike various left critics the neoconservatives did not locate the sources of this crisis in the social-economic structures, but treated them as mainly arising from the cultural

condition itself, from the state of our mores and beliefs. Neoconservatives hardly varied at all in their analysis of this cultural crisis. One
favorite category in their analysis was Lionel Trilling's idea of the
adversary culture, an oppositionist mentality critical of all authority
and institutions, which had once been in the possession of the avant-
garde minority, but, through mass higher education, had recently
spread to great numbers of individuals in what was termed the "new
class," a group reportedly having a great impact on the media and on
social policy. In neoconservative eyes, the interaction of this "new
class" with a vaguely defined group called the "underclass" produced
social demands, in the name of the underclass and under the banner of
egalitarianism, that the government was simply unable to meet. The
result was what neoconservatives called overload, namely the inability
of government to meet these claims, with a consequent undermining of
legitimate government authority. Similar themes of adversarial mentality, egalitarianism, and a loss of confident authority were voiced in
the area of foreign policy, which I'm not going to expand upon now.
These are the themes which inspired the neoconservatives' interpretations of facts, determined, for example, by their tendency to examine
bureaucratic failings in the government sector far more than in the
private sector. In short, neoconservatism is not a simple movement
from facts to knowledge; it is instead a preexisting viewpoint that inter-
prets reality.

Now I found a number of virtues in neoconservatism, at least
enough for one neoconservative reviewer to suggest that I was actually
a closet neoconservative. But the virtues of neoconservatism are going
to be well represented this evening, so I would like to stress criticism.

There are two familiar reactions to neoconservatism One claims
that neoconservatism is irrelevant: a bunch of eastern academics
carrying on their old quarrels in a new form, divorced from real
politics and the rest of the country. On the right Kevin Phillips is an
articulate spokesman for this point of view, and there are others who
say much the same on the left. Their position is reinforced by the
striking fact that here we have what both neoconservatives and non-
neoconservatives recognize as one of the most influential movements of
intellectual opinion, and yet you cannot clearly identify a single
neoconservative policy on the major issues facing the country. There is
no neoconservative energy policy; there is no neoconservative unemployment policy; there is no neoconservative inflation policy.

On the other hand, you can find a set of cues which neoconservatives use to establish which participants in the discussions of major

questions come in with two strikes against them, which are to be considered as having the burden of proof on their shoulders rather than on other shoulders. In this sense I belong to the second family of critics, those who think that neoconservatism is extremely important as a cultural force.

It has been and will be important for two reasons. The first has to do with the contradictory impulses of the American public on such questions as containing the size of government and tax expenditures, and on a whole series of citizen concerns, from education, to health, to environment, and so on. In a situation where the citizenry seems to be pulled in two different directions, a set of selective views which can shape the discussion has a particularly powerful place.

Second, neoconservatism is especially important in relation to the existence of the so-called "new class." It is true that, however vaguely defined, some large group of people, who are relatively affluent and educated, and who work in large organizations, seems to be so located as to have their shifts in opinion magnified by the media; and they are an important element in the legitimation of various social concerns and social programs. In linking the significance of neoconservatism to the existence of a "new class" I am not endorsing the neoconservative theory of the "new class." In fact, that theory is an example of how little facts may have to do with this discussion. That is, the idea of the "new class" was set forth by neoconservatives long before any of them, as far as I know, made any effort to get the facts. This effort was made only recently in a volume edited by Bruce-Briggs.

The notion of the "new class" as a highly adversary oppositionist group in society was from the beginning contradicted by available facts including those gathered, for example, by Seymour Martin Lipset and Everett Ladd in the late sixties, at the high point of volatility in American politics. Their study of academics, who should have been the heart of the "new class," found out that while busing, to take one instance as a test case, was much more popular among college professors than among the general public, it was still opposed by over half of the professors. Fifty-eight percent of the professors disapproved strongly of student and faculty radicalism, and almost all of those who approved did so with reservations. Only three percent had no reservations. Finally Lipset and Ladd concluded, after redoing some of this study several years later, that although American academics constitute the most politically liberal occupational group in the United States, they are not in any way radical. "They manifest values, expectations, orientations to governments, moods, and concerns that broadly reflect those of the American public. Most faculty liberals are far from supporting demands for basic changes in the society, and most of them, like their fellow citizens, support the prevailing economic and political order."

If problems are not arising from this adversarial "new class," where are the problems in our society arising from? By and large, neoconservatives do not examine this question. Yet a number of theories can be proposed to answer it. They are expressed in terms such as the "era of limits," and the title of Lester Thurow's book, *The Zero-Sum Society*. My own term has been "the veto society." In any case, all these theories recognized that the magic of economic growth no longer works. We've reached the point where it has become obvious that any social or economic policy will have clear winners and losers. Pick any energy policy, whether it's nuclear, coal, or oil, and you'll quickly be able to see who will gain from it and who will lose from it in disproportionate ways. Investment policy, too, will require winners and losers, and so will ecological concerns. In any case the sticking point is that today the losers, or rather potential losers, are able to veto the initiatives that would make them losers, even if they cannot impose their own alternative policies. The result: we're paralyzed in many areas of national policy.

This has implications for questions of equality and of democracy. In terms of equality, what has kept the distribution of income equal, and furthermore has improved the lot of most households during recent years, are three things. The first is government transfer of income. In that sense, our government social policies have been very successful. It's also true that neoconservatives who advised us to follow what they called an income strategy rather than a service strategy were giving good advice, because the transfer programs have made the difference between what would otherwise be a slightly increasing inequality and the actual maintenance of equality. The second thing that has maintained the level of equality or even improved it is the emergence of second wage earners within the family. The third thing, of course, is government employment, which has played a particular role among the middle class, especially among women and minorities.

Today all of these factors, it seems, are threatened with limits if not actually with decrease. Income transfer programs are being tightened, squeezed, taxed. There is no longer a reservoir of spouses, or second income earners, who can go to work to maintain household income levels. In fact from here on, those spouses who go to work are largely from more highly educated groups, and the effect of the second income for most families will be to increase rather than decrease inequality. And finally there will most likely be cutbacks in government employment, disproportionately affecting women and minorities in the middle class. In other words, the eighties and the nineties are very likely to be decades of growing inequality and perhaps even absolute drops in the standard of living for the lower sixty percent of the American population.

What does all of this have to do with neoconservatism? They have described today's situation as one of a "new class" battling with the business class for leadership in our country. But I think we are seeing, instead, a revolt of the nobles, a reassertion of business leadership in an attempt to bulldoze its way out of the veto society. This effort will have a political component, and we've seen the vast expansion of political action committees and direct electoral activity by corporate leadership. It will also have an ideological component sounding certain themes. One will naturally be a steady disparagement of government which, after all, is the main source of transfer payments and equalizing jobs. Another will be the effort to honor the market as the only guide to efficient and legitimate distribution. A third will be a distinction between the "productive" and the "unproductive" as a justification for increasingly unequal distribution, with the understanding, of course, that the "productive" are those with sufficient income to save and to invest. It is difficult to get figures on exactly how much is being invested in this ideological effort. In short, however, in order to legitimate continuing and, in all likelihood, increasing inequality, business leadership is beginning to launch an all-out political and ideological offensive that, in my opinion, threatens to eviscerate our democracy.

In this effort, neoconservatism, to my disappointment, has almost entirely linked itself to business leadership. I could cite someone like Michael Novak, who in an Exxon-funded publication for the American Enterprise Institute provides an appendix advising corporations on ways in which business can hire intellectuals to carry on ideological warfare. Though Novak is perhaps an exaggerated instance, what neoconservatism does, it seems to me, is first, habitually ignore the capitalist and economic sources of our problems, including those cultural problems it has had the good sense to focus attention on. I hasten to add that Daniel Bell is an exception. Second, neoconservatism has proclaimed egalitarianism and redistribution to be dangerous and unjustified goals of public policy at a time when growing inequality is apt to be the problem. Third, neoconservatism has announced a need to save democracy by having a little less of it, continually offering criticism of programs of citizen participation. Fourth, it wants to construct a positive correspondent to what it claims (wrongly, I think) is the negative "new class." The positive correspondent is some kind of militant clericy which will do the work of cultural discipline in order to keep social thought from growing too turbulent and boiling over into mischievous and dangerous initiatives. The power of "new class" in the symbolic and ideological arenas will then be mobilized to reinforce rather than counter-balance the power of corporate wealth. In my estimation—and this does have a lot to do with one's overall judgment of the leading issues—this neoconservative effort is likely, by and large, to narrow the range of alternatives the society would have before it, socially, economically, and politically.

William Phillips: Peter Steinfels has made an interesting and balanced criticism of the positive aspects, the programmatic aspects, of neoconservative thought. But there's another aspect here. In my opinion, the main contribution of neoconservatism has been to point out the foolishness of a good deal of liberal and radical opinion. Our neoconservatives here should be pushing that side of it. Perhaps Norman Birnbaum and Peter Steinfels might be responding to that. Anyway, the next speaker is James Q. Wilson.

JAMES Q. WILSON

I was struck by our moderator's suggestion that one of the purposes of tonight's meeting was for neoconservatives to explain how they are going to solve the problems of the country. I find that odd. I would think that those who propose changes have the principal obligation to defend them, to explain how they might work, and to explain the errors of the past, almost all committed in the name of liberalism. Neoconservatives, I suppose myself included, point out that these errors are primarily with the use of facts and, as Peter Steinfels has rightly pointed out, with the dispositions behind those facts.

We are contributing to a discussion. Now in bringing my views to this I'm at a profound disadvantage. I was not given the benefits of being raised in New York or in other places where one is a participant from early childhood in the struggles and factional quarrels of the left.

My friend Nathan Glazer says we were all socialists when we were young. I was not.

I didn't know what a Trotskyite was until Dan Bell explained it to me. I'm still not sure I can repeat the definition. I was raised in Southern California, in Los Angeles, where people don't ordinarily say you're beautiful unless you are, but where a large proportion of the people are. I was raised in a Catholic family of parents who were from the south and the west in a community overwhelmingly midwestern and Protestant in its orientation. The only distinctive ethnic group was the Mexican-Americans, whom we didn't understand, and who didn't understand us.

Coming to the east, coming to the University of Chicago, and then at Harvard, I discovered that the things I had learned about politics in my life—what I was brought up to believe in my home, church, and community—were not believed by my intellectual peers. I came to realize I was a dissident, a heretic. I had wandered (many of my colleagues assumed by accident) into a citadel of orthodoxy. If you held the views that are characteristic of most Americans, the citadel either tolerated you kindly, or placed on you (somewhat benign) labels, such as neoconservative. And you were expected to justify yourself. I've been teaching now for nearly twenty years at Harvard. I am struck by the relationship between my opinions, which I am told are neoconservative, and popular opinions. That relationship is formed by my own experiences, not in the eating halls of CCNY, but on the playing fields of David Starr Jordan High School in Long Beach, California. In both the popular views and in neoconservative opinion are certain tensions and ambiguity.

First, people in general have due regard for their self-interest; when they engage in that sober reflection which is required by citizenship, they think of their self-interest, rightly understood. They wish freedom, but they wish amenity—personal benefits—as well. When intellectuals state this, they discuss the virtues and defects of the market; when they speak of amenity they debate alternative ways of achieving it. Conservative or neoconservative intellectuals are interested in achieving amenity in ways that are consistent with the market, if possible produced by the market, because we feel that the market tends to produce, if properly induced and constrained, solutions that are more desirable than planned solutions. This is not how the average citizen would state it. He is concerned about his job, the security of his home, his environment, and the quality of his schools. Intellectuals discuss the matter in somewhat more abstract ways.

314 / Writers' Political Documents

Secondly, the public is concerned about family, religion, community, and decency. The public has become quite tolerant of things that seem to threaten those values, but never mistake their great instinctive loyalty to them and the importance of these institutions and values in shaping their lives. To most people, most of the time, the government is far less important. Neoconservatives share these concerns, though we phrase them differently. We speak of traditional values; of mediating institutions; of taking crime seriously (and not regarding it as a code word for racism as so many liberals did in the 1960s).

And finally, the popular mood is pragmatic; it wants to know what works. It judges what works in its own daily environment, and it is dismayed that governmental things often don't work. But as Peter Steinfels rightly pointed out, they want the government to keep trying because they do want clean air, safe food, pure water, decent schools, and safe streets, and they hope that smart people are trying not only harder but more intelligently.

Neoconservatives seek to provide an intellectual statement of this concern and try, as Nathan Glazer says, to get the facts, comprehensively and systematically. But note how the tensions which are implicit in popular opinion become explicit in intellectual opinion. There is a great tension between libertarianism and self-interest on the one hand, and the concern for traditional values, family, mediating structures, continuity, and history on the other hand. There is a great tension between the desire to see your own circumstances improved dramatically, and a realization that the government programs often do not work well. As a result, there is no such thing as a neoconservative manifesto, credo, religion, flag, anthem, or secret handshake. As a tendency, it is shot through with inner tensions. The magazines to which I contribute are edited and written by people who in most cases are aware of these tensions, and usually find easy answers hard to come by. This often leads to the statement that neoconservatives never favor anything. That's untrue. But they are rarely in favor of things that can be stated simply. Neoconservatism is a mood, not an ideology, and a mood that has not only intellectual sources, but popular ones as well.

To me, and I suppose to most neoconservatives, Alexis de Tocqueville is one of the most important authors. So is Aristotle. But I think what I find in de Tocqueville, in the Federalist Papers, and in Aristotle, is a combination of theory and practice, a desire to test ideas by the sober second thought of a decent citizen—to ask whether institutions can be made to display the best qualities of people without imposing upon people the worst qualities of the institutions.

Peter Steinfels concluded by mentioning that the two major contemporary issues are democracy and equality. He is quite right. He has pointed out the ways in which equality has been helped by government transfer payments, second wage earners, and public employment. I would add that it has also been helped, decisively, by a (until recently) growing economy. A zero-growth society is a society that will not only condemn all of us to suffer a bit, it will condemn the weakest among us, the least advantaged, the poor, the blacks, to suffer the most. Businessmen must be encouraged to invest. But there are important limits as to the appropriate form of the encouragement. Indeed, the whole relationship between neoconservatism and the business establishment is an uneasy one. I don't feel very comfortable before business audiences because I know that in many ways they are part of the problem. Given a large government they will attempt to seize control of some of its parts to use for their own advantage. One of the arguments for a modest government with modest ambition is that it provides fewer points at which any interest group—political or economic or Ralph Nader—can seize control of some bureau and turn it to its own advantage.

The other issue is democracy. Democracy is not an end in itself, but a means to an end. The ends to which it is a means are listed in the preamble to the Constitution. There are six of them, and they involve domestic tranquility, justice, liberty, and the national defense. This view should guide us as we judge democracy as the principle for governance for any institution: the university, the corporation, or the labor union. The question is not whether democracy should exist in order to "achieve democracy," but rather, what internal arrangements are best suited to the nature of an institution so that it can perform its proper social function and serve its highest purposes. Sometimes the answer is democracy, almost always in voluntary associations, and sometimes it is not. But you'd never know this if you read the statements that have been made by many anti-big business groups. Of all of the criticisms of big businesses that can be made, and I have made many, the notion that the corporation is insufficiently democratic strikes me as one that is least helpful and flows most clearly form an *a priori* political position which has not been tested either by popular concerns or by the facts.

———————

William Phillips: I'm puzzled by two statements that James Wilson made. One is that he seems to assume that there is no obligation on the part of neoconservatives to offer any program or any type of solution for the problems confronting us. That strikes me as quite significant. I think it's the first time any social intellectual movement was not able to justify itself on the basis of what ideas or programs it had for the solution of existing social problems, for the improvement of existing society. The second thing that puzzled me is the definition of democracy. Maybe I misunderstood James Wilson, but it does seem to me that from what I know of history, most, if not all antidemocratic movements got their source, their energy, and their rationale from the idea of the slogan that democracy wasn't working, that democracy was not achieving superior ends which were of greater value to society. Anyhow, Norman Birnbaum is the next speaker.

NORMAN BIRNBAUM`

It seems to me that so-called neoconservatism is an incomplete or unachievable amalgam of very diverse themes and very diverse groupings and movements, of different impulses, and I think James Wilson was quite right to contrast his own background with that of the cultural background of some of the other proponents of what can hardly be called a movement. It is, rather, a tendency, a mood, a tempo, or even a fashion. However, if we try to analyze that, a number of themes emerge.

The first theme is the primacy of the market, that is to say, a belief in the efficacy of the free market and of a relatively unregulated form of corporate capitalism. And the arguments are made in the first instance from efficiency, that this is the best way to get goods produced and distributed, and secondly from liberty, the maintenance of an extremely strong private sector is indeed a guarantor of political liberty. And of course in these arguments the negative sides tend to be overlooked, in some cases jeered at: mainly the argument that a pure cost benefit or social market cost benefit analysis would not necessarily produce or give us socially valuable or desirable goods and services, and second that the present structure of the American economy entails an enormous concentration of decision-making power in the economic sector, and a large capacity to influence the political sector of government, politics, and opinion formation.

The second theme is the critique of large government, or centralized government, of government initiative. The critique of big government rests on several familiar ideas: bureaucratization, the autonomy of bureaucrats, their remoteness from popular will or legislative control, deficiencies of decentralization. And here some of our neoconservative thinkers exhibit a frightening provincialism which is evident in Nathan Glazer's litany of the difficulties with socialism, and in the repudiation of nationalization by the democratic socialist parties of western Europe. And it is interesting that the critique of government in neoconservative thought in many instances takes no account of our own political tradition.

A third theme of the neoconservatives has to do with the fear of egalitarianism. Peter Steinfels has pointed out in his book how the publication of John Rawls's book produced a kind of ideological St. Vitus reaction on the part of some of our conservative thinkers. And here a series of rather contradictory arguments again make their appearance: in the first place, a great fear of the destruction of elites, and indeed a threat to western culture. Secondly, the notion of an enormous wave of unnatural egalitarianism, a leveling downward. This theme coincides with the belief that the classification of people by racial and sexual groups is bad, but the classification of people by neighborhood groups, certain kinds of class coherence, is somehow good.

The fourth theme is the familiar phrase about the adversary culture, and the notion that modernism has taken to the streets. At the same time there is in fact a very old-fashioned defense of progressivism, of the historical value of technology, of productivity. Here neoconservatives are at one with Soviet leaders, with very old-fashioned nineteenth-century Marxists like those to be found in the Soviet and French communist parties.

They also defend what could be called traditional familial values which the neoconservatives don't always practice in their own lives, but which they think are certainly good for others. But the defense of traditional culture, of course, comes up against the difficulty that there is no traditional culture to defend, and that it is quite true that the fragmentation of our kind of cultural existence, its division into competing and fragmented class, ethnic, and regional notions, makes the defense or the consolidation of a national community about one set of cultural values exceedingly difficult and artificial.

Finally, there is the maintenance, or defense of American power in the world, and again in the area of foreign affairs, very different themes emerge. One is the notion of the United States as the best, or the most important bastion of freedom in the world. This is generally accompanied by a systematic campaign of disparagement of the western

Europeans, who are thought to have no experience, for being somewhat cowardly and retrograde, as Dr. Brzezinski suggested of the West Germans and others.

On the other hand there's a kind of hard-headed realism expressed by Robert Tucker, a professor of International Relations at Johns Hopkins, who several years ago proposed the occupation of the sources of oil in the Persian Gulf and the Middle East and argued that this was in our national interest. One of the aspects of the debate of American power is the extent to which it is not so much about concrete issues of foreign policies, defense policies, and so on, but about the nature of American Society. And the debate about foreign policy is really an extension of the debates about America's position in the world.

Now if we look at the groupings that seem to be united in what is called neoconservatism, or the publics to which this grouping appeals, there are in fact very different groupings. There are traditional conservatives, generally Protestant, antisecular, committed to what could be called an individualistic and familial model of a society, believing in the free market, and an uncomplicated notion of American society. There are others, and I hope James Wilson will pardon me if I've put him in this category to some degree, whom one might call technocratic, or technocratic liberals, who think that social experiment for the time being demands nothing so much as a pause for reflection, and who appear to preclude much further social experimentation or institutional change and concentrate on trying to make the system work. Irving Kristol frightens businessmen with the "new class," who to some extent are proponents of the radical social programs, but who are quite content to work in the professional and managerial hierarchies of our society, and who pose no danger. There are also the theological conservatives, if we take theology in a philosophical sense, and I think some of the ex-radicals fit here. They seek a coherent and enlarged vision of American society, and they see not the system that needed changing when they were younger, but America as a realized utopia, and they resist even minor changes which might be in order from time to time.

On our position in the world, there's a group we might call the liberal imperialists, a word first used to describe Max Weber and his generation in Imperial Germany. They are liberal insofar as you find a lot of them in the coalition for a democratic majority, and grouped around figures like John Kennedy or Hubert Humphrey, as well as in some sections of the AFL and CIO. There are also conservative realists who don't much care about the liberal or libertarian content of foreign policy, but who are interested in defending what they take to be concrete and visible national interests. And there are also messianics who think of an American mission in the world. Finally, of course, we come to the business of the corporate elites, some of whom are very glad to purvey these ideas, and some of whom have their doubts.

It seems to me that the neoconservatives in a sense are not conservatives at all. It's very hard to trace a direct line of descent from Edmund Burke and Joseph De Maistre to the more vulgar of our contemporaries. In any case their espousal of certain notions of the free market also marks a break with profound American tendencies in conservatism. These were perhaps better expressed by theologians like Niebuhr. Obviously they ignore the threats to liberty, and to choice, and to the forging of a more equitable, a more just, a more sane, national community.

There seems to be a compulsive note of affirmation in much of what the neoconservatives say, or at least a withdrawal from the problems posed not alone by the eighties but by the foreseeable human future—a kind of sacrilization of the present.

I have disagreed with Peter Steinfels on this before. I am not convinced the movement is important. I think it will probably fragment and regroup in ways that at the moment are very difficult to foresee.

William Phillips: Our speakers have waived their rights of argument and refutation and have suggested that we open up the discussion. I have one question. What I find missing from Norman Birnbaum's strong criticism of the neoconservative position is any indication why the neoconservatives have attracted so much intellectual support. They must be responding to or putting their finger on some problems in our society that are not being responded to properly by the liberals and the left. Also, I disagree with Norman Birnbaum's view of culture in its historical or experimental forms. One of the illnesses of our time is the breakdown of the traditional culture, the fragmentation of tradition, the loss of intellectual authority. The answer is not in "cultural pluralism," which is the slogan of people who have no use for intellectual traditions. Also, America is not solving its foreign policy problems. Therefore, unless we believe the neoconservatives have some kind of validity, we must ascribe their influence on other intellectuals to stupidity.

Robert Nozick: William Phillips said that the neoconservative movement is the only movement that he has ever heard of that doesn't propose answers to social problems, and is just saying how hard the answers are. And we know that there are problems with liberal answers and with radical answers.

I would like to ask, and I hope that this doesn't sound boringly philosophical, how one decides what a problem is, and what a social problem is, as opposed to just a fact out there that one accepts. What are the criteria for deciding what social problems are, and presumably for deciding what social problems are within the proper orbit for the government to handle? I constructed a list of problems. Inequality of income: is that a social problem or just something that's happening out there that arises by a certain process that's perfectly okay? Fewer than one hundred percent of the young people go to universities: is that a social problem or not? Many people think that being overweight is a social problem in the United States. Ought one to propose solutions for it or not? Or for the current divorce rate? These are things that are addressed in social problem text books, but do government programs cause the problems that they're supposed to cure?

But Irving Kristol has proposed that there are ties, and has talked seriously about one apparently governmental problem, namely censorship to preserve certain bourgeois and middle-class virtues, virtues that one might find admirable. But is it a social problem that there are changes taking place in some of those? Is a difference between the average age of men and women in the United States a social problem? It causes some problems about insurance policies. . . . And that is a social fact. These things can be altered in various ways. One can go either for great expenditures in raising the average age of men, or in handicapping women in various age groups to lower their life expectancy, to eliminate that inequality. Is it a social problem that sport is a common bond that brings out more crowds than would ever show up in a meeting like this? That only fifty percent of the people vote in presidential elections? Or that the weather is worse in the northeast than it is in California?

Hanna Papanek: I think, to come back to an earlier point, the appeal of the neoconservatives may be that they fail so singularly to put their finger on any of the social problems of the future. I'm appalled by the omissions both of the neoconservatives and of their critics. I don't know what vision of the future you people have, but to my mind, the world includes parts that go beyond western Europe and the United States. What are the neoconservatives and their critics thinking about a major issue, that is the North-South dialogue? Another problem you seem to have conveniently overlooked has to do with women. I'd like to know what your position is on the Equal Rights Amendment, or on the fact that women get fifty-nine cents to every dollar that men earn.

James Q. Wilson: I'll start. One of the tendencies of public discourse that I find most lamentable is that everybody must have an instant opinion on issues, and the list of issues could go on and on. I'm not sure I'm obliged to have an instant sloganized opinion on those questions. The North-South question, that is to say the relationship between rich and poor nations, is a question on which a different answer must be given depending on the country and the commodity. To generalize about it would deny everything that is important to intellectuals. With respect to women it would do little good to give my views on the Equal Rights Amendment. I signed a petition to have it placed on the ballot. On the whole I think I'm in favor of it. On the other hand I really don't think that is what you're getting at, because you're really getting at the status of women in society as a social fact and not as a legal hypothesis. This social fact is an issue that cannot be summarized by asking people to raise their hands to vote for or against women. Or to say that it is lamentable that women earn fifty-nine percent of men's salaries. I don't know all of the reasons for those facts. Some may be lamentable. Some may be explicable. Some, probably the largest number, are unknown.

Norman Birnbaum: I'm not sure that Hanna Papanek is right in saying that the neoconservatives have an appeal precisely because they don't have answers to these questions. There is, sometimes by implication, a neoconservative program as inchoate as the different components of the movement are. It seeks a break on further movement toward equality, income redistribution, and economic planning. It seeks an end to, or at least a slowing down of, movements like the women's movement. With respect to foreign policy, the North-South issues are very important to neoconservatives who are for regrouping the Atlantic alliance into a global one for defending the United States against "excessive demands" by the Third and Fourth Worlds. I think the program will fail, because it entails not only starting another set of journals like *The Public Interest*, which cannot be created by funding from the American Enterprise Institute. It involves the forging of a political consensus in the United States, which members of the intelligentsia and other groups are not prepared to go along with. That is why we have many hawks who are perfectly willing to demand action against Iran but refrain from volunteering for military service, and who are unwilling to provoke the domestic consequences of conscription. So it seems to me that we get a program unlikely to be put into effect even if Ronald Reagan were elected. If his election were to produce a decade of unprecedented civil strife and social turbulence in this country, the neoconservatives would learn that there is, in fact, a difference between advocating moderation and stability and so on, and in enforcing it.

Nathan Glazer: Nobody is enforcing anything on anyone. Norman Birnbaum really does get carried away, and I don't know what carries him away. There is no movement. I am not on the road plugging anything, and I don't think James Wilson is either, even if I talk to audiences about things I know about, like affirmative action and a few other modest topics. I think he feels that we're not rising to his grand views of the world, all stemming out of the great socialist tradition in which everything is connected to everything else. I'm not rising to this grand view, and I'm certainly not engaged in some monumental power struggle. I find it odd that he insists I am.

Leon Wieseltier: I'm rather disturbed by James Wilson's particular defense of neoconservatism. But I would like to make one brief comment on Norman Birnbaum's defense of liberalism. I think liberals should be candid about the failings of liberalism. It's difficult when you're faced with liberals like Ramsey Clark not to go with people who write in *Commentary* on this issue. But more generally I am very concerned with the kind of defense James Wilson makes for neoconservatism. I agree with him and probably with all the people on the panel that the famous adversary attitude did not deserve the glamour that it won on the upper west side. And yet I'm troubled by the idea that one should recommend any particular position because of the extent to which it is in harmony with what are the perceived wishes or ideas of large groups of people. It confirms my main impression that one of the attractions of neoconservatism, certainly in the case of certain Jewish intellectuals, is that it has finally allowed the middle class and the intellectuals to kiss and make up. To James Wilson, Rousseau is the enemy, and yet I find that his defense of neoconservatism relies to a certain extent upon some notion of a general or common will. I'm not sure where this will exists. In the first place, popular attitudes change. But more specifically, at any given moment, the political perceptions of Jordan High School in Long Beach are not the perceptions of Erasmus High School in Brooklyn. And it seems to me that there is a kind of spurious notion of commonalities you're operating with, which leads to a certain amount of sentimentality. If one is going to defend neoconservatism, then either one speaks to the merit of the argument itself, or one should be more candid about calculating which groups or constituencies benefit from which principles or programs, and then perhaps advance the argument that the benefit of a specific group enhances the welfare of the larger community or group.

James Q. Wilson: I certainly agree with what you've just said, and I don't think my views were meant to persuade you that I didn't agree. I suggested that men and women are by nature social and political communal creatures who do not have wholly idiosyncratic, random, ephemeral values; that some of these core values tend to be permanent and unchanging, or change very slowly. And to identify those and to understand them more fully is, I think, where classical political philosophy began, and where much contemporary political thought could probably return. I think there is a long way between that view and whatever people want at a particular moment. Then I went on to say that given the instincts that come from what I regard as natural sentiments evinced by men and women living in communities, one tries to make an intellectual defense of core values, and to see how they influence policy. But first you must examine evidence and describe consequences because now you have responsibility for affecting many people. Secondly, you quickly become aware of the tensions and inconsistencies in those views, and reconciling tendencies and inconsistencies intellectuals have been trained for. We are simplifiers; we tend to be doctrinaire. It is a sobering experience when you realize that you can't do that and be truthful to the core values. Now all of this strikes me as common sense. My colleagues on the panel describe it as an "ism," as a movement, so that they can point out that it is either trivial or irrelevant or wrong. I don't think of it as a movement or as an ideology. They disagree as to whether it is important. The one who thinks it is important thinks it is wrong. The one who thinks there may be something to say for it thinks it is unimportant. I don't think it really makes a lot of difference, because, as you rightly said, each argument has to be judged on its merits, and what I find attractive about the magazines I write for is that one attempts to make an argument that is capable of being judged on its merits, and one expects it to be criticized on its merits. And one is not expected to subordinate that argument to some larger theoretical interest.

Norman Birnbaum: I think, too, that the failure of liberalism might have generated some of the different approaches. It seems to me that this question may suggest at least implicitly that there may be more continuity amongst the so-called neoconservatives than we generally think, and that this continuity also accounts for the success of the neoconservative movement, particularly after the mistakes and excesses of the sixties, some of which were due to the absence of a long socialist tradition in this country. A great many were due, as well, to the absence of a strong organized union component in a movement for social change.

Jean Layzer: I wanted to reclaim Nathan Glazer for the liberals, because I consider myself liberal, and I find that when I read him on the subject of welfare policy I believe him to be just a smarter liberal than I am. I find that he informs my views. I think we part company where we view what is happening, and what it is we are reacting against. I believe that we either ought to include work, or have a much more sweeping welfare policy rather than the weak and ineffective one that isn't put into effect either by radicals or by good liberals, but by very placating neoconservatives. They have no long-range goals for many problems. But there are no long-range liberal goals either. So I think we're coming from pretty much the same position.

Nathan Glazer: I have the problem of always being overwhelmed by the complexity of small issues, let alone large ones. I think that welfare, compared to some of the things that we are talking about tonight, is small, although it is a big issue. For a lot of issues there is the problem of premature analysis. Inevitably, if you look at the history of any of these problems, they have gotten more complicated in our understanding, even such issues as how you look at a policy, or whether it helps the capitalists or the poor. It may be true that cutting fifty billion dollars from corporation income taxes may be doing more for the poor than distributing fifty billion to them. It is hard to give fast answers.

Eugene Goodheart: I'd like to pursue the line that Leon Wieseltier took in questioning James Wilson. I think it is pretty clear that one understands what neoconservatism is about negatively—a resistance to certain liberal pieties of the past fifteen to twenty-five years. But there is also a desire to know what neoconservatism stands for. And when neoconservatives are asked that, they feel that this is a question about a theory or system. I think it is fair for neoconservatives, and even for certain liberals, to resist this desire for a systematic response. But I think it's also perfectly understandable that one wants some sense of a positive idea, because without it you don't have a critical stance. All you have is some kind of instinctive resistance. In a way James Wilson dramatized the problem, because he spoke about some relationship between popular feeling and neoconservatism. Then, under questioning, he retreated and said that he doesn't mean popular feeling at any given moment, but something more traditional; and then he speaks of core beliefs. Core beliefs, I suppose, have always characterized society. But once he invokes the idea of core beliefs, it seems to me that he has concealed a philosophical idea, and .he goes to the philosophers for that. One of them is de Tocqueville. In his talk I found a very facile conflation between his notion of popular feeling as it exists in America today, and de Tocqueville's idea of the citizen which was often the basis for a critique of popular feeling and of popular passion. And the neoconservatives can't just say we know facts, and the liberals have historically or traditionally been ignorant, and we'll give them the facts, and somehow together we will work out some solution to the problems we all recognize.

James Q. Wilson: I can see why they call it the *Partisan Review*. There are two levels at which I can make a brief response. The first is that since I do not think of myself as a philosopher, or as a person who has an ideology that is worked out with respect to political objects, I don't feel myself under an obligation to have those views that many intellectuals feel all intellectuals must have. I find that stifling. Secondly, with respect to the question of core beliefs, you put your finger on an essential point. And it becomes incumbent upon persons who are evaluating public policy and using facts to be explicit about what those beliefs are that lead them to make judgments. Most people develop very early in life an almost instinctive sense of justice which informs virtually everything they judge. Much of public policy today does serious violence to this elemental sense of justice. That equals should be treated equally is an empirical question which most people can agree on. This leads to the following problem, which is one of the reasons why people are called neoconservatives instead of frustrated liberals. And that is the issue of integration. When I formed views on this subject, they were based on the principle of equal opportunity to all, and on proportional division of benefits. With respect to political things, most people were equal, and therefore most things distributed politically should be distributed equally. This implied that you favor civil rights laws, you favor ending inhibitions on people expressing political rights, you opposed manifestly unjust distributions of public goods and services. Now suddenly comes the arrival of quotas and goals, affirmative action, and a form of advanced ethnic political patronage in which what is being sought for is more, not the good but the more. And at this point most people in society feel that an elemental standard of justice has been either violated or made obscure. Now that is an area in which one can show the linkage between a philosophical conception that is not trivial, a set of empirical observations, and a comment on public policy.

Norman Birnbaum: The sense of justice exists, but its structure, content, and concrete application varies from group to group in such a way that we do have political conflict and controversy of an implicitly philosophical nature.

Joan Axelrod: Nathan Glazer, I imagine that your transition from socialism to neoconservatism has been a gradual one. I was wondering if you could briefly outline the little bends and twists along the road that have brought you this far. And do you think this movement, which is really a nonmovement, is going to last?

Nathan Glazer: No, but fortunately I can give you a reference for the first question. It is a book of essays I published called *Remembering the Answers.* I will mention one key moment. It was when I read the first issue of *Dissent,* maybe in 1956, and I found one socialist attacking another socialist for having sold out. I won't say who the two were; they're both well known sociologists. But as I knew at the time, the first one was making more money than the second. I felt that was a rather odd form of polemic which turned me somewhat against the first socialist who was attacking the second. I must confess I've seen some of it in Norman Birnbaum, whose insinuation was that we are serving power. I don't feel we do.

Henri Zerner: I have a very distant point of view. I'm not a native, so I'm a little puzzled. The alternatives seem to be between liberalism and neoconservatism. Now it seems to me to be pretty clear that neoconservatives are very liberal. My question would be rather to the representatives of liberalism, which is that since liberalism seems to have posed very serious problems, and many liberals apparently go so far as to talk about the failure of liberalism, which I would sympathize with, maybe the alternative is not neoconservatism, but rather a left.

William Phillips: Since both representatives of liberalism here call themselves democratic socialists, they probably ought to make some effort to explicate and defend these positions. But that ought to be the subject of a future *Partisan Review* panel.